Teacher's Resource Book

Bruce Wade

with

Maria Karyda

B1+

Business Partner

Coursebook contents

Contents

Overview

Business Partner is a flexible course designed for a variety of learners. It is suitable for students with mixed abilities, requirements and interests and for varied class sizes where the common requirement is to learn professional English language and develop key skills for the workplace.

When talking to learners, their reasons for studying business English almost always relate to their employability. Many tertiary students want to maximise their chances of finding a job in an international environment, while in-work professionals want to communicate more effectively in their workplace and improve their future career prospects. Other learners may simply need to study and pass a business English exam in order to complete their overall degree.

In all three cases, teachers need to be able to engage and motivate by providing learning materials which:

- are interesting and relevant to their life experiences.
- match their learning needs and priorities.
- are appropriate for the amount of study time available.

Business Partner has been designed to enable teachers to meet these needs without spending many hours researching their own materials. The content and structure of the course is based on three key concepts: **employability**, **flexibility** and **learner engagement**.

Course aims and key concepts

Employability

Balance between language and business skills training

In order to achieve their employability goals, learners need to improve their knowledge of English language as it is used in the workplace and also develop key skills for the international workplace. *Business Partner* provides this balance.

In addition to building their vocabulary and grammar and developing their writing skills, *Business Partner* trains students in Communication and Business skills. Language being only one aspect of successful communication, students also require an understanding of different business situations and an awareness of different communication styles, especially when working across cultures.

- 'Communication skills' (Lesson 3) provides the soft skills needed in order to work effectively with people whose personality and culture may be different from your own. This includes teamwork, decision-making and influencing skills.
- 'Business skills' (Lesson 4) provides the practical skills needed in different business situations, such as taking part in meetings, presentations and negotiations.

Flexibility

The modular approach means that *Business Partner* can be adapted to suit a variety of teaching requirements from extensive lessons to intensive short courses. In addition to the Coursebook, a wide variety of additional optional activities and resources are provided which can be used to focus on and extend material which is most useful to learners' needs.

Extra activities and extra grammar points

You can extend your lessons or focus in more depth on certain areas by using the large bank of extra activities in MyEnglishLab (clearly signposted for you throughout the Coursebook). These include extra vocabulary and grammar practice exercises for use in class as well as activities which draw attention to useful language in reading texts.

 Teacher's resources: extra activities

These are PDFs in MyEnglishLab that you can download and print or display on-screen.

 Teacher's resources: alternative video and activities

Alternative videos with worksheets are available for some units and are clearly signposted. You can use this in the classroom as an alternative approach to the topic in Lesson 1, depending on your students' needs.

 The summary contains examples of how to order information in sentences. Go to MyEnglishLab for optional grammar work.

Business Partner offers a flexible approach to grammar depending on whether you want to devote a significant amount of time to a grammar topic, or focus on consolidation only when you need to. There is one main grammar point in each unit, presented and practised in Lesson 2.

In addition, the Writing section (Lesson 5) includes a link to an optional second grammar point in MyEnglishLab, where students can watch short video presentations of the grammar points and do interactive activities.

---

 page 112 See Pronunciation bank — Pronunciation activities are included at the back of the book. This allows teachers to focus on aspects of pronunciation which are most useful for their students.

Teacher's Resource Bank: Photocopiables, Writing bank, Reading bank and Functional language bank

You can use these resources as and when needed with your classes. The Photocopiables further activate and practise, vocabulary from Lesson 1 and grammar from Lesson 2 as and when needed.

The Reading bank for each unit gives students more reading practice and can be also used for self-study. The activity types reflect those found in a range of business English exams. The Writing bank provides supplementary models of professional communication and the Functional language bank extends useful phrases for a range of business situations.

Learner engagement

Video content: We all use video more and more to communicate and to find out about the world and we have put video at the heart of *Business Partner*. There are two videos in every unit with comprehension and language activities:

- an authentic video package in Lesson 1, based on real-life video clips and interviews suitable for your learners' level of English.
- a dramatised communication skills training video in Lesson 3 which follows characters in an international team as they deal with different professional challenges.

Authentic content: Working with authentic content really helps to engage learners, and teachers can spend many hours searching for suitable material online. *Business Partner* has therefore been built around authentic videos and articles from leading media organisations such as the *Financial Times* and news channels. These offer a wealth of international business information as well as real examples of British, U.S. and non-native-speaker English.

Relevance for learners without work experience: Using business English teaching materials with learners who have little or no work experience can be particularly challenging. *Business Partner* has been carefully designed to work with these students as well as with in-work professionals. In the case of collaborative speaking tasks and roleplays, the situation used will either be:

- one that we can all relate to as customers and consumers; OR
- a choice of situations will be offered including a mix of professional and everyday situations.

Both will allow learners to practise the skill and language presented in the lesson, but in a context that is most relevant to them.

Business workshops: Learners have the opportunity to consolidate and activate the language and skills from the units in 8 business workshops at the end of the book. These provide interesting and engaging scenarios where students simulate real-life professional situations such as roleplaying meetings, negotiations or presentations.

Approach to language and skills

Business Partner offers fully integrated skills, including the essential critical thinking and higher-order thinking skills, which are built into the activities.

Vocabulary and video The main topic vocabulary set is presented and practised in Lesson 1 of each unit, building on vocabulary from the authentic video. Teachers are given lots of opportunities to use the vocabulary in discussions and group tasks, and to tailor the tasks to their classroom situations.

Functional language (such as giving advice, summarising, dealing with objections) supports learners' capability to operate in real workplace situations in English. Three functional language sets are presented and practised in every unit: in Lessons 3, 4 and 5. You will be able to teach the language in group speaking and writing tasks. There is a Functional language bank at the back of this Teacher's Resource Book which students can also find in MyEnglishLab so that they can quickly refer to useful language support when preparing for a business situation, such as a meeting, presentation or interview.

Listening and video The course offers a wide variety of listening activities (based on both video and audio recordings) to help students develop their comprehension skills and to hear target language in context. All of the video and audio material is available in MyEnglishLab and includes a range of British, U.S. and non-native-speaker English. Lessons 1 and 3 are based on video (as described above). In four of the eight units, Lesson 2 is based on audio. In all units, you also work with a significant number of audio recordings in Lesson 4 and the Business workshop.

Grammar The approach to grammar is flexible depending on whether you want to devote a significant amount of time to grammar or to focus on the consolidation of grammar only when you need to. There is one main grammar point in each unit, presented and practised in Lesson 2. There is a link from Lesson 5 to an optional second grammar point in MyEnglishLab – with short video presentations and interactive practice. Both grammar points are supported by the Grammar reference section at the back of the Coursebook (p.118). This provides a summary of meaning and form, with notes on usage or exceptions, and business English examples.

Reading *Business Partner* offers a wealth of authentic texts and articles from a variety of sources, particularly the *Financial Times*. Every unit has a main reading text with comprehension tasks. This appears either in Lesson 2 or in the Business workshop. There is a Reading bank at the back of this Teacher's Resource Book which students can also find in MyEnglishLab and which has a longer reading text for every unit with comprehension activities.

Speaking Collaborative speaking tasks appear at the end of Lessons 1, 3, 4 and the Business workshop in every unit. These tasks encourage students to use the target language and, where relevant, the target skill of the lesson. There are lots of opportunities to personalise these tasks to suit your own classroom situation.

Writing *Business Partner* offers multiple opportunities to practise writing. Lesson 5 in every unit provides a model text and practice in a business writing skill. The course covers a wide range of genres such as reports, proposals, note-taking and emails, and for different purposes, including formal and informal communication, summarising, invitations, replies and project updates. There are also short writing tasks in Lesson 2 which provide controlled practice of the target grammar. There is a Writing bank at the back of this Teacher's Resource Book which students can also find in MyEnglishLab and which provides models of different types of business writing and useful phrases appropriate to their level of English.

Pronunciation Two pronunciation points are presented and practised in every unit. Pronunciation points are linked to the content of the unit – usually to a video or audio presentation or to a grammar point. The pronunciation presentations and activities are at the back of the Coursebook (p.112), with signposts from the relevant lessons. This section also includes an introduction to pronunciation with British and U.S. phonetic charts.

Approach to Communication skills

A key aspect of *Business Partner* is the innovative video-based communication skills training programme.

The aims of the Communications skills lessons are to introduce students to the skills needed to interact successfully in international teams with people who may have different communication styles from them due to culture or personality. Those skills include teamwork, decision-making and influencing.

These lessons are based on videos that provide realistic examples of work situations. This is particularly important for pre-service learners who may not have direct experience of the particular situations they are about to see. In each of these videos students watch two possible scenarios (Option A and Option B) in which a different cwommunication style is used. These options give students the opportunity to engage in critical viewing of each option and gain awareness of the impact of different communication styles.

Approach to testing and assessment

Business Partner provides a balance of formative and summative assessment. Both types of assessment are important for teachers and learners and have different objectives. Regular review and on-going assessment allows students to evaluate their own progress and encourages them to persevere in their studies. Formal testing offers a more precise value on the progress made on their knowledge and proficiency.

Formative assessment: Each Coursebook lesson is framed by a clear lesson outcome which summarises the learning deliverable. The lesson ends with a self-assessment section which encourages students to reflect on their progress in relation to the lesson outcome and to think about future learning needs. More detailed self-assessment tasks and suggestions for further practice are available in MyEnglishLab. (See also section on the Global Scale of English and the Learning Objectives for Professional English.)

The Coursebook also contains one review page per unit at the back of the book to recycle and revise the key vocabulary, grammar and functional language presented in the unit; they are structured to reflect the modularity of the course.

Summative assessment: Unit tests are provided and activities are clearly labelled to show which section of the unit they are testing to reflect the modular structure of the course. The tests are available in PDF and Word formats so that you can adapt them to suit your purposes. They are also available as interactive tests that you can allocate to your students if you wish to do so.

These Unit tests are based on task types from major business English exams. There is also an additional LCCI writing task for professional English for every unit. This approach familiarises learners with the format of the exams and gives them practice in the skills needed to pass the exams.

MyEnglishLab also contains extra professional English practice that can be used as additional revision material.

The Global Scale of English

The Global Scale of English (GSE) is a standardised, granular scale from 10 to 90 which measures English language proficiency. The GSE Learning Objectives for Professional English are aligned with the Common European Framework of Reference (CEFR). Unlike the CEFR, which describes proficiency in terms of broad levels, the Global Scale of English identifies what a learner can do at each point on a more granular scale – and within a CEFR level. The scale is designed to motivate learners by demonstrating incremental progress in their language ability. The Global Scale of English forms the backbone for Pearson English course material and assessment.

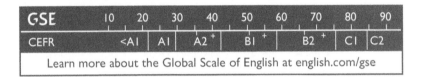

GSE	10	20	30	40	50	60	70	80	90
CEFR		<A1	A1	A2 +	B1 +	B2 +	C1	C2

Learn more about the Global Scale of English at english.com/gse

Business Partner has been written based on these Learning Objectives, which ensure appropriate scaffolding and measurable progress. Each Lesson outcome in each lesson in the Coursebook encapsulates a number of specific Learning Objectives which are listed in this Teacher's Resource Book in the Teaching notes. These Learning Objectives are also listed in the Self-assessment sheets available to students in MyEnglishLab. (See also Self-assessment above in Approach to testing and assessment.)

Course structure

Business Partner is an eight-level course based on the Global Scale of English (GSE) and representing the CEFR levels: A1, A2, A2+, B1, B1+, B2, B2+, C1.

	For the teacher	For the student
print	Teacher's Resource Book with MyEnglishLab	Coursebook with Digital Resources Workbook
blended	Presentation tool	Coursebook with MyEnglishLab

Business Partner is a fully hybrid course with two digital dimensions that students and teachers can choose from. MyEnglishLab is the digital component that is integrated with the book content.

Access to MyEnglishLab is given through a code printed on the inside front cover of this book. As a teacher, you have access to both versions of MyEnglishLab, and to additional content in the Teacher's Resource folder.

Depending on the version that students are using, they will have access to one of the following:

Digital Resources includes downloadable coursebook resources, all video clips, all audio files, Lesson 3 additional interactive video activities, Lesson 5 interactive grammar presentation and practice, Reading bank, Functional Language bank, Writing bank, and My Self-assessment.

MyEnglishLab includes all of the **Digital Resources** plus the full functionality and content of the self-study interactive workbook with automatic gradebook. Teachers can also create a group or class in their own MyEnglishLab and assign workbook activities as homework.

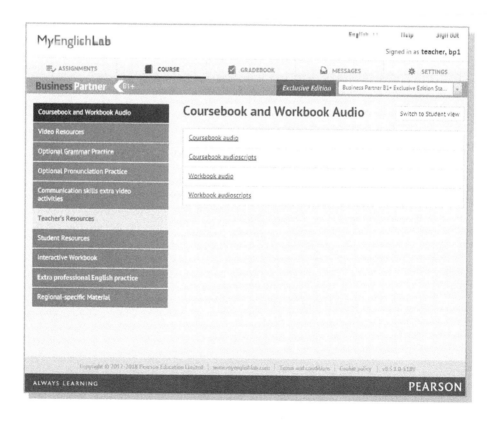

Coursebook
(with access code for MyEnglishLab)

- Eight units, each containing five lessons (see pages 2–3 for unit overview)
- Eight Business workshop lessons relating to each of the eight units
- A one-page Review per unit to revise key language and grammar
- A Pronunciation section which practises two points from each unit
- A Grammar reference with detailed explanations and examples
- Videoscripts and audioscripts
- A glossary of key business vocabulary from the book

Coursebook video and audio material is available on MyEnglishLab.

 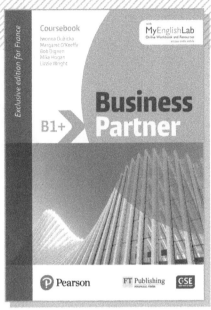

MyEnglishLab digital component

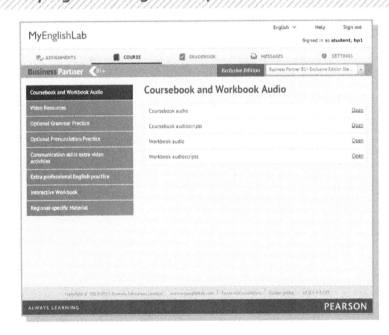

Accessed using the code printed on the inside cover of the Coursebook. Depending on the version of the course that you are using, learners will have access to one of the following options:

Digital resources powered by MyEnglishLab
- Video clips
- Audio files and scripts
- Extra Coursebook activities (PDFs)
- Lesson 3 extra interactive video activities
- Lesson 5 interactive grammar presentation and practice
- Reading bank
- Writing bank
- Functional language bank
- Extra professional English practice
- My Self-assessment
- Workbook audio files and scripts

Full content of MyEnglishLab
- All of the above
- Interactive self-study Workbook with automatic feedback and gradebook

Workbook

- Additional self-study practice activities, reflecting the structure of the Coursebook. Activities cover vocabulary, grammar, functional language, reading, listening and writing.
- Additional self-study practice activities for points presented in the Coursebook Pronunciation bank.
- Answer key
- Audioscripts

Workbook audio material is available on MyEnglishLab.

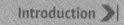

Teacher's Resource Book (with access code for MyEnglishLab)

- Teaching notes for every lesson including warm-ups, background/culture notes and answer keys
- Business brief for every unit with background information on the unit topic and explanations of key terminology; it gives teachers an insight into contemporary business practices even if they have not worked in these particular environments.

- Photocopiable activities – two per unit with teaching notes and answer keys
- Reading bank – an extended reading text for every unit with comprehension activities (+ answer keys)
- Writing bank – models of different types of business writing with useful phrases
- Functional language bank – useful phrases for different business situations, e.g. meetings, interviews
- Videoscripts and audioscripts

MyEnglishLab digital component

Accessed using the code printed on the inside cover of the Teacher's Resource Book.

Coursebook resources
- Video clips and scripts
- Audio files and scripts
- Extra Coursebook activities (PDFs)
- Lesson 3 extra interactive video activities for self-study
- Lesson 5 interactive grammar presentation and practice for self-study
- Extra professional English practice
- My Self-assessment: a document that students can use to record their progress and keep in their portfolio

Workbook resources
- Self-study interactive version of the Workbook with automatic feedback and gradebook
- Teachers can assign Workbook activities as homework
- Workbook audio files and audioscripts

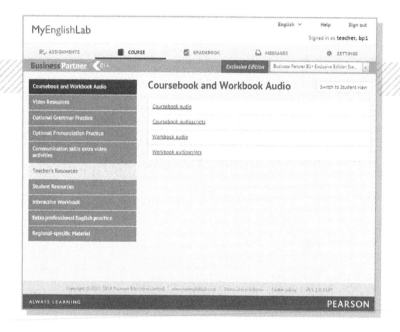

Teacher's Book resources
- Alternative video and extra activities (units 2 and 6)
- Photocopiable activities + teaching notes and answer keys
- Reading bank + answer keys
- Writing bank
- Functional language bank

Tests
- Unit tests (PDFs and Word)
- Interactive Unit tests, with automatic gradebook
- Tests audio files
- Tests answer keys

Presentation tool

- Digital version of the Teacher's Resource Book
- Digital version of the Coursebook with classroom tools for use on an interactive whiteboard
- Video clips and scripts
- Audio files and scripts
- Extra Coursebook activities (PDFs)

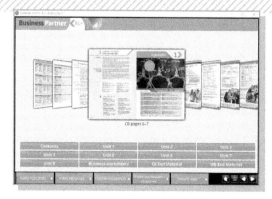

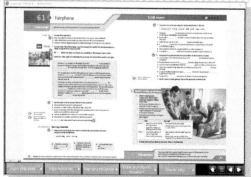

Unit overview page ≫

① A well-known or provocative quote related to the unit topic is provided as a talking point. There are suggestions for how to use the quote in the Teacher's Resource Book notes for each unit.

② The Unit overview summarises the contents of each lesson as well as the lesson outcomes.

③ Content at the back of the book which extends the unit is highlighted: the Business workshop, Review, Pronunciation bank and Grammar reference.

Entrepreneurs 6 ≫

① *'It's not about ideas. It's about making ideas happen.'*
Scott Belsky, co-founder of Behance

Fresh Squeezed LEMONADE! 50¢

② **Unit overview**

6.1	**Fairphone**	**Video:** The world's first ethical smartphone
	Lesson outcome: Learners can use vocabulary related to starting and financing a business.	**Vocabulary:** Running a business
		Project: Brainstorm and present new business ideas

6.2	**Young entrepreneurs**	**Reading:** Leaving Harvard to start a business
	Lesson outcome: Learners can use reported speech to report what other people have said and asked.	**Grammar:** Reported speech
		Speaking and writing: Talk to a journalist about your start-up

6.3	**Communication skills:** Influencing	**Video:** Influencing styles: push and pull
	Lesson outcome: Learners are aware of different ways to influence other people and can use a range of phrases for dealing with objections.	**Functional language:** Dealing with objections
		Task: Influencing others to overcome objections

6.4	**Business skills:** Presenting facts and figures	**Listening:** A presentation based on visual data
	Lesson outcome: Learners can use a range of phrases to present facts and figures using visual information.	**Functional language:** Presenting visual information
		Task: A presentation to an investor

6.5	**Writing:** Summarising	**Model text:** Summary of a business talk
	Lesson outcome: Learners can write a simple summary of factual work-related information.	**Functional language:** Summarising
		Grammar: Order of information in sentences
		Task: Listen to a talk and write a summary

③

≫ 57 ≪

Lesson 1 ➤➤

The aims of this lesson are:

- to engage students with the unit topic through a video based on authentic material.
- to present and practise topic business vocabulary, drawing on vocabulary from the video.
- to encourage students to activate the language they have practised in a group project.

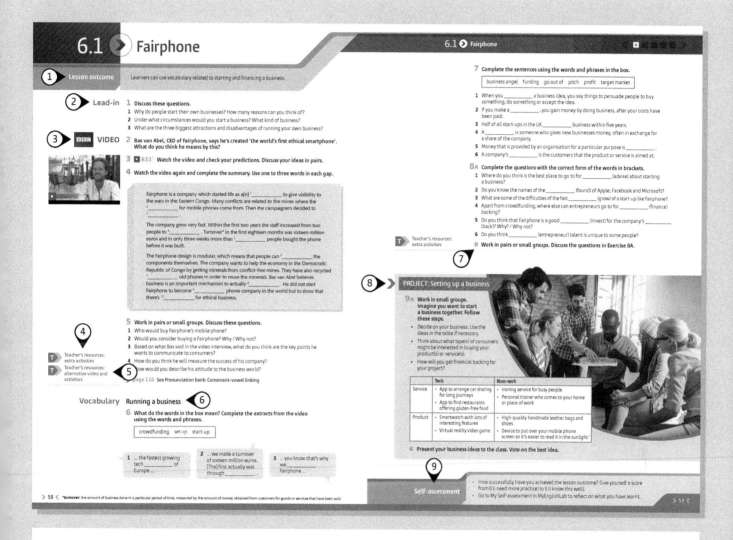

① The Lesson outcome defines a clear learning outcome for every lesson. Each Lesson outcome encapsulates a number of specific Learning Objectives for Professional English which are listed in this Teacher's Resource Book in the Teaching notes.

② Every lesson begins with a short Lead-in activity to engage learners with the lesson topic on a personal level.

③ Lesson 1 is based on an authentic video of about 4 minutes with comprehension activities.

④ **T** Teacher's resources: extra activities Extra activities are clearly signposted. These are PDFs in MyEnglishLab to display on-screen or print. They can be used to extend a lesson or to focus in more depth on a particular section.

⑤ **T** Teacher's resources: alternative video and activities Alternative videos with worksheets are available for some units and are clearly signposted.

⑥ The main unit vocabulary set is presented and practised in Lesson 1, building on vocabulary from the video. Extra activities are available in MyEnglishLab.

⑦ Follow-up questions provide an opportunity for personalisation.

⑧ The Project at the end of Lesson 1 is a collaborative group task with a strong emphasis on communication and fluency building. It can be done in class or in more depth over several weeks in and out of class.

⑨ Every lesson ends with a short Self-assessment section which encourages learners to think about the progress they have made in relation to the lesson outcomes. More detailed self-assessment tasks and suggestions for extra practice are available in MyEnglishLab.

Lesson 2 ❯ Reading or Listening

The aims of this lesson are:

• to provide students with meaningful reading or listening skills practice based on engaging, relevant and up-to-date content.

• to present and practise the unit grammar point, drawing on examples from the text.

• to encourage students to activate the grammar point they have practised through communicative speaking or writing activities.

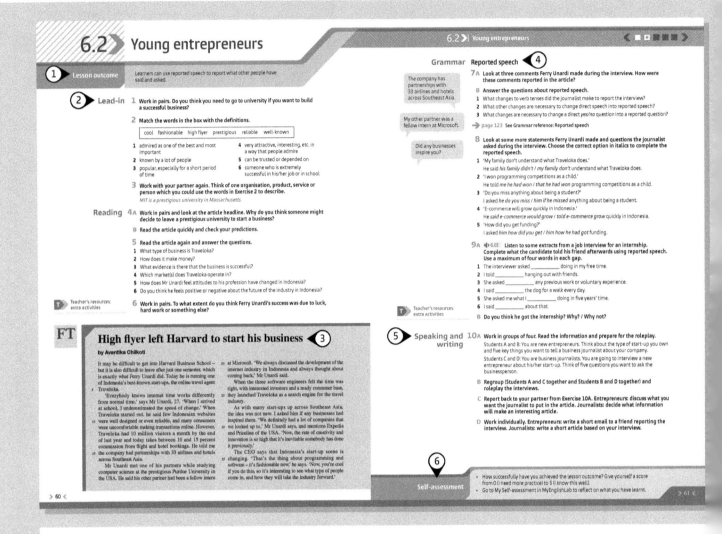

① The Lesson outcome defines a clear learning outcome for every lesson.

② Every lesson begins with a short Lead-in activity to engage learners with the lesson topic on a personal level. This section includes pre-teaching of vocabulary needed for the reading or listening to come.

③ The reading text is generally an article, often from the *Financial Times*. The text focuses on a particular aspect of the unit topic which has an interesting angle, and it contains examples of the grammar point presented.

④ There is one grammar point in each unit, presented in Lesson 2. In general a guided discovery (inductive) approach has been taken to the presentation of grammar. The grammar is presented with reference to examples in the reading (or listening) text, followed by controlled practice.

⑤ Discussion questions and communicative practice of vocabulary and grammar is provided in the final Speaking or Writing section of this lesson.

⑥ Every lesson ends with a short Self-assessment section which encourages learners to think about the progress they have made in relation to the lesson outcomes.

Lesson 3 > Communication skills

The aims of this lesson are:

- to introduce students to the skills needed to interact successfully in international teams.
- to encourage students to notice different communication styles and the misunderstandings that can arise as a result, by watching the scripted skills training video.
- to present and practise functional language associated with the communication skill in the lesson.

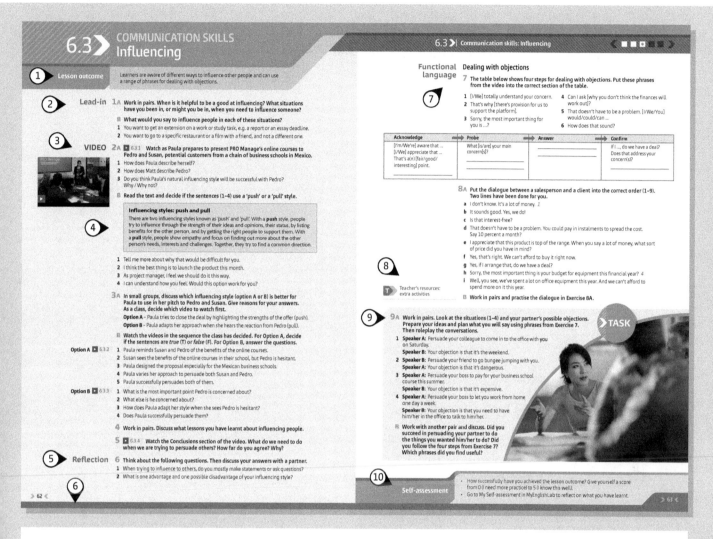

① The Lesson outcome defines a clear learning outcome for every lesson.

② Every Communication skills lesson begins with a short Lead-in activity to engage learners with the lesson topic on a personal level and to set-up the video which follows.

③ The Communication skills training video introduces learners to the skills needed to interact successfully in international teams, with people who may have different communication styles due to culture or personality. There is a storyline running through the eight units, with the main characters appearing in different situations. Note: Each clip, however, can be watched separately and each lesson done independently without the need to watch the preceding video clips.

④ In each Communication skills lesson, you will:
  a watch a set-up video which introduces the main characters and challenge of the lesson;
  b watch the main character approach the situation in two different ways (Options A and B);
  c answer questions about each approach (Option A and Option B) before watching the conclusion.

⑤ Students work alone on a short reflection activity. The approach to this reflection activity may change to suit each lesson. The idea is to encourage students to think about communication styles and their implications.

⑥ The lesson to this point works as a standalone lesson for teachers who have a limited amount of time to work on communication skills. In other teaching situations, the lesson can be extended using the activities on functional language.

⑦ This page presents and practises a set of useful functional language from the video in the Communication skills lesson.

⑧ **T** Teacher's resources: extra activities The optional extension activities for this lesson provide controlled practice of the functional language.

⑨ The lesson ends with a collaborative group task designed to practise the functional language and the communication skill presented in the lesson. There is a scenario or scenario options which pre-work students can relate to, as well as an element of personalisation in the scenario to help with mixed-ability classes.

⑩ Every lesson ends with a short Self-assessment section which encourages learners to think about the progress they have made in relation to the lesson outcomes.

Lesson 4 ❯ Business skills

The aims of this lesson are:

- to give students exposure to a functional business skill or sub-skill using a listening comprehension, encouraging them to notice successful and unsuccessful techniques.
- to present and practise relevant functional language drawing on examples from the listening.
- to encourage students to activate the skill and language they have practised by collaborating on a group task.

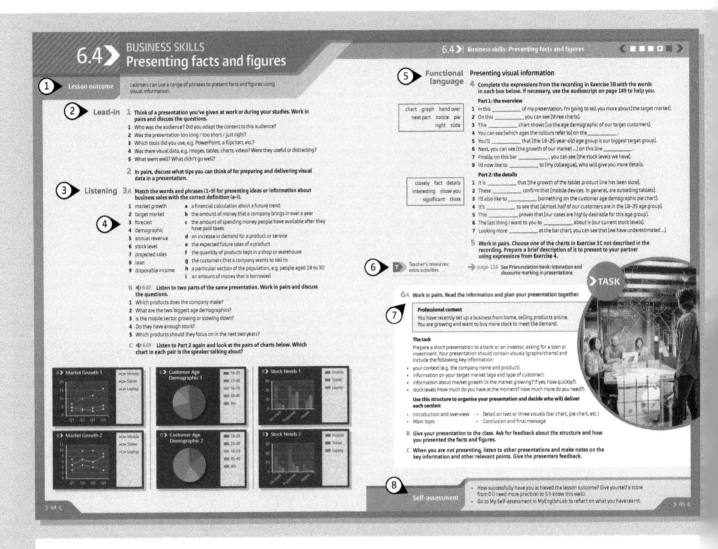

① The Lesson outcome defines a clear learning outcome for every lesson.

② Every Business skills lesson begins with a short Lead-in activity to engage learners with the lesson topic on a personal level.

③ An original listening comprehension introduces the business skill and related key techniques and key functional language.

④ Listening comprehension activities check that students have understood the meaning of key concepts or vocabulary, and move on to listening for detail.

⑤ The section on Functional language offers presentation and practice of a set of useful functional language related to the business skill of the lesson. The language exponents come from the audioscript, and common tasks include gap-fill activities.

⑥ **T Teacher's resources: extra activities** The optional extension activities for this lesson provide controlled practice of the functional language and additional listening practice using the lesson listening text.

⑦ The lesson ends with a significant collaborative group task to practise the target business skill and provide an opportunity to use the functional language presented. A scenario or several scenario options are provided to help with mixed classes, and often include an opportunity for personalisation.

⑧ Every lesson ends with a short Self-assessment section which encourages learners to think about the progress they have made in relation to the lesson outcomes.

Lesson 5 ❯ Writing

The aims of this lesson are:

- to present and practise a specific aspect of business writing, focusing on either genre, function or register.
- to present and practise relevant functional language, drawing on examples from the model text.

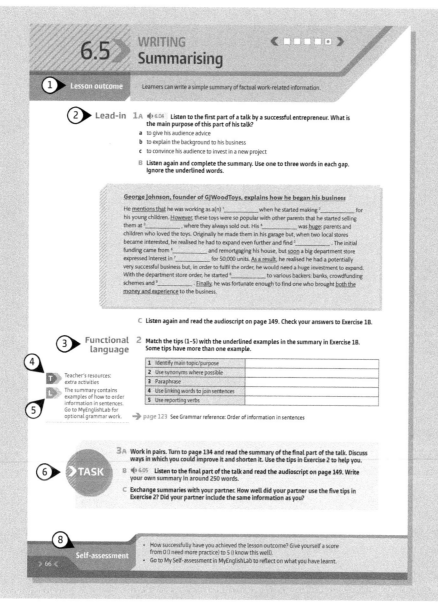

1. The Lesson outcome defines a clear learning outcome for every lesson.

2. Every Writing lesson starts with a writing model with an associated task. The task often requires students to notice or do something with the language within the model text. In specific cases, this section may also include an element of listening, if for example the writing skill refers to 'taking notes from a phone call or presentation', or 'summarising what a speaker or colleague says'.

3. The functional language is presented in a table summarising useful language associated with the target writing skill, and includes a related activity. The table is likely to be categorised according to the different sections of the writing model. Tasks include completing exponents in the table or identifying which ones are formal and informal.

4. **T** Teacher's resources: extra activities   The optional extension activities for this lesson provide controlled practice of the functional language.

5. **L** The summary contains examples of how to order information in sentences. Go to MyEnglishLab for optional grammar work.

There is a signpost to the optional second grammar point. Some examples of the target language point are included in the writing model. The teacher's notes include instructions to focus students on the examples before directing them to the activities in MyEnglishLab if they choose to do so.

6. The lesson ends with at least two writing tasks, from controlled to freer practice.

7. Every lesson ends with a short Self-assessment section which encourages learners to think about the progress they have made in relation to the lesson outcomes.

Business workshops »

The aims of the Business workshops are:

- to simulate a real-life professional situation or challenge which is related to the theme of the unit.
- to provide multiple opportunities for free, communicative practice of the language presented in the unit.

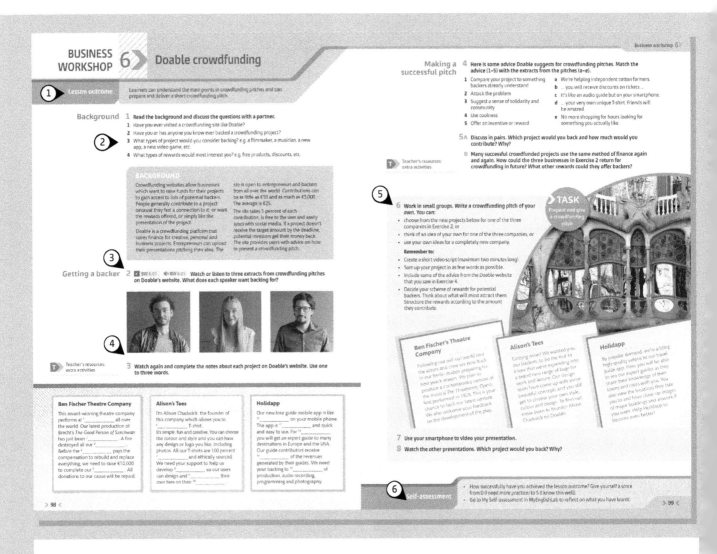

(1) The Lesson outcome defines a clear learning outcome for every lesson.

(2) The workshop begins by providing some background information on the company and the situation or challenge the scenario focuses on.

(3) In units where Lesson 2 contains a reading text, the Business workshop contains a significant listening section, as in Business workshop 6 here. Where Lesson 2 contains a listening, the Business workshop contains a reading text.

(4) This section includes an activity to check understanding.

(5) The task is a practical, collaborative task which addresses the challenge set out in the background section. It focuses on speaking, but usually also includes an element of writing. The Business workshops provide a good variety of output task types.

(6) Every lesson ends with a short Self-assessment section which encourages learners to think about the progress they have made in relation to the lesson outcomes.

Extra material ❯

Extra coursebook activities (PDFs)
❯ go to MyEnglishLab, Teacher's Resources

Photocopiables (PDFs)
❯ at the back of this Teacher's Resource Book, and on MyEnglishLab, in the Teacher's Resources

Resource Bank: Reading bank, Writing bank, Functional language bank (PDFs)
❯ at the back of this Teacher's Resource Book, and on MyEnglishLab, in the Teacher's Resources

Unit tests, with audio files and answer keys (PDFs and Word documents)
❯ go to MyEnglishLab, Teacher's Resources; also available as Interactive tests

Regional-specific material
❯ go to MyEnglishLab, Regional-specific material

1 ▶ Organisation

Unit overview

	CLASSWORK	FURTHER WORK

1.1 ▶ A news organisation

Lead-in	Students look at vocabulary related to typical departments in a company and the roles of each department.
Video	Students watch a video featuring five employees from ITN, a British news organisation. The employees explain their roles and responsibilities, and how the organisation works.
Vocabulary	Students look at vocabulary related to roles and responsibilities in the workplace.
Project	Students roleplay showing someone around an organisation/ campus, putting the language from this lesson into practice.

FURTHER WORK:
MyEnglishLab: Teacher's resources: extra activities; Reading bank

Pronunciation bank: p.114 Word stress

Teacher's book: Resource bank Photocopiable 1.1 p.136

Workbook: p.4 Exercises 1 and 2

1.2 ▶ Innovative organisations

Lead-in	Students discuss the differences, advantages and disadvantages of tall and flat organisational structures.
Listening	Students listen to a radio discussion with an organisation consultant, where she talks about tall and flat company structures, and their benefits and drawbacks.
Grammar	Students study and practise future forms.
Writing	Students practise using future forms by writing an email.

FURTHER WORK:
MyEnglishLab: Teacher's resources: extra activities

Grammar reference: p.118 Future forms

Teacher's book: Resource bank Photocopiable 1.2 p.137

Workbook: p.4 Exercise 3, p.5 Exercises 1–3, p.6 Exercises 1 and 2, p.7 Exercise 3

1.3 ▶ Communication skills: Managing first meetings

Lead-in	Students think about being polite and building relationships in first meetings.
Video	Students watch a video about different ways to approach first meetings in the workplace. Two possible options are introduced, which students explore and discuss.
Reflection	Students think about different communication styles during first meetings and how they themselves approach first meetings.
Functional language	Students look at questions and answers that are commonly used when we meet people and help to develop a business relationship.
Task	Students practise the functional language from the lesson through a mingling activity.

FURTHER WORK:
MyEnglishLab: Teacher's resources: extra activities; Interactive video activities; Functional language bank

Pronunciation bank: p.114 Intonation and politeness

Workbook: p.7 Exercise 1

1.4 ▶ Business skills: Small talk in first meetings

Speaking	Students think about small talk in first meetings.
Listening	Students listen to an interview with a communication coach about using small talk to manage first meetings.
Functional language	Students look at useful language for managing small talk in first meetings.
Task	Students roleplay a first meeting with a visitor and practise making small talk.

FURTHER WORK:
MyEnglishLab: Teacher's resources: extra activities; Functional language bank

Workbook: p.7 Exercise 2

1.5 ▶ Writing: Emails – Organising information

Lead-in	Students think about the organisation of an email and look at some useful phrases for different parts of an email.
Functional language	Students look at more useful phrases for the different parts of an email.
Task	Students write a reply to an invitation email.

FURTHER WORK:
MyEnglishLab: Teacher's resources: extra activities; Interactive grammar practice; Writing bank

Workbook: p.8 Exercises 1–3

Business workshop 1 ▶ Office space

Listening	Students listen to employees giving their views on their workspace.
Reading	Students read two texts about millennial-friendly workspaces.
Task	Students brainstorm, discuss and present their ideas for the design of a new office space.

FURTHER WORK:
MyEnglishLab: Teacher's resources: extra activities

Business brief

The main aim of this unit is to introduce students to the concept of **organisation**. An organisation is a group of people that operate together for a particular purpose. An organisation could be a company, a government department, a service like a hospital or a worldwide organisation like UNESCO or the World Health Organization. Note that all companies are organisations but not all organisations are companies.

The word *organisation* also refers to the way something is **structured**. For example, many companies are organised into departments. Each **department** performs certain **functions**, for example, the human resources department is responsible for recruiting people, providing training, promotion and discipline.

Each member of staff or employee in a company or organisation has a **role** and **responsibilities**. For example, 'Human Resources Director' is a role and that person's responsibilities include recruiting and training new employees. The operations of the various departments must be **coordinated** and teams work together.

We also think of 'organisation' in terms of the **shape** of a company. For example, some companies are **flat**, i.e. they do not have many layers and most of the employees have a similar status. There are usually only a small number of managers and often the manager will be hands-on and have direct contact with the staff.

Typically, **start-ups** are flat and small – a start-up may have only a few staff. Twitter, for example, started with four people. Smaller companies with a flat structure are thought to be more **innovative** and more adaptable. Staff are more directly involved in the decision-making process. However, smaller companies have less security and are often in danger of being bought by bigger companies. Career opportunities for staff can be limited.

Other companies are **tall**, i.e. there are lots of layers between the bottom and the top of the organisation. We also describe this kind of structure as **hierarchical**. Higher levels of management usually have limited direct contact with the staff, in many cases because the company is simply too big. Walmart, the American retail corporation, has about 2.3 million employees worldwide, so a large structure of **middle management** is required to run the various branches and departments in each country. Large companies have the advantage of providing employees with the opportunity for **promotion**, **training** and developing a career within the company. At the same time, large companies can be impersonal and make staff feel remote from the decision-making process.

It is important to note, however, that not all large companies are necessarily hierarchical or impersonal. Often the culture of the company will depend on the approach of the CEO, and these days some CEOs prefer to avoid the stereotype of a large company and continue to operate with the flexibility and speed of a smaller company, maintaining a flat decision-making process and keeping all members of staff involved.

Organisations and your students

It is important that students are aware of the different ways in which companies and organisations are structured. For students who are not yet working, understanding what kind of company they want to work for and the kind of role they want to take on will help them when they enter the job market. Working students will probably already be aware of their own company's structure but may need to develop a wider range of understanding about how other companies work and how businesses do not always conform to the small–large stereotypes.

Unit lead-in

Elicit a brief description of the main photo and then look at the quote with the class. Check that students understand *be your best* and give students 2 minutes to discuss in pairs or small groups: do they agree with the quote? Once students have discussed in their pairs/groups, you could broaden this into a class discussion.

1.1 > A news organisation

GSE learning objectives

- Can understand a large part of a video on a work-related topic.
- Can describe what someone likes or dislikes about their job or workplace.
- Can use key words and phrases related to company structure, departments, jobs and duties.
- Can extract the meaning of unknown words from context if the topic discussed is familiar.
- Can write descriptions of familiar job roles and responsibilities.
- Can understand duties and responsibilities listed in job descriptions.
- Can describe job roles and responsibilities they would like in the future.
- Can provide a basic description of professional goals.
- Can make formal introductions in a professional or work-related situation.
- Can describe a range of jobs in their department or company.

Warm-up

Write the names of three organisations on the board that you think students will know (e.g. *Google, BMW, the World Wildlife Fund*). Ask students what the three names have in common (they are all organisations) and in what ways they are different (Google is a company that provides a service; BMW is a company that makes cars and motorcycles / sells products; the World Wildlife Fund is an organisation, not a company, that protects endangered species). Ask the class to think of more examples for each of the three groups (e.g. Facebook, Ferrari, the World Trade Organization).

Lead-in

Students look at vocabulary related to typical departments in a company and the role of each department.

1 Go through the words in the boxes before students begin and get them to check the meanings of any unknown words in a dictionary. Then put students in pairs and ask them to discuss question 1. Go round the class and help each pair where necessary. As feedback, elicit a description for each department from a pair, and a list of activities for that department. Encourage other pairs to add more details for each department. Do question 2 as a whole class. Give some ideas and clues if necessary (e.g. *This department looks after all the computers, online security, downloading software, etc.* (IT)). Finally, discuss question 3 as a whole class. Make sure students give reasons for their answers.

Possible answers

1 **Finance** is the part of an organisation that manages its money and cash flow. The business functions typically include planning, organising, auditing, accounting for and controlling its company's finances. It raises invoices and chases payment. The department also usually produces the company's financial statements.
Human resources is responsible for recruiting, interviewing and contracting workers. It may also handle employee relations, health and safety, payroll, benefits and training.
The **marketing department** is responsible for market research, promotional campaigns, brand promotion and brand image as well as customer relationship programmes such as social media management. Its main role is to increase revenue for the business.
Operations department's primary functions include the design and management of products, services and processes. It controls the supply chain. The operations department of a manufacturing company is in charge of making the products that a company sells and is therefore often called the production department instead. Performing quality assurance or audits are also functions of an operations department.
Production is the functional area responsible for making sure that raw materials are provided and made into finished goods effectively through a series of production processes.
Sales is the division of a business that is responsible for selling products or providing services such as after-sales customer services. The role of a sales department varies and different companies interpret 'sales' and 'marketing' in widely varying ways. In some companies sales may be part of the marketing department. In general the sales team works closely with the marketing department to plan promotion campaigns and sales strategies.
2 research and development, legal, logistics, customer service, IT
3 Students' own answers

Video

Students watch a video featuring five employees from ITN, a British news organisation. The employees explain their roles and responsibilities, and how the organisation works.

2A Discuss the questions with the class. If students answer *yes* to the first question, ask them which jobs they would like to do.

2B Check that students understand *stressful* and get them to give examples of things they find stressful in their lives. Ask them how working for a news organisation might be stressful. Do the same for *glamorous* and *interesting*.

Possible answers

a It's probably stressful because they have deadlines every day to produce news programmes.
b It could be glamorous if they meet and interview powerful and famous people.
c It is interesting in the sense that the world and the news is changing constantly and dramatic things can happen.

3A ▶ 1.1.1   Tell students they are going to watch a video about five people who work for ITN. You could pre-teach *hub, gather, deploy* and *bulletin,* which are used in the video and will help students answer the questions. Check that students understand the meaning of the jobs in the box, then play the video, twice if necessary, and get students to complete the task. Encourage students to listen just for the information they need to complete the task. Check answers with the class.

> **1** News Editor   **2** News Reporter   **3** Programme Director
> **4** Director of Human Resources   **5** Finance Supervisor

3B Discuss the question as a whole class, getting students to justify their answers.

> Arti Lukha and Nick Thatcher probably work closely together on a daily basis since she would pass the news to him to report on. Nick probably also works closely with John, who has to coordinate the news programmes.

4 ▶ 1.1.1   Explain to students that sentences 1–8 are spoken by the people in the video. Give students a few minutes to read the sentences and try to guess the missing words where possible. Then play the video again, pausing after each sentence where the gaps occur for students to complete the information. Check answers with the class.

> **1** roles   **2** coordinating   **3** reporter   **4** operator
> **5** teams   **6** conductor   **7** operational   **8** payments

5 Put students in pairs or small groups. Suggest they write the name of each person and *Likes most* and *Likes least* on the right to make a table and note down their ideas. Go round the class and monitor. Then check answers with the class, encouraging students to justify their answers.

Extra activities 1.1

A ▶ 1.1.1   This activity gives further practice of key vocabulary from the video. Ask students to complete it individually, then check answers with the class. Alternatively, you could play the video again for students to check their answers.

> **1** leading   **2** hub   **3** deploy   **4** covering   **5** bulletins
> **6** base   **7** ongoing   **8** broadcast live   **9** build-up
> **10** tightly   **11** behind the scenes   **12** billing

B Students could do this individually or in pairs.

> **1** behind the scenes   **2** base   **3** broadcast live
> **4** covering   **5** hub   **6** bulletins   **7** billing   **8** tightly
> **9** deploy   **10** leading   **11** ongoing   **12** build-up

---

Vocabulary: Roles and responsibilities

Students look at vocabulary related to roles and responsibilities in the workplace.

6 Explain that sentences 1–4 are used by the people in the video to talk about their jobs. Go through the words and phrases in the box with the class, then ask students to complete the exercise individually. During feedback, point out the verb form after *involves* and *responsible for* (*-ing*).

> **1** involves (If an activity or situation involves something, that thing is part of it or a result of it.)
> **2** lead (the position of having control of or responsibility for a group of people or an activity)
> **3** running (organising or being in charge of an activity, business, organisation or country)
> **4** make sure (check that something has been done)

7 You could ask students to do this exercise in pairs or get them to complete it individually and then check answers in pairs before class feedback. Encourage students to record the expressions in their notebooks.

> **1** to   **2** of   **3** with   **4** after   **5** of   **6** for   **7** of   **8** with

8 Tell students that this is an opportunity to practise the words and phrases from Exercises 6 and 7, and get them to complete the texts individually or in pairs. Check answers with the class.

> **1** lead   **2** involves   **3** charge   **4** report   **5** care
> **6** responsible   **7** coordinate/work   **8** sure

9 Put students in pairs. Depending on whether your students are in work or not, ask them to describe either their own job, a job they would like to do or a job from the box. You may want to go through the job titles in the box as a class before students begin, to check that they understand the meanings. Go round monitoring, and help students with any extra vocabulary they may need.

Extra activities 1.1

C Explain to students that this activity will help them check their vocabulary from this lesson, and get them to complete it individually as a quick vocabulary quiz. You could get them to compare answers in pairs before checking answers with the class.

> **1** look after   **2** report   **3** involves   **4** charge
> **5** closely   **6** head   **7** lead   **8** Running

> **Pronunciation bank**
p.114: Word stress

Warm-up

Check that students can identify the number of syllables in a word. Write *vacation* on the board and ask the class how many syllables it has (three). Ask students to break the word up into the three syllables: *va-ca-tion*. Now ask students to identify which syllable is stressed (the second syllable, *ca*).

Get students to read the explanation in the box. Check they understand by getting a few students to pronounce *photographer* correctly. Model its pronunciation if necessary. Finally, ask a student to come up to the board and mark the pronunciation pattern for *vacation* (oOo).

1 Put students in pairs for this activity. Do *advertising* as an example with the class, then give pairs 3–4 minutes to categorise the rest of the words in the box.

2 🔊 P1.01 Play the recording for students to check their answers. Then play the recording a second time for students to listen and repeat. You could drill the words chorally first, then individually.

1 Oo: programme, website
2 Ooo: manager, marketing
3 Oooo: advertising, operator
4 oO: involves, report
5 oOo: director, resources
6 oOoo: coordinate, responsible

3 Put students into pairs. Make sure each pair has one large coin and three small coins. Alternatively, you could use paper circle cut-outs. Do an example with a stronger student: put coins/circles into one of the patterns (e.g. Oo) for the student to say a word from Exercise 1 with this stress pattern (e.g. *website*). Then ask him/her to use this word in a sentence. Students then practise in their pairs. Monitor and make a note of any errors/points to highlight during feedback.

Project: Showing someone around
Students roleplay showing someone around an organisation/campus, putting the language from this lesson into practice.

10A Put students in pairs or small groups and explain the situation. Working students are going to show a new member of staff around their organisation. Students who are not yet working are going to show a new/overseas student around their campus. Go through the bullet points so students are clear about what they need to decide, and give students some time to prepare for their roleplays. Encourage them to make notes, and to also think about questions they could ask the three people they are being introduced to. Depending on your class size, you could put students into larger groups, and ask them to also assign roles for the people who are being introduced.

10B Students roleplay the situation. Depending on your teaching situation and the time available, students could do their roleplays in the classroom or you could get them to physically walk around the building, showing their partner(s) around. Monitor and note down any errors or points to highlight during class feedback.

MyEnglishLab: Teacher's resources: extra activities; Reading bank
Pronunciation bank: p.114 Word stress
Teacher's book: Resource bank Photocopiable 1.1 p.136
Workbook: p.4 Exercises 1 and 2

1.2 › Innovative organisations

GSE learning objectives

- Can compare the advantages and disadvantages of different types of company structure.
- Can understand charts and visual interpretations of company structure.
- Can understand the key points of a radio programme on a work-related topic.
- Can express opinions and attitudes using a range of basic expressions and sentences.
- Can use a range of future forms to talk about intentions, plans and predictions.
- Can write an email giving some detail of work-related news and events.

Warm-up

Write on the board: *small companies vs. large companies*. Put students in small groups and ask them to think about and discuss the differences and the advantages/disadvantages of each. To help them, you could write prompts on the board of different aspects to think about (e.g. *structure? number of employees? layers of management? security? career opportunities? training? contact between management and staff?*). You could also ask them to discuss whether they would prefer to work for a smaller or larger company. Give students 4–6 minutes to share their ideas. Once students have discussed in their groups, you could broaden this into a class discussion.

Lead-in

Students discuss the differences, advantages and disadvantages of tall and flat organisational structures.

1 Ask students to look at the two organisational structures and describe the main differences. Ask a few questions to check that students understand the difference between the two structures, e.g. *Who is the person at the top of each structure? How many layers are there in each structure?* Then discuss the question as a whole class. You could put students' ideas on the board into a table with two columns (*Advantages* and *Disadvantages*) and two rows (*Tall organisation* and *Flat organisation*). This will allow you to come back to the list when students do Exercises 2B and 7.

2A Students could do this individually or in pairs, using their dictionaries if necessary.

> **1** promotion **2** innovative **3** hierarchy **4** bureaucracy
> **5** centralised **6** decentralised

2B Put students in pairs and give them 2–3 minutes to discuss the question. Go round the class and help pairs where necessary by asking questions, e.g. *Which structure is more complicated / involves more communication, emails, meetings, etc.?* Then refer students to page 126 and give them another 2–3 minutes to read the information and compare their answers. As feedback, ask students if they disagree with any of the criticisms in the descriptions.

Listening

Students listen to a radio discussion with an organisation consultant, where she talks about tall and flat company structures, and their benefits and drawbacks.

3 Put students in pairs and ask them to look at the company profiles and discuss the questions. If your students have access to the internet, you could ask them to find out more information about each company (e.g. its history, what sort of products it makes, where it is based). Invite a few students to share their ideas with the class, but do not confirm answers yet.

> **Notes**
>
> W. L. Gore was founded in 1958 and is based in Delaware, USA. It specialises in products derived from fluoropolymers and is best known for the fabric Gore-Tex.
>
> Zappos is an online shoe and clothing store, founded in 1999 and based in Las Vegas, USA. In 2009, Amazon.com Inc. acquired Zappos for about $1.2 billion, but lets it operate as an autonomous subsidiary.

4 🔊 1.01 Tell students that they are going to listen to an organisation consultant talk about the two companies. Play the recording for them to check their answers to Exercise 3.

> W. L. Gore started out as a company with a flat structure in the 1950s. Zappos changed to a flatter structure two years ago.

5 🔊 1.01 Ask students to read the sentences and see if they can answer any of the questions from memory. Then play the recording, twice if necessary, for them to complete the activity. Check answers with the class.

> **1** F (Organisations with tall structures can be slow to change and innovate.)
> **2** F (in the 1950s)
> **3** T
> **4** T
> **5** T
> **6** F (The CEO of Zappos says the transition will take two to five years to complete.)

6 Give students 3–4 minutes to complete the activity, individually or in pairs. If necessary, play the recording again. During feedback, you could get students to explain their answers using the audioscript on page 146 (e.g. *I think Janet Wood is critical of hierarchies because she says '… this traditional pyramid hierarchy has many problems'.*).

> **1** a **2** b **3** b **4** c

7 Put students in pairs. Remind them of the list of advantages and disadvantages of tall and flat companies they discussed in Exercise 2. When students have had enough time to discuss the question in pairs, have a whole-class discussion. You could also take a class poll on who would prefer to work for a tall or flat organisation.

> **Notes**
>
> A lot will depend on each student's personality. Some people will enjoy the creative freedom of the boss-free environment. They'll feel more engaged and empowered. Some will not be happy in an organisation that does not offer a clear career path, and will be concerned about how to get promotion and pay rises. (See Zappo's voluntary redundancy scheme.)
>
> Completely manager-free companies are the extreme version of a more general recent trend to flatten out management hierarchies. In flatter hierarchies the remaining managers can have much more responsibility and work.

> **Extra activities 1.2**
>
> **A** 🔊 Ext 1.01 Students could do this individually or in pairs, using a dictionary if necessary. Give them 3–5 minutes to complete the exercise, then play the recording for them to check their answers.
>
> > **1** decision-making **2** bureaucratic **3** successful
> > **4** fabric **5** organisational chart **6** job title
> > **7** delegated **8** join

Grammar: Future forms: Present Simple, Present Continuous and *be going to*

Students study and practise future forms.

8A You could do this as a quick whole-class exercise, checking answers as you go along. Check that students understand the difference between *intention* and *arrangement*.

> **1** a **2** d **3** b **4** c

8B Refer students to the Grammar reference on page 118. Check that they understand the explanations and clarify any points as necessary. Then give them 2 minutes to match the future forms with the examples. Check answers with the class.

> **1** *be* + *going to* + infinitive **2** Present Simple
> **3** Present Continuous **4** *be* + *going to* + infinitive

9 Get students to do the exercise individually. Make it clear that there is more than one answer to some questions and remind students that they can refer to page 118. Go round the class and help where necessary. When students have finished, get them to check their answers in pairs. Monitor again and if there are any points that are still causing problems, go through them with the class during feedback.

> 1 a – scheduled event
> 2 c – personal intention
> 3 b – plan/arrangement with the client (Option c is also possible if viewed as an intention and the speaker doesn't have a fixed arrangement with the client.)
> 4 c – personal intention
> 5 b – plan/arrangement with the friends (As in question 3, option c is also possible if viewed as an intention and the speaker doesn't have a fixed arrangement with his/her friends.)
> 6 c – prediction
> 7 a – scheduled event
> 8 c – The speaker is asking for a prediction.

10A Tell students to work individually and, again, clarify that there may be more than one possible answer to some questions. Remind students to use contractions where possible. Do not confirm answers at this stage.

10B 🔊 1.02 Play the recording and ask students to check if they have used the same future forms as the speakers. Then play the recording a second time, pausing after each line of the conversation. Ask students to explain each answer and discuss any answers that are different from theirs. If time allows, you could put students in pairs and ask them to practise the conversation.

> 1 does the department meeting start – scheduled event
> 2 'm going to be – prediction
> 3 Are you going to be – prediction
> 4 'm giving – plan/arrangement
> 5 's going to be – prediction
> 6 're moving – plan/arrangement
> 7 'm not going to tell – personal intention
> 8 'm going to sit – personal intention

Extra activities 1.2

B This activity gives further practice of future forms. Get students to complete the exercise individually and then check their answers in pairs before checking with the class. During feedback, ask students to explain their answers.

> 1 going to have (prediction)
> 2 are you doing (question about a plan/arrangement, i.e. the exam)
> 3 are meeting (plan/arrangement)
> 4 going to rain (prediction)
> 5 closes (scheduled event)
> 6 going to look (personal intention)
> 7 doesn't finish (scheduled event)
> 8 going to ask (personal intention)

Writing

Students practise using future forms by writing an email.

11 Go through the task with students. Brainstorm ideas as a whole class and write students' ideas for each bullet point on the board (e.g. *a holiday in Japan, flying and taking bullet train; old-fashioned Japanese inn; may be hot; visit temples in Kyoto*). As the email is quite short, this exercise could be done in class. This gives you an opportunity to go round the class and give students individual advice and feedback.

> **Model answer**
>
> Hello Paul,
>
> Guess what! We're going to Madrid for a long weekend in December. We're taking the high-speed train from Barcelona on Thursday 1st and coming back home the following Monday. I expect it's going to be cold there at this time of year but I don't mind. There's so much to see and do in Madrid.
>
> The train gets to the city at 11 a.m., so we're going to leave our bags at the hotel and then explore. On Saturday we're going to the Renoir exhibition. I've booked tickets for that. We're staying right in the centre and it's going to be easy to walk to lots of interesting places.
>
> Write soon and tell me your news.
>
> Best wishes,
> Caroline

MyEnglishLab: Teacher's resources: extra activities

Grammar reference: p.118 Future forms

Teacher's book: Resource bank Photocopiable 1.2 p.137

Workbook: p.4 Exercise 3, p.5 Exercises 1–3, p.6 Exercises 1 and 2, p.7 Exercise 3

1.3 ❯ Communication skills
Managing first meetings

> ### GSE learning objectives
>
> - Can make simple recommendations for a course of action in familar everyday situations.
> - Can extract key details from conversations between colleagues about familiar topics.
> - Can initiate, maintain and close simple, face-to-face conversations on familiar topics.
> - Can make formal introductions in a professional or work-related situation.

> ### Warm-up
>
> Write on the board: *First meetings: creating a good first impression*. Put students in pairs or small groups and ask them to think about what might help them make a good impression when they first meet someone. You could limit this to a business context and ask students to think about a first meeting with a particular person (e.g. a new colleague, a potential employer). Give students 3–4 minutes to discuss in their pairs/groups, then elicit ideas from different students and list them on the board. You could then discuss the list on the board as a whole class.

Lead-in

Students think about being polite and building relationships in first meetings.

1 Tell students they are going to look at how we behave when we meet people for the first time and also at how we approach business relationships. Put students in pairs and ask them to discuss the questions. Tell them that it is important that they think about other cultures as well as their own. Encourage them to think of the different situations in which we meet people (at work, socially, in other countries, etc.). They should also think about verbal communication (what we say) and non-verbal communication (how we behave, our gestures, body language, etc.). Once students have discussed in their pairs, you could broaden this into a class discussion.

> **Possible answers**
> 1 In different cultures and between individuals, there is often a significant variation in what people say and do during first meetings. For example, in some cultures, it may be polite to ask lots of questions and to show curiosity. In other cultures, it may be more respectful to be silent or say very little. For body language, handshakes are expected in some contexts; in others, a kiss and hug may be typical; in others, it may be appropriate to bow.
> 2 Many differences exist with both verbal and non-verbal behaviour, and practices such as gift-giving, types of clothing worn, where the relationship is built (at home or in a restaurant), etc.
> 3 This is an important question as there are significant differences here across cultures and personalities in terms of which comes first; in many cultures, for example, it is impossible to do business until a relationship and a level of trust has been established. In addition, there are different expectations about how long to spend on relationship-building and how deep and trustful the relationship must be before you can do business together.

Video

Students watch a video about different ways to approach first meetings in the workplace. Two possible options are introduced, which students explore and discuss.

2A ▶ 1.3.1 In the first sequence, two people who work for the same company, Matt and Stefanie, meet for the first time. Stefanie is visiting Matt's office. Matt has two options: to focus on developing a good relationship or to focus on work, and students are asked to think about and discuss which option is best. Explain to students that they are going to watch a short video about two businesspeople who are going to meet each other for the first time. Give them a minute to read questions 1–3 and then play the video. Check answers with the class.

> 1 Stefanie works in Germany (Cologne), and a little in Switzerland. Matt works in London.
> 2 Matt heads the UK operations. Stefanie is the manager of the German office.
> 3 Matt is the project lead. Stefanie will provide all technical support.

2B ▶ 1.3.1 Go through the adjectives in the box with students and check that they understand the meanings. Ask students if they remember which adjectives Matt and Stefanie used to talk about themselves. Go through the rubric and play the video for students to match the adjectives with the speakers. Check answers with the class. You could play the second part of the video again, asking students to note down what other words the other speakers use to describe Stefanie (see answer key below).

> **M:** open, flexible, informal
> **S:** efficient, effective, organised, work-focused
> **Other speakers:** work-focused, rude
> **Not used:** friendly, polite, professional, quiet
> (other words the speakers use to describe Stefanie: excellent, demanding, gets results, good person to have on a team)

2C Discuss the question with the whole class. Encourage students to give reasons based on the video and also to use some of the adjectives in Exercise 2B.

> **Possible answer**
> It's difficult to predict how they will work together. They are similar in important ways, e.g. both are work-focused and want to be polite and manage relationships with others effectively. But Matt's fun and more informal approach contrasts with Stefanie's more serious style, which might make it difficult for them to cooperate.

3A Explain to the class the idea of Matt having two options when he meets Stefanie and go through the details of options A and B with the class. Make it clear to students that they can choose which option they want to see first. Put students in small groups and ask them to discuss the two options, giving reasons for their answers. Elicit ideas from a few students and then, as a class, decide which video to watch first.

3B ▶ 1.3.2 ▶ 1.3.3 Tell the class to answer the questions for Option A or B depending on their choice, and play the video. You could ask students to discuss the questions in their groups first (the same groups they worked in for Exercise 3A), and then check answers as a class. Do the same for the second video.

> **Possible answers**
> **Option A**
> 1 with first name only (Matt)
> 2 showing the office and meeting people – because it's important to build a relationship to work well together
> 3 In this meeting Matt focuses on relationships first. He tries to be informal, friendly and positive, and wants Stefanie to meet the team in the office. Matt believes it is important to build relationships as a basis for a project's success. His approach is unclear and confusing to Stefanie at the beginning. However, the result is positive as Matt convinces Stefanie of the importance of strong relationships, and she makes the decision to stay in London to help drive the project.

Option B
1 with first name (Matt), surname (Farnham) and job title (Head of Operations)
2 because Stefanie only has two hours and there are a few issues he would like to discuss
3 In this meeting Matt focuses on the project work. Stefanie is comfortable with this approach and the meeting allows them to discuss important topics for the project. However, Matt is unclear at the end of the meeting if Stefanie is the right person for the project because he has left no time to get to know her, and he will now have to wait a long time before he meets her again.

4 Put students into pairs and give them 3–4 minutes to discuss the questions. Encourage them to think about the speakers' reactions and how each communication style affected the outcome of the meeting. Once students have discussed this in their pairs, open this up into a class discussion. Encourage students to make notes, which they can use in Exercise 5.

Possible answers
1 In Option A, Matt was very relationship-focused, asked lots of questions, and wanted to introduce Stefanie to people to build relationships. In Option B, Matt stayed more task-focused to be polite and tried to get down to business immediately.
2 In Option A, Stefanie seemed uncomfortable during her time with Matt and his team. She said she found it 'unclear and confusing' to focus on relationships rather than work. However, at the end she says she can see the benefit of strong relationships and plans to move to London to get to know the team better. In Option B, the focus on work issues suits Stefanie and she leaves feeling positive. Matt sees that Stefanie is good at her job, but seems frustrated that he didn't get to know her better as a person.

5 ▶ 1.3.4   Students should do this in the same pairs as in Exercise 4. Explain that they are going to watch the last section of the video, where the speaker is commenting on the different communication styles they looked at in Options A and B. Play the video and give students 3–4 minutes to discuss and make notes, then discuss the questions as a whole class. Make sure students give reasons for their answers to question 3.

1 Students' own answers
2 1 Know your own communication style.
  2 Understand the communication style of the other person.
  3 Decide on the best communication style to manage the meeting and have a positive impact on the other person.
3 Students' own answers

Reflection

Students think about different communication styles during first meetings and how they themselves approach first meetings.

6 Allow students to work individually on this so that they can reflect on their own preferences and ideas. Ask them to think of their own answers to the questions and to make notes. Then put students in pairs to discuss and compare their answers. Check answers with the class.

Functional language: Greetings, introductions and goodbyes

Students look at questions and answers that are commonly used when we meet people and help to develop a business relationship.

7 Explain to students that this activity highlights expressions that we use when we meet people for the first time. Go through the table with the class, and then ask students to complete it with phrases 1–8. You could get students to compare answers in pairs before checking with the class.

Meeting and greeting: 2, 6, 8
Introducing people: 3, 4
Saying goodbye: 1, 5, 7

8A Explain that sentences a–e are the visitor's responses to what Suzanne, the host, says (sentences 1–5), and that students need to match them in order to form a dialogue. Check answers with the class. You could ask students to practise reading the dialogue, while you go round monitoring, checking their pronunciation and intonation. However, do not focus on pronunciation/intonation in detail at this stage; this will be the focus of the pronunciation bank activities.

1 b **2** d **3** e **4** a **5** c

8B Put students in pairs for this activity. Point out that they should use phrases from the table in Exercise 7, and that their dialogue can follow the same pattern as the one in Exercise 8A. Give students time to prepare and roleplay their dialogues while you go round monitoring and helping where necessary. If time allows, invite a few pairs to act out their dialogues to the class.

8C Join pairs together into groups of four and go through the rubric with the class. Encourage students to develop the conversation, ask questions and be natural. The conversations should finish with students saying goodbye and giving a reason for leaving. Before students begin, you could brainstorm a few reasons for leaving (e.g. *have to take a phone call, have an appointment / a meeting, must talk to another person*). Allow enough time for students to prepare and roleplay their conversations. If time allows, you could ask each group to roleplay a second dialogue, so that both hosts in each group get to introduce their visitors. Again, you could invite a few groups to act out their conversations to the class. During class feedback, highlight any points/errors you noted while monitoring.

Model dialogue
A: Guys, this is Suzanne Jones.
C: Hi, Suzanne.
D: Nice to see you again.
A: Do you know Suzanne?
D: Yes, we met in Paris last year.
B: Hello, Tom. How's it going?
D: Very well, thanks.
C: Excuse me. I must go to a meeting.
B: Have a good meeting.

Extra activities 1.3

A This activity gives further practice of useful language for managing first meetings. You could do it as a whole class, checking answers as you go, or ask students to do it individually and compare their answers in pairs before checking with the class.

1 How's it ~~doing~~ going?
2 Thank you for ~~going~~ coming today.
3 Did you have a good ~~travel~~ trip?
4 Good to finally ~~know~~ meet you in person.
5 Have you ~~known~~ met Stephanie before?
6 ~~Take~~ Have a good trip home.
7 Let's go ~~to~~ and have lunch.
8 Lovely to see you ~~more~~ again.
9 Sorry ~~for~~ to leave so soon.
10 Alistair, ~~she~~ this is Stephanie.

➤ Pronunciation bank
p.114: Intonation and politeness

Warm-up

Write on the board: *What do you do exactly?* Turn to a student and ask him/her the question, using flat, uninterested intonation. Then turn to another student and ask the same question using rising, interested intonation. Ask the class what they think the difference is between the two versions. Elicit or explain that there is a wider range of intonation in the 'interested' version, and stronger stress on individual words. Get students to read the explanation in the box, and point out the importance of intonation when asking questions: incorrect intonation may result in misunderstandings or listeners even taking offence!

1 🔊 P1.02 Explain that students will hear two versions of each of the three questions: one sounding polite and interested and one sounding impolite and uninterested. Play the recording for students to identify the intonation patterns, and check answers with the class.

1 A polite and interested; B impolite and uninterested
2 A polite and interested; B impolite and uninterested
3 A impolite and uninterested; B polite and interested

2 🔊 P1.03 Explain that this time students will only hear the polite and interested version of each question. Play the recording for students to mark the stressed words, and get them to check answers in pairs before checking with the class. Then play the recording a second time, pausing after each question for students to repeat.

1 Are you very <u>busy</u> at the moment?
2 Where are you <u>based</u>?
3 Do you travel a <u>lot</u> for work?

3 Put students in pairs and explain the activity. With weaker classes, you could do an example with a stronger student. Give students 3–4 minutes to practise in their pairs. Go round monitoring and help, correct or model as necessary. As a round-up, you could ask students if intonation for sounding polite and interested is used in the same way / is also important in their language.

Task

Students practise the functional language from the lesson through a mingling activity.

9A With the whole class, choose an industry from the box and write it on the board (e.g. *architecture*). Elicit a fictional company name (e.g. *DPE Architects*), a job title (e.g. *Head of Planning*), and a (fictional) location for the company (e.g. *Helby, UK*). Put students in pairs and ask them to choose an industry and do the same. Explain that they will use these details in a roleplay in the next stage.

9B Explain the scenario and make sure students have a pen and paper to make a note of any useful contacts they find. They should stand up, mingle and try to speak to different people at the public event. Each time, they should introduce themselves and their colleague, ask about the other person, start some small talk and finally say goodbye, having made a note of the person's name if they wish to. During the activity, monitor and make note of any errors students make with the functional language for this lesson to highlight later.

9C Get students to feed back to the rest of the class on people they met and contacts they think are useful. Encourage students to give as much detail as possible.

9D In the same pairs, students reflect on and discuss the roleplay: which phrases from Exercise 7 they used and any difficulties they had in communicating. As feedback, get students to share their ideas with the class and highlight any errors you noted during the roleplay. Round off the task by asking how students will handle first meetings in the future. You could get them to write three action points starting *In future first meetings I will …*

MyEnglishLab: Teacher's resources: extra activities; Interactive video activities; Functional language bank
Pronunciation bank: p.114 Intonation and politeness
Workbook: p.7 Exercise 1

1.4 ❯ Business skills
Small talk in first meetings

GSE learning objectives

- Can follow a recorded interview or talk on work-related topics.
- Can understand the details of someone's personal and professional experience from an interview or presentation.
- Can recognise the use of small talk when welcoming guests and visitors.
- Can use polite questions to build rapport in work-related social situations.
- Can initiate, maintain and close simple, face-to-face conversations on familiar topics.

Warm-up

Write the following questions on the board: *When was the last time you met someone for the first time? What questions did you ask him/her? What questions did he/she ask you? How did you feel about being asked those questions?* Put students in pairs or small groups and give them 3–4 minutes to discuss. Once students have discussed in their pairs/groups, ask different students to share their answers with the class. Try to elicit/pre-teach *small talk*.

Lead-in

Students think about small talk in first meetings.

1 Put students into pairs and give them 3–4 minutes to discuss the questions. Then discuss as a class. Ask students for some examples of small talk and put them on the board (e.g. *How was your journey? It's hot/freezing today, isn't it?*).

Possible answers

1 Small talk is a form of polite conversation which people use in first meetings and informal moments or between discussions of more serious topics.
2 When meeting in business, it is typical to ask questions about travel to the meeting place, to offer a drink, etc.
3 Asking questions puts some pressure on your counterpart to answer, which may be stressful. Additionally, some people may feel that asking too many questions, especially on personal topics, is impolite.

Listening

Students listen to an interview with a communication coach about using small talk to manage first meetings.

2A 🔊 1.03   Tell students that they are going to listen to an interview with a communication coach about small talk and the importance of getting to know people in a business context. You could ask students to think of possible answers to the questions before they listen. Play the recording and discuss the answers as a class.

1 People are strangers; they don't know each other and they (often) have to communicate in a foreign language.
2 You learn about the other person and so can build a relationship.
3 Short, simple, starter questions with follow-up questions. They allow an easy answer, they're not too personal, they can quickly break the ice and get the conversation flowing.
4 Ask about work responsibilities and the organisation behind the person; on a personal note, travel is a good topic.

2B 🔊 1.03   Give students time to read the questions, then play the recording again. If necessary, pause at key points to allow students enough time to note down their answers. Check answers with the class.

1 Silence in some cultures is a way to signal respect, but she thinks silence slows down the process of getting to know another person.
2 The content of some questions doesn't matter, but the questions do help to break the ice and get the conversation flowing.
3 You trust people you know well. Questions help you get to know a person and so are essential to trust-building.

2C Put students in pairs to discuss the questions, then discuss as a whole class.

Possible answers

1 People from different backgrounds respond to questions in very different ways – some more positively and some less positively. Some will feel engaged; others might feel the questions are impolite in some way. At work and in life generally, we need to ask questions which are right for the other person if we want to motivate them to have a conversation. The challenge is to find out which questions motivate others. This is often a process of trial and error.
2 Conversations can be easier if both people have something to say about a topic which they know.
3 Conversations need many things to be successful. Fundamentally, people must bring a positive attitude – to want to talk – to the conversation. Finding topics which both people are interested in will motivate interaction. Finally, balancing participation – letting people talk and listen in silence – in a way which is comfortable for everyone is important.

3A 🔊 1.04   Check that students understand the statements, then play the recording. You could get students to compare answers in pairs before checking with the class.

1 T
2 F (It's her second visit.)
3 F (She works 20 percent in Geneva.)
4 T
5 F (Paul is leading the project.)

3B 🔊 1.04 Go through the list of tips with students and ask them if they can remember Paul using any of these tips when he greets Eva. Then play the recording again for students to check their answers. With students who are working, you could ask them if they ever do any of the things on the list in first meetings.

> b, c, d, e, g, h, i, j, k

3C You could ask students to discuss the question in pairs or groups and then broaden this into a class discussion. Make sure students justify their answers.

> Paul handles the meeting well as Eva responds positively to his questions and general style of first meeting.

Functional language: Asking and answering questions in first meetings

Students look at useful language for managing small talk in first meetings.

4A Check that students understand the headings in the table before they begin. Explain that these are questions from the recording and refer them to the audioscript on page 146 if necessary. You could do this as a whole class, checking answers as you go along, or ask students to complete it individually and check answers in pairs before checking with the class.

> **1** take **2** offer **3** have **4** time **5** work **6** join
> **7** report **8** free

4B Again, this could be done as a whole class: nominate a student to read a question from Exercise 4A at random and then ask another student to find the matching answer in Exercise 4B. Alternatively, get students to do this individually and then check answers with the class.

> **a** 4 **b** 5 **c** 7 **d** 6 **e** 1 **f** 2 **g** 3

Extra activities 1.4

A/B These activities provide further practice and consolidation of the functional language from this lesson. Ask students to complete both exercises individually and get them to compare answers in pairs before checking with the class.

> **A 1** e **2** d **3** a **4** f **5** c **6** b
> **B 1** My flight was delayed for two hours.
> **2** The taxi driver couldn't find the office.
> **3** My battery was flat so I couldn't call you.
> **4** I think I left my laptop on the train.
> **5** The hotel couldn't find the booking you made for me.
> **6** I need to buy some clothes because my luggage didn't arrive.

Task

Students roleplay a first meeting with a visitor and practise making small talk.

5A Put students in groups of three and explain the task. There are three roles: a host, a visitor and an observer, and three scenarios so that each student has the opportunity to play each role once. Allocate roles A, B and C and refer each student to the relevant page for their role card. If you don't have the right number of students, give priority to having A and B roles. Explain that the observers can take notes while listening. Clarify that students will roleplay each scenario separately, and that each student will take the role of host, observer and visitor once.

5B Follow these steps for each scenario: give students time to read their cards and ask you questions if anything is not clear, and allow 4–6 minutes' preparation time. Set a time limit for the roleplay. During the activity, go round monitoring, but only help out if a group or student is struggling. It is important that students learn to deal with silences and not being sure about what to say.

5C Keep students in the same groups. It is now the observers' role to give feedback to the other two students. Try to keep in the background at this stage. Students A and B should also talk about their performance and their opinions about how to manage a first-time meeting. You could do a whole-class round-up at the end if you feel that it would be useful. It is often good for students to hear the opinions of others, to get a balanced perspective on their own performance and an objective view of the task as a whole.

MyEnglishLab: Teacher's resources: extra activities; Functional language bank
Workbook: p.7 Exercise 2

1.5 ➤ Writing
Emails – Organising information

GSE learning objectives

- Can understand standard emails on work-related topics.
- Can organise a work-related email to emphasise the main point.
- Can reply to a work-related email confirming arrangements.
- Can tell when to use the Present Simple and when to use the Present Continuous.

Warm-up

Do this quick warm-up activity to help familiarise students with the organisation and different parts of an email. Write the parts of an email in random order on the board (given in the correct order here): *subject line, greeting/opening, reason for writing, details / main body, concluding, closing, signature*. Put students in pairs and ask them to put the parts in the correct order. List them in the correct order on the board, and leave the list on the board for students to refer to during the lesson.

Lead-in

Students think about the organisation of an email and look at some useful phrases for different parts of an email.

1 Check that students understand *induction day* before they begin, then ask them to do this individually. Get them to compare their answers in pairs before checking with the class.

> **1** Dear Jill **2** Just a quick email to let you know **3** Firstly **4** Then **5** After **6** feel free to call me if you have any questions **7** All the best

Functional language

Students look at more useful phrases for the different parts of an email.

2A If you did the warm-up activity above, go straight into the task. Otherwise, check that students understand the headings in the table and briefly discuss the organisation / different parts of the email. Ask students to complete the exercise individually or in pairs, then check answers with the class. For this and the next exercise, you could copy the table onto the board and invite different students to come up and write the answers in the correct column.

> See phrases in italics in answer key to Exercise 2B below.

2B Before students begin, you could go through the phrases in the box with the class or let students check any words they don't know in a dictionary (e.g. *further to, confirm, hesitate*). Elicit or explain when *Dear Sir/Madam* is used (when we don't know the name of the person we are writing to).

Greeting/ Opening	*Dear Jill*
	Dear Sir/Madam,
	Good morning Jacques
	Hello/Hi George
Reason for writing	*Just a quick email to let you know ...*
	I'm writing to inform you that ...
	Further to our conversation, I confirm that ...
	Thank you for your email.
Ordering information	*Firstly,*
	Then,
	After,
	Finally,
	Thirdly,
Concluding email	*Feel free to call me if you have any questions.*
	Hope to hear from you soon.
	I look forward to hearing from you.
	Please do not hesitate to contact me if you have any questions.
Closing	*All the best,*
	Yours,
	Kind regards,
	Regards,
	Yours sincerely,

Extra activities 1.5

A This activity gives further practice of useful phrases for the different parts of an email. Ask students to complete it individually and then get them to check answers in pairs before checking with the class.

> **1** Dear **2** for **3** Further **4** confirm **5** Firstly **6** that **7** Finally **8** hesitate **9** seeing **10** regards

Optional grammar work

The email in Exercise 1 contains examples of the Present Simple and Present Continuous, so you could use it for some optional grammar work. Refer students to the Grammar reference on page 118 and use the exercises in MyEnglishLab for extra grammar practice.

Task

Students write a reply to an invitation email.

3A Put students in pairs and refer them to the information on page 126. Explain that they will be using this information to reply to Greg's email, and check that they understand *re* (= about, on the subject of) in e. If you did the warm-up activity, you could refer students to the list on the board to help them. Check answers with the class.

> **Possible answers**
> **1** e **2** d **3** g **4** a **5** c **6** b **7** f

3B Set a time limit for the writing task and remind students to use the information from Exercise 3A and phrases from Exercises 2A and 2B. Students can write their emails individually and then come back together for Exercise 3C. Alternatively, they can write their emails in pairs and then work with a different partner for Exercise 3C.

> **Model answer**
> Dear Greg,
>
> Thank you for your email about the induction day next week, which I am very keen to attend.
>
> Unfortunately, I am unable to attend on Thursday as I'm going to an important conference with the Finance Manager and will be away from the office all day. Therefore, I hope that it will be alright for me to have the induction day on Friday. However, I may be slightly late in the morning on Friday as I have a dentist's appointment at 8.30 a.m.
>
> I look forward to hearing from you.
>
> Kind regards,

3C In their pairs, students evaluate and discuss each other's answers. Monitor and make a note of any errors/points to highlight during feedback.

MyEnglishLab: Teacher's resources: extra activities; Interactive grammar practice; Writing bank
Workbook: p.8 Exercises 1–3

Business workshop ⟩1

Office space

GSE learning objectives

- Can summarise the main message from simple diagrams (e.g. graphs, bar charts).
- Can infer speakers' opinions in conversations on everyday work-related topics.
- Can identify and exchange key information in an extended text or article.
- Can express opinions as regards possible solutions, giving brief reasons and explanations.

Background

Students read about Ditigal, an internet media organisation.

1 Put students in pairs and ask them to read the background and discuss the questions. Check answers with the class. For question 2, you could use your classroom to check/elicit/explain features like noise level, light, space, windows, view, furniture, etc.

> 1 *Arbejdsglæde* means 'happiness at work'.
> 2 **Possible answers:** People in dark, noisy offices with very little personal space may feel more stressed and therefore less happy and productive. People with more space and nicer views from the window may feel more relaxed at work and therefore happier and more productive. Office temperature and lighting can also affect a person's productivity.

Finding out what employees think

Students study a bar chart showing employees' views on their workspace and then listen to employees giving their views.

2A Refer students to the bar chart and check they understand *communal, distractions and acoustic.* You may also want to check they understand the phrase *X in Y* in terms of percentages, e.g. *one in four* = 25 percent. Check answers with the class.

> 1 nicer communal areas 2 more private meeting rooms, bigger personal work space 3 half / 50 percent of
> 4 access to outdoors 5 work away from the office

2B Once students have discussed the question in pairs, you could broaden this into a class discussion.

Possible answers

The survey suggests that staff want more space in general, including personal workspace as well as private meeting rooms and nicer communal areas where staff can gather. It also seems clear that staff don't like current noise levels nor the fact that they don't have much 'visual and acoustic privacy', perhaps when talking on the phone or due to being seen by colleagues and managers.

3 ◀⟩ BW 1.01 Play the recording once only and check answers with the class.

> **a** Speaker 3 **b** Speaker 1 **c** Speaker 2

4 ◀⟩ BW 1.01 Play the recording again and tell students that they can make notes while listening. If they are struggling, you could play the recording a third time.

> Speaker 1 wants more flexible work spaces such as more meeting rooms and quiet zones for individual work.
>
> Speaker 2 wants the office design, furniture and artwork to reflect the company's innovative, fun-loving, techy image of itself.
>
> Speaker 3 wants to have more public spaces for communication and collaboration between departments such as a bigger kitchen / dining room, a ping-pong table and an outside space where staff can go.

Extra activities Business workshop 1

A ◀⟩ BW 1.01 This activity practises key vocabulary from Exercises 1–4. Go through the words/phrases in the box before students begin, and ask them to do the exercise individually. Play the recording for them to check their answers, and clarify any vocabulary queries as necessary.

> 1 cramped 2 tied down 3 open-plan
> 4 distractions 5 fun-loving/tech-savvy
> 6 tech-savvy/fun-loving 7 work–life
> 8 working hours 9 presenteeism 10 tiny
> 11 welcoming 12 mingle

The office as somewhere to enjoy

Students read and discuss two articles on millennial-friendly workspaces.

5A Put students in pairs and assign A and B roles. Explain that students are going to read one article each and summarise the article for their partner. Refer students to their articles and give them time to read and make notes on the main points.

5B In their pairs, students summarise their articles for their partner and then discuss the question. Point out that they should use their own words in their summaries and not read from their texts. If time allows, discuss the two companies as a whole class and have a vote on the top three features.

Possible answers

GoCardless in London has an open-plan design, informal furniture (picnic tables) and game consoles (Xbox) to create an informal atmosphere. The company spends money on staff meals and entertainment. They want staff to like actually being at the office rather than choosing to work from home.

A small but growing number of companies in Poland are introducing features found in hi-tech U.S. companies in order to attract the most talented young employees. These include areas designed for different types of work, such as creative spaces with walls for writing notes, 'silence boxes' where people can concentrate in peace, as well as relaxation rooms with games consoles and spacious kitchens with full fridges. Some modern office buildings now have restaurants, hotel-like lounges in the reception, cycle racks and showers as well as green areas with ponds, amphitheatres, art galleries and cafés.

Extra activities Business workshop 1

B This reading comprehension task can be done in class or set as homework. Explain that students need to read *both* texts for this exercise, and ask them to underline the parts of each text that lead them to the answers. With weaker classes, it might be better to do this activity in class and allow students to work in pairs.

1 c **2** a **3** b **4** a **5** c **6** b **7** b **8** c **9** a **10** a

Task

Students brainstorm, discuss and present their ideas for the design of a new office space.

6A Put students in small groups and go through the instructions and checklist with them. Answer any questions they may have and allow 4–6 minutes for the activity.

6B Put students in pairs. Ensure each student is working with someone from a different group. Allow students 4–6 minutes to exchange ideas. At this point, you may want to elicit ideas from different pairs and write them on the board.

7 Refer students to page 130 and give them time to read the email. Let them discuss their ideas in pairs, then broaden this into a class discussion. Ensure students justify their answers.

MyEnglishLab: Teacher's resources: extra activities

Review ◀ 1

1 **1** involves **2** reports **3** for **4** leads **5** Head **6** after **7** with **8** makes **9** care **10** charge

2 **1** 'm going to get **2** opens **3** Are we going to sell **4** 's going to ask **5** are you meeting **6** I'm going to **7** 's going to snow **8** 'm seeing

3 **1** Not bad, not bad **2** A bit of a delay **3** Have you met **4** see you again **5** in such a rush **6** let's go and say hello **7** in person **8** first time **9** for coming

4 **1** offer **2** would **3** based **4** report **5** worked **6** join **7** free

5 **1** i **2** d **3** j **4** a **5** e **6** g **7** h **8** b **9** c **10** f

Brands

2

Unit overview

	CLASSWORK	FURTHER WORK
2.1 › The life of luxury	**Lead-in** Students discuss luxury brands. **Video** Students watch a BBC report on the recent history of the luxury brand Bulgari and how the brand and products have been developed. **Vocabulary** Students look at vocabulary related to marketing and brands. **Project** Students choose an advertising campaign to research and discuss.	**MyEnglishLab:** Teacher's resources: extra activities; Alternative video worksheet; Reading bank **Pronunciation bank:** p.114 Stress in compound nouns and noun phrases **Teacher's book:** Resource bank Photocopiable 2.1 p.138 **Workbook:** p.9 Exercises 1–3
2.2 › Asian brands go west	**Lead-in** Students discuss global brands and study collocations with *brand*. **Reading** Students read a newspaper article about Asian brands. **Grammar** Students study and practise connectors for adding and contrasting ideas, referring to time, giving examples and sequencing. **Speaking** Students practise using connectors while discussing brands.	**MyEnglishLab:** Teacher's resources: extra activities **Pronunciation bank:** p.114 Connectors: intonation and pausing **Grammar reference:** p.119 Connectors **Teacher's book:** Resource bank Photocopiable 2.2 p.139 **Workbook:** p.10 Exercises 1–3, p.11 Exercises 1–3
2.3 › Communication skills: Supporting teamwork	**Lead-in** Students discuss team- and groupwork as a lead-in to the video topic. **Video** Students watch a video about supporting team colleagues and how this can affect the performance of a team. **Reflection** Students reflect on the learning points and conclusions from the video and discuss effective teamwork. **Functional language** Students look at phrases for giving and responding to advice. **Task** Students practise the functional language from the lesson by roleplaying and then discussing different situations.	**MyEnglishLab:** Teacher's resources: extra activities; Interactive video activities **Workbook:** p.12 Exercises 1 and 2
2.4 › Business skills: Making a presentation	**Lead-in** Students discuss giving and attending presentations and look at the dos and don'ts of opening a presentation. **Listening** Students listen to different presentation openings and then discuss techniques for opening presentations. **Functional language** Students look at useful signposting phrases for presentations. **Task** Students practise giving a short presentation.	**MyEnglishLab:** Teacher's resources: extra activities; Functional language bank **Workbook:** p.12 Exercise 3
2.5 › Writing: Formal and semi-formal emails	**Lead-in** Students analyse an invitation email and learn to distinguish between formal and semi-formal language. **Functional language** Students look at useful phrases for formal and semi-formal invitation emails. **Task** Students write a reply to a formal invitation email.	**MyEnglishLab:** Teacher's resources: extra activities; Interactive grammar practice; Writing bank **Grammar reference:** p.119 Verbs + *-ing* vs. infinitive **Workbook:** p.13 Exercises 1–3
Business workshop 2 › Kloze-Zone	**Listening** Students listen to customers and staff giving feedback on a clothing store. **Task** Students hold a brainstorming meeting for a brand awareness campaign. **Writing** Students write an email summarising their ideas from the brainstorming meeting.	**MyEnglishLab:** Teacher's resources: extra activities

Business brief

The main aim of this unit is to introduce students to the concept of **brands**. A **brand** is a product or service combined with various elements that create a unique **image** – a **logo**, the product **design**, a **slogan** and the impression created by **marketing** and **advertising campaigns**.

Brands exist in many **sectors**: car manufacturing, fashion, hotels, food and, increasingly, technology and online services – the list of top global brands today contains several technology-based companies like Apple, Google, Microsoft and Amazon. Top global brands also include car brands like Toyota and BMW, and food and drink brands like Coca-Cola and McDonald's. Brands are found in the both the **luxury market** (e.g. Porsche) and in the mainstream (e.g. Zara).

Companies **maintain** their brands by **updating** and improving successful products; for example, Apple releases new versions of the iPhone at regular intervals. At the same time, a company's brand has to be reliable in order to maintain **brand loyalty**. If changes are made, the brand can be damaged; for example, Coca-Cola lost a lot of customers in 1985, when it changed the formula of what was then the world's most popular soft drink.

Companies use **marketing** and **advertising** to help develop and maintain a brand. This could take the form of a logo – famous logos include Nike's swoosh and McDonald's golden arches. The design of a product is also key; for example, a Ferrari sports car has a shape and colour that is instantly recognisable and is unique to the brand. Slogans like 'Think different' (Apple), 'Just do it' (Nike), and 'I'm lovin' it' (McDonald's) also play a part in establishing the brand personality.

Brand awareness is often developed by **brand ambassadors** and celebrity **endorsement**. Famous entertainers and sportspeople often become associated with a particular brand, which helps to create a **brand image** that appeals to the desires and **aspirations** of consumers. The overall impression created in the consumer's mind by these elements is a brand's **personality**.

Growing the brand is another element of marketing. Companies can expand the **range of products** that they offer; for example Bulgari, which has gone from jewellery to fragrance to hotels. Another way of developing is to buy other brands to create a super-brand like LVMH (Louis Vuitton Moët Hennessey), which is a group of over 70 brands. Companies also grow by finding new markets. Brands produced in Asian markets have been a growing part of the global market since the emergence of Japanese brands Sony and Toyota in the 1980s, Uniqlo and Muji in the 2000s, and Taiwanese brands like HTC and Asus gaining in popularity in the 2010s. Brands never stand still.

Brands and your students

Working students should be aware of their company's image and any brands that they produce. They should be able to describe them and explain their importance to the company. Students who are not yet working will be aware of brands as consumers, and should be able to analyse how a brand works. Using brands they are familiar with is a good jumping-off point for further exploration into how marketing and advertising work.

Unit lead-in

Ask students to look at the photo and quote. Check that they understand *project, perceive* and the job title *brand strategist*. Ask: *How do you think the photo is relevant to the quote?* Elicit a few ideas from students. Then discuss the quote: Do students agree? Why / Why not? This can be done in pairs, small groups or as a whole-class discussion.

2.1 ❯ The life of luxury

GSE learning objectives

- Can give or seek personal views and opinions in discussing topics of interest.
- Can understand a large part of a video on a work-related topic.
- Can use language related to advertising and branding.
- Can express and comment on ideas and suggestions in informal discussions.
- Can ask and answer questions in a face-to-face survey.
- Can prepare a simple questionnaire in order to gather data.
- Can present findings from a research project in a simple way.

Warm-up

Ask the class to think of some brand names. Write *Luxury* and *Mainstream* on the board in two columns, and elicit ideas from students. They should tell you which of the two categories on the board each brand name they suggest fits in (e.g. *Patek Philippe* (Swiss watch manufacturer) goes in the *Luxury* category; *Timex* (American watch manufacturer) goes in the *Mainstream* category). Briefly discuss some of the brand names as a class, eliciting what students know about them.

Lead-in

Students discuss luxury brands.

1 Students could discuss the questions in pairs or groups first, and then as a whole class. For question 1, help students with any vocabulary they may need, and list their ideas on the board. For question 2, point out that the items do not have to be expensive – a Louis Vuitton key ring counts as an example. Students may say they don't buy luxury brands, but some of them may have designer trainers, jewellery, mobile phones, etc. Ask question 3 in a neutral way so that students who disagree feel confident to speak up.

Possible answers

1 cars, technology, watches and jewellery, perfumes/ fragrances, cosmetics, designer clothes, accessories (e.g. sunglasses), furniture

Video

Students watch a BBC report on the recent history of the luxury brand Bulgari and how the brand and products have been developed.

2 ▶ 2.1.1   If Bulgari did not come up in the warm-up or lead-in activities, ask students what they know about it. (It is an Italian company that produces jewellery, fragrances and luxury goods, founded in 1884 by a Greek jeweller, Sotirios Voulgaris.) Explain that students are going to watch a video about Bulgari and check that they understand *extend the brand* in the rubric. Play the video and check the answer with the class.

> They moved into hotels. (Fragrances were also added at an earlier stage.)

3 Give students a minute to go through the questions before they watch again. Check that they understand *over-extending* and *launched*. Play the video and get students to check answers in pairs before checking with the class.

> **1** stretch it
> **2** in Rome, more than 100 years ago
> **3** jewellery, watches, accessories and fragrances (perfumes)
> **4** Milan (in a building that used to be a convent), next to the Botanical Gardens
> **5** from the 1600s and 1970s
> **6** It has a 25-metre pool, although it's a small hotel.
> **7** The brand is devalued if a company goes into areas or sectors where it is less credible.
> **8** It has launched three hotels so far but it will launch three more in the future.

4 ▶ 2.1.1   Go through the statements with the class and clarify any unknown words (e.g. *devalued, ultimately*). Play the last part of the video again (2:55–4:24) for students to match the statements with the speakers. To check answers, you could play the last part of the video again, pausing after each statement is heard and eliciting the answer.

> **1** Peter York **2** Silvio Ursini **3** Silvio Ursini **4** Peter York

5 Put students in pairs or small groups and explain the activity. You could point out to students that copying includes products that are similar but not exactly the same. Give pairs/groups 2–3 minutes to discuss the first question, then get brief feedback from the class, noting students' ideas on the board. Then give them another 2–4 minutes to brainstorm other categories and think of examples for each one. Elicit ideas from different students.

Extra activities 2.1

A ▶ 2.1.1   This activity practises key vocabulary from the video. Students should do this activity individually. Give them time to read the sentences and play the first part of the video again (0:00–2:54). If necessary, pause after each sentence is heard, to give students time to complete their answers. Check answers with the class and check that students understand the collocations.

> **1** seen **2** worn **3** was **4** began to **5** had
> **6** came about **7** decided to **8** came up
> **9** set about **10** kept

Alternative video worksheet: Power of the internet

1 Refer students to the photo and get them to discuss the questions in pairs or small groups. Remind them to give reasons for their answers. You could then broaden this into a class discussion. Try to elicit *digital marketing* and students' opinions of it.

Possible answers

weddings, celebrations; use online or digital marketing, advertise in wedding/events magazines, promote services at wedding or events conferences

2 ▶ ALT2.1.1 Explain to students that they are going to watch a video about the power of digital marketing, and go through the statements with the class. Play the video, twice if necessary in weaker classes, then check answers with the class.

1 F **2** T **3** F

3 ▶ ALT2.1.1 Go through the questions with the class and check students understand *niche market* in question 2. Play the video for students to answer the questions. Get them to compare and discuss their answers in pairs before checking with the class.

1 It is a cheaper alternative.
2 through social networks
3 create a Facebook page, create a video
4 in the 60s 'to crush Adidas', now 'to bring inspiration and innovation to every athlete in the world'
5 blogger; 60,000 followers
6 to feature the website in the blog and speak to Jo about becoming a featured supplier
7 growth in her business

4 Put students in pairs or small groups and give them 3–5 minutes to discuss the questions. Then get brief feedback from the class.

Possible answers

1 newspaper/magazine advertising, flyers, brochures, billboards, etc.
2 People who do not have easy access to the internet or some older consumers might prefer traditional channels. Younger consumers who frequently use smartphones and digital devices might respond to digital marketing.
3 specialised publications such as wedding magazines, advertisements in local papers or at wedding events

5 ▶ ALT2.1.1 Students could do this individually or in pairs, using their dictionaries if necessary. Play the first part of the video again (0:00–0:27) for them to check their answers; check they understand the meanings of the collocations.

1 c **2** a **3** b

6 Explain that the sentences are extracts from the video. You may want to let students use their dictionaries for this exercise. With weaker classes, you could allow students to work in pairs. Check answers with the class and clarify any vocabulary as necessary.

1 transactional **2** social media
3 catches **4** develop **5** about
6 on trend **7** prestige
8 cost-effective **9** unique selling point
10 target markets

7 Again, weaker students could do this exercise in pairs. Allow them to use their dictionaries. During class feedback, check that students understand all the words in italics, not just the correct answers.

1 blog **2** content **3** hits **4** viral
5 comments **6** links

8 Put students in pairs and give them 3–5 minutes to discuss the questions. As class feedback, elicit ideas from different students, ensuring they justify their answers. For question 2, you could ask students if they have ever decided to buy a product based on online consumer reviews. Ask them about the products they bought and whether they regretted their decision in the end: how accurate were the comments they read and how far did students agree with the reviews after trying the products?

Vocabulary: Marketing and brands

Students look at vocabulary related to marketing and brands.

6 Explain that sentences 1–10 are from the video and look at the words in the box with the class. This exercise can be done individually or in pairs.

1 Stretching **2** cautious approach **3** base of clients
4 further afield **5** ultra-luxury **6** core business
7 bad history, devalued **8** brands **9** fast growth
10 venture into

7 Ask students to do this individually and then check answers in pairs before checking with the class. As homework, you could ask students to write their own example sentence for each word.

1 product placement **2** interactive marketing
3 brand stretching **4** customer engagement
5 awareness **6** logo **7** loyalty **8** image

8 Put students in pairs and give them 3–5 minutes to discuss the questions. Go round monitoring and helping where necessary. Once students have discussed in their pairs, you could broaden this into a class discussion.

Extra activities 2.1

B Write *control* on the board and ask students to think of adjectives that collocate with it (e.g. *complete, total*). Refer students to the activity and explain that two words in each question collocate with the noun and one doesn't. Give students time to complete the activity individually and get them to compare answers in pairs before checking with the class. Encourage them to record the collocations in their notebooks, with an example sentence for each.

> **1** fast **2** longest **3** placement **4** tight
> **5** devalued **6** image **7** vital **8** business **9** thin
> **10** engagement **11** approach **12** further
> **13** stretching **14** logo **15** long

❯ **Pronunciation bank**
p.114: Stress in compound nouns and noun phrases

Warm-up

Write *jewellery brand* on the board. Say the two words out loud, with the stress on *jewellery*. Ask a student to come up to the board and underline the word they thought was stressed. Do the same with *soft drink*. Refer students to the explanation in the box and clarify as necessary. Drill the pronunciation of both examples.

1 Put students in pairs for this activity. Alternatively, you could ask them to work individually first, and then get them compare their answers in pairs. Do not confirm answers yet as students will check them in the next exercise.

2 🔊 P2.01 Play the recording for students to check their answers. Then play the recording a second time for students to listen and repeat.

> <u>adverti</u>sing campaign   brand <u>image</u>
> <u>client</u> base   company <u>logo</u>   core <u>business</u>
> <u>luxury</u> brand   mobile <u>phone</u>
> online <u>advertisement</u>   <u>product</u> placement
> <u>TV</u> programme

3 Put students in pairs and give them 3–4 minutes to write their sentences. You could ask them to take turns to say the sentences to their partner, who checks if the correct word is being stressed for each compound noun / noun phrase. Go round monitoring and correcting students' pronunciation as necessary.

Project: Research an advertising campaign
Students choose an advertising campaign to research and discuss.

9A Put students in pairs and go through the instructions with the class. Explain the stages of the project: choose an advertisement; analyse the advertisement using the ideas on page 135; do a class survey to test people's reactions; compare your analysis with other students. Students will need access to one or more of the following:
- a PC, tablet or smartphone (They can use these to research both online and TV ads – most TV ads can be found on websites like YouTube.).
- recent magazines or newspapers.

Give students time to read the information on page 135 and ask you questions if anything is unclear. Then set a time limit for the first part of the activity and let students work in their pairs to research their campaign, while you monitor and help as necessary. Finally, set a time limit for the class survey. Again, monitor and provide help if needed.

9B Join pairs together into groups of four. Groups now work together to compare their analyses and decide on the most effective campaign. As class feedback, ask a few students to share their opinions with the class, giving reasons.

MyEnglishLab: Teacher's resources: extra activities; Alternative video worksheet; Reading bank
Pronunciation bank: p.114 Stress in compound nouns and noun phrases
Teacher's book: Resource bank Photocopiable 2.1 p.138
Workbook: p.9 Exercises 1–3

2.2 ❯ Asian brands go west

GSE learning objectives
- Can use language related to advertising and branding.
- Can give or seek personal views and opinions in discussing topics of interest.
- Can scan short texts to locate specific information.
- Can extract key details from an article on a business-related topic.
- Can link clauses and sentences with a range of basic connectors.
- Can use limited discourse devices to link sentences smoothly into connected discourse.
- Can ask and answer questions about advertising and brands.

Warm-up

Write the following quote on the board: *'Great companies that build an enduring brand have an emotional relationship with customers that has no barrier. And that emotional relationship is on the most important characteristic, which is trust.' (Howard Schultz, Chairman and CEO, Starbucks).* Put students in groups and ask them to discuss how far they agree with the quote, giving reasons. Give them 3–4 minutes to discuss in their groups, then broaden this into a class discussion.

Lead-in

Students discuss global brands and study collocations with *brand*.

1 Put students in pairs or small groups. Check they understand *accessories* and *associate sth with sth*. Give them a few minutes to go through questions 1–2, then elicit a few ideas from different students. Move on to question 3, asking students to discuss it in pairs/groups first. You could then broaden this into a class discussion, eliciting ideas from different students and listing qualities they suggest on the board.

2 Refer students to the diagram first. You could ask them to check the meanings in their dictionaries or go through the collocations with the class (see Notes below). Students then work through questions 1–3 in the same pairs/groups as for Exercise 1. When they have finished, invite students from different pairs/groups to share their ideas with the class.

Notes

brand ambassador: a real or fictional character who embodies the characteristics of a brand (e.g. Beyoncé for Pepsi, George Clooney for Nespresso and Omega, Leonardo DiCaprio for Chinese EV-maker BYD Auto and other brands, Novak Djokovic for Uniqlo, Kendall Jenner for Estée Lauder, Marc Jacobs for Calvin Klein, Karlie Kloss for Swarovski, Taylor Swift as the face of L'Oréal Paris, Wonder Woman (fictional) as the UN ambassador for the empowerment of women and girls)

brand image: a clear set of customer ideas about the practical benefits of a product

brand logo: a small design which is a brand's official sign (e.g. Twitter's blue bird logo)

brand loyalty: the extent to which people always buy the same brand even if similar products or services are available at a cheaper price or superior quality

brand personality: customers' emotional associations with a brand

Reading

Students read a newspaper article about Asian brands.

3 Ask students to read the article quickly and answer the questions. Explain that they should not read in detail at this point – they only need to scan for the information they are looking for.

Six brands are mentioned in the article:

Qeelin: Asian brand of fine jewellery

Chanel: French brand famous for fashion, fragrances and accessories, e.g. handbags

Louis Vuitton: French brand famous for its accessories, especially travel luggage

Chow Tai Fook: Asian brand of fine jewellery

Shang Xia: luxury Asian label now operated by Hermès

Hermès: French luxury group

4 Students read the article again, this time in more detail, and decide if the statements are true or false. Get them to compare answers in pairs before checking with the class.

1 T
2 T
3 F (Chow Tai Fook has more than 2,000 stores in mainland China.)
4 T
5 T
6 F (Qeelin and Shang Xia are Asian luxury labels, and Shang Xia is now operated by the French luxury group Hermès.)
7 T
8 F (Building a brand overseas will take time.)

Extra activities 2.2

A This activity looks at key vocabulary from the reading text. You could ask students to complete it using their dictionaries and, in weaker classes, allow them to work in pairs. Check answers with the class.

1 retail **2** millennial **3** label **4** wealthy
5 expand **6** store **7** jeweller **8** iconic

Grammar: Connectors

Students study and practise connectors for adding and contrasting ideas, referring to time, giving examples and sequencing.

5 Ask students to look at the underlined words and phrases in the article. Explain or elicit what type of words they are (connectors) and what their function is (to link sentences/ideas). You could refer students to the Grammar reference on page 119 at this point, and go through the explanations as a class. Ask students to complete the exercise individually and get them to compare answers in pairs before checking with the class.

Adding ideas: and, as well as
Contrasting ideas: however, but, While
Referring to time: Recently, Previously, In recent years, Earlier this year, now
Giving examples: such as, for example
Sequencing: Then

> **Pronunciation bank**
> **p.114: Connectors: intonation and pausing**
>
> ### Warm-up
> Write the example sentence on the board: *Recently, Asian brands have started to appear in U.S. shops.* Read the sentence out loud with no pauses and a flat intonation. Then read the sentence again, using a fall-rise intonation on *recently*, and a slight pause before *Asian*. Ask students if they could hear any differences, and which sentence they thought sounded better. Then look at the explanation and example in the box with the class, explaining intonation and pausing with connectors. Invite a few students to repeat the sentence.

1/2 🔊 P2.02 Play the recording, pausing after each sentence for students to repeat it. Then put students in pairs for Exercise 2. They should take turns to say the sentences, checking each other's use of intonation and pausing. Go round the class and monitor. If students are not able to use the intonation or pausing correctly, model the sentences for them and get them to repeat.

6 Ask students to do this exercise individually and get them to check answers in pairs before checking with the class. With stronger classes, during class feedback, you could ask students to explain why the incorrect option is wrong.

1 Although   2 for instance   3 such as   4 first of all, now
5 To start with   6 However, also, as well as

7 Ask students to use their dictionaries to check the meaning of the connectors. Check answers with the class.

Adding ideas: also, in addition
Contrasting ideas: although
Referring to time: –
Giving examples: for instance
Sequencing: first of all, to start with

Extra activities 2.2

B Explain that for this activity students will need to refer to Exercises 5 and 7 on page 21, and point out that there may be more than one possible answer to some questions. As this is consolidation of the language presented in the main lesson, it would be better for students to do this exercise individually.

1 For example / For instance   2 addition   3 But
4 To start with / First of all   5 such as / for example / for instance   6 As well as   7 and   8 However / Then
9 also   10 and

C Again, it would be better to ask students to do the exercise individually. During feedback, ask them to explain why the incorrect options are wrong.

1 b   2 c   3 a   4 c   5 a   6 b

Speaking

Students practise using connectors while discussing brands.

8A Explain that there may be more than one possible answer to some questions. Check answers with the class, eliciting the different possible answers for questions 2–5.

1 Although   2 such as / for instance / for example
3 as well as / and   4 recently / in recent years
5 while / although

8B Put students in pairs or small groups to ask and answer the questions from Exercise 8A. Monitor and make notes of any errors with connectors for some brief class feedback afterwards.

MyEnglishLab: Teacher's resources: extra activities
Pronunciation bank: p.114 Connectors: intonation and pausing
Grammar reference: p.119 Connectors
Teacher's book: Resource bank Photocopiable 2.2 p.139
Workbook: p.10 Exercises 1–3, p.11 Exercises 1–3

2.3 ❯ Communication skills
Supporting teamwork

GSE learning objectives

- Can give or seek personal views and opinions in discussing topics of interest.
- Can evaluate the effectiveness of participants in a meeting on a familiar topic.
- Can recognise a speaker's feelings or attitudes.
- Can give advice on a wide range of subjects.
- Can identify when speakers agree or disagree in work-related conversations.
- Can express and comment on ideas and suggestions in informal discussions.

Warm-up

Write the following quote on the board: *'Alone we can do so little, together we can do so much.'* (Helen Keller, American author and lecturer) Ask students how true they think this is in the workplace and why. Elicit ideas from different students, and then ask them to think about the advantages and disadvantages of *teamwork*. You could do this as a class discussion or let students discuss in pairs/ groups first, and then get brief class feedback.

Lead-in

Students discuss team- and groupwork as a lead-in to the video topic.

1 Put students in pairs to discuss the questions. Check they understand *challenges* and *problematic* before they begin. Once students have discussed in their pairs, elicit ideas in open class and encourage a whole-class discussion about working with similar and different types of people.

Possible answers
1 Team problems inside and outside the workplace are usually due to lack of clear goals, poor leadership, personality clashes, a lack of resources, intercultural differences, etc.
2 Diversity is potentially an advantage as different people bring different points of view and help innovation. However, different views and working styles can lead to conflict.
3 Students' own answer.

Video

Students watch a video about supporting team colleagues and how this can affect the performance of a team.

2 ▶ 2.3.1 Explain the situation to the class and ask a few questions to check students' understanding (e.g. *What is the purpose of the conference call? Who will be leading the call? What type of project will they discuss? What do you need to listen for?*). Play the video and check answers with the class.

> **Matt:** to create a real team
> **Stefanie:** the U.S. IT department must deliver on budget and schedule
> **Dan:** to focus on quality, and to have happy customers
> **Paula:** a high standard of final product

3 ▶ 2.3.1 Play the video again and discuss the answers with the class. Get students to give reasons for their answers.

> 1 On a positive note, Matt makes a relatively clear introduction to the meeting and tries to moderate between the different opinions to find a consensus. However, he seems to lose control a little to Dan, who interrupts and upsets others with his strong, opinionated style.
> 2 Stefanie is clearly unhappy with Dan and is not sure she can work with him. She finds him arrogant.

4A Explain to students the idea of Matt having two options and go through the details of Options A and B with the class. Make it clear to students that they can choose which option they want to see first on the video. Put students in small groups and ask them to discuss the two options, giving reasons for their answers. Elicit ideas from a few students and then, as a class, decide which video to watch first.

4B ▶ 2.3.2 ▶ 2.3.3 Give students a minute to read the questions for Option A or Option B, depending on their choice, and play the video. You could get them to compare answers in pairs or small groups before class feedback, if time allows. Do the same for the second video.

> **Option A**
> 1 Dan and Matt know each other; Dan has a strong personality, Matt knows how to manage him, it will be easier if Stefanie works with Paula as they get on.
> 2 She agrees. She sees Dan as very different.
> 3 She understands that Dan's ideas were correct and that she should be working with him more closely to deal with quality problems faster.
> 4 Relatively well. He is sensitive to check in with Stefanie, and suggests a logical solution which she is happy with. However, he learns that Stefanie and Dan fail to communicate at all, which leads to unnecessary project problems.

> **Option B**
> 1 Their experience is complementary; it's a great opportunity for Stefanie to learn about the U.S. market, which is the most important; it could be career-changing; she can improve/demonstrate ability to manage different people (which is important if she wants promotion).
> 2 She is not keen. She says they are very different.
> 3 She has found working with Dan challenging, but sees the advantages of working more closely with him and they are working together to resolve the quality problems.
> 4 Matt takes a more challenging approach to her and advises Stefanie to step outside her comfort zone. Overall, this is a more dynamic management of diversity, but one with potentially more risks of failure if conflict arises.

4C Put students in pairs and give them 3–4 minutes to discuss the questions. Check answers with the class.

> 1 **Possible answer:** In Option A Matt tells Stefanie to focus on Mexico and let him worry about Dan. In Option B Matt tells Stefanie it's important for her to work with Dan.
> 2 **Possible answer:** In both options Stefanie followed Matt's advice. As a result, in Option A there was a problem with the project because Stefanie was not in contact with Dan. In Option B Stefanie was learning from Dan and thanks to direct communication they were able to work together to solve problems.
> 3 Students' own answers

5 ▶ 2.3.4 For this activity, students should work in the same pairs as for Exercise 4C. Explain that they are going to watch the last section of the video, where the speaker is talking about successful teamwork. Get students to read the questions and then play the video. Go through the answers with the class and encourage students to agree or disagree with the conclusions presented in the video.

> The three main learning points are:
> 1 You have to make an effort and be patient to build relationships.
> 2 People will need advice and support when working in international teams so be there for others.
> 3 There are two main options when advising: advise people to just work with people like themselves or encourage people to work with different types of people, which is more challenging but may lead to better teamwork.

Reflection

Students reflect on the learning points and conclusions from the video and discuss effective teamwork.

6 Allow students to work individually first, so that they can reflect on their own preferences and ideas. Then put them in pairs to discuss their answers. As feedback, elicit ideas from different students for each question, and encourage brief class discussion.

Functional language: Giving and responding to advice

Students look at phrases for giving and responding to advice.

7A As a brief lead-in to giving and responding to advice, ask the following questions and elicit answers from different students: *Does it ever annoy you when someone gives you advice? Why / Why not? In what ways is giving advice a way to show you care?* Now explain that students will be looking at useful phrases for giving and responding to advice. Get them to do the exercise individually and then compare answers in pairs before checking with the class.

> **1** c **2** e **3** b **4** a **5** g **6** f **7** d

7B This exercise can be done individually or in pairs. The second option may be easier for weaker classes.

> **1** *quality should* + infinitive (b)
> **2** *Why don't you* + infinitive (b)
> **3** *Maybe it would be better (for you)* + *to* + infinitive (a)
> **4** *Have you tried* + verb + -*ing* (c)
> **5** *You need* + *to* + infinitive (b)
> **6** *Don't be afraid* + *to* + infinitive (a)
> **7** *I think it's important* (for you) + *to* + infinitive (a)

8A Put students in pairs. Get them to say the phrases out loud to each other and ask them to listen for which phrases sound stronger. This is an opportunity for students to think about not just the words, but also the pronunciation and intonation. A higher pitch at the end of a phrase can sound less strong than flat or falling intonation. Discuss this with the class and get them to think of phrases in their own language which sound strong. You could also ask them to think about why this is important in terms of building and maintaining relationships (i.e. being too strong can damage a relationship).

> 1, 2, 5, 6 and 7 sound stronger and more direct in English. The explorative question in 1 (*Have you tried ... ?*) and the tentative and hypothetical language in 3 (*Maybe it would ...*) make these less direct ways to give advice.

8B This question is a chance for students to think about how the language we use does depend in part on our relationship with the person we are talking to. There are no correct answers to the question, but students should note that we are usually less direct with people we don't know well or who we have just met.

9A To demonstrate the activity, tell the class that you feel very tired, ask for some advice and respond positively or negatively (e.g. T: *I feel really tired.* S: *Why don't you have a rest?* T: *That's a great idea, but I'm too busy teaching!*). Put students in pairs to practise conversations in the four situations given. Point out that they should use the phrases in the box to respond to advice, and phrases from Exercise 7A to give advice. Go round the class and monitor, correcting and helping where necessary. Make sure students follow the three steps: situation – advice – response. Point out that a negative response needs to be carefully worded, e.g. *That's a good idea, but ...* , to avoid sounding impolite.

9B This activity can be done in class or set for homework.

Extra activities 2.3

A This activity provides further practice in language for giving advice. Ask students to complete it individually and get them to compare answers in pairs before checking with the class. To practise language for responding to advice, you could extend this activity by putting students in pairs to roleplay the situations; they should take it in turns to read the advice for their partner to respond.

> **1** I think you should tell her it's unacceptable.
> **2** Why don't you tell him to stop it?
> **3** Have you tried using headphones to block out the noise?
> **4** Maybe it would be good for you to just do some relaxation classes.
> **5** I think it's important for you not to listen to him.
> **6** Don't be afraid to ignore them until you're back at work.
> **7** You need to ask your boss for help.

B Put students in pairs for this activity. Explain that they should say if they agree with the advice in Exercise A and change the advice they disagree with.

Task

Students practise the functional language from the lesson by roleplaying and then discussing different situations.

10A Put students in groups of three and refer them to page 126. Explain that they are going to roleplay different situations in which they ask for and give advice. Give them time to read the situations on page 126 and ask some check questions to make sure they understand what to do (e.g. *Who do you ask for advice in situation 1? What's the problem in situation 2? What sort of advice do you expect in situation 3?*). Give groups 6–8 minutes for their roleplays. Go round the class and make notes of good examples of advice and also any errors to highlight during feedback. You may prefer to do class feedback after each stage or at the end of the task, after Exercise 10C.

10B In the same groups, students now think of a situation they could ask advice on *from their colleagues*. Ask them to explain the situation in detail, assign roles for each and then roleplay it in their groups. Point out that the situation can be real or imaginary. Again, give students 6–8 minutes for their roleplays, and go round monitoring and making notes for class feedback.

10C Groups now discuss the situations they practised in Exercises 10A and 10B. Get students to think about when it might be more appropriate to use 'politer' forms of advice, e.g. when you are not an expert or when you don't know a person very well and don't want to risk offending them.

MyEnglishLab: Teacher's resources: extra activities; Interactive video activities

Workbook: p.12 Exercises 1 and 2

2.4 › Business skills
Making a presentation

GSE learning objectives

- Can answer questions about professional experience.
- Can express belief, opinion, agreement and disagreement politely.
- Can extract key information in a presentation about a company.
- Can use appropriate linking expressions to signal transitions within a presentation.
- Can write a brief plan to prepare for a presentation.
- Can highlight important information in each section of a short presentation.
- Can give an effective presentation about a familiar topic.
- Can ask questions about the content of a presentation or lecture aimed at a general audience, using simple language.
- Can answer questions about the content of a presentation or lecture aimed at a general audience.
- Can evaluate the effectiveness of a simple presentation on a familiar topic.

Warm-up

Write the following questions on the board: *Have you attended/given many presentations? How do you think a presenter feels before, during and after a presentation? How would you feel about giving a presentation in English? What advice would you give to someone giving a presentation for the first time?* Put students in pairs or small groups and give them 4–5 minutes to discuss the questions. Then invite different students to share their ideas with the class.

Lead-in

Students discuss giving and attending presentations and look at the dos and don'ts of opening a presentation.

1A Discuss the questions as a class. Ask students if they have ever attended a presentation they found particularly interesting/funny/bad, etc. If so, ask them to share their experience with the class.

1B Put students in pairs and explain that they are going to read a blog extract about the dos and don'ts of opening a presentation (in a foreign language). Give pairs 6–8 minutes to read the extract, discuss the questions and brainstorm ideas to add to the list. Go through the answers with the class.

Listening

Students listen to different presentation openings and then discuss techniques for opening presentations.

2A ◀)2.01 Explain the activity and, if necessary, give students 1–2 minutes to look at the tips in the blog extract again. Then play the recording and check answers with the class.

Speaker 1
Begin with a warm welcome
State your name
Confirm the objective of the presentation
Say how long you will talk for
Let the audience know when to ask questions – during or at the end of the presentation
Speaker 2
Begin with a warm welcome – thank the audience for coming
State your name and job title
Confirm the objective of the presentation
Explain the structure of the presentation
Move smoothly to the first point in the presentation
Speaker 3
Begin with a warm welcome
State your name and job title
Apologise for your English
Confirm the objective of the presentation
Let the audience know when to ask questions
Move smoothly to the first point in the presentation

2B Before students discuss the questions, you could ask them if they have ever attended a presentation where the speaker began by using one of these techniques.

Possible answer

Standard openings are useful because they are highly structured and offer information in a logical and clear way. However, some audiences might find this approach boring and welcome a less standard approach which engages and motivates them in some way to listen.

2C ◀)2.02 Play the recording and check answers with the class.

Speaker 1: Begin by telling the audience about a conversation you had recently.
Speaker 2: Open with questions.
Speaker 3: Start with a personal story.

2D You could discuss the questions as a class or let students discuss in pairs or small groups first.

Possible answer

The effectiveness of these presentation openings will depend on how the audiences react and engage with the presentation.

3A ◀)2.03 Explain to students that they will now hear the next part of the first speaker's presentation. Play the recording and get students to compare answers in pairs before checking with the class.

When established: three years ago
Main strength: innovation
Size of workforce: 56, 20 nationalities, average age 29
Countries of operation: five
Plan for growth: rising to 65 employees; plans to remain small

3B Ask students what question was asked during the presentation. If necessary, especially in weaker classes, replay the last part of the recording. Discuss the questions as a class.

> **Possible answer**
>
> The presenter reacted with very positive feedback that it was a great question. This form of positive feedback can show respect for the audience member who asked the question and encourage more questions, which helps the flow of information between presenter and audience.

> **Extra activities 2.4**
>
> **C** ◀) 2.01 ◀) 2.02 Put students in pairs. Ask them to look at the techniques in the box and refer them to audioscripts 2.01 and 2.02 on page 146. In their pairs, students create an alternative opening for one of the presentations they listened to.
>
> **D** Give students time to practise their openings in their pairs. Then join pairs together into groups of four. Students take it in turns to present their openings to each other. Finally, they decide on the best alternative opening, giving reasons. When they have finished, invite different students to present their openings to the class. For homework, you could ask students to prepare a different opening for one of the other presentations in the audioscript. They could then present it to the class in a future lesson.

Functional language: Signposting in presentations

Students look at useful signposting phrases for presentations.

4 Students could do this individually or in pairs and if necessary, they can refer to audioscripts 2.01 and 2.02 on page 146. Before they begin, go through the headings in the left-hand column – the different functions for each phrase. Check answers with the class.

> **1** today **2** begin **3** make **4** take **5** said **6** feel
> **7** close **8** hand

> **Extra activities 2.4**
>
> **A** This activity practises phrases for signposting in presentations. Students could do it individually or, in weaker classes, in pairs. Check answers with the class.
>
> > **1** c **2** h **3** e **4** g **5** a **6** d **7** f **8** b
>
> **B** Put students in pairs. Explain that they can use the ideas in the table or their own and allow 3–5 minutes' preparation time. Then give them plenty of time to practise their presentation openings. If time allows, you could invite a few students to present their openings to the class. With weaker classes, you could do the first opening in the table as an example with the class. Ask individual students to use the information in the table with the signposting phrases they have learnt (e.g. *Good morning, everyone, and good to see you here. I'm Bob Jones and I am the head of HR.*)

Task

Students practise giving a short presentation.

5A Explain that students are going to prepare and give a presentation and go through the instructions and list of possible topics with them. Refer them to the techniques they looked at in Listening and the signposting phrases in Exercise 4. Ask them to work individually for this stage and give them sufficient time to prepare. Encourage them to make notes. You could let them compare and discuss their ideas in pairs if time allows, but students should prepare their presentation on their own. Go round the class and help where necessary.

5B Put students in small groups. Students take turns to give their presentations. Point out that the 'presenters' should invite questions from the 'audience', and that the 'audience' should ask questions for each presentation. Also explain that the 'audience' should take notes on things done well and things that could be improved. Go round the class and note any points students need to work on.

5C In their groups, students share their feedback, decide on the most effective presentation and discuss the questions in the rubric. When they have finished, open this up into a class discussion, and add your own suggestions and any points you noted while monitoring.

MyEnglishLab: Teacher's resources: extra activities; Functional language bank
Workbook: p.12 Exercise 3

2.5 ❯ Writing
Formal and semi-formal emails

> **GSE learning objectives**
>
> • Can identify formal and informal register in emails and letters.
> • Can write a formal email accepting or declining a work-related invitation.
> • Can use a range of common verb + verb combinations using the *-ing* form.

> **Warm-up**
>
> Write the following questions on the board: *How do you feel about exchanging emails with friends? With business contacts? Why? What do you find easy/difficult?* Put students in small groups to discuss the questions for 3–4 minutes, then open this up into a class discussion. If there is time at the end of the lesson, you could come back to this and ask students if they would answer any of the questions differently.

Lead-in

Students analyse an invitation email and learn to distinguish between formal and semi-formal language.

1 Go through the instructions with the class and point out that both options are correct, but one is more appropriate for a formal email. Let students complete the activity individually first, then get them to compare answers in pairs. Check answers with the class.

1 Dear Mr Vesely **2** I'd like **3** will be held **4** provided
5 delighted to announce **6** collaborated
7 Please confirm your attendance **8** We look forward
9 Kind regards

Functional language

Students look at useful phrases for formal and semi-formal invitation emails.

2 Before students begin, go through the phrases with them and clarify the meaning of any unknown words. Then ask students to complete the activity, individually or in pairs, and check answers with the class.

Inviting
I'd like to invite you to ... – F
I'm writing to invite you to ... – F
We are delighted to invite you to ... – F
It would be great if you could come ... – SF

Accepting
Many thanks for the invitation. – SF
Thanks for inviting me. – SF
I'd (would) be delighted to accept your invitation/offer. – F
Although Mr ... is unable to attend, ... will be happy to take his place. – F

Declining
I'm sorry but I won't be able to come. – SF
I'm afraid (that) I will be unable to attend. – F
I'd love to come but ... – SF
I'm afraid I can't make it. – SF
Unfortunately, I have already made other arrangements. – F

Closing
We (very much) look forward to seeing you. – F
We are looking forward to seeing you. – F
Looking forward to seeing you soon! – SF
Best wishes – SF
Kind regards – F
All the best – SF

Extra activities 2.5

A Ask students to do the exercise individually and get them to compare answers in pairs before class feedback. With weaker classes, students can refer to the table on page 26 of the Coursebook. With stronger classes, you could ask students to cover the box and see how many of the sentences they can complete. They then uncover the box and check/complete their answers.

1 thanks **2** Thank **3** would be **4** great
5 Looking **6** Unfortunately **7** Sorry **8** am writing
9 am looking

Optional grammar work

The email in Exercise 1 contains examples of verbs followed by -*ing* or infinitive, so you could use it for some optional grammar work. Refer students to the Grammar reference on page 119 and use the exercises in MyEnglishLab for extra grammar practice.

Task

Students write a reply to a formal invitation email.

3A Put students in pairs and refer them to the email on page 127. Explain that it is a reply to the email in Exercise 1, which they need to rewrite in order to make it more formal. Remind them that they should use phrases from Exercise 2 and, depending on the level of your class, set a time limit of 10–15 minutes for the task. Go round monitoring and helping students where necessary. If there is time, when they have finished, do some peer correction: join pairs together into groups of four and ask students to read each other's emails and make suggestions for improvement.

Model answer

Dear Ms Pannu,

Thank you for inviting me to the preview. I would have loved to come but, unfortunately, I have already made other arrangements and will not be available that day as I am away on business.

However, the event sounds extremely interesting and my colleague, Marisa Shields, has expressed an interest in attending. I was wondering if it would be possible to add her name to the guest list.

I hope the preview evening is successful.

I look forward to seeing you again soon.

Kind regards,
Ted Vesely

3B Students now write their own reply, this time accepting the invitation. Point out the word limit, set a time limit and remind students to use appropriate phrases from Exercise 2.

Model answer

Dear Ms Pannu,

Thank you so much for inviting me to the preview of the Street Art Exhibition at the NGMA on 22nd November. As you know, modern art is a great interest of mine and this exhibition sounds fascinating.

I am writing to let you know that I would be delighted to accept your invitation to the event. Moreover, I am very keen to hear what Karla Lansing has to say about street art and marketing.

I very much look forward to seeing you there.

Kind regards,
Ted Vesely

3C Students now work in the same pairs as for Exercise 3A for some peer correction. Explain the activity and set a time limit (5–10 minutes, depending on the level of your class). Once students have discussed in their pairs, ask a few pairs to share their answers with the class.

MyEnglishLab: Teacher's resources: extra activities; Interactive grammar practice; Writing bank
Grammar reference: p.119 Verbs + -*ing* vs. infinitive
Workbook: p.13 Exercises 1–3

Business workshop ❯2

Kloze-Zone

GSE learning objectives

- Can identify key information in a concise business-related text or article.
- Can understand the main points of feedback from clients and colleagues.
- Can interpret and discuss main information in diagrams and graphs.
- Can express ideas and suggestions, discuss options and present conclusions in meetings.
- Can write a description of a future event or activity.
- Can write an email giving some detail of work-related news and events.

Background

Students read about Kloze-Zone, a Japanese fast-fashion retailer.

1 Put students in pairs and ask them to read the background and discuss the questions.

> 1 Kloze-Zone is a successful Japanese fast-fashion retailer that has expanded globally.
> 2 It has a reputation for quality clothing for young people at affordable prices.
> 3 The assistant store managers have to help the store manager, supervise staff, deal with deliveries, help customers, etc.
> 4 The Berlin store has problems with its brand awareness, poor sales, long queues and demotivated staff, while shop assistants say they are under-staffed and work long hours.
> 5 If they solve these problems, the assistant store manager will be promoted in the near future.

Customer and staff satisfaction

Students brainstorm questions they could ask to check customer and staff satisfaction.

2A/B Put students in pairs. Go through the instructions and bullet points with the class and give students 3–5 minutes to write their questions. You could do the first bullet point as an example, brainstorming possible questions for customers with the whole class. When the time is up, go through suggestions with the whole class. For Exercise 2B, follow the same process, this time focusing on staff.

> **Possible answers**
> **2A**
> - Do you think the window displays are attractive? Do the window displays attract customers in your age group?
> - What do you think of the store's promotional offers compared to other retailers?
> - Are you happy with in-store customer service? Are store staff always helpful, friendly and polite?
> - What do you think of the customer service when you are using the fitting rooms? Are staff helpful in the fitting rooms? Do you have to wait long to try on clothes? Are there enough fitting rooms?
> - Do you have to wait long to pay for items? How long do you have to wait on average? Are you satisfied with the payment experience?
>
> **2B**
> - Does the store provide enough training? Are there opportunities for promotion?
> - What do you think of the working hours, breaks and holidays? / Are you happy with the working hours, breaks and holidays?
> - What do you think of the staff discount compared to other retailers where you have worked?
> - What do you think of the staff turnover rate? Do you think it's higher or lower than other retailers?
> - Do you think Kloze-Zone is a good place to work? Would you recommend working for the store to your family and friends?

Feedback from customers and staff

Students listen to customers and staff giving feedback on Kloze-Zone.

3A 🔊 BW 2.01 Explain that the recording is of customers and staff talking about Kloze-Zone. Make sure students understand that there are more comments than speakers. Play the recording and check answers with the class.

> **a** Speaker 1 **b** Speaker 3 **c** Speaker 5 **d** Speaker 2
> **e** Speaker 3 **f** Speaker 4 **g** Speaker 6 **h** Speaker 6

3B You could do this exercise as a whole class, checking answers as you go.

> **Customers:** a, b, d, e
> **Staff:** c, g
> **Both:** f, h

Extra activities Business workshop 2

A 🔊 BW 2.01 This activity provides students with extra listening practice. Give them some time to go through the statements before you play the recording. You may need to play the recording twice: the first time for students to decide if the statements are true or false, and the second time for students to correct the false statements. Check answers with the class.

> 1 T
> 2 F (The member of staff thinks it helps to increase brand awareness, although it doesn't increase sales that much.)
> 3 F (The customer says men often buy two of the same thing.)
> 4 F (The customer says the mobile app is easy to use and is really cool because you can mix and match clothes online before you come to the shop.)
> 5 T
> 6 T

Consumer ratings

Students study and discuss a bar chart showing consumer ratings for Kloze-Zone and its main competitor.

4 Put students in pairs. Explain the activity and go through the example with the class. While students are speaking, go round monitoring and make notes for brief class feedback afterwards.

Possible answers

The bar chart shows a lower customer service rating of only 40 percent for Kloze-Zone, which should be higher. In-store experience is also very poor at 40 percent, while Fun & Sun has a slightly higher rating of 60 percent. The consumer rating for innovation is also lower than that of its competitor, at 60 percent. However, as we can see, both fashion retailers have excellent design, which consumers rate at 80 percent. They also think both brands offer good value for money. But the worst thing is that brand awareness is much lower for Kloze-Zone: it's only 55 percent compared to Fun & Sun's 75 percent.

Extra activities Business workshop 2

B Explain that the conversation is about the consumer ratings for Kloze-Zone, and refer students to the bar chart on page 91. Get students to complete the exercise individually, then check answers with the class. If there is time, you could put students in pairs and ask them to practise the conversation.

1 As you can see **2** when it comes to **3** although
4 also **5** In addition **6** but **7** However
8 For example

Task

Students hold a brainstorming meeting for a brand awareness campaign and then write an email summarising their ideas from the meeting.

5 Put students in small groups and go through the instructions and discussion points with them. Make sure they understand *brainstorming meeting*, and refer them to the definition of *brainstorming* at the bottom of the page. Point out that students should decide on their roles / job titles, and that they should take it in turns to chair the meeting. Encourage them to take notes. During the activity, go round and check that the meetings are being chaired and that decisions are made about assigning actions points to people.

6 Go through the instructions and steps with the class. In their groups, students prepare to present their ideas to the rest of the class. Encourage them to use their notes from Exercise 5 and to take new notes for this stage – to help them during their presentation. Give them sufficient preparation time. After groups have completed their presentations, the class votes on the most innovative event, slogan and campaign. Make sure students give reasons for their votes.

7 This exercise can be done in class or for homework. Explain the writing task to students and point out or elicit that they need to write a *formal* or *semi-formal* email. If students write their emails in class, you could encourage some peer correction afterwards: put them in pairs and ask them to read their partner's emails and make suggestions for improvements.

Model answer

Dear Bernd Franzke,

At our meeting, we decided that the promotional event needs to be original and fun to engage customers. We suggest a fun-run in collaboration with a well-known gym. Participants will receive a free T-shirt and shopping bag with the company logo and the new slogan: 'Look good, feel great'.

The marketing campaign will have the same slogan and will use traditional advertising as well as interactive marketing, using social media to attract younger consumers.

The campaign will focus on the excellent design and good value of our products as our consumer ratings in these areas are very good.

In addition, we want to highlight that we are now using new technologies to improve customer service – for example, three stores are trialling an app that lets shop assistants know when a loyal customer enters the store. We can use the social media campaign to get customers to sign up for this service.

We look forward to receiving your feedback.

Regards,
Valentina De Angelis

MyEnglishLab: Teacher's resources: extra activities

Review ◀ 2

1 1 approach **2** history **3** stretching **4** devalued
5 loyalty **6** marketing **7** base **8** growth
9 core **10** venture
2 1 Recently **2** and **3** Then **4** In addition
5 Although **6** Now
3 1 Have you tried **2** We need **3** It's important
4 You shouldn't **5** Why don't we **6** this would be
4 1 begin **2** Firstly **3** take **4** Finally **5** earlier
6 important **7** more **8** listening
5 1 h **2** e **3** f **4** d **5** g **6** c **7** a **8** b

Job-hunting

Unit overview

	CLASSWORK	FURTHER WORK
3.1 A job search	**Lead-in** Students discuss CVs and applying for a job or internship. **Video** Students watch a video in which an internship applicant discusses her CV with experts. **Vocabulary** Students look at vocabulary related to job-hunting. **Project** Students write and then discuss a job advertisement.	**MyEnglishLab:** Teacher's resources: extra activities; Reading bank **Pronunciation bank:** p.115 Stress in derived words **Teacher's book:** Resource bank Photocopiable 3.1 p.140 **Workbook:** p.14 Exercises 1–3
3.2 Job interview questions	**Lead-in** Students talk about preparing for a job interview and the importance of body language during the interview. **Listening 1** Students listen to extracts from a job interview and look at some common job interview questions. **Grammar** Students learn how to form and use indirect questions. **Listening 2** Students look at useful strategies and useful language for answering interview questions effectively. **Speaking** Students roleplay a job interview.	**MyEnglishLab:** Teacher's resources: extra activities **Pronunciation bank:** p.115 Voice range and intonation in indirect questions **Grammar reference:** p.120 Direct and indirect questions **Teacher's book:** Resource bank Photocopiable 3.2 p.141 **Workbook:** p.15 Exercises 1 and 2, p.16 Exercises 1 and 2
3.3 Communication skills: Listening actively	**Lead-in** Students discuss managing emotions in the workplace. **Video** Students watch a video about the importance of active listening in the workplace. **Reflection** Students reflect on the conclusions from the video and discuss their own active listening skills. **Functional language** Students look at phrases they can use during conversation to demonstrate they are listening actively. **Task** Students play a game and then discuss the importance of active listening.	**MyEnglishLab:** Teacher's resources: extra activities; Interactive video activities; Functional language bank **Workbook:** p.17 Exercise 1
3.4 Business skills: Interviews	**Lead-in** Students discuss their experiences of job interviews. **Listening** Students listen to two job interviews in which the candidates deal with questions in different ways. **Functional language** Students look at useful phrases for the different stages of a job interview. **Task** Students create/choose a job advertisement and roleplay an interview for it.	**MyEnglishLab:** Teacher's resources: extra activities; Functional language bank **Workbook:** p.17 Exercises 2 and 3
3.5 Writing: Covering letters	**Lead-in** Students read a covering letter and complete an error correction task. **Functional language** Students look at the organisation of and some useful phrases for a covering letter. **Task** Students assess a covering letter and then write their own.	**MyEnglishLab:** Teacher's resources: extra activities; Interactive grammar practice; Writing bank **Grammar reference:** p.120 Past Simple and Present Perfect **Workbook:** p.18 Exercises 1 and 2
Business workshop 3 Social media manager required	**Video and listening** Students watch (or listen to) video CVs of applicants for a position with a media company. **Listening** Students listen to extracts from the applicants' first interviews. **Reading** Students analyse the applicants' covering letters / emails. **Task** Students roleplay the second interview of one of the applicants.	**MyEnglishLab:** Teacher's resources: extra activities

Business brief

This unit looks at the various aspects of **applying for** and getting a job. There are two sides involved in the process: the company or organisation and the **applicant**. A company's **human resources (HR) department** is responsible for **recruitment** and applicants will need to follow the HR department's application procedure. This includes writing a **covering letter**, **submitting a CV** (or résumé) and **attending an interview**. The applicant will also be expected to research the company they are applying to and write or customise their CV to fit the job they are applying for.

The application may be accepted or rejected at the initial stage. This is why it is important for a CV and covering letter to be well presented, accurate and relevant to the company and position being applied for. Spelling mistakes, grammatical errors or poor presentation can instantly disqualify a candidate.

A CV needs to clearly list an applicant's **qualifications**, starting with their educational history, examination results and degree. CVs differ in style and content. One style is to be neutral and simply state facts. The other is to self-promote and emphasise all the applicant's good qualities. Applicants need to be aware of the culture of the company they are applying to and adapt their CV accordingly.

Competition for the best jobs is tough and job seekers need to persuade potential **employers** that they are the best candidates and that they can offer what the company needs. This means identifying and highlighting their strong points and unique skills specific to the role. These are divided into two categories: hard and soft. **Hard skills** refers to concrete things like qualifications, grades and experience. **Soft skills** refers to the aspects of someone's **character**, for example leadership, **motivation**, flexibility and the ability to communicate.

If the application is accepted, the candidate will be invited to attend an interview. At this stage their physical appearance, behaviour and social skills will all be judged. **Verbal** and **non-verbal communication skills**, for example smiling and positive body language, are both important. Very often there is a **second interview** and candidates are given a **task** to do before the interview. This could be to prepare a presentation or answer a set of questions.

Jobs and your students

Knowing how to apply for a job and performing well in an interview are two of the most important skills for students. Students who are not yet working will need plenty of practice and confidence-building in order to be competitive. Working students have already cleared the first hurdle, but must continue improving their skills in order to develop their careers.

Unit lead-in

Ask a student to briefly describe the photo. They will probably mention that the man is looking for a job, but if not, ask: *What is the man trying to do?* Elicit or refer to the fact that this is an old photo, then encourage a brief class discussion about how the process of seeking employment and applying for a job has evolved over the years (e.g. the shift from paper to digital information, social media, online job searches, networking). Refer students to the quote and check that they understand *in itself* (in its true nature; considered separately from other facts). Then discuss the quote as a class. What do students think it means? Elicit students' ideas but do not confirm at this stage – explain that they will find out and discuss this quote further in Lesson 3.1.

3.1 ❯ A job search

GSE learning objectives

- Can answer questions about professional experience.
- Can understand a large part of a video on a work-related topic.
- Can understand advice on a work-related situation.
- Can describe skills and abilities related to work.
- Can use language related to aptitude, ability, knowledge and skills.
- Can understand information in advertisements for jobs and services.
- Can express and comment on ideas and suggestions in informal discussions.
- Can write a job posting describing duties and responsibilities.

Warm-up

Write the following sentence on the board: *Only _____ percent of job applicants will get a first interview.* Invite different students to try to guess the missing number. Give them the answer (2 percent), then discuss as a class: Do students find this fact surprising? Why do they think the number is so low?

Lead-in

Students discuss CVs and applying for a job or internship.

1 Give students a minute to read the questions and check they understand *internship* (a job that lasts for a short time, that someone, especially a student, does in order to gain experience). Then discuss the questions with the class.

Video

Students watch a video in which an internship applicant discusses her CV with experts.

2 ▶ 3.1.1 Explain to students that they are going to watch a video where a student applying for an internship is discussing her CV with experts; they should watch and listen out for the three rules for writing a CV. Play the video and then check answers with the class.

Rule 1: Employers hate spelling mistakes (in your CV).
Rule 2: Keep it relevant.
Rule 3: Don't use clichés. Be different.

3 ▶ 3.1.1 Give students a minute to read questions 1–7. Make sure they understand *entrepreneur* and play the video. Get students to compare answers in pairs before checking with the class. During feedback, you may want to remind students that the quote in question 7 is the one they discussed on page 27, the unit lead-in.

1 He thinks that Esther isn't selling herself well with her CV.
2 She has spelt *intermediate* incorrectly – she wrote 'intimidate'.
3 soft skills: commitment, flexibility and imagination; hard skills: knowledge and diplomas
4 irrelevant information, e.g. *I like eating pizzas.* (*'It isn't impressive.'*)
5 opportunity, role, value
6 One, but she will probably get a second interview.
7 It means that it is hard work looking for a job and job-seeking can take a lot of time, e.g. looking at job advertisements, writing and updating your CV and covering letter, preparing for and going to interviews.

4 ▶ 3.1.1 Give students a minute to read the extract. With stronger classes, you could ask students to try to complete as many of the gaps as they can before watching, then watch and check/complete their answers. Play the video from 2:30 to 2:56 and then check answers with the class.

1 mistakes 2 language 3 team player 4 self-starter
5 motivated 6 candidate

5 Put students in pairs or small groups to discuss the questions. For question 1, make sure they understand *stand out from the crowd*. For question 2, clarify that students should work *individually* to write down the three characteristics and three skills, then compare and discuss their answers with their partner(s). During the activity, monitor and help/correct students as necessary.

Extra activities 3.1

A ▶ 3.1.1 Ask students to do this individually, then play the first part of the video for them to check their answers. Check answers with the class and clarify any new vocabulary (e.g. *progress* (v), *potential employer*, *jobseeker*, *competitive*).

1 f 2 b 3 a 4 d 5 c 6 e

B Give students a minute to read the sentences. You could ask them to try to guess who might have said each sentence before watching. Play the video again and check answers with the class. With weaker classes, you may need to play the video twice.

1 James Caan 2 Simon Dolan 3 Presenter
4 John Lees 5 Simon Dolan 6 Interviewer
7 James Caan

Vocabulary: Getting a job

Students look at vocabulary related to applying for and getting a job.

6 Explain that the words on the left are from the video. Students could do this individually or in pairs, using their dictionaries to help them.

> **1** h **2** j **3** g **4** a **5** b **6** l **7** c **8** d **9** k **10** f **11** i **12** e

7 Again, this exercise can be done individually or in pairs – the second option may be easier for weaker classes. Before students begin, point out that the grammar of the sentence can help them choose the correct answer in some cases – they should think about what type of word is needed (a noun, an adjective, etc.). You could let students use their dictionaries if they need help. During feedback, ask students to give reasons for their choices (e.g. in 1, *competition* does not fit the sentence because it is a noun).

> **1** competitive **2** employer **3** motivated **4** communicative
> **5** responsible **6** interns **7** position **8** flexible **9** skills
> **10** passionate **11** Recruitment **12** interview

8 Put students in pairs to discuss the questions. Explain that students who have no experience in looking for a job should discuss the questions on the left, and those with experience should discuss the questions on the right.

Extra activities 3.1

C This activity practises key vocabulary from the lesson. You could ask students to do it individually, as a quick vocabulary quiz, and then get them to compare answers in pairs before checking with the class. With weaker classes, you could help students by providing the last letter of each missing word.

> **1** employer, CVs **2** jobseekers, apply
> **3** gained, intern **4** came across, recruitment
> **5** sort out, position **6** motivated, communicative
> **7** clichéd **8** interview, value **9** résumé, stands out
> **10** responsible, flexible

› Pronunciation bank
p.115: Stress in derived words

Warm-up

Write the following two pairs of words on the board and underline the stressed syllables: *develop – development, personal – personality*. Get students to say the words and ask: *Look at the stressed syllables in each pair. How is the second pair different from the first?* (In the first pair, the stress is on the same syllable in both words. In the second pair, the stress shifts from the first to the third syllable.) Refer students to the explanation in the box and drill the pronunciation of the example words. Ask students if they can think of any other examples for each pair (e.g. *impress – impression; technology – technological; economy – economical*).

1 Ask students to complete the exercise individually and then compare answers in pairs. Do not confirm answers yet as students will check them in the next exercise.

2 ◆) P3.01 Play the recording for students to check their answers. Then play the recording a second time for students to listen and repeat.

> character – characteristic
> communicate – communication
> effect – effective
> interview – interviewer
> responsible – responsibility

3 Put students in pairs and ask them to complete the sentences using words from Exercise 1. Check answers with the class and then get pairs to ask and answer the questions. Walk round and monitor to check that students are using the correct word stress.

> **1** character **2** effective, communication
> **3** responsibility, interviewer

Project: Write a job advertisement

Students write and then discuss a job advertisement.

9A Put students in pairs and go through the instructions with the class. Students will need to do some online research before they write their advertisement, so you may want to suggest some websites which might be useful (online newspapers are a good place to start). Answer any questions students may have before they begin, and set a time limit. During the activity, monitor and help students as necessary.

9B Join pairs together into groups of four. Students now read each other's adverts and say whether they would apply for the job. Allow 4–6 minutes for this and then give students feedback: suggest areas for improvement and highlight any errors that made communication difficult.

Model answer

Key Account Managers needed for immediate start

Do you have a degree in chemistry or marketing? Are you interested in managing our key client accounts? At ASTRA Pharmaceuticals we are looking for candidates who are motivated, organised and have excellent communication skills. In this position you will be responsible for managing our key clients.

ASTRA Pharmaceuticals is based in Birmingham and we have a proven track record of offering successful candidates an exciting career in the pharmaceutical industry. Candidates with a minimum of two years' experience in a similar position are preferred. Working hours are Mon–Fri, 9.00 a.m.–6.00 p.m. The salary is negotiable, according to experience.

If you think you have the right profile, please send your CV with a covering letter to our Head of Recruitment at hr@astrapharma.com.

We look forward to hearing from you.

MyEnglishLab: Teacher's resources: extra activities; Reading bank
Pronunciation bank: p.115 Stress in derived words
Teacher's book: Resource bank Photocopiable 3.1 p.140
Workbook: p.14 Exercises 1–3

3.2 ❯ Job interview questions

GSE learning objectives

- Can express and comment on ideas and suggestions in informal discussions.
- Can understand a range of questions in a job interview.
- Can use a range of direct and indirect questions.
- Can understand the details of someone's personal and professional experience from an interview or presentation.
- Can give information in a job interview.
- Can ask for information in a job interview.
- Can carry out a prepared interview, checking and confirming information as necessary.
- Can ask and answer questions about professional experience.

Warm-up

Write the following on the board and ask students to put the words in the correct order to form questions:
1 what / day-to-day / be / would / responsibilities / my ?
2 the / interview process / are / what / the / in / next steps ?
Check answers with the class (1 What would be my day-to-day responsibilities? 2 What are the next steps in the interview process?). Elicit or explain that these are questions candidates often ask at the end of a job interview. Put students in pairs or groups and ask them to think of other questions a candidate might ask the interviewer. What would students, as candidates, want to know? Elicit students' ideas and list them on the board. You could come back to the list after Exercise 7 and ask students to rewrite the direct questions on the board as indirect questions.

Lead-in

Students talk about preparing for a job interview and the importance of body language during the interview.

1 Put students in pairs to discuss the question. If necessary, help them with prompts on the board (e.g. research, CV, clothes, questions to expect). Once students have discussed in their pairs, you could broaden this into a class discussion.

Possible answers

I would find out about the company on the internet. I might ask who is going to interview me or how many people will interview me and check their profiles on the internet. I would make sure my CV is updated. I would make sure I have something smart to wear, e.g. a suit. I would check how to get there and arrive early for the interview. It's also a good idea to anticipate some questions and practise them with a friend/colleague, and prepare questions I'd like to ask them.

2 Ask students to look at the photos and go through the instructions with them. Give pairs 3–4 minutes to discuss, then broaden this into a class discussion: elicit ideas about the interviewee's facial expressions, posture, and what these suggest about how he feels. Highlight the importance of body language during job interviews.

Possible answers

a nervous and a bit negative   **b** confident and positive
c thoughtful, listening carefully, but a bit negative
d speaking confidently, more positive than c

Listening 1

Students listen to extracts from a job interview and look at some common job interview questions.

3 Put students in pairs. Students with little or no experience of job interviews should do the task on the left, referring to the job interview questions on page 127. Students with experience should do the task on the right. Explain the task and give students plenty of time to discuss. Go round the class and monitor while they are speaking. For the task on the left, check answers with the class when students have finished. For the task on the right, as feedback, elicit students' ideas and put them on the board.

Possible answers

I don't have much experience in going for interviews.
Appropriate questions for a job interview:
2, 4, 5, 6, 9, 10, 11, 13, 14, 16, 18, 19 and possibly 20 (Some interviewers sometimes ask these kinds of psychological questions to see how you see yourself or how creative you are.)

Inappropriate or irrelevant questions for a job interview:
 1 (irrelevant, but a possible question for younger candidates or those who have been out of work for a long period)
 3 (irrelevant, and a personal question)
 7 (In many countries it is unacceptable to ask this kind of personal question.)
 8 (irrelevant, although some interviewers may offer you a drink if you've travelled far)
 12 (irrelevant)
 15 (irrelevant unless perhaps you're going to work in a restaurant or the food industry)
 17 (irrelevant, and a personal question)

I have some experience in going for interviews.
Do you have any experience as a (job position) / in (field or sector)?
What qualifications do you have?
Why did you leave your last job?
Why did you go travelling for one year?
How did you get on with your previous employer?
How would you describe yourself?

4 ◀》3.01   Explain the context for the listening and make sure students understand that they are listening for similar questions to those they worked on in Exercise 3. Play the recording, then check answers with the class.

5 ◀》3.01   Students could do this individually or in pairs. Play the recording for them to check their answers, then check with the class.

1 What are your strengths and weaknesses?
2 Are you working at the moment?
3 How long have you worked as a chemical engineer?
4 Do you have any experience in green technologies?
5 Why would you like to work for us?
6 What would you do on your first day at work?
7 Do you have your original certificates with you?
8 Where do you see yourself in five years' time?

Grammar: Indirect questions

Students learn how to form and use indirect questions.

6A 🔊 3.02 Play the recording for students to complete the sentences and get them to compare answers in pairs before checking with the class.

1 Can you tell me what   2 Could you tell me about
3 Can you tell me about   4 I'd like to know if
5 Could you tell me how   6 I'd like to know if
7 I'd like to know who

6B Ask students how the questions in Exercise 6A are different from those in Exercise 5. Elicit or explain that they are indirect questions. Refer students to the Grammar reference on page 120 and clarify any points as necessary.

They are indirect questions, starting with *Can/Could you tell me …* or *I'd like to know if/wh-* question word.

They are different from the direct questions in Exercise 5 because they are longer and the word order changes. In addition, if it's a *yes/no* question without any question words (*what, when, where, how,* etc.), we need to remember to use *if* or *whether*.

> **Pronunciation bank**
> **p.115: Voice range and intonation in indirect questions**
>
> **Warm-up**
> Write an example question on the board: *Can you tell me why you'd like to work for us?* Say the question, starting at a higher pitch, then falling to a low pitch. Drill the question, then refer students to the explanation in the box. Explain that using this intonation and voice range makes us sound friendlier and more polite.
>
> **1** 🔊 P3.02 Play the recording for students to listen and repeat, copying the voice range and intonation. You could drill the questions chorally first, then individually. Repeat as many times as necessary until students get the voice range and intonation right.
>
> **2A** Ask students to do this exercise individually. Monitor and check they are forming indirect questions correctly.

> **Possible answers**
> Can you tell me about your holiday plans?
> Could you tell me what you're doing at the weekend?
> I'd like to know why you decided to study business English.
> Can you explain how indirect questions are made?

2B Put students in pairs. They should take turns to ask and answer their questions from Exercise 2A. Monitor and check that students are using the correct voice range and intonation.

7 Go through the example with the class and ask students to complete the exercise individually. Point out that there is a mistake in *both* questions in each pair. You could get students to compare answers in pairs before checking with the class.

1 Direct: What **is** your greatest strength?
  Indirect: Can you tell me what your greatest strength **is**?
2 Direct: Have **you** ever managed a team?
  Indirect: I'd like to know if **you** have ever managed a team.
3 Direct: Who **was** your previous employer?
  Indirect: I'd like to know who your previous employer **was**.
4 Direct: **What** do you enjoy about working in teams?
  Indirect: **Could** you tell me what you enjoy about working in teams?
5 Direct: When **was** the last time you solved a problem successfully?
  Indirect: Could you tell me about a time **when** you solved a problem successfully?

> **Extra activities 3.2**
>
> **A** Students could do this exercise individually and then compare answers in pairs, or you may prefer to do it as a whole class, eliciting the answers as you go.
>
> 1 if 2 tell 3 about 4 Could 5 what 6 where
> 7 tell 8 when

Listening 2

Students look at useful strategies and useful language for answering interview questions effectively.

8 🔊 3.03 Ask students what they think a good answer to question 1 in Exercise 7 might be (an effective answer would directly answer the question and demonstrate the candidate's positive qualities). Explain the task and play the recording for students to assess the candidates' answers. Go through the answers with the class, asking students to give reasons for their choices.

1 Poor – he doesn't know what to say and when he answers, it's a cliché.

2 OK – he doesn't have much work experience but he answers positively.

3 Good

4 Good

5 Good

6 Good

7 OK – he should perhaps mention the references in his CV, or in the interview.

9 🔊 3.03 Give students a minute to look at the expressions and check that they understand them. Play the recording and if necessary, pause after each expression to give students time to identify it. Check answers with the class.

1 e 2 d 3 g 4 b 5 f,h,a 6 i 7 c

10 Go through the strategies with the class and check they understand the expressions *buying time* and *repeating yourself*. You could do the matching exercise with the whole class, checking answers as you go. Then give students 2–3 minutes to think of more expressions for each strategy. You could also ask if they can think of other strategies to deal with difficult questions and expressions for them (see answer key below). Elicit students' ideas, write them on the board and encourage students to record them in their notebooks.

A d B g,i C b,c,h D a E f F e

Other expressions for strategies A–F

A Being honest: Well, sometimes I become nervous when … , but … To be honest, I haven't thought about that before.

B Answering positively: Yes, definitely. Absolutely.

C Buying time: That's a good / an interesting question. Let me see.

D Repeating yourself: As I mentioned previously, …

E Asking for repetition: Sorry? Could you repeat that, please? Would you mind repeating the question, please?

F Expressing uncertainty: It's difficult to say, but …

Other strategies and suggested expressions

Asking for clarification: Do you mean … ? Is that … ? When you say … , do you mean … ?

Paraphrasing: So, you're asking me if I … ? So you'd like to know if/wh- … ?

Extra activities 3.2

B 🔊 3.03 Give students time to read the four summaries and clarify any unknown words. Then play the recording and check answers with the class.

> **3** doesn't have much work experience but he has a PhD specialising in waste water management and has done related voluntary work

Speaking

Students roleplay a job interview.

11A Put students in pairs. Go through the instructions and refer students to the advertisement on page 127. Give them time to read it, and set a time limit for pairs to write their questions. Monitor and help students as necessary, making sure they include some indirect questions.

Possible answers

Do you surf? Have you ever been surfing?

Have you ever worked in sales?

Do you have any references?

Do you prefer working independently or in a team?

Are you prepared to work long hours?

What is your greatest passion?

What do you know about us / our company?

Who was a mentor for you at university / in your previous job?

Can you tell me about a time when you worked well in a team?

Could you tell me about a successful project you've worked on?

Could you tell me about a time when you dealt with a difficult customer?

I'd like to know / Tell me about your proudest achievement.

I'd like to know about a time when you negotiated something successfully.

Could you give me the names and phone numbers of two referees?

11B Students work in the same pairs and discuss possible answers to the questions they wrote in Exercise 11A. Explain that they should *not* roleplay asking and answering the questions at this point; they should only think about what a good answer to each question should include. When they have finished discussing the answers, they should write five questions the candidate could ask the interviewer. Again, monitor and help students if needed.

Possible answers

How many people are there in the team/department?

Who would I work with?

Who do/would I report to?

What are the working hours?

What kind of training do you give for this position?

Are there any opportunities for promotion?

How many weeks' holiday will I have?

How much is the starting salary for this position?

When will I hear from you?

When do I start? / When does the job start?

12 Students now roleplay their interview. When they have finished, they should change roles and repeat. Before they begin, refer them to the useful phrases and strategies they looked at in Exercises 8–10 and tell them that they should try to use them in their interviews. Go round monitoring during the roleplays and allow time for some class feedback afterwards. Ask different students what they think went well and what could be improved. Suggest areas for improvement and highlight errors that made communication difficult.

MyEnglishLab: Teacher's resources: extra activities

Pronunciation bank: p.115 Voice range and intonation in indirect questions

Grammar reference: p.120 Direct and indirect questions

Teacher's book: Resource bank Photocopiable 3.2 p.141

Workbook: p.15 Exercises 1 and 2, p.16 Exercises 1 and 2

3.3 ❯ Communication skills
Listening actively

GSE learning objectives

- Can express belief, opinion, agreement and disagreement politely.
- Can recognise when someone is clarifying or checking information in a work-related conversation.
- Can understand the main points of feedback from customers or work colleagues.
- Can recognise when a speaker is checking that the listener has understood something in a conversation conducted slowly and clearly.
- Can ask someone to clarify or elaborate on what they have just said.
- Can use simple appropriate language to check that information has been understood on the phone.
- Can ask someone to paraphrase a specific point or idea.
- Can explain the main points in an idea or problem with reasonable precision.
- Can correct mistakes if they have led to misunderstandings.

Warm-up

Write the following quote by Stephen Covey on the board: *'Most people don't listen with the intent to understand; they listen with the intent to reply.'* Check that students understand *intent* and ask them what they think the quote means (that during a conversation, most people are either speaking or preparing to speak – they are not really listening to what the other person has to say). Ask students: *Does this sound familiar? Do you know anyone who 'listens' in this way?* Invite students to share their experiences with the class. Finally, ask: *What problems might 'listening' in this way cause in the workplace?* Invite students to share their views with the class. You could use this activity as an opportunity to pre-teach *active listening / listening actively*, which is the main topic of this lesson.

Lead-in

Students discuss their views on managing emotions in the workplace.

1A Put students in pairs. Give them 3–4 minutes to discuss the questions, then invite different students to share their ideas with the class.

1B Discuss the question as a class. You could draw two columns on the board with the headings *Advantages* and *Disadvantages* and add students' ideas as the discussion develops. You could then use the list on the board to elicit different students' ideas. Point to an item on the list and ask individual students: *What do you think of this point?*

Possible answers

Statement 1
Advantage: People who don't mix work and private life may find it easier to connect with you. They may also perceive this approach as professional.
Disadvantage: If you are too neutral, you risk coming across as cold or not valuing relationships in business. People may find it difficult to connect with you.

Statement 2
Advantage: If you show your feelings, it can enable you to build better relationships with others, as they can see more of who you really are as a person and not just as a colleague or business partner. People may perceive you as authentic.
Disadvantage: Being too emotional in business may be seen as unprofessional or inappropriate.

Video

Students watch a video about the importance of active listening in the workplace.

2A ▶ 3.3.1   If the class watched the Unit 2 video, ask them for a short summary: a description of the situation and the main characters' roles. If this is the first communication skills video for your students, briefly explain the situation and characters yourself. Go through the questions with students and play the video. Check answers with the class.

1 Paula describes herself as expressive about her feelings and results-focused.
2 Paula thinks Matt sounded tense. He said he has concerns about Paula's ability to meet her targets and perform successfully on the team and is a little worried.
3 The issues raised by her previous line manager: her ability to meet targets and perform as part of a team.

2B Discuss the question as a class.

Possible answer

It's uncertain how their meeting will go. Paula has said she is expressive about her feelings and Matt is going to ask her about her poor past performance. She might not react well to this line of questioning. Matt may be too focused on project success and results when speaking to her.

3A Put students in small groups. Read Matt's two options with the class, then give the groups 2–3 minutes to discuss and decide on the best approach for Matt to take when he meets Paula. Make it clear to students that they can choose which option they want to see first on the video. Elicit ideas from a few students and then, as a class, decide which video to watch first.

3B ▶ 3.3.2   ▶ 3.3.3   Give students a minute to read the questions for Option A or Option B, depending on their choice, and help them with any unknown words. Play the video and then check answers with the class. Do the same for the second video. For Option B, you may need to play the video a second time for students to answer question 2.

Option A

1 Matt focuses on points a, c and e.
2 Paula responds somewhat defensively. She probably feels defensive and frustrated that this issue from a past project is coming up in her new project. She might also feel that Matt is not listening to her responses or trying to understand her perspective.
3 Matt makes statements rather than asking more open, clarifying questions. He fails to adapt to Paula's answers, but interprets them in terms of his own assumptions. He could have asked questions to better understand why she was saying what she was saying and feeling. He could focus on points b and d.

Option B

1 In this version Matt adapts his approach when Paula starts using emotionally driven key words like *incompetent* or *difficult*. He asks open questions to understand her feelings. This approach helps him to understand how to best work with Paula on this project and leads to positive responses from her. This, in turn, helps lead to a positive outcome.
2 **a** say, describe **b** important **c** rushed **d** mean

4 Ask students to discuss the questions in pairs or groups first, and then have a whole-class round-up.

5 ▶ 3.3.4 Explain that students are going to watch the last section of the video, with conclusions on and tips for successful active listening. Play the video, twice if necessary. Check answers with the class, then get students to discuss the tips given in the video. This could be a class discussion or you may prefer students to discuss in pairs / small groups first.

The four tips are:
1 Listen carefully to identify key words.
2 Try to understand by asking clarifying questions.
3 Summarise to check understanding.
4 Be open – don't just focus on what you want to talk about.

Reflection

Students reflect on the conclusions from the video and discuss their own active listening skills.

6 The main aim of these questions is to help students reflect on their own natural style: Are they active listeners? Put them in pairs and give them 4–6 minutes to discuss the questions, then broaden this into a class discussion. Ask students to write down their answer to question 4 so their commitment to it is stronger. Follow this up with students in a future lesson.

Functional language: Active listening

Students look at phrases they can use during conversation to demonstrate they are listening actively.

7 Ask students why active listening is important (it avoids misunderstanding/frustration, helps resolve conflict, etc.) and ask them for some examples of how we can show we are listening actively. These can include body language (e.g. nodding, eye contact) as well as asking questions,

responding appropriately, correcting, etc. Explain to students that phrases a–g are useful when they want to show someone that they are listening actively, and ask them to complete the table. After checking answers, you could ask students to think of another way to complete each phrase (e.g. *OK, why don't you tell me [how you feel]? No, that's not what I [meant].*).

1–3 a, d, g **4** c **5** e **6** f **7** b

8A Put students in pairs and explain the activity. Point out that there are no correct ways to respond, and that the main aim is to show they are listening actively. It may also help students to think about what the person responding needs to know/check/correct in each situation. Give pairs 3–5 minutes for the activity, then elicit ideas from different students.

Possible answers

1 What do you mean by a bit late? / I can see you're busy.
2 How would you describe 'difficult to work with'? / Sorry, I don't understand what you said about 'difficult to work with'.
3 Why did you refuse the invitation? / I'm not clear about why you refused.
4 So, he doesn't want to do any more business trips. / OK, that's useful to know.
5 I can see you are upset. / OK, why don't you tell me a bit more?
6 Sorry, that's not what I meant. / No, that's not what I said.

8B Students stay in pairs to develop one of the situations from Exercise 8A into a dialogue. Monitor and make sure they are using the phrases from Exercise 7 correctly. Get pairs to act out their dialogues for the class. Alternatively, if time is short, this exercise can be set as homework.

Extra activities 3.3

A Get students to do this individually and then compare answers in pairs before checking with the class. After checking answers, you could put students in pairs to practise the dialogues. For further practice, especially with stronger classes, you could ask students to write alternative responses for speaker B in each conversation. They could do this in class or as homework.

Conversation 1
1 a **2** d **3** b **4** h **5** e **6** c **7** g **8** f
Conversation 2
1 a **2** d **3** h **4** f **5** e **6** c **7** g **8** b
Conversation 3
1 a **2** e **3** d **4** g **5** b **6** f **7** h **8** c

Task

Students play a game and then discuss the importance of active listening.

9A The main aim of the task is for students to notice how much more they remember and understand if they listen actively. Start by putting students in groups of three for the listening/distraction game. For this first stage, students work individually and prepare to talk about a topic for two minutes. Encourage them to make notes and suggest each student chooses a different topic, which will probably make the game more interesting.

9B Students play the game in their groups. Before they begin, go through the instructions with them and make sure they understand how the game works and what they have to do while each of their partners is speaking (listen actively in one case, focus on something completely different in the other).

9C/D In their groups, students now assess the outcome of the activity by comparing how much they could remember when they listened actively compared with when they did not. They should also assess how many active listening phrases their partners used, and whether they used them appropriately. Feed back by asking the class what they learnt from the activity.

MyEnglishLab: Teacher's resources: extra activities; Interactive video activities; Functional language bank

Workbook: p.17 Exercise 1

3.4 ❭ Business skills

Interviews

GSE learning objectives

- Can give detailed accounts of experiences, describing feelings and reactions.
- Can understand a range of questions in a job interview.
- Can understand the details of someone's personal and professional experience from an interview or presentation.
- Can give information in a job interview.
- Can ask for information in a job interview.
- Can carry out a simple informal job interview.
- Can carry out a prepared interview, checking and confirming information as necessary.
- Can discuss their own achievements in previous jobs during a job interview.

Warm-up

Write the following on the board: *dressing inappropriately, arriving late, being uninformed about the company, criticising previous employer(s), being too relaxed.* Explain to students that these are five common mistakes candidates make during a job interview. Put students in pairs or groups and ask them to rank the mistakes in order of importance. After 3–5 minutes, ask a few pairs/ groups to share their lists with the class, giving reasons. Encourage a whole-class discussion on why it is important to avoid these things and/or what other things students think candidates should avoid.

Lead-in

Students discuss their experiences of job interviews.

1 Put students in pairs to discuss the questions. For students who are not yet working, you could ask them to talk about other interviews they may have attended (e.g. for university entrance). As feedback, invite a few students to share their answers with the class.

> **1** Organisations hold interviews to check if the person can do the job (if they have the right skills and qualifications) and if they are a good fit for the organisation and the working environment.

Listening

Students listen to two job interviews in which the candidates deal with questions in different ways.

2A Go through the tips with students and check they understand *improvise, two-way, cheat* and *concise.* Then put them in small groups for the activity. Explain that they should choose one tip in each pair, and encourage them to explain their answers. Ask a few students to share their opinions with the class, giving reasons.

> **Possible answers**
> **1** a **2** b **3** b **4** b

2B Put students in pairs or small groups and give them 2–4 minutes to brainstorm ideas. As feedback, elicit ideas from different students.

> Students' own answers

3A ◀» 3.04 Explain the activity and play the recording, twice if necessary. Check answers with the class.

> <u>Max</u>
> **Positive:** hard-working, flexible, good at working with both colleagues and customers, has relevant experience and skills
> **Negative:** no regional sales experience, no driving licence, not very organised
>
> <u>John</u>
> **Positive:** hard-working, flexible, good at working with both colleagues and customers, has relevant experience and skills, good transferable skills, is aware of weaknesses and is working on them, taking driving test in two weeks
> **Negative:** no driving licence, not very good at administrative work and paperwork

3B ◀» 3.04 Elicit or explain what open and closed questions are. (An open question encourages a fuller, more detailed answer, and cannot be answered with 'yes' or 'no'. Open-ended questions usually start with a *wh-* word. A closed question can be answered with a 'yes' or 'no'.) Play the recording and, if necessary, pause after each question to give students time to write. Check answers with the class.

1 you are the right person for this job (open question)
2 in a regional sales team (closed question)
3 driving licence (closed question)
4 your weaknesses (open question)

3C Discuss the questions with the class.

Possible answers

The interviewer uses a mix of open and closed questions to get more or less detailed answers in each case.

Closed questions generally lead to answers such as 'yes' or 'no'. Open questions give the person more freedom and flexibility to give more or less detail.

4 Put students in pairs to discuss the questions. If necessary, replay the recording or refer students to audioscript 3.04 on page 147 for questions 2 and 3. Check answers with the class. There is no correct answer to question 4, though students' perceptions may enable you to have a discussion on why they feel they way they do. On the surface, John appears the better candidate.

1 In the first interview, Max answers closed questions in a closed way. In the second interview, John adds more details to his answers to closed questions. Especially when the answer might be bad for him, he gave more details so he could focus on the positive.
If the answer to a closed question may be negative for you, give more details about relevant and related points that are positive and shift the focus from the negative (e.g. John doesn't have a driving licence, but emphasises the fact that he's taking his test soon. He's also aware that he isn't good at paperwork, but is working on it.).
2 He says he has worked in different local offices of the same company so he has a good perspective on the balance between local and regional priorities. While his experience is local, he has a good awareness of the sales focus from regional perspectives, too. He has also indirectly supported a regional project with local information.
3 Sue references why she has called him in for the interview. This, in theory, should have given John some confidence and removed any nerves he may have been feeling.

Functional language: Useful phrases for candidates

Students look at useful phrases for the different stages of a job interview.

5A Explain that this section looks at useful phrases a candidate can use during the different stages of a job interview. Ask students to do the exercise individually, referring to audioscript 3.04 on page 147. Check answers with the class.

1 question **2** asked that **3** day or week in this job would be like **4** steps **5** hear from you

5B Students could do this exercise individually and then compare answers in pairs before checking with the class.

A 3,8 **B** 4,6 **C** 1,2 **D** 5,7

Extra activities 3.4

A Ask students to do the exercise individually and get them to compare answers in pairs, giving reasons for their choices. During feedback, elicit or explain why the correct answer would be a better response in each case.

1 c **2** c **3** b **4** a **5** b **6** c **7** b

B Students could do this exercise in pairs, giving reasons for their answers.

a, c, f

C Make sure students understand that there are two seats of sentences: they need to match 1–5 with a–e, and 6–10 with f–j.

1 e **2** d **3** b **4** a **5** c **6** j **7** i **8** h **9** f **10** g

---

Task

Students create/choose a job advertisement and roleplay an interview for it.

6A Put students in pairs and go through the instructions with them. Clarify that they can choose to create their own job advertisement or use one of the advertisements on the page.

6B Ask pairs to assign roles, and refer students to their role cards on pages 126 and 127. Give them some time to read their cards, and answer any questions they may have. Then, depending on the strength of your class, set a time limit of 5–10 minutes for students to prepare for their interviews.

6C Go through the instructions with students and set a time limit for the roleplay. Point out that they need to make notes during the interview so they can give their partner feedback afterwards. When students have finished their roleplays, allow plenty of time for peer-assessment. Monitor and make note of any points to highlight during class feedback.

6D Ask students to swap roles and roleplay their interview again. They can use the same job advertisement or create/choose a different one. If time is short, ask students to use the same advertisement, as a new one will require more preparation time. Again, monitor and make notes during the roleplay and peer-assessment stages. Feed back by asking students to share with the class what they think went well and what could be improved. Then highlight any points you noted while monitoring.

MyEnglishLab: Teacher's resources: extra activities; Functional language bank
Workbook: p.17 Exercises 2 and 3

3.5 ❯ Writing
Covering letters

GSE learning objectives

- Can write a covering letter addressing specific information mentioned in a job post.
- Can write a letter of application with appropriate register and supporting details, given a model.
- Can tell when to use the Past Simple and when to use the Present Perfect.

Warm-up

Write the following questions on the board: *Have you ever written or read a covering letter? What do you think an effective covering letter should include?* Get students to discuss the questions in pairs or groups first, and then as a class. You could come back to the second question at the end of the lesson, asking students to say what they have learnt about covering letters and how they would answer this question having completed today's lesson.

Lead-in

Students read a covering letter and complete an error correction task.

1 Before students read the letter, refer them to the job advertisement on page 127 and give them 1–2 minutes to read it. Draw their attention to the correction on the first line of the letter and explain that they need to find nine more mistakes. If necessary, explain the type of mistakes they need to look for by giving examples on the board (e.g. spelling: *aplication application*; grammar: *I write am writing to apply for …*; missing words: *With reference (to) your advertisement in …*). Get students to compare answers in pairs before checking with the class.

> **Para 2:** degrees = degree (singular noun); interntional = international (spelling), experience = experienced (adjective needed), we have won = we won (definite past time – *last year*)
>
> **Para 3:** spent last three = spent **the** last three (missing article), helped me to increasing = helped me to increase (infinitive needed), significant = significantly (adverb needed as describes the verb *increase*), would be suitable = would be **a** suitable (missing article)
>
> **Para 5:** look forward to hear = look forward to hearing (*-ing* form needed)

Functional language

Students look at the organisation of and some useful phrases for a covering letter.

2 Students could do this individually or in pairs, using their dictionaries if necessary. Check answers with the class and clarify any vocabulary if necessary. It would be worthwhile to spend some time on the organisation of the letter at this point. Look at the different parts of the letter with students and elicit what type of information each one includes. You could get students to annotate the letter, labelling the different parts (e.g. greeting

→ subject line → para 1: opening (reason for writing) → para 2: qualifications, experience → para 3: why you are the right person for the job → para 4: concluding → signing off).

> **1** enclosed **2** vacancy **3** advertised **4** considered **5** have been **6** degree **7** experience **8** exceeding **9** confident **10** allow **11** asset **12** grateful

Extra activities 3.5

A This exercise practises useful phrases for covering letters. It is a consolidation exercise, so it would be better for students to do it individually. Check answers with the class.

> **1** g **2** e **3** f **4** i **5** h **6** c **7** j **8** b **9** d **10** a

Optional grammar work

The email in Exercise 1 contains examples of the Past Simple and Present Perfect, so you could use it for some optional grammar work. Refer students to the Grammar reference on page 120 and use the exercises in MyEnglishLab for extra grammar practice.

Task

Students assess a covering letter and then write their own.

3A Put students in pairs. Refer them to page 130 and give them time to read the job advertisement and covering letter, and discuss how the letter could be improved. As feedback, elicit and discuss students' suggestions.

3B Students write their own covering letter in response to the advertisement on page 130. Remind them to use the functional language from Exercise 2, and point out the word limit. Monitor and help students as necessary.

3C Put students in pairs. Go through the instructions with them and give them 4–6 minutes for the activity. If time allows, you could also ask them to suggest ways in which their partner could improve their letter.

Model answer

Dear Mr Slater,

I would like to apply for the position of Digital Technology Sales Trainee as advertised on your website and which interests me very much.

Having completed my degree in multimedia three months ago, I am now looking for an opportunity to use my skills working for an innovative company such as MolMedia. I have spent every vacation working in a similar company to yours. My duties included calling potential clients and explaining how we could help them, experience which is very relevant to your vacancy.

This year my team and I have already won an award for some of our designs, which have now been entered into an international competition. Being very competitive, we are hoping to win an award there, too. I also represented my university at an international media conference in Barcelona last year where I gave a presentation on new developments in digital technology.

I would very much appreciate having the opportunity of an interview to learn more about your company and demonstrate to you how I could be of value to your company.

I look forward to hearing from you.

Yours sincerely,

MyEnglishLab: Teacher's resources: extra activities; Interactive grammar practice; Writing bank

Grammar reference: p.120 Past Simple and Present Perfect

Workbook: p.18 Exercises 1 and 2

Business workshop ⟩ 3

Social media manager required

GSE learning objectives

- Can understand duties and responsibilities listed in job descriptions.
- Can understand the details of someone's personal and professional experience from an interview or presentation.
- Can compare a resumé/CV against a job posting to determine if key requirements have been met.
- Can ask for information in a job interview.
- Can give information in a job interview.
- Can discuss their own achievements in previous jobs during a job interview.
- Can understand a range of questions in a job interview.

Background

Students read about Media Solutions, a media company.

1 Put students in pairs and ask them to read the job advert and discuss the questions. Ask them to make notes, which they will need for Exercise 2. Check answers with the class.

1 Social Media Manager
2 Media Solutions, a company that specialises in media and PR (Public Relations) solutions for clients around the world
3 The candidate should have relevant experience in social media and experience in communication and marketing is also required (*proven track record*). Previous experience in management is not necessary.
4 The candidate must be a team player, they must be able to work to tight deadlines and, if possible, speak languages. They also want someone who has a passion for social media (*a social media addict*).
5 Students' own answers
6 Students' own answers
7 Possible answers: It's more immediate and engaging. A video CV would test a candidate's communication skills and whether they are confident and good at speaking in public. It would also test their level of English.

Video CVs

Students watch (or listen to) video CVs of applicants for a position with Media Solutions, then read and discuss the applicants' CVs.

2 Put students in new pairs. Explain that they are going to take on the roles of Human Resources Manager and Head of Communications at Media Solutions. Ask how these two people relate to the job. (The HR Manager is responsible for interviewing and deciding who will get the job. The Head of Communications will be the new employee's manager.) Allocate a role to each student and give them a few minutes to discuss their ideal candidate. Remind them to refer to their notes from Exercise 1.

Possible answers

A candidate who loves working with social media, has excellent communication skills, is a team player, is good at writing, can meet deadlines, is good at languages and has experience in social media, marketing or PR.

3A ▶ BW3.01 ◀) BW3.01 Students should do this exercise individually. Explain the task and play the video or recording. If necessary, allow students to watch/listen a second time to complete their notes.

Possible answers

Amalia

Qualities/Experience: highly qualified, with experience in marketing; hard-working; reliable; good communication skills, especially writing; language skills

First impressions: She seems a bit shy and nervous, but comes across as conscientious, reliable and friendly. She looks smart but is older than the other candidates. This could be an advantage or a disadvantage.

Birte

Qualities/Experience: degree in marketing; did an internship (in father's company); doesn't have much experience, but she is social, creative and loves sports and social media

First impressions: She is wearing sports clothes in the video, which is very informal, but it gets our attention. She comes across as very communicative, confident and very motivated, which helps to compensate for her lack of experience.

Cindy

Qualities/Experience: doesn't have a degree in marketing/communication, but is currently working as a manager, so has experience of deadlines and working under pressure; is studying marketing online; loves social media; writes a blog in her free time

First impressions: She comes across quite well in the video CV, although she does get distracted by her phone at one point. She dresses smartly and comes across as confident.

3B Put students in the same pairs as Exercise 2, to compare their notes from Exercise 3A. Then give them a few minutes to decide who the best candidate is. Point out that they should give reasons for their choice. When they have finished, invite a few pairs to share their decisions with the class.

Possible answer

Birte and Cindy are good at selling themselves.

4A Keep students in the same pairs and explain the activity: they need to work together to add the missing headings to Birte's CV, but they each read only one of the other candidates' CVs. Refer students to the appropriate pages and give them 5–7 minutes for the activity. Check answers with the class.

Possible answers

1 Personal Information / Contact Information
2 Profile / Personal Summary
3 Work Experience / Employment History
4 Education / Qualifications
5 (Hobbies and) Interests

4B Keep students in the same pairs. They each make notes in the space provided about the two CVs they read and then compare notes and decide which candidate they would hire. Go through the examples with students before they begin. During the activity, monitor and help students as necessary. As feedback, invite a few pairs to share their decision with the class, giving reasons.

Possible answers

I'd hire Amalia because of her experience as a marketing and PR professional; she has managed people while working as an assistant store manager and she is used to working in a team. I also think we should employ Amalia because she has studied Communications and Public Relations, which would be very useful for the post. In addition, the candidate needs to be someone with very good communication skills and she says she has excellent written communication and language skills. I'd prefer someone who can write well and her CV is more complete than Birte's.

I'd hire Cindy because she 'has a proven track record of achieving excellent results'. I also think we should hire her because she has experience working as a Customer Service Manager in a call centre, although she has only worked in marketing as an intern for six months. Another reason to hire Cindy is that she spent one year doing the Erasmus exchange programme in the University of Copenhagen, Denmark, which is an advantage. I'd prefer someone who works well in a team and who is more results-oriented. Her CV is also more complete than Birte's.

I wouldn't employ Birte because her CV is poorly organised and incomplete compared to Amalia's and Cindy's. However, she is a possible candidate because she has a degree in Marketing and Event Management. She doesn't seem to have much work experience, apart from working as a children's Taekwondo instructor, as a monitor in a summer camp and doing voluntary work. But she comes across as enthusiastic – she says she loves social media and writes a blog, which is very useful for this post.

Extra activities Business workshop 3

A ▶ BW3.01 This activity provides students with extra listening practice. Give them time to read the questions first, so they know what to watch for. Then play the video, twice if necessary, and check answers with the class. If time allows, you could ask students to look at the videoscript on page 145 and underline the parts which give the answer to each question.

1 Amalia 2 Cindy 3 Birte 4 Cindy 5 Birte
6 Cindy 7 Amalia 8 Birte 9 Amalia

Analysis of covering letters

Students read and analyse the applicants' covering letters / emails.

5 Refer students to the covering letters/emails on page 133 and give them sufficient time to read and assess them. Then discuss the questions as a whole class. Ask students to justify their opinions.

Both Amalia and Cindy's emails/letters are well written, in a formal style. Birte's email has spelling and punctuation mistakes (e.g. 'i') and is much too informal.

Students' own choice of candidate based on the video CVs and the covering letters (probably either Amalia or Cindy).

First interviews

Students listen to and discuss extracts from the applicants' first interviews.

6 ◀) BW3.02 Explain the activity and encourage students to take notes as they listen. Play the recording and ask students to think about who they would hire and why. Again, ask them to make notes. Put students in pairs and get them to compare and discuss their ideas. As feedback, elicit ideas from different students.

Students' own answers; the candidates give interesting answers for different reasons, and all of the candidates refer to their proudest moment being related to social media. Although both Amalia's and Birte's achievements are not work-related, they are perhaps more inspiring and engaging than Cindy's.

Extra activities Business workshop 3

B This activity provides students with extra reading practice. Ask them to read the questions first, and help them with any unknown vocabulary. Then refer them to the CVs on pages 132, 134 and 137 and set a time limit for the activity. Depending on the ability of your class, ask students to complete it individually or in pairs. Check answers with the class.

1 T
2 T
3 F (Birte writes 'with excellent communication and leadership skills'.)
4 F (Amalia writes 'I am familiar with most office software packages'.)
5 F (This refers to Cindy. Birte has a degree in Marketing and Event Management.)
6 T
7 F (This refers to Cindy: 'one year Erasmus exchange programme with the University of Copenhagen'.)
8 T
9 T
10 F (Amalia speaks English, French, Spanish and Portuguese. Cindy doesn't mention languages, although she speaks English, and we can imagine she speaks German and Spanish.)

C ▶ BW3.02 This activity provides students with extra listening practice. Give them time to read through the sentence halves, then play the recording, twice if necessary. Get students to compare answers in pairs before checking with the class.

1 c 2 d 3 h 4 e 5 f 6 a 7 b 8 g

Task

Students roleplay the second interview of one of the applicants.

7 Put students in new pairs. Go through the instructions with them and answer any questions they may have. Encourage them to make notes in preparation for the interview. Allocate roles and allow students 4–6 minutes to prepare. When the time is up, ask students to roleplay their interviews. You could set up the interviews with chairs facing each other. Monitor and note down any points to highlight during feedback. When students have finished, ask a few HR Managers if they would hire the candidate, and a few candidates if they think their second interview went well. Then highlight any points you noted while monitoring.

Social media profiles

Students read about and discuss Media Solutions' final decision.

8A/B Explain Exercise 8A and get students to read the information on page 136. When they are ready, put them in pairs to discuss the company's decision. Then, as a whole class, discuss the questions in Exercise 8B.

Students' own answers, depending on the second interviews. But students will probably have chosen either Cindy or Amalia, although Amalia seems too nervous or shy for the position. Birte has a degree in marketing and lots of enthusiasm but her social media presence might be inappropriate in a business context when dealing with key clients. Colleagues also might find her difficult to work with because she has a strong personality and is over-confident.

Other factors that could influence their choice of candidate: references, and, from the candidates' perspective, the pay and working conditions (e.g. Cindy might prefer to carry on working in the call centre).

MyEnglishLab: Teacher's resources: extra activities

Review ◀ 3

1 1 jobseeker 2 applied 3 employer 4 come
  5 competitive 6 gained 7 internship 8 motivated
  9 stand 10 sort 11 clichés 12 character
2 1 what degree you did
  2 why you want to work for us
  3 where you expect to be in five years' time
  4 what my responsibilities will be
  5 why you think you're the right person for this job
  6 how long you were working in China
3 1 tell me a bit more 2 exactly do you mean
  3 don't understand what 4 what I meant
  5 you are frustrated
4 1 time 2 about 3 like 4 with 5 hear
5 1 attached 2 completed 3 considered 4 post
  5 proved 6 appreciate

4 ▶ Business strategy

Unit overview

		CLASSWORK	FURTHER WORK
4.1 ▶ **Food industry strategies**	**Lead-in**	Students discuss famous food brands and trends in the food industry.	**MyEnglishLab:** Teacher's resources: extra activities; Reading bank
	Video	Students watch a video about problem-solving strategies in the food industry and the risks involved in tackling corporate problems.	**Teacher's book:** Resource bank Photocopiable 4.1 p.142
	Vocabulary	Students look at vocabulary related to business strategy.	**Workbook:** p.19 Exercises 1–3
	Project	Students research a food brand and its attitudes to health.	
4.2 ▶ **PEST analysis**	**Lead-in**	Students discuss different everyday situations when developing a strategy is necessary.	**MyEnglishLab:** Teacher's resources: extra activities
	Listening	Students listen to a lecture on business strategy.	**Grammar reference:** p. 121 Modal verbs
	Grammar	Students study and practise modal verbs for obligation, prohibition, necessity and recommendation.	**Teacher's book:** Resource bank Photocopiable 4.2 p.143
	Writing	Students write a PEST analysis of a company/organisation.	**Workbook:** p.20 Exercises 1–3, p.21 Exercises 1–3
4.3 ▶ **Communication skills:** Solving problems	**Lead-in**	Students discuss communication styles in different cultures.	**MyEnglishLab:** Teacher's resources: extra activities; Interactive video activities; Functional language bank
	Video	Students watch a video about direct and indirect communication styles in the workplace and think about the advantages and disadvantages of each.	**Pronunciation bank:** p.115 /iː/, /ɪ/, /eɪ/ and /aɪ/
	Reflection	Students think about and assess their own communication style.	**Workbook:** p.22 Exercise 1
	Functional language	Students study and practise useful phrases for offering help, asking for help and responding to offers of help.	
	Task	Students practise the functional language from the lesson by roleplaying and then discussing different situations.	
4.4 ▶ **Business skills:** Problem-solving meetings	**Lead-in**	Students read and discuss tips for leading problem-solving meetings effectively.	**MyEnglishLab:** Teacher's resources: extra activities; Functional language bank
	Listening	Students listen to extracts from a problem-solving meeting.	**Pronunciation bank:** p.115 Intonation in 'OK'
	Functional language	Students look at useful language for leading and participating in problem-solving meetings.	**Workbook:** p.22 Exercise 2
	Task	Students practise the functional language from the lesson by roleplaying a problem-solving meeting.	
4.5 ▶ **Writing:** Reporting reasons and results	**Lead-in**	Students read a model answer and study linkers of reason and result.	**MyEnglishLab:** Teacher's resources: extra activities; Interactive grammar practice; Writing bank
	Functional language	Students look at more linkers of reason and result.	**Grammar reference:** p.121 Comparison
	Task	Students write a report extract.	**Workbook:** p.23 Exercises 1 and 2
Business workshop 4 ▶ Supermarket wars	**Reading**	Students read an article about changing consumer habits.	**MyEnglishLab:** Teacher's resources: extra activities
	Speaking	Students analyse visual data about three supermarket chains.	
	Task	Students discuss and develop growth strategies for a supermarket chain.	
	Listening	Students listen to a news report about the supermarket industry.	

Business brief

The main aim of this unit is to introduce students to the concepts related to **business strategy**. All companies and organisations have **aims** and to achieve these aims, a company needs a business strategy, i.e. they need to answer the question 'How?'.

Most companies aim to **improve their performance**, **grow** the company by **expanding** into new markets and **developing** new products, improve their **profit margins** (the difference between the cost of producing something and the price you sell it at). If they are ambitious, they may also aim to **take over** or **merge** with another company. Examples of this are when Disney bought Pixar in 2006 to form a large film-making company or when the two food companies Kraft and Heinz merged in 2015 to form Kraft Heinz.

To create a strategy, an organisation needs to **analyse** the economic and business situation. This analysis needs to be systematic. For example, **PEST analysis** involves analysing the **Political**, **Economic**, **Social** and **Technological** factors. These are the **external** events and background situations which might affect the company – for example, if the economy goes into recession or the government decides to raise corporation tax, or if there is a significant technological advance. Variations of PEST include SLEPT (including 'L' for 'Legal') and PESTLE (including 'L' for 'Legal' and 'E' for 'Environment').

Other analytical tools include **SWOT** – Strengths, Weaknesses, Opportunities and Threats. **Strengths** and **Weaknesses** refer to **internal** factors such as a new groundbreaking product or a poorly designed company website. **Opportunities** may relate to economic factors such as a reduction in inflation or unemployment that leads to people spending more. **Threats** could refer to other bigger or more aggressive companies which are competing in the same market.

A company cannot achieve all its aims at once, so it needs to prioritise – decide which aims are more important or urgent. These decisions may be based on financial factors, such as the company being short of money, or may be based on strategic factors such as getting into a new market before a competitor. Finally, the company's managers need to take action using the strategy they created to achieve their aims.

Business strategy and your students

It is important for students, whether they have started working or not, to understand business analysis. It is a central part of Business Studies courses and is part of any company's business. Using simple but effective analytical tools like PEST is a good way to help students understand the basic principles and apply them to everyday examples in the business world.

Unit lead-in

Look at the quote with the class and check that students understand the difference between *distant* and *distanced*. Ask students if they agree that 'taking a distanced view of close things' is good business strategy. What problems could not distancing yourself from 'close things' create? If time allows, you could let students discuss in pairs or small groups first, and then broaden this into a class discussion.

4.1 ❯ Food industry strategies

GSE learning objectives

- Can give or seek personal views and opinions in discussing topics of interest.
- Can understand a large part of a video on a work-related topic.
- Can present findings from a research project in a simple way.

Warm-up

Write *ketchup, breakfast cereal, instant coffee* and *cookies* on the board and ask students what they have in common (they are all types of (processed) food and drink). Tell students that they have 30 seconds to write down as many types of food as they can. When the time is up, elicit students' ideas and write them on the board. You could make this into a competition: the student with the most ideas is the winner.

Lead-in

Students discuss famous food brands and trends in the food industry.

1 Students could discuss the questions in pairs first and then as a whole class. In a multinational class, you could pair up students from different countries, to discuss how trends in the food industry differ in their countries. For question 2, point out the different topics in the box. Students should try to think about these and include them in their discussion: What brands are famous in their country? Are prices going up or down? What health issues are there? Are people becoming more or less healthy? What are some typical health problems related to food/diet? Are people eating more or less organic food? What changes have there been in lifestyles? Has this led to more people eating prepared meals? Once students have discussed in their pairs, open this up into a class discussion. List students' ideas for question 1 on the board so that they can refer to them when they do Exercise 4.

Notes

2 Students may feel food prices are always rising, although in general, in Europe, since the economic crisis started in 2008, there has been enormous competition in the food industry. Consumers are spending less on branded goods these days and major food brands have seen their profit margins slashed. There's also been huge competition in prices in the supermarket sector. Students may mention global concerns about obesity and the responsibilities of the processed food and drink industry. Again, lifestyle changes see more people eating ready meals which are often not that fresh or healthy.

Video

Students watch a video about problem-solving strategies in the food industry and the risks involved in tackling corporate problems.

2 ▶ 4.1.1 Go through the question with students and encourage them to take notes while watching. Play the video and check answers with the class.

> Kraft, Cadbury, Heinz; Kraft took over / acquired / now owns Cadbury. Kraft merged with the other food giant, Heinz. The company is now called Kraft Heinz.

3 ▶ 4.1.1 Give students a minute to go through the sentences and point out the word limit. Play the video again, then check answers with the class.

> **1** was poor **2** demand for (the)
> **3** its home U.S. market / the U.S. market
> **4** costs (were too high) **5** around the world / worldwide **6** cut costs **7** changing consumer preference
> **8** rose 17 percent

4 Put students in pairs or small groups and go through the questions with them. Check that they understand *consolidation* and *inevitable*. For question 1, you could refer them to the list on the board from Exercise 1. Give students 3–4 minutes to discuss in their pairs/groups, then get brief feedback from the class.

Extra activities 4.1

A ▶ 4.1.1 Give students a minute to read the sentences. If there is time, you could put them in pairs to check if they can answer any of the questions before watching again, and then watch the video to check/complete their answers. Play the video, then check answers with the class. To check answers, you could play the video again, and tell students to ask you to pause it when an answer is heard.

> **1** c **2** b **3** a **4** b **5** b **6** c **7** a **8** c

Vocabulary: Business strategy collocations

Students look at vocabulary related to business strategy.

5 Students could do this activity individually or in pairs. With stronger classes, ask students to use their dictionaries to check the meaning of any unknown words. With weaker classes, go through the words in the boxes with students before they complete the sentences. Check answers with the class, clarifying meaning as necessary.

> **1** major player **2** profit margin **3** emerging markets
> **4** takeover bid **5** product lines

6 Again, you could let students complete this activity individually or in pairs. After checking answers with the class, encourage students to record the collocations from this and the previous exercise in their vocabulary notebooks.

> 1 b 2 c 3 d 4 a 5 f 6 g 7 h 8 e

Word building – verbs, nouns and adjectives

7 Do the first item as an example with the class. Ask students to complete the exercise individually, using their dictionaries to help them if necessary, then get them to compare answers in pairs before checking with the class. Write the answers on the board so students can check their spelling. You could then use the completed table for some pronunciation work: model and drill the pronunciation of each group of words, and point out the shift in stress in some cases (e.g. _acquire – acquisition_; _compete – competition_).

> **1** acquisition **2** compete **3** competitive
> **4** development **5** developed **6** expand **7** expanding
> **8** fail **9** growth **10** innovation **11** innovative
> **12** merge **13** performance **14** profit **15** risky
> **16** success **17** successful **18** take over

8 You could do this exercise as a whole class, checking the gapped words and discussing each question as you go. Alternatively, give students time to complete the questions, check answers with the class, then put students in pairs to discuss the questions.

> **1** competition **2** competitive **3** growing **4** growth
> **5** successful **6** succeed
> (The answer to question 3 is China and India, in this order.)

Extra activities 4.1

B This activity practises key vocabulary from the lesson. Ask students to do it individually, as a quick quiz, then get them to compare answers in pairs before checking with the class.

> **1** acquires **2** come up with **3** developing
> **4** innovative **5** major player **6** merge
> **7** performance **8** profit margin **9** tackle
> **10** takeover

Project: Attitudes to health

Students research a food brand and its attitudes to health.

9A Put students in pairs or small groups and go through the headlines with them. Check they understand _drive_, _obesity_ and _turn to_. Allow 3–4 minutes for students to discuss the question in their pairs/groups, then invite different students to share their views with the class.

9B Students will need access to the internet for this activity. Put _Additives_, _Ingredients_, _Labelling_ and _Product lines_ in four columns on the board and ask students to copy them in a table into their notebooks. Clarify meaning as necessary, and explain that students should choose a food brand to research online and make notes in the table they have in their notebooks. Point out that they will need their notes for the next stage of the project.

9C Join pairs/groups together into groups of four / larger groups and allow plenty of time for them to exchange and discuss their findings. As feedback, you could ask a few pairs/groups to share their findings with the class.

MyEnglishLab: Teacher's resources: extra activities; Reading bank
Teacher's book: Resource bank Photocopiable 4.1 p.142
Workbook: p.19 Exercises 1–3

4.2 ❯ PEST analysis

GSE learning objectives

- Can express and comment on ideas and suggestions in informal discussions.
- Can recognise examples and their relation to the idea they support.
- Can follow most of a clearly structured presentation within their own field.
- Can predict the content of a simple presentation or lecture by listening to the introductory statement.
- Can use a range of modals to talk about obligation, prohibition, necessity and recommendation.
- Can use language related to ways of expressing necessity and obligation.
- Can write a simple PEST analysis.

Warm-up

Write the following quote on the board: _Leaders establish the vision for the future and set the strategy for getting there._ (John P. Kotter, author, Harvard professor, entrepreneur) Check that students understand _vision_, and discuss the quote as a class. Do students agree? How important is strategy in achieving goals? Is it possible to achieve a goal without a sound strategy? Does it depend on the goal?

Lead-in

Students discuss different everyday situations when developing a strategy is necessary.

1A Ask students to choose one of the situations and give them 1–2 minutes to think about their strategies individually. Then put them in pairs to exchange and discuss their ideas for their chosen situation. Alternatively, start by putting students in pairs, and have each pair choose and discuss one situation. Set a time limit for the students' discussions, then ask different pairs to explain their strategies to the class.

Possible answers

1 You will need to find out what subjects you have to study to get into medicine at university (e.g. biology, chemistry) and choose those subjects. You will need to find out which universities offer degrees in medicine and what type of applicants they accept. You could do some voluntary work for a health organisation to get experience to support your application.

2 You could get a job to help pay for your driving lessons or get some financial help from your family. You need to find out where you can study for the licence and how much it will cost. You'll also need to calculate how long it will take you to pass the test and what you will do if you fail. You will need to study for the theory test. You could get an experienced driver to help you with extra practice.

3 You and your team members will need to prepare mentally and physically for the match. You may all need to study the rival's tactics and adapt the way you play in order to beat them.

4 You could plan your nutrition and exercise carefully for the year ahead, including dieting and joining a gym.

1B Students could brainstorm ideas in pairs first, then discuss as a class.

Possible answers

planning a wedding, organising a summer holiday, deciding what to do with the children during the school holidays, getting to a more senior position in your profession, changing careers, finding a job

2 Look at the dictionary definition with students, then discuss the question as a whole class. Encourage students to give reasons and to think of examples in their own country/area.

Possible answer

Companies, large and small in every industry, in every part of the world, need a strategy or strategies in order to plan for the future and respond to an ever-changing environment. Also governments (and NGOs) need strategies to help them to prepare for the future.

Listening

Students listen to a lecture on business strategy.

3A 🔊 4.01 Refer students to the diagram and ask what they think *PEST* means. Do not confirm the answer yet – students will find out when they listen. Play the recording for students to check their ideas and complete the headings in the diagram.

Political, Economic, Social, Technological

3B 🔊 4.01 Ask students if anyone can remember the answers to the questions. If necessary, play the recording again for students to answer the questions or check their answers.

1 All four factors are external to the company / outside influences (and in general, companies have little or no control over these factors).
2 It can be extended to *PESTLE*, which includes *L* for 'Legal factors' and *E* for 'Environmental factors'.

4A 🔊 4.02 Explain that students now have to complete the examples in the diagram in Exercise 3A. Point out the word limit (1–3 words per gap) and play the recording. Check answers with the class.

1 stability or instability 2 employment 3 economic recession 4 exports and imports 5 consumer preferences 6 growing 7 production lines 8 smartphone

4B You could do this as a whole class or get students to brainstorm ideas in pairs or small groups first.

Possible answers

Political: wars, diplomatic crises, levels of corruption, nationalisation policies
Economic: employment levels, salaries, interest rates
Social: cultural differences, health concerns, immigration
Technological: rapid changes to technology and products / IT systems becoming outdated

5A 🔊 4.03 Go through the instructions and list of tasks with the class, and check that they understand *prioritise*. You could get them to briefly discuss their ideas in pairs first. Elicit students' ideas but do not confirm the order yet – let them listen to check their predictions. Check answers with the class.

c, b, d, a

5B 🔊 4.03 Play the recording and check the answer with the class.

Example of an opportunity: a new technology to improve production processes and reduce costs
Example of a risk: If consumer demand is falling in one part of its market, should the company develop new product lines?

Extra activities 4.2

A 🔊 4.01 🔊 4.02 🔊 4.03 This activity practises key vocabulary from the recordings. Students could do it individually or in pairs, using a dictionary if necessary. Give them 3–5 minutes to complete the sentences. You could play all three parts of the recording again for students to check their answers before class feedback. During feedback, check that students understand the words in the box and ensure they can pronounce them correctly.

1 tool 2 acronym 3 face 4 stand for 5 closely
6 emerging 7 prioritise 8 improve 9 threats
10 come up with

Grammar: Modal verbs

Students study and practise modal verbs for obligation, prohibition, necessity and recommendation.

6 You could do this exercise as a whole class, checking and explaining each answer as you go along. Briefly check the grammar of modal verbs: elicit that *should* and *must* are the same in all persons and are followed by an infinitive without *to*; then check the form of *have to*. Finally, refer students to the Grammar reference on page 121, give them time to go through the explanations and examples (or go through them as a class), and clarify any points as necessary.

> **1** d **2** b **3** c **4** a **5** c

7 You may want to do the first item as an example with the class. Explain that more than one answer may be possible in some items, and ask students to do the exercise individually. Get them to compare answers in pairs before checking with the class.

> **1** must / have to **2** don't have to **3** should **4** shouldn't **5** must / have to **6** will have to (no future form of *must*)

8 Again, explain that there may be more than one possible answer in some items before students begin. Check answers with the class and if there is time, put students in pairs to practise the conversation.

> **1** must / has to **2** have to **3** mustn't **4** have to **5** should **6** must **7** should **8** don't have to

9 Put students in pairs. Give them 3–5 minutes to discuss the questions, then get brief feedback from the class. For question 2, encourage students to say if they agree with the rules. For question 3, encourage them to give reasons for their recommendations.

Extra activities 4.2

B This is a consolidation exercise, so you may prefer students to do it individually and compare answers in pairs before class feedback. Before they begin, point out that both options are possible in some items.

> **1** mustn't **2** → (Both modals express obligation or necessity.) **3** → (*Should* is a recommendation and *must* is a strong recommendation.) **4** don't have to **5** not having to **6** shouldn't **7** shouldn't **8** mustn't **9** must **10** don't have to

Writing

Students write a PEST analysis of a company/organisation.

10 Put students in pairs or small groups and explain that they are going to write a short PEST analysis of a company or organisation they know well. Go through the instructions with them and check that they understand what they have to do and what they need to include in their analysis. Refer them to page 129 and give them a few minutes to go through the model answer. Give students sufficient time to write their analyses. Monitor as they are writing and help them with any vocabulary they may need. Finally, invite pairs/groups to present their analyses to the class.

Teacher's resources: extra activities
Grammar reference: p. 121 Modal verbs
Teacher's book: Resource bank Photocopiable 4.2 p.143
Workbook: p.20 Exercises 1–3, p.21 Exercises 1–3

4.3 ❱ Communication skills
Solving problems

GSE learning objectives
- Can understand problem and solution relationships in informal conversation.
- Can offer and ask for help or assistance.
- Can use simple, fixed expressions to accept offers in a simple business transaction.
- Can decline offers politely using a range of formal and informal expressions.

Warm-up
Ask students to think about a time when they strongly disagreed with someone (with an opinion they expressed, with the way they handled a difficult situation, etc.). Ask them if they chose to show their disagreement directly, stating facts as they were and not worrying about how the other person might feel, or to simply not say anything in order not to hurt the other person's feelings. Put them in pairs or small groups and ask them to describe the situation to their partner(s), explaining what happened, how they reacted, whether or not they expressed their disagreement and why. Invite a few students to share their stories with the class. Encourage them to explain why they chose to express/hide their disagreement.

Lead-in
Students discuss communication styles in different cultures.

1 With books closed, write *direct* and *indirect* on the board. Ask students what they think a 'direct communication style' is and put their ideas on the board. Do the same for 'indirect communication style'. Ask students to open their books and give them time to read the texts and check their ideas. Put them in pairs and give them 3–5 minutes to discuss the two questions, then broaden this into a class discussion. Highlight that 'disadvantages' often relate to how other people may interpret your style, not how the style is intended. However, stress that people often view their interpretations as facts, which is why communication skills are so important.

Possible answers
1 Direct style
Advantage: People trust you.
Disadvantage: People think you are rude.
Indirect style
Advantage: People think you are polite.
Disadvantage: People don't believe you are saying what you really think.

Video

Students watch a video about direct and indirect communication styles in the workplace and think about the advantages and disadvantages of each.

2A ▶ 4.3.1 If students watched the Unit 3 video, ask them for a short summary of the situation so far. If this is the first communication skills video for your students, briefly set up the context and explain Matt's role yourself. Go through the instructions and questions with students and play the video. Check answers with the class.

> 1 not very happy as the Japan side has a three-week delay
> 2 Kenji lacks experience of international projects. Stefanie has provided little support as she has focused on Mexico.
> 3 Talk straight – tell Kenji that he has to perform or he is off the project. Make his expectations as project leader clear.
> 4 He doesn't want to offend Kenji by doing things in what he thinks is a non-Japanese way – directly. Also, Matt prefers a less direct approach in general – it's his personal style.

2B Discuss the question with the whole class. Encourage students to give reasons. Highlight the fact that leadership today always involves some balance of both 'push' and 'pull', and that knowing when to apply each style, although immensely difficult, is part of the art of leadership.

3A Go through the instructions and details of Options A and B with the class. Check that students understand *confront*, *impose* and *instincts*. Put them in small groups and give them 1–2 minutes to discuss which communication style they think Matt should adopt, giving reasons. Elicit ideas from a few students. Clarify that students can choose which option they want to see first on the video and then, as a class, decide which video to watch first.

3B ▶ 4.3.2 ▶ 4.3.3 Give students a minute to read the questions and play the video for Option A or Option B, depending on the students' choice. With weaker classes, you may need to play the video a second time for students to complete their answers. Check answers as a class, then explain that students will need to answer *the same* questions for the second option. Repeat the process for the second video.

> **Option A**
> 1 more than three weeks (a major delay)
> 2 Kenji says it is not ideal, but they are working very hard to correct things. Matt is not happy about what looks like an understatement of the seriousness of the situation.
> 3 Stefanie will fly to Tokyo and provide support; Stefanie will talk to Kenji about this the next day. Matt suggests the solution.
> 4 Kenji, despite the initial upset of the direct feedback, now sees it as a useful learning experience.

> **Option B**
> 1 just over three weeks (a slight delay)
> 2 Kenji admits they are struggling with resources and workload of local projects, which local management wants to be prioritised. Matt shows understanding and invites Kenji to come up with possible solutions.
> 3 Stefanie will support Kenji and visit him on Friday, and stay a week or so until things are back on track. Kenji will call Stefanie to confirm this and talk to Matt again in a couple of weeks.
> 4 Matt had to make a second call to ensure things happened as he wanted them to happen. The project is back on track and team spirit is high.

4 Put students in pairs and give them 3–4 minutes to discuss the questions. Remind them to discuss what they can learn from Matt's experience. Check answers to questions 1 and 2, and invite different students to share their views for question 3, giving reasons.

> 1 In Option A, Matt focused very quickly on the problem – the three-week project delay – and said very openly that he was unhappy. He disagreed very strongly with Kenji's explanation, and gave Kenji the solution (Stefanie will talk to him and deal with things). In Option B, Matt asked about family at the beginning, showed understanding, offered help and negotiated a solution, with Kenji agreeing to call Stefanie.
> 2 Things went well in both videos. In Option A, Kenji accepted the feedback as a useful learning experience. In Option B, Matt had to step in and phone Stefanie, but there is a very positive team spirit in addition to the project being back on track.
> 3 Students' own answers

5 ▶ 4.3.4 Keep students in the same pairs and explain that they are going to watch the last section of the video, where the speaker discusses the learning points from Matt's situation and comments on the effectiveness of the two communication styles. Play the video and give pairs a few minutes to compare what is said on the video with their answers to Exercise 4. Then play the video a second time and ask students to note down the three main learning points. Check answers with the class and invite different students to share their views with the class: do they agree with these points?

> 1 Direct communication can work, but it can create conflict, so use it carefully.
> 2 Indirect communication can work, but it can take longer to be effective.
> 3 Individuals should choose the communication style which fits the situation, not simply the style they prefer when solving problems.

Reflection

Students think about and assess their own communication style.

6 Allow students to work individually on this so that they can reflect on their own preferences and communication style. Then put them in pairs to discuss their answers. As feedback, elicit ideas from different students for each question and encourage brief class discussion. Ask if any students will consider changing their style after today's lesson.

Functional language: Offering and asking for help

Students study and practise useful phrases for offering help, asking for help and responding to offers of help.

7 You could do this exercise as a whole class, checking and explaining answers as you go. Write the phrases in two columns on the board for students to refer to during the lesson. Point out that *I think I / we can manage* is a polite way to reject an offer of help, and highlight the importance of being polite – especially in business situations.

> **a** 2, 4 **b** 1, 3, 5, 6

8A Again, this exercise can be done as a whole class or you may prefer students to work individually and compare answers in pairs before class feedback. Add the phrases to the lists on the board (adding a third column for *Asking for help*).

> **a** 1, 3, 4, 6 **b** 5, 7 **c** 2, 8

8B Do this activity with the whole class. After checking the answers, you may want to use the lists on the board for some pronunciation work: model the pronunciation of each phrase, focusing on intonation. Highlight the fact that intonation can project attitudes, and so it is important to use the correct intonation in order not to sound rude. Drill the phrases.

> 4 and 6 are informal.

9A/B Ask students to do Exercise 9A individually. Refer them to Exercises 7 and 8A or to the lists of phrases on the board. Go round the class, making sure students are using the phrases correctly. Then put students in pairs for Exercise 9B. As feedback, invite different pairs to act out their exchanges to the class.

> **Possible answers**
> **9A**
> 1 I can show you how it works if you like.
> 2 Let me open the window.
> 3 Need a hand to look for them?
> 4 Would you like me to get you a sandwich?
> **9B**
> 1 I think I can manage.
> 2 Yes, that would be good.
> 3 Thanks for offering but I'll be fine.
> 4 Thanks! I appreciate it.

Extra activities 4.3

A Ask students to do this individually. Then put them in pairs to compare their answers and practise the exchanges. Remind them to use intonation to sound polite. Check answers with the class.

> **1** there, manage **2** can, appreciate **3** like me, would **4** Let, for **5** hand with, that **6** mind

❯ Pronunciation bank
p.115: /iː/, /ɪ/, /eɪ/ and /aɪ/

Warm-up
Help students with recognising the vowel sounds: write an example of each on the board, underline the vowel sound and write its phonetic symbol next to it (e.g. w**ee**k – /iː/, tr**i**p – /ɪ/, w**ay** – /eɪ/ and l**ie** /aɪ/). Then go through the explanation in the box as a class. Check they understand by saying a word for each vowel sound and inviting a student to write it next to the correct symbol on the board (e.g. r**ea**d, k**i**tch**e**n, m**a**de, wh**y**).

1 Put students in pairs and give them 3–4 minutes to complete the table. Do not confirm answers yet as students will check them in the next exercise.

2 🔊 P4.01 Play the recording for students to check their answers. Then play the recording a second time for students to listen and repeat. You could drill the words chorally first, then individually.

> /iː/: briefed, colleague, people
> /ɪ/: business, limited, opinion
> /eɪ/: change, day, raise
> /aɪ/: advice, idea, style

3 Do an example with a stronger student: point to a word on the board and ask him/her to say a sentence containing that word. Check and correct pronunciation of the vowel sound(s) as necessary. Then put students in pairs and ask them to do the same for the words in Exercise 1. Monitor and help/correct students' pronunciation as necessary. Make note of any persistent pronunciation errors to highlight during feedback.

Task

Students practise the functional language from the lesson by roleplaying and then discussing different situations.

10A Go through the instructions with students and remind them that they can refer to Exercises 7 and 8A. Allow plenty of time for students to write their dialogues while you monitor and help/correct them as necessary. Set a time limit for the roleplay and let students practise their dialogues. Monitor and make note of any errors to highlight during feedback.

10B In the same pairs, students swap roles and repeat the process for a different situation. During class feedback, highlight any errors you noted while monitoring and, if time allows, invite a few pairs to act out their dialogues to the class.

MyEnglishLab: Teacher's resources: extra activities; Interactive video activities; Functional language bank
Pronunciation bank: p.115 /iː/, /ɪ/, /eɪ/ and /aɪ/
Workbook: p.22 Exercise 1

4.4 › Business skills
Problem-solving meetings

GSE learning objectives

- Can understand problem and solution relationships in informal conversation.
- Can understand advice and instructions for resolving a problem with a product or piece of equipment.
- Can explain why something is a problem.
- Can express opinions as regards possible solutions, giving brief reasons and explanations.
- Can suggest solutions in a problem-solving meeting.

Warm-up

Ask the class if they have taken part in a problem-solving meeting recently, how the meeting was structured, the positive and negative aspects of the meeting and the outcome. With students who are not yet working, ask what they think makes an effective problem-solving meeting.

Lead-in

Students read and discuss tips for leading problem-solving meetings effectively.

1 Put students in pairs and give them a few minutes to read the texts. Before they begin their discussion, check that they understand *commitment* and remind them to give reasons for their choices. Ask a few pairs to share their ideas with the class. If time allows, you could give pairs a few more minutes to brainstorm more ideas for each heading.

Listening

Students listen to extracts from a problem-solving meeting.

2A/B 🔊 4.04 🔊 4.05 Go through the instructions for Exercise 2A with the class, then play the recording. Get students to compare answers in pairs before checking with the class. For weaker students, you may need to play the recording twice. In stronger classes, after checking answers, you could refer students to the audioscript on page 148 and ask them to highlight the parts that give the answers. Follow the same procedure for Exercise 2B.

2A
1 The problem is a lack of language competence among existing staff to deal with enquiries from customers from new markets using their own language.
2 Failure to deal with the problem could result in losing these new customers.
3 training internal staff, working via an external call centre, hiring new people with relevant language skills
2B
1 Recruitment of new people with the relevant language skills.
2 Annette has to create a job description by the end of the week, and advertise the post the following week.
3 The problem will hopefully be solved by the end of the month (in three weeks) with the recruitment of the new people.

2C Elicit or remind students of the tips in Exercise 1. You may also wish to play the recording again or refer students to the audioscript on page 148 before they discuss the questions. Students could discuss in pairs or groups first and then as a whole class.

Possible answers

All the team members are engaged at the beginning and through the meeting.
They work hard to define the problem.
They are creative and offer a lot of ideas proactively.
They agree explicitly with the decision, and commit to implement it.
Annette shows responsibility by offering to deal with the job profile.
Bibi shows commitment to the team by agreeing with the decision and offering to help.
Overall, the meeting was effective with a clear decision and way forward which everyone agreed with.

› Pronunciation bank
p.115: Intonation in 'OK'

Warm-up

Say: *Now let's work on our pronunciation, OK?* Turn to a student and ask again: *OK?* Keep asking different students if necessary until one responds with *OK*, then ask the class: *What word did I use to check if (the student) agrees?* (*OK*.) *And what word did (the student) use to answer 'yes'?* (*OK*.) Refer students to the explanation in the box and highlight that what gives *OK* a different meaning/function each time is our intonation.

1 🔊 P4.02 Go through the instructions with the class and play the recording. Get students to compare answers in pairs before checking with the class.

a 1 **b** 4 **c** 3 **d** 2

2 Put students in pairs to practise the exchanges. Go round monitoring and check that students are using the correct intonation patterns. Help/Correct them as necessary.

Functional language: Leading and participating in problem-solving meetings

Students look at useful language for leading and participating in problem-solving meetings.

3A Go through the phrases with students and check that they understand *doable*, *take on* and *competence*. Give them 2–4 minutes for the matching activity, then check answers with the class.

> **a** 4 **b** 6 **c** 1 **d** 5 **e** 3 **f** 2

3B This exercise could be done individually or in pairs. Check that students understand the categories before they begin, especially *Building on others' ideas*.

> **a** 4,6 **b** 2,9 **c** 1,5 **d** 7 **e** 3 **f** 8

4 Put students in pairs and go through the steps they need to follow in their conversation. Remind them to use phrases from Exercises 3A and 3B, and set a time limit for the activity. Go round monitoring and make sure students are using the phrases correctly. If time allows, you could ask them to swap roles and discuss a second problem. During feedback, highlight any errors you noted while monitoring.

> **Extra activities 4.4**
>
> **A** Students could do this individually or in pairs. It may be better to check the sentences first, before students match them with the tips.
>
> > **a** That's a really good suggestion. (tip 4)
> > **b** What's a realistic deadline for us to do this? (tip 6)
> > **c** Many thanks for finding time for this important meeting. (tip 1)
> > **d** We need to come to a decision on this. (tip 5)
> > **e** What other ideas do you have to solve the problem? (tip 3)
> > **f** The main problem is a lack of investment in people. (tip 2)
>
> **B** Explain the activity and point out that students can only use each problem-solving phrase once. Monitor and make sure students are using the phrases correctly.
>
> **C** Put students in groups to share their ideas and decide on the best solution for each problem. Invite groups to share their chosen solutions with the class.

Task

Students practise the functional language from the lesson by roleplaying a problem-solving meeting.

5A Put students in small groups and explain that they are going to roleplay a problem-solving meeting. Give them time to read the information, and answer any questions they may have. Then ask a few questions to check they understand the task, for example: *Which department do you work in? What are the recommendations for? What is your budget?*

5B Explain that students need to do this individually and tell them that they should not yet share or discuss their ideas with anyone in their group. Refer them to the tips in Exercise 1, remind them of their budget and set a time limit for the activity. Encourage them to make notes.

5C In their groups, students first decide who will lead, and then hold their meeting. Set a time limit before they begin. During the activity, monitor and make note of any points you would like to highlight during feedback, but try to keep in the background – do not interrupt the meetings.

5D Give groups a few minutes to reflect on how effective their meetings were, which of the tips from Exercise 1 they used and if/how the tips helped them find a solution to the problem. As feedback, ask students to share their ideas with the class and highlight any points you noted while monitoring.

MyEnglishLab: Teacher's resources: extra activities; Functional language bank
Pronunciation bank: p.115 Intonation in 'OK'
Workbook: p.22 Exercise 2

4.5 ⟩ Writing
Reporting reasons and results

> **GSE learning objectives**
>
> - Can write a short, simple work-related report outlining key issues.
> - Can show a basic direct relationship between a simple problem and a solution.
> - Can write a brief standard report conveying factual information, stating reasons for actions.
> - Can support a main idea with examples and reasons.
> - Can use all forms of comparatives and superlatives of adjectives.

> **Warm-up**
>
> Draw a table with two columns on the board, headed *Problem* and *Reason*, and ask students to copy it in their notebooks. Put students in pairs and ask them to imagine they are representatives of a big supermarket group, with several stores around the country. The group has faced several problems over the last year. Ask pairs to think of problems the group might be facing, and the reasons for them. They should make notes in the table. Give students 2–4 minutes to brainstorm in their pairs, then elicit ideas from different students and write them in the table on the board.

Lead-in

Students read a model answer and study linkers of reason and result.

1 Ask students to read the report quickly and tell you what it is about (problems a supermarket group is facing) and in which three areas there have been problems (decrease in sales (in out-of town stores), negative customer feedback, increased competition). Get students to complete the exercise individually and check answers with the class.

> **reason:** 1, 4 **result:** 2, 3, 5, 6

Functional language

Students look at more linkers of reason and result.

2 You may want to let students use their dictionaries for this exercise. With weaker classes, you may prefer to do this as a whole class, checking and explaining answers as you go.

> **1** because **2** so **3** as a result of **4** resulting in **5** due
> **6** has led **7** in order to **8** has resulted in

Extra activities 4.5

A Depending on your students' needs, ask them to do this exercise individually, as a quick quiz, or in pairs. Check answers with the class and clarify any errors as necessary.

> **1** due **2** resulted **3** so **4** a result **5** because
> **6** leading **7** in order **8** so **9** because

Optional grammar work

The report in Exercise 1 contains examples of comparative forms, so you could use it for some optional grammar work. Refer students to the Grammar reference on page 121 and use the exercises in MyEnglishLab for extra grammar practice.

Task

Students write a report extract.

3A Put students in pairs to brainstorm ideas. With weaker classes, you may prefer to brainstorm ideas for the first problem as a class, then let them think about the other two problems in their pairs. If time allows, you could then join pairs together into groups of four to discuss their ideas. Elicit ideas from students and list them on the board.

Possible answers

- **customers unhappy:** unhelpful staff, poor-quality products, late deliveries, price increases
- **staff unhappy:** poor pay or working conditions, too much work, no pay increases, promotion difficult
- **sales falling:** out-of-date products, poor product quality, weak advertising campaigns, prices too high, not enough sales staff

3B Ask students to turn to page 130 and give them time to read the information. Explain the task and let students ask you any questions they may have. Refer them to the model in Exercise 1 and briefly discuss the structure and style of a report with them. Remind them to divide their report into clear sections, using headings, and to use appropriate linkers to introduce reasons and results. If time is short, students can write their reports for homework.

Model answer

This report aims to outline problem areas within the company and details reasons and results.

Problems

Customer complaints

There has been a big increase in customer complaints over the past few months. The main problem seems to be that customers are unable to get through to customer service by phone. Secondly, when they manage to speak to someone, staff are very rude and are unable to explain the situation to them. As a result, many customers have cancelled their contracts with us.

Phones not working

There appears to be a big problem with some of our phones, which do not work properly. We have investigated and found that in order to reduce costs, we had changed supplier, but some of the materials proved to be substandard. This has resulted in the failure of two models and, to solve this, we have had to replace many of the handsets.

Poor network service

Some customers say they are experiencing poor network service since there are not enough masts around the country and their phones are useless in some areas.

3C If students write their reports for homework, you could do this exercise in the next lesson. Put them in pairs and ask them to read each other's reports and think about how they have used linkers of reason and result: How many did they use? Did they use them correctly? Could they add any more?

MyEnglishLab: Teacher's resources: extra activities; Interactive grammar practice; Writing bank
Grammar reference: p.121 Comparison
Workbook: p.23 Exercises 1 and 2

Business workshop ❯4
Supermarket wars

GSE learning objectives

- Can recognise significant points and arguments in straightforward newspaper articles on familiar topics.
- Can interpret the main message from complex diagrams and visual information.
- Can briefly give reasons and explanations for opinions, plans and actions.
- Can understand the key points about a radio programme on a familiar topic.

Background

Students discuss their shopping habits and read about the supermarket industry.

1 Do the first part of the activity as a whole class. Ask students to look at the two photos and briefly describe and compare them: What are the differences between the two types of shop? Nominate different students to add ideas. Then put students in pairs to discuss the questions. Broaden this into a class discussion. You could use this as an opportunity to pre-teach some useful vocabulary from the texts in Exercises 2 and 3A (e.g. *grocery market, convenient, major player, hypermarket, aisle, shopping trolley, convenience store*).

> **Possible answers**
> **Large supermarket:** cheaper, especially when buying in bulk; special offers; much more choice; further to travel; more time shopping; tendency to buy more than you need
> **Local stores:** more expensive; less choice; convenient; closer to home; saves time; less waste; more 'human' way to shop; easier to shop for a couple of items

2 Put students in pairs and ask them to read the background and discuss the questions. Broaden this into a class discussion and, to lead into Exercise 3A, ask if the situation in the students' country/-ies has changed / is changing.

Consumer habits

Students read an article about changing consumer habits.

3A Give students 4–6 minutes to read the text and answer the questions. They should compare answers in pairs before class feedback.

> The four ways to shop are: at a hypermarket, at a smaller neighbourhood shop, online with home delivery, and the Click & Collect option to buy online but collect the shopping yourself.
>
> The reasons for the change are that consumers want more convenience, e.g. shops closer to home or work and online shopping. This is because they are busy and want to spend less time shopping. They also want to waste less.
>
> Other possible reasons: e.g. younger consumers order more takeaway food and eat out more than in the past.

3B Ask students to find the changes in business strategies mentioned in the text (big supermarket chains have reintroduced smaller convenience stores; big retail chains have started to offer the Click & Collect option). Then put students in pairs and give them a few minutes to think about other possible changes in the business strategies of big supermarket chains. Get feedback from the class.

> **Possible answers**
> Supermarkets may need to sell off some less frequented 'big box' stores and find smaller locations in high-street, town/city-centre locations. They may also need to think about how to rent out underused retail space in hypermarkets or convert these into warehouses for online shopping orders. They may need to invest in further online shopping options such as Click & Collect.

Three supermarket chains

Students analyse visual data about three supermarket chains.

4A Put students in groups of three, but explain that they need to work individually for now. Refer them to their texts and give them time to read and note down their answers.

> Mulberry's is one of the major players in the food retail industry.
> White's is a high-end food retailer.
> C&C is a discount supermarket.

4B Again, students should work individually and not share any of their information with their group. Allow students enough time to read the texts again and note down their answers.

> **Possible answers**
> **Mulberry's**
> 1 It makes very little profit from online shopping due to delivery costs. It has cut costs by introducing self-service checkouts.
> 2 Stores are big, there are self-service checkouts, it probably takes a long time to choose and shop.
> 3 vast, overwhelming for customers
> 4 It risks losing market share to discounters. It has high distribution costs due to the wide product ranges. Its out-of-town hypermarkets are losing business and revenue due to changing consumer habits. It needs to stop discounters from taking its market share.
>
> **White's**
> 1 It does not compete on price with the big supermarkets and discounters.
> 2 There are lots of staff.
> 3 high-quality, premium, specialist
> 4 It needs to keep innovating to meet the needs of demanding customers paying premium prices.
>
> **C&C**
> 1 cheapest price guaranteed
> 2 old-fashioned store design and poor cleanliness
> 3 very limited – under 800 items
> 4 Its cheapest price guaranteed strategy will not allow it to grow in the future. At the same time, it needs to spend money on improving stores and introducing fresh produce, all of which will initially increase costs.

5A Explain that students will now share the information from their texts in order to complete the pie chart and bar chart. Before they begin, check that they understand the charts: ask what each one refers to (total market share of the supermarket business, the details of which supermarket has which percent of the market; and the number of products in each supermarket's product range). Allow plenty of time for the group discussion as students need to share information first, complete the charts and then think about what conclusions they can draw from them. Check answers with the class and invite groups to share their conclusions.

Market share
16% Mulberry's; 6% C&C; 5% White's
Product range on sale in stores
25,000 Mulberry's; 10,000 White's; under 800 (750) C&C

Possible conclusion: Mulberry's product range is probably too big and C&C's is too small.

5B Students could discuss this question in their groups first and then as a whole class.

Mulberry's has the most to lose because it has high distribution costs due to a massive product range and unprofitable online shopping, a large number of increasingly unpopular hypermarkets and intense competition from discounters who are driving prices down.

Extra activities Business workshop 4

A Refer students to the three profiles on pages 128, 133 and 137. Explain that they have to read *all three* profiles and answer the questions. Point out that more than one answer may be possible. With weaker classes, you may prefer students to work in pairs for this activity, or let them compare answers in pairs before checking with the class.

1 Mulberry's and C&C 2 Mulberry's 3 White's
4 C&C 5 C&C and White's 6 Mulberry's 7 C&C
8 Mulberry's

B This activity practises useful vocabulary from the lesson. Students could do it individually or in pairs. Depending on the level of your class, you could go through the words in the box with students before they begin, or ask them to use their dictionaries instead. Check answers with the class, clarifying meanings as necessary.

1 checkout 2 convenience store 3 own-brand
4 upmarket 5 aisle 6 sell off 7 Groceries
8 retailer 9 outlet 10 core business

Task

Students discuss and develop growth strategies for a supermarket chain and listen to a news report about the supermarket industry.

6A Put students in small groups and go through the instructions and the list of strategies with them. Check that they understand what they have to do and before they begin, refer them to the list of points to think about. Set a time limit. During the discussion, monitor, helping students as necessary and making sure they are giving reasons for their suggestions and decisions.

6B Put students in new groups so that they are working with students who discussed one of the other supermarkets. They share and explain their decisions from their previous group.

7 ◀) BW 4.01   Play the recording, twice if necessary, pausing at short intervals to give students time to make notes. If they are struggling, allow them to refer to the audioscript on page 151. Give them a few minutes to discuss their answers in their groups, and then ask a few groups to tell the class how the supermarkets' chosen strategies compare with their own ideas.

White's has introduced a loyalty scheme to provide better value, expanded its own brand range and promises 'price matches' with major supermarket chains like Mulberry's. It's also investing in promotions, pushing into food-to-go.

Mulberry's 'back-to-basics' strategy includes selling off non-core activities, spending less on special promotions in order to simplify its strategy and also cutting the number of product ranges to 20,000 to cut costs.

C&C has just announced its ambitious expansion plan including the construction of 50 new stores and it will refurbish 150 existing stores. The retailer is also doubling its product range, including more fresh meat and a new own-brand low-price luxury range to rival the main supermarket chains.

MyEnglishLab: Teacher's resources: extra activities

Review ◀ 4

1 1 takeover 2 lines 3 emerging 4 major 5 tackle
  6 missed 7 developed 8 cut 9 margin 10 risks
2 1 innovative 2 expansion 3 failure 4 acquisition
  5 took over 6 succeeds
3 1 shouldn't 2 don't have to 3 must 4 should
  5 should 6 mustn't
4 1 Would you like me 2 Thanks for 3 I can manage
  4 Is there anything else 5 I'd really like 6 Would you
  mind 7 would be 8 Need a hand
5 1 explain 2 possible 3 do 4 pick 5 makes 6 take
6 1 Sales fell due to poor product quality.
  2 Poor product quality (has) led to unhappy customers.
  3 As a result of (the) high costs, customers bought
    cheaper rival products. / Customers bought cheaper
    rival products as a result of (the) high costs.
  4 The product was redesigned in order to attract new
    customers.
  5 The new strategy (has) resulted in production
    problems.

Logistics

Unit overview

	CLASSWORK	FURTHER WORK
5.1 E-commerce	**Lead-in** Students discuss questions related to the delivery of goods. **Video** Students watch a video about e-commerce logistics and recent innovations in product delivery. **Vocabulary** Students look at vocabulary related to logistics and the delivery of goods. **Project** Students debate the pros and cons of product delivery by drone.	**MyEnglishLab:** Teacher's resources: extra activities; Reading bank **Pronunciation bank:** p.116 Pausing and stress in presentations **Teacher's book:** Resource bank Photocopiable 5.1 p.144 **Workbook:** p.24 Exercises 1 and 2
5.2 Driverless technology	**Lead-in** Students talk about driverless vehicles. **Reading** Students read an article about self-driving technology. **Grammar** Students study and practise the passive. **Speaking** Students practise using the passive by describing a process.	**MyEnglishLab:** Teacher's resources: extra activities **Pronunciation bank:** p.116 Auxiliary verbs in passives **Grammar reference:** p.122 Passive forms **Teacher's book:** Resource bank Photocopiable 5.2 p.145 **Workbook:** p.25 Exercises 1–3, p.26 Exercises 1–3
5.3 Communication skills: Collaborating	**Lead-in** Students are introduced to the idea of collaborating by reading and discussing an email about a missed deadline. **Video** Students watch a video about effective collaboration with external partners. **Reflection** Students reflect on the main points and conclusions from the video and discuss different collaboration styles. **Functional language** Students look at useful phrases for agreeing and disagreeing. **Task** Students practise the functional language from the lesson by roleplaying a meeting.	**MyEnglishLab:** Teacher's resources: extra activities; Interactive video activities **Workbook:** p.27 Exercise 1
5.4 Business skills: Negotiating	**Lead-in** Students think about their own negotiation skills and discuss the qualities of a good negotiator. **Listening** Students listen to a negotiation meeting and think about the different stages of a negotiation. **Functional language** Students look at useful phrases for negotiation meetings. **Task** Students roleplay a negotiation meeting.	**MyEnglishLab:** Teacher's resources: extra activities; Functional language bank **Workbook:** p.27 Exercises 2 and 3
5.5 Writing: Letter of complaint	**Lead-in** Students read a letter of complaint and look at some useful vocabulary. **Functional language** Students think about the structure and organisation of a letter of complaint and look at some useful phrases. **Task** Students write a letter of complaint.	**MyEnglishLab:** Teacher's resources: extra activities; Interactive grammar practice; Writing bank **Grammar reference:** p.122 Linking **Workbook:** p.28 Exercises 1 and 2
Business workshop 5 Robots wanted for warehouse	**Listening** Students listen to a discussion on criteria for choosing suppliers, and to teleconferences between Meble BDB and two suppliers. **Task** Students roleplay a negotiation between Meble BDB and suppliers. **Writing** Students write a formal email confirming the points agreed during the Task.	**MyEnglishLab:** Teacher's resources: extra activities

Business brief

The main aim of this unit is to introduce students to concepts related to **logistics**. The simplest definition of **logistics** is 'the practical arrangements needed for the **transportation** of **goods** from location A to location B'. When an item is produced – a pair of jeans, for example, the **raw material** (cotton) needs to be grown, harvested and then **transported** to a factory to be processed. The cotton may come from one country and the **processing** may be done in another, so the cotton has to be **packaged** and stored in a **warehouse**. It is then transported by **container lorry** to a **port** where it is **loaded** onto a **container ship**. **Containers** are a standard size worldwide and reduce **loading** and **unloading** time as the items can remain in the container when they arrive at the dock and be transferred directly to container ship.

The various forms of transport need to be arranged well in advance, and all the **legal documents** required for exporting material from one country to another need to be processed along with **payments** to the various transport companies. Safety is a major factor and all the items must be **insured** against accidents such as fire, theft and damage whilst being transported. The items must arrive at the **right place** at the **right time** in **good condition**. Between the stages of production, items must be stored in **warehouses**. The time they stay in a warehouse needs to be as short as possible to reduce costs. At the final stage, items are **distributed** to the various **retail outlets** or **delivered** to individual customers who order online.

At the consumer end of the process, a customer may order a pair of jeans online, in which case the order is processed by computer and a message is sent to the nearest **distribution centre**. If the jeans are in stock, they will be **dispatched** and **delivered** to the customer, usually within a few days. One of the main objectives of logistics is to make sure that the goods customers want are available at the time of ordering and to avoid any delay in the customer receiving the item. Computer systems check **stock levels** and make sure that new stock is ordered in time.

The main forms of transportation are **container lorry**, **container ship** and **freight** (or **goods**) trains. **Cargo aircraft** are used for smaller **shipments** that need to be transported quickly over long distances. For smaller items or loads, bicycles, motorbikes or **vans** are used. In specialist cases, for emergencies and delivery to inaccessible areas, **helicopters** or **drones** may be used. Drones are able to deliver to places that are not accessible to larger vehicles and are significantly cheaper. **Driverless** vehicles are another form of transport that businesses are developing to reduce costs.

Logistics and your students

It is important for students, both those who are working and those who have not yet started work, to understand logistics as it is a fundamental part of the business process. Students who are not yet working need to be aware of the various stages of the process and understand basic examples of this as given above. Working students should be aware of the logistics involved in products related to their own business, and details such as transportation and legal documents.

Unit lead-in

Ask students to look at the unit title and photo. Ask them how the photo may be related to the title and elicit or give a brief definition of *logistics* (see Business brief on page 78). Then discuss the quote with the class: What do they think it means? Do they agree? How could poor logistics create *disorder*?

5.1 ❯ E-commerce

GSE learning objectives

- Can give or seek personal views and opinions in discussing topics of interest.
- Can understand a large part of many TV programmes on familiar topics.
- Can extract specific details from a TV programme on a business-related topic.
- Can justify and sustain views clearly by providing relevant explanations and arguments.
- Can make and justify a simple point of view on a work-related topic.

Warm-up

Write *A* and *B* on the board and connect them with an arrow. Ask students to think of an item of food they have bought in the supermarket. Ask them which country they think it came from and how it got from there to their local supermarket. Write the country name(s) under *A* and *supermarket* under *B* on the board. Get students to think of means of transport (trains, lorries, vans, etc.) which may have helped get their chosen item from point A to point B. Explain that the process of getting items from one place to another is what they will be looking at in this unit, and elicit once again what it's called (logistics).

Lead-in

Students discuss questions related to the delivery of goods.

1 Discuss the questions as a class. For question 1, check that students understand *parcel* (something wrapped in paper or put in a special envelope so it can be sent by mail or delivered) and *package* (something wrapped in paper and packed in a box so it can be sent by mail or delivered). For question 2, encourage students to use transport vocabulary introduced in the warm-up. For question 3, check that students understand *e-tailer*. Encourage them to think of other examples of successful e-tailers.

Video

Students watch a video about e-commerce logistics and recent innovations in product delivery.

2 ▶ 5.1.1 Tell students that they are going to watch a video about logistics in e-commerce and go through the questions with them. Play the video and check answers with the class.

Three people are interviewed: Allen Lyall, Amazon's Vice President of European Operations; Jukka Rosenberg, Project Director of the drone postal service in Finland; Jim McAuslan, a spokesperson for commercial pilots. The two new ways of delivering packages are delivery by robot (using a mobile app) and drones.

3 ▶ 5.1.1 Give students a minute to go through the statements, and clarify any unknown vocabulary (e.g. *dispatched, in transit*). After playing the video, allow students enough time to correct the false statements. You could get them to compare answers in pairs before checking with the class. With weaker classes, you may want to do this activity in two stages: play the video for students to decide if the statements are true or false. Check answers, then play the video a second time so they can correct the false statements.

> **1** F (One day Amazon dispatched **2.1 million** items and last year a truck left the warehouse every two minutes **thirty seconds**.)
> **2** T
> **3** T
> **4** F (There are now robots that **deliver packages**; **customers arrange to collect their goods/packages from the robot** using a mobile app.)
> **5** T
> **6** F (Airline pilots are worried about issues such as **safety and congestion**.)

4 ▶ 5.1.1 Give students time to read the sentences. Explain that there is one gap for each word, so they know how many words they are looking for in each sentence. Stronger students could try to fill as many of the gaps as they can before watching again, then watch and check/complete their answers. You may want to pause the video after each answer is heard. Play the video from 1:48 to 3:06, then check answers with the class.

> **1** convenience, at home, left, pick them up, PIN
> **2** robot, designed, goods, robot, app
> **3** drones, drone, developed
> **4** order, delivered, drone, little

Extra activities 5.1

A ▶ 5.1.1 This activity provides students with listening practice and then teaches some key vocabulary from the video. It is best done in two stages: start by giving students a minute to read the sentences. Play the video from 3:08 to the end for students to order the sentences, and check answers with the class. For the vocabulary practice, you could go through the words in the box with students or ask them to use their dictionaries. Let students compare their answers in pairs, then check answers with the class, clarifying meanings as necessary.

> **1** d; changes, concerns **2** a; congestion
> **3** f; Airline, issues, pilots **4** b; operation, technology
> **5** e; properly **6** c; safety, convenience, delivery

5 Put students in pairs or small groups and check that they understand *physical stores*, *implications* and *distributors*. Give pairs/groups 4–6 minutes to discuss the questions, then encourage a whole-class discussion.

Vocabulary: Logistics

Students look at vocabulary related to logistics and the delivery of goods.

6 This exercise can be done individually or with the whole class, checking answers as you go. The second option might be easier for weaker classes. If you choose the first option, you may want to do the first item as an example, and also let students compare answers in pairs before checking with the class.

> **1** items (This is the only noun in the group. *Deliver* and *collect* are verbs.)
> **2** transport (*Goods* and *packages* are things/products that are packed; but *transport* refers to the delivery process.)
> **3** collection locker (A *collection locker* is a place where you can pick up your ordered goods; but *postal services* and *courier companies* are responsible for delivering goods.)
> **4** couriers (*Couriers* are people who deliver goods, whereas *robots* and *drones* are not human.)
> **5** packed (*Damaged* and *broken* are near synonyms.)
> **6** badly (*Properly* and *correctly* both mean something is done well.)
> **7** congestion (*Pick up* and *receive* are verbs, and they relate to the delivery process. *Congestion* is a noun, and it is used to talk about traffic.)
> **8** balanced (*Congested* and *crowded* have the meaning of being full – although *congested* is usually used to talk about traffic but *crowded* refers to the number of people.)

Word building – verbs, things and people

7 Write *invest – investment – investor* on the board. Underline the endings *-ment* and *-or* and ask students which is used for things (*-ment*) and which for people (*-or*). Then ask students to look at the table and find more endings like these: used for things (*-tion*, *-y*, *-ing*,) and for people (*-ian*, *-er*). Depending on the strength of your class, you could then ask them to complete the table individually or in pairs.

> **1** collection **2** deliver **3** distributor **4** fulfilment
> **5** logistics **6** manufacture **7** operate **8** operation
> **9** package **10** package **11** packaging **12** produce
> **13** producer **14** retail **15** supply **16** supplier
> **17** transport (Br. Eng.) **18** transportation (Am. Eng.)

8 Ask students to do the first part of this exercise individually: explain that some of the words in bold are incorrect and that students need to correct them. Check answers with the class, and then put students in pairs for the speaking activity. Check that they understand *feasible* and *adapt*, and give them 3–5 minutes to discuss the questions. As feedback, invite different pairs to share their ideas with the class.

1 How feasible or safe is it for items to be ~~delivery~~ **delivered** by drone where you live/work? Consider different kinds of ~~good~~ **goods** ...
2 What are the advantages and disadvantages of **manufacturers** (✓) using robotics (robot technology) in warehouses?
3 If drones become a popular method of delivering goods to customers, how will ~~supplies~~ **suppliers** and ~~distributes~~ **distributors** need to adapt their **operations** (✓)?

Extra activities 5.1

B This is a word formation exercise practising key vocabulary from the lesson. Students could do it individually or in pairs. Encourage them a) to read the whole sentence first and look at the words before and after the gap to decide what part of speech they need and b) to read the completed sentence carefully, to check that it makes sense. Remind them to check not only that they have used the correct part of speech, but also that it is in the correct form (e.g. If it's a noun, should it be singular or plural? If it's a verb, what form should it be in?).

> **1** delivery **2** collected **3** distributors **4** fulfil
> **5** packaging **6** Logisticians **7** operates
> **8** suppliers **9** product **10** manufacturing

> **Pronunciation bank**
> **p.116: Pausing and stress in presentations**

Warm-up

Ask students to listen to the first couple of sentences of a presentation. Say the following sentence with flat intonation, no pauses and minimum sentence stress: *Hello, my name is ... . Welcome to my presentation on teamwork.* Ask the class what they thought of the way you said the sentence and elicit ideas from different students. Highlight that intonation, pausing and sentence stress are very important in public speaking, and explain that this is what you will be looking at in this lesson. Refer students to the explanation in the box.

1 ◆ P5.01 Go through the instructions with students and play the recording. Discuss the answers as a whole class.

> Version 2 is more effective because the speaker uses stress and pausing to good effect.

2 ◀) P5.02 Explain the activity and refer students to the text in Exercise 1. Play the recording and get students to compare answers in pairs before checking with the class.

> Online shopping is now a major part of the retail sector. | It is convenient | and often cheaper | than buying in traditional stores. | E-commerce operators have invested heavily | in their logistics systems | so that consumers receive a quick | and efficient service.

3 Put students in pairs. You could let them listen once more before they practise giving the presentation themselves. While pairs are practising, go round monitoring and correcting any errors with stress and pauses as necessary.

Project: The drone debate

Students debate for and against product delivery by drone.

9A Put students in small groups and assign a letter, A or B, to each group. Go through the instructions and the statement with the class, and ask groups to read their information – box A or box B. Next, go through the steps students need to follow to prepare for the debate: they should first prepare arguments for their own group considering the points in the box, and then prepare to counter the other group's arguments. Refer students to the examples. Give groups sufficient time to prepare their arguments. Go round and help students with ideas and/or any language they may need.

9B Students now hold their debate. This could be done in groups, with A groups working with B groups, or as a whole class. As feedback, ask the groups / the class which side they think 'won' and take a class vote: ask for a show of hands for those who are for and those who are against the proposal.

MyEnglishLab: Teacher's resources: extra activities; Reading bank
Pronunciation bank: p.116 Pausing and stress in presentations
Teacher's book: Resource bank Photocopiable 5.1 p.144
Workbook: p.24 Exercises 1 and 2

5.2 ▶ Driverless technology

GSE learning objectives

- Can give or seek personal views and opinions in discussing topics of interest.
- Can extract key details from a company blog or article.
- Can use passive forms to describe a process.
- Can decribe a familiar process in detail.

Warm-up

Write *driverless vehicles* on the board and elicit or explain its meaning. Then put students in pairs or small groups and ask them to discuss the advantages and disadvantages of driverless vehicles. Give them 3–4 minutes to discuss in their pairs/groups, then ask different students to share their ideas with the class.

Lead-in

Students talk about driverless vehicles.

1 Put students in pairs to discuss the questions. Before they begin, go through the vocabulary in the box with them and answer any questions they may have. Give pairs 3–4 minutes to discuss, then invite different students to share their answers with the class.

> **Possible answer**
> It's possible because car **manufacturers** are testing **new technologies** and **self-driving systems**. The **driver** in the picture can rest on a **long-haul** journey, read a book and doesn't need to use the **steering wheel** or **pedals**.

2 This activity can be done in pairs or as a whole-class discussion. Encourage students to give examples and explain their ideas in detail.

> **Possible answer**
> **3** the business of transporting things such as goods to the place where they are needed

Reading

Students read an article about self-driving technology.

3 Go through the instructions with students and explain that they should not read the text in detail at this point – they should only *scan* it to find the information they are looking for. Check answer with the class.

> Five automotive companies are mentioned:
> **1** Volvo, the Swedish bus and lorry maker
> **2** ZF, the German car parts maker
> **3** Bosch, the world's largest automotive supplier by revenue
> **4** Daimler, the world's biggest manufacturer of commercial vehicles
> **5** Mercedes-Benz, a subsidiary of Daimler

4 Tell students not to worry about any unknown words in the text – they should focus on finding the information they need to answer the questions. When they have finished, get them to compare answers in pairs and while checking with the class, ask students to say where in the text each answer is found.

1 Because of the opportunities in buses and lorries (public transport and long-haul freight), which are ahead of passenger cars in terms of self-driving systems. Technology developed in these areas will be used in passenger cars.

2 buses = public transport; lorries = long-haul freight (vehicles) / commercial vehicles

3 logistics and efficiency

4 Because commercial vehicles can be tested in areas far away from humans so people's lives are not put at risk.

5 (i) Technology used in lorries (to improve predictive cruise-control systems) will be used in other areas, including self-driving cars.
(ii) We will probably see big advances in self-driving technology because investments can reduce truck operators' costs.

6 (i) The driver will be able to get out of the truck and rest while it is unloaded and loaded.
(ii) Drivers will be given new tasks to plan routes or process shipping documents and will work more as logistics managers.

7 It is battery-powered. It doesn't have pedals or a steering wheel. It is equipped with drones.

8 There will be more changes to trucks than in the last 120 years, according to the head of Daimler's buses and lorries unit.

5 You could start the discussion by asking students about current problems with ordering and delivery (e.g. the wrong goods are delivered, deliveries are often late, customers are not at home when the goods are delivered). Then put students in pairs to discuss the question. Elicit ideas from different pairs as feedback.

Extra activities 5.2

A This activity provides students with extra reading practice. Explain to students all the sentences refer to the article on page 50, and give them time to complete the exercise. Ask them to underline the parts of the text where they find each answer. If time allows, you could get them to compare answers in pairs before checking with the class.

1 b 2 c 3 a 4 c 5 a 6 c 7 b 8 b

B This exercise practises useful noun/adjective + noun collocations from the reading text. It can be done individually or in pairs. Before discussing the answers and meanings as a class, you could ask students to check their answers by finding the collocations in the text.

car parts, commercial vehicles, cruise control, logistics managers, public transport, shipping documents, steering wheel

C This activity practises common verb + noun collocations related to the topic of the text. Again, students could do it individually or in pairs. Point out that some verbs can be combined with more than one noun. Check answers with the class, and encourage students to record the collocations from this and the previous exercise into their vocabulary notebooks.

drive a vehicle/a lorry/trucks; plan routes; process goods/documents; (un)load a vehicle/goods/a lorry/trucks

Grammar: Passive forms

Students study and practise the passive.

6 Refer students to the example from the article or copy it onto the board and highlight/underline the passive forms. Point to the highlighted passive forms and ask: *What form are these in, active or passive?* (passive). Point to the first passive form (*has been used*) and ask: *Do we know who used the technology?* (No.) Point to the second passive form and ask: *Do we know who will deploy the technology?* (No.). Ask students to identify the verb tenses. At this point, you could refer students to the Grammar reference on page 122 and go through the explanations and examples as a class, clarifying any points as necessary.

Present Perfect Simple, Future Simple (*will*); no, we don't know – automotive companies in general

---

▶ Pronunciation bank
p.116: Auxiliary verbs in passives

Warm-up

Refer students to the box and go through the explanations and examples with them. Model and drill the pronunciation of the weak (/bɪn/, /həz/) and strong forms (/hæz/) of the auxiliaries in the examples. To check that students understand the difference, before starting on the exercises, you could model and drill the pronunciation of the weak/strong forms of some more auxiliary verbs, listing them on the board:

	Strong	Weak
can	/kæn/	/kən/
were	/wɜː/	/wə/
was	/wɑːz/	/wəz/
have	/hæv/	/həv/
am	/æm/	/əm/
are	/ɑː(r)/	/ə(r)/

1 Ask students to do this individually and encourage them to try saying the words to themselves in order to decide. Do not confirm answers yet.

2 ◀) P5.03 Put students in pairs to compare their answers. Encourage them to say the sentences to each other but do not correct them yet. Play the recording for students to check their answers, then check as a class.

(underlined = weak; **bold** = strong)
1 A: <u>Has</u> the order <u>been</u> sent?
  B: Sent? It's already <u>been</u> delivered!
2 A: When <u>were</u> these invoices paid?
  B: I think they <u>were</u> paid last week. Let me check – yes, they **were**, on Wednesday.
3 A: I don't think driverless vehicles <u>can</u> be tested safely.
  B: They **can** be – they <u>can</u> be tested in closed areas.

3 Put students in pairs to practise the exchanges in Exercise 1. Go round monitoring and correcting any errors in the use of strong/weak forms in auxiliaries.

7A/B Ask students to do these exercises individually and give them time to compare their answers in pairs before checking as a class. If this didn't come up in Exercise 6, elicit or point out that we only use the agent when it adds important information in the sentence.

> **7A** There are eight more examples of the passive in the article:
> **1** technology developed in these areas <u>will be used</u> in passenger cars (para 1) – Future Simple (*will*)
> **2** these commercial vehicles <u>can be tested</u> (para 3) – present modal
> **3–4** while the truck <u>is unloaded</u>, and then (is) <u>loaded</u> again (para 4) – Present Simple
> **5** drivers <u>can be given</u> new tasks – modal passive
> **6** delivery van that <u>was made</u> by its Mercedes-Benz subsidiary – Past Simple
> **7–8** It <u>is equipped</u> with drones <u>to be used</u> – Present Simple and present infinitive
> **7B 6** delivery van that was made <u>by its Mercedes-Benz subsidiary</u>. (We use the preposition *by*.)

8 Do an example on the board to quickly review how the adverbs are used and where they go in the sentence. Write on the board: *The technology has been tested. The technology hasn't been tested. Has the technology been tested?* Underneath the three sentences, write: *already, just, yet.* Ask students which of the three adverbs we usually use in questions and negative sentences (*yet*), which one we use to talk about a very recent action (*just*), and which one to mean 'before a time in the past' (*already*). Ask students to tell you how you could change the three sentences to include these adverbs. (*The technology has **already** been tested. The technology has **just** been tested. The technology hasn't been tested **yet**. Has the technology been tested **yet**?*) Ask students to complete the exercise individually, then check answers with the class.

> **1** Has the order been delivered <u>yet</u>? (We can also say, 'Has the order been delivered <u>already</u>?' or 'Has the order <u>already</u> been delivered?' to express surprise.)
> **2** The order hasn't been delivered <u>yet</u>.
> **3–4** The order has <u>just</u> been delivered. / The order has <u>already</u> been delivered.
> **5** Have these invoices been paid <u>yet</u>? (We can also say, 'Have these invoices been paid <u>already</u>?' or 'Have these invoices <u>already</u> been paid?' to express surprise.)
> **6** These invoices haven't been paid <u>yet</u>.
> **7–8** These invoices have <u>just</u> been paid. / These invoices have <u>already</u> been paid.
>
> The most recent actions are:
> The order has <u>just</u> been delivered.
> These invoices have <u>just</u> been paid.

9 Depending on the level of your class, students could do this exercise individually or in pairs. The second option might be easier for weaker classes. Check answers with the class.

> **1** have been developed
> **2** were talked about / were being talked about
> **3** has already been designed
> **4** has been developed, hasn't been developed yet
> **5** are taken off, (are) put on
> **6** will be done / are going to be done
> **7** has just been revealed
> **8** can be made

Extra activities 5.2

> **D** It might be better for students to do this exercise individually, as it is a consolidation exercise. You could get them to compare answers in pairs before checking with the class. If they are struggling, remind them that they can refer to the Grammar reference on page 122 to help them.
>
> > **1** is ~~make~~ made **2** was first ~~implement~~ implemented **3** are ~~choosing~~ chosen
> > **4** have been ~~designing~~ designed **5** ~~are~~ often made
> > **6** can be ~~damaging~~ damaged
> > **7** must ~~been~~ be avoided **8** ~~have~~ has not been fulfilled

Speaking

Students practise using the passive by describing a process.

10A Give students a minute to read the text and identify the process being described. You could also ask them to identify the words we use to signpost the stages of a process (*First, Next, After that, When ... has (finished), Finally*) and list them on the board for students to refer to when they do Exercise 10C.

> using a washing machine

10B Explain the activity and give students 3–5 minutes to make notes. Point out that they should not let anyone see their notes. As an additional or alternative activity, if your students have internet access, you could ask them to research a process online.

10C Put students in pairs or small groups. They should take turns to describe their process, using their notes from Exercise 10B. Explain that they should not show their notes to their partner/group or use any keywords that will give away the answer – their partner/group has to guess what process is being described. Also tell students that they should try to use the passive where possible. Go round monitoring and make note of any errors in the use of passive forms to highlight during feedback.

Pronunciation bank: p.116 Auxiliary verbs in passives
Grammar reference: p.122 Passive forms
Teacher's book: Resource bank Photocopiable 5.2 p.145
Workbook: p.25 Exercises 1–3, p.26 Exercises 1–3

5.3 > Communication skills

Collaborating

GSE learning objectives

- Can understand factual details in work-related emails.
- Can extract key details from conversations between colleagues about familiar topics.
- Can express support in a manner that shows they were actively listening to the other person.
- Can express disagreement in a manner that shows they were actively listening to the other person.
- Can express belief, opinion, agreement and disagreement politely.
- Can express limited opinions and arguments during work-related meetings.

Warm-up

Dictate or write the following questions on the board: *Have you ever missed a deadline? If not, what/who helped you meet it? If so, why? What happened? What could you have done differently?* Put students in pairs or small groups and give them 3–4 minutes to discuss the questions. When the time is up, invite students who answered *yes* to the first question to share their stories with the class.

Lead-in

Students are introduced to the idea of collaborating by reading and discussing an email about a missed deadline.

1A Students could discuss the question in pairs or small groups first and then as a class.

1B If your students watched the Unit 4 video, ask them to give you a brief summary of the situation and a short description of Matt and Stefanie's roles. If this is the first communication skills video for your students, briefly explain the situation and the characters' roles yourself. Put students in pairs and give them 4–6 minutes to read the email and decide if the statements are true or false. Check answers with the class.

> **1** F **2** T **3** T

1C Students discuss the questions in the same pairs as Exercise 1B. Help them with any vocabulary they may need to describe Matt's feelings in question 1 (e.g. *frustrated, sympathetic, understanding*).

Possible answers

1 Matt could react in a number of ways. He could feel frustrated that the project is delayed and that costs will increase, especially as Raj promised to solve the problems at their last meeting. Matt may also have understanding and sympathy for Raj's situation.
2 Matt could communicate in different ways. For example, he might insist Raj meets the deadline agreed at the first meeting and could refuse to pay any additional costs. Alternatively, Matt may decide to work positively and collaboratively to find a new timeline and costing to manage the project.

Video

Students watch a video about effective collaboration with external partners.

2 ▶ 5.3.1 Explain to students that they are going to watch the first sequence of the video, where Matt discusses the situation after Raj's email with his colleague Stefanie. Encourage them to make notes in answer to the questions while watching, and play the video, twice if necessary. Check answers with the class.

> **1** Matt thinks that Raj could not say 'no' directly when asked by Matt in the first meeting if he could solve the problem.
> **2** Stefanie thinks this cultural analysis is too simplistic and stereotypical.
> **3** Stefanie thinks Matt should put pressure on Raj to make the project a priority – for example, by calling his manager.
> **4** Matt doesn't want to make the atmosphere difficult; Raj may react badly to pressure.

3A Put students in small groups. Go through Matt's two options with the class, then give the groups 2–3 minutes to discuss and decide on the best approach for Matt to take when he talks to Raj. Make it clear to students that they can choose which option they want to see first on the video. Elicit ideas from a few groups and then, as a class, decide which video to watch first.

3B ▶ 5.3.2 ▶ 5.3.3 Give students a minute to read the questions for Option A or Option B, depending on their choice, and play the video. If time allows, put students in the same groups as in Exercise 3A and get them to compare answers before checking with the class. Do the same for the second video. With weaker classes, you may need to play each video twice for students to complete their answers.

> **Option A**
> 1 increased costs, no clear timeline to sort out the technical problems
> 2 risk of delaying the pilot, might lose customers
> 3 deliver all additional work at own cost
> 4 Matt is successful in paying none of the extra costs for the project, and the regular telephone calls will help track and manage the project. However, Raj may be demotivated and leave the project, especially because of family issues, which could cause major problems.
>
> **Option B**
> 1 to share the costs between them (Matt will take ten percent)
> 2 Matt's team changed and added some requirements which meant more resources and people were needed to be put into the project.
> 3 give Raj someone from his internal IT team
> 4 It's successful in the sense that he now only pays ten percent of the extra project costs as agreed. The placement of an internal IT staff member in the project can help Matt manage the project better. Raj is also motivated, and positive relationships may open up future contracts. However, Matt has the problem of discussing with his own management the extra cost of the internal project resource.

4 Put students in pairs and give them 3–4 minutes to discuss the questions. Encourage them to make notes and remind them to give reasons for question 3. If there is time, you could join pairs into groups of four to exchange ideas. After checking answers to questions 1 and 2, invite different students to share their views on question 3 with the class.

> **1** In Option A, Matt was demanding, telling Raj to deal with the issues and cover the cost for extra work on the project. In Option B, Matt was supportive and offered to work with Raj to find a solution.
> **2** In Option A, there are no extra costs to Matt's team and Matt and Raj establish a workflow to fix things. But Matt is worried that Raj is demotivated and may leave the project, which would be a huge problem. In Option B, Matt agrees to take 10 percent of the costs and to send someone from IT to help Raj's team. Matt has also built a positive relationship with Raj.
> **3** Students' own answers

5 ▶ 5.3.4 Explain that students are going to watch the last section of the video, with conclusions and tips for effective collaboration with external partners. Play the video and get students to compare what the speaker says with their own answers to Exercise 4, and note down the three main learning points mentioned. With weaker classes, you may wish to let students watch twice: once to compare the speaker's points with their answers to Exercise 4, and a second time to note down the learning points. Discuss the answers and students' views as a whole class.

> **1** It's sometimes important to be demanding to get a good result. However, demanding has risks – Raj is demotivated and may leave the project.
> **2** External parties can respond positively to a supportive approach. But you may need to invest time and money to achieve an acceptable outcome.
> **3** Be flexible and choose the style that best fits the situation.

Reflection

Students reflect on the main points and conclusions from the video and discuss different collaboration styles.

6 Allow students to work individually first so that they can reflect on their own preferred style. When they have had enough time to reflect, put them in pairs to discuss their answers. You could then broaden this into a class discussion on different collaboration styles and their advantages and disadvantages.

Functional language: Agreeing and disagreeing

Students look at useful phrases for agreeing and disagreeing.

7A Give students time to look at the phrases and elicit the functions. Ask: *What are these phrases for?* (to agree, disagree and express doubt). Get students to do the exercise individually and then compare answers in pairs before checking with the class. Check that they understand that *That's rubbish/ nonsense!* is very direct and should only be used with people you know well and not used in a formal discussion or meeting.

> **Direct agreement:** 3, 4, 5
> **Expressing doubt:** 1, 2, 6

7B Discuss the questions as a class. Encourage students to think about the importance of maintaining relationships and not 'losing face'.

> ### Notes
> Direct disagreement might cause offence in formal situations and with people we don't know well. It's a common communication strategy to express disagreement as doubt, at least at first. This allows people to explain an alternative point of view and explore the disagreement further.

8A You may want to do the first item as an example with the class. Ask students to read the first exchange and discuss with them which of the options in the 'Expressing doubt' column of the table in Exercise 7A would be appropriate, and how to modify the employee's response to fit the dialogue (e.g. *I know we're busy, but …* or *I'm not sure that's a good idea / the best solution.*). Explain that more than one option is possible and give students time to rewrite the employee's responses. Check answers with the class.

> See Exercise 8B below.

8B Put students in pairs to expand and practise the dialogues. Remind them to use phrases from Exercise 7A and encourage them to be natural and at the same time avoid any direct disagreement. For weaker classes, you could read out one of the suggested dialogues in the answer key below. Ask different pairs to act out their dialogue and the other students to give feedback and comment on the use of expressions for expressing doubt.

> **Possible answers**
> **1**
> **M:** We're very busy. We need to cancel all staff holidays in August.
> **E:** I'm not sure that's the best solution.
> **M:** Why not?
> **E:** People might not be happy. Many of them have booked and paid for holidays.
> **M:** I know they have, but we need them.
> **E:** That's one way of looking at it, but we could find some temporary staff.
> **M:** Good thinking.
> **2**
> **M:** I think we should outsource the IT department.
> **E:** I know the IT staff are expensive, but they are also very good at their jobs.
> **M:** They are good yes, but the costs are very high.
> **E:** I know you're right, but we could discuss this with the IT manager.
> **M:** That makes sense.
> **3**
> **M:** Karine is the best person to negotiate with these clients.
> **E:** That might not work.
> **M:** Why not?
> **E:** Because she doesn't speak very good English. Let's send Patricia with her.
> **M:** That would be a good solution.

Extra activities 5.3

A This activity practises the functional language from this lesson. It is best done individually, to check students' understanding and see if any remedial work is needed. You could get students to compare answers in pairs before class feedback.

1 I ~~am~~ completely agree with you.
2 That would ~~to~~ be a good solution.
3 That makes ~~the~~ sense.
4 Good ~~your~~ thinking.
5 That's one way of looking ~~for~~ at it.
6 He ~~don't~~ might not react well.
7 I'm not sure that's ~~no~~ the best solution.
8 That's ~~a~~ nonsense!
9 I don't agree at ~~in~~ all.
10 I'm afraid I ~~am~~ disagree.

Task

Students practise the functional language from the lesson by roleplaying a meeting.

9A Put students in groups of four divided into two pairs, A and B. If you have a larger class, you could create bigger groups, divided into two sub-groups of, e.g. three students A and three students B. This could help create a more dynamic interaction during the discussion. Go through the instructions with students and give them enough time to prepare their arguments. Go round the class and help students with any language they may need. Check that they are following the instructions and have thought of some strong arguments to support their opinion (e.g. having an earlier starting time may not be possible for staff with children at school).

9B Students now hold their meetings. Remind them to use phrases from Exercise 7A and set a time limit for the activity. Monitor while the students are speaking, noting down any good examples and also any significant errors to highlight after Exercise 9C.

9C In their groups, students evaluate and comment on their performance. When they have finished, invite a few groups to share their comments with the class, and then highlight any good examples and errors you noted during Exercise 9B.

MyEnglishLab: Teacher's resources: extra activities; Interactive video activities
Workbook: p.27 Exercise 1

5.4 ❯ Business skills
Negotiating

GSE learning objectives

- Can understand main proposals in a negotiation.
- Can signal agreement in a simple negotiation using fixed expressions.
- Can use simple language to convey the basic facts about a negotiating position.
- Can negotiate simple terms and conditions of a basic sale or contract.

Warm-up

Write the following quote on the board: *In business, as in life, you don't get what you deserve; you get what you negotiate.* (Chester L. Karrass, Author, Founder of Karrass Negotiating Ltd) Put students in pairs to discuss the quote. Do they agree? Is it the same in life as in business? Allow pairs 3–4 minutes to discuss, then broaden this into a class discussion.

Lead-in

Students think about their own negotiation skills and discuss the qualities of a good negotiator.

1A Put students in pairs, go through the instructions with them and give them 2 minutes to discuss. If necessary, give them an example to get them started (e.g. a daughter negotiating with her mother about watching her favourite TV programme: the mother wants the daughter to help with the housework, the daughter agrees to do the washing-up in exchange for watching the programme). When the time is up, get brief feedback from the class.

1B Students could discuss the question in the same pairs as Exercise 1A or in groups. Check that they understand *structured*, *analytical*, *competent* and *firm*. Let them discuss the question in their pairs/groups first, then invite different students to share their answers with the class.

Notes

Discussion around negotiation skills often emphasises qualities such as:
- listening skills – understanding the counterparts' position.
- rhetorical skills – explaining your own arguments clearly and concisely.
- confidence – having a belief in yourself and your own arguments.
- goal–relationship balance – focusing on the goal and the relationship at the same time.
- determination – having the resilience to not give up even when the person disagrees with you.

1C Keep students in the same pairs/groups. Start the activity by asking what a bad negotiator is (e.g. someone who gives in too easily). Give students a few minutes to discuss in their pairs, then get brief feedback from the class.

Listening

Students listen to a negotiation meeting and think about the different stages of a negotiation.

2 Put students in pairs, explain the activity and give them time to read the background and agenda. Ask a few check questions, e.g. *What does Anne Roberts do?* (buys the sports clothes for DesignPro); *Who is she going to meet?* (Anders Rik, a travel service salesman); *What are they going to discuss?* (the services Anders Rik's company offers). Let students discuss in their pairs, then ask them to share their suggestions with the class. During feedback, point out that the approach outlined in the agenda is a classic four-step approach for a negotiation (see answer key below).

The agenda lacks detail, but outlines a classic four-step approach for a negotiation with:
1 an opening, which will include confirmation of the agenda and possibly who is present.
2 a proposal phase, where each party presents their view of the situation, with space for clarification.
3 a discussion or bargaining phase, where proposals, responses and counter-proposals are made and agreement is reached.
4 a final summary where the agreement (if reached) is confirmed, minuted and the next steps agreed.

3A ◀» 5.01 Explain to students that they are going to listen to the first part of the negotiation. Play the recording, twice if necessary, and check answers with the class.

1 For pushing (i.e. insisting) to have the meeting at very short notice. It was urgent for her.
2 price, cancellation policy and quality
3 Anders to give his first ideas on these topics, based on previous meetings he had with his management.

3B ◀» 5.02 Explain that students need to listen for the proposals for the three items they identified in question 2 of Exercise 3A. To help them with recording their answers, you could put the following table on the board and suggest that they copy it in their notebooks and complete it while listening. Play the recording, check answers with the class and write them into the table on the board. Leave the table on the board for the next exercise.

	Anne	Anders
price		
cancellation terms		
quality		

	Anne	Anders
price	1.5% increase	2% increase
cancellation terms	3 hours' advance notice	8 hours' advance notice
quality	book only four-star hotels at three-star price	no change

3C ◀» 5.03 Add a fourth column to the table on the board, headed *Agreement*. Tell students that they are going to listen to the third stage of the negotiation. Play the recording and ask students to complete the new column in their table. Check answers with the class and add them to the table on the board.

	Agreement
price	1.5% (review again in the future)
cancellation terms	6 hours' notice for any travel cancellation (allows same-day cancellation for Anne's company)
quality	book only 4-star hotels at 3-star prices, but limit choice to two hotels per city location

3D ◀» 5.04 Play the recording and check answers with the class.

1 The three-star hotel cost agreed is based on an average of three-star hotel prices in the city location.
2 Anne focuses back on a personal topic – the trip to Copenhagen. At the close of the negotiation, this is an approach which can work if the negotiation ending is positive and it matches the general tone of the relationship which exists between the two negotiating parties.

4 Discuss the question with the class. You could also ask students who they think the better negotiator was – Anne or Anders. Ask them to explain their choice (e.g. Anne was well prepared and flexible).

Possible answer

In general, it is very effective. It is well structured and clear about what is to be negotiated and how (Anders first, and then Anne). It is positive and collaborative in tone, with both parties showing flexibility. It is also successful in terms of outcome; an agreement is reached which is acceptable to both parties.

Functional language: Negotiating

Students look at useful phrases for negotiation meetings.

5A Go through the four steps of negotiating with students and explain that 1–12 are some useful phrases for each step of a negotiation. Give them plenty of time to work through the steps and phrases and complete the activity. Get them to compare answers in pairs, then go through the answers as a class, step by step.

a 4 **b** 10 **c** 1 **d** 12 **e** 6 **f** 2 **g** 9 **h** 5 **i** 11 **j** 3 **k** 8 **l** 7

5B This exercise can be done individually or in pairs. Explain that these are all examples of step 3 from Exercise 5A above.

1 c **2** e **3** b **4** f **5** a **6** d

Extra activities 5.4

A Ask students to do the exercise individually and get them to compare answers in pairs before class feedback. With stronger classes, you could ask students to cover the box and see how many of the gaps they can complete on their own. They can then uncover the box and check/ complete their answers. After checking answers, you could put students in pairs to practise the dialogue.

> **1** agree **2** suggest **3** include **4** prefer **5** need
> **6** confirm

B Again, students could do this individually and then check answers in pairs before class feedback.

> **a** Thanks for coming today.
> **b** … would you like to start?
> **c** How does that sound?
> **d** … this form of consultancy is very expensive.
> **e** OK, 2 percent sounds fair.
> **f** Then we agree 5 percent on products and
>   2 percent on support.
> **g** I appreciate your flexibility here.

Task

Students roleplay a negotiation meeting.

6A Explain that students are going to hold a negotiation meeting and divide the class into two groups, A and B. Group A are ATAX negotiators and group B are LAURA negotiators. Give students a minute to read the professional context.

6B Put students in A–A and B–B pairs, go through the instructions with them and refer them to their information on page 129 or 131. Give them plenty of time to read through their information and ask you any questions they may have. Remind students of the four steps of a negotiation. Set a time limit and encourage students to make notes. During the activity, monitor, helping and guiding students as necessary.

6C When the time is up, join pairs together into groups of four (A–A and B–B) to hold their negotiation meetings. Before they begin, remind them to follow the four steps in Exercise 5A and use phrases from the page. Set a time limit. While students are negotiating, monitor and make notes of any points to highlight during feedback, paying attention to whether they are keeping to the stages, using appropriate language and negotiating successfully.

6D Allow plenty of time for this stage. Groups should reflect on their performance and then share their ideas with the class. Finally, highlight any points you noted while monitoring.

MyEnglishLab: Teacher's resources: extra activities; Functional language bank
Workbook: p.27 Exercises 2 and 3

5.5 ❯ Writing
Letter of complaint

GSE learning objectives

- Can understand basic types of standard letters and emails on familiar topics (e.g. enquiries, complaints).
- Can write a letter or email of complaint with supporting details.
- Can write a basic email/letter of complaint requesting action.
- Can use a range of common linking words to sequence events or activities.

Warm-up

Ask students to give you examples of products (or services) they have bought which they were not happy with. Tell them to imagine they were going to write a letter of complaint about these products/services. Ask the following questions, eliciting ideas from different students and correcting/explaining answers as necessary: *Who could you write the letter to?* (e.g. to the manager of a company; to customer support); *What information do you think a letter of complaint should include?* (a description and details of the problem, a request for action, a desired outcome); *What tone do you think you should use: friendly and warm, polite and formal, or aggressive?* (polite and formal); *Why would you write such a letter? What would you expect?* (e.g. a refund, a replacement).

Lead-in

Students read a letter of complaint and look at some useful vocabulary.

1 Ask students to quickly read the letter to find out the main topic (a complaint about the delivery of dishwashers). Then ask them to read it again and do the exercise individually, using their dictionaries to check the words in italics if necessary. Get them to compare answers in pairs, then check answers with the class, clarifying meanings as necessary.

> **1** ordered **2** delivered **3** assured **4** damaged **5** calls
> **6** respond **7** forced **8** collect **9** prompt

Functional language

Students think about the structure and organisation of a letter of complaint and look at some useful phrases.

2 Point out that the headings in the table show the main structure of a letter of complaint – the number of main paragraphs and what each paragraph should include. Ask students to complete the exercise, individually or in pairs, then check answers with the class.

> **1** ordered **2** damaged **3** calls **4** assured us
> **5** contact **6** do not respond **7** shall be forced
> **8** request (that) **9** (sincerely) hope **10** mutual
> satisfaction **11** to receiving

Extra activities 5.5

A Tell students that they can use the headings in the table on page 56 to help them with the structure of a letter of complaint. With weaker classes, it may be easier for students to do this exercise in pairs.

1 c **2** f **3** g **4** b **5** d **6** e **7** a

Optional grammar work

The letter in Exercise 1 contains examples of linking words, so you could use it for some optional grammar work. Refer students to the Grammar reference on page 122 and use the exercises in MyEnglishLab for extra grammar practice.

Task

Students write a letter of complaint.

3A Put students in pairs and give them a minute to list as many situations as they can in which a letter of complaint may be written. Elicit ideas from different pairs and list them on the board. Refer students to the table on page 130 and point out the headings: explain that for each **Problem**, a letter of complaint should include **Details** and a **Demand**. Give pairs a few minutes to complete the table, then elicit ideas from different students. You could list students' ideas in a table on the board for them to refer to when they do Exercise 3C.

Problem	Details	Demand
late payments	month overdue	immediate payment /court
damaged goods	scratched, broken, not working	replacement, refund, different product
wrong goods	order for correct goods, reference number, details of goods required and received	collect and replace immediately, need discount/ compensation
invoice incorrect	wrong goods, agreed price incorrect, discount not applied	won't pay until new invoice received/ send correct one immediately
inferior quality	cheap and easily breakable, materials used not as good as usual product, product fails to work	if cannot supply quality products, we must find another supplier
late deliveries	two deliveries arrived late over last month	if deliveries cannot be guaranteed, will be forced to find another supplier

3B Set a time limit, highlight the word limit (180 words) and remind students to use the structure in and phrases from Exercise 2. Monitor and help students as necessary. Depending on the time available, students could plan their letter in class and write it for homework.

Model answer

Dear Sirs,

Re: Order number 34 B/101

On 12 November we placed an order for 1,000 units of your robot cleaning appliance, catalogue number XYG 54. You assured us that the delivery date would be 20 November. However, the goods did not arrive until 23 November.

When we checked the items, we discovered that they were catalogue number XYG 3 and not XYG 54 as we had ordered. When we contacted your company, they informed us that we had ordered XYG 53 but I attach a copy of our original order, which was correct. As this is obviously your company's mistake, we expect you to resolve the situation immediately.

We have been customers of your company for several years now, and are surprised by this failure. However, if you are unable to supply the correct order, we will be forced to find another supplier.

Nevertheless, we sincerely hope that this matter can be resolved to our mutual satisfaction considering our good working relationship over the years.

We look forward to receiving your prompt response.

3C If students write their letters for homework, you could do this exercise in the next lesson. Put them in pairs and ask them to read each other's letters and think about how their partner has a) organised the letter and b) used phrases from Exercise 2.

MyEnglishLab: Teacher's resources: extra activities; Interactive grammar practice; Writing bank
Grammar reference: p.122 Linking
Workbook: p.28 Exercises 1 and 2

Business workshop ❯ 5
Robots wanted for warehouse

GSE learning objectives

- Can extract the key details from discussions in meetings conducted in clear, standard speech.
- Can maintain rapport during a negotiation using personal pronouns of inclusion (i.e. *we* vs. *I, you*).
- Can summarise the position at the end of a negotiation in a simple way.
- Can refer to a related email or conversation in an email message.

Background

Students read about Meble BDB, a Polish furniture company.

1 Ask students what the photo shows (a warehouse). Put them in pairs and ask them to read the background and answer the questions. Check answers with the class.

1 a quality furniture manufacturing company based in Poznań, Poland
2 The Minister of Development wants Polish furniture to be exported all over the world with a 'Made in Poland' label.
3 to minimise human error, avoid damage and deal more efficiently with the goods being prepared for shipment

Criteria for choosing suppliers

Students discuss criteria for choosing suppliers and then listen to a discussion on these criteria.

2A Put students in pairs, assign roles and check that students understand the criteria in the box. Remind them that they should work individually at this point and not show their answers to their partner.

Students' own answers, but one possible option is:
1 price 2 quality 3 after-sales service and maintenance
4 guarantees 5 delivery terms

2B In their pairs, students compare and discuss their answers. Refer them to the examples using comparative structures and encourage them to use some in their answers as well. After comparing answers, pairs should try and think of more criteria for choosing suppliers. Discuss the answers with the class.

Possible answers

installation procedures; training for operating the robots; instruction manuals in Polish, not just English; shipping agents; possible job losses and impact on the employees

3 ◀) BW 5.01 Give students a minute to read the questions, and check that they understand *automation*. Play the recording, then check answers with the class. With weaker classes, you may need to pause after each answer is heard to give students time to write their answers, and/or play the recording a second time.

Possible answers

1 Quality – Anna says both suppliers offer quality automation.
Price – Ted is worried about costs and thinks the Japanese supplier will be expensive.
Maintenance – Ted is also concerned about this.
2 Anna says both suppliers provide training.
Anna is concerned about the transition period, when they'll have to deal with the old system and the new technology at the same time.
Ted also mentions that people are worried about robots taking their jobs.
Ted adds that HR want to discuss possible job losses, although some employees can be retrained.
3 Anna is more in favour of automation. ('We have to move with the times', 'we need this automation if we're going to stay competitive', 'It's going to make everything much easier.')
Ted is more sceptical. ('What do we do when the robots break down?' 'Are there local people who can fix it?' 'We're going to be taken over by robots.')
4 There will be two interviews. Tadeusz will interview the supplier from Singapore and Anna will talk to the supplier from Japan. They will then compare notes.

Extra activities Business workshop 5

A ◀) BW 5.01 Give them a minute to read the sentences, then play the recording for students to number them in the correct order. Get them to compare answers in pairs, then check answers with the class.

1 d 2 a 3 e 4 h 5 g 6 b 7 f 8 c

Analysis of proposal

Students listen to teleconferences between Meble BDB and two suppliers and then analyse the suppliers' proposals.

4A ◀) BW 5.02 Explain to students that they will hear two teleconferences: the first one is between the Company Director and potential supplier Novarobot. The second one is between the Logistics Manager and potential supplier Bot-automation. Play the recording, twice if necessary, and get students to compare answers in pairs before checking with the class.

Possible answers

Supplier A: Novarobot, Singapore

Strength(s): They are specialists in industrial automation. They have worked with clients in Poland. They offer an easy/smooth transition period between manual and automated systems.
Installation: They will install the automated system in two phases: three days are required for each phase. It can be done over a weekend.
Guarantee: They offer a two-year guarantee.
Training: Basic training is provided during installation.
Maintenance: They offer a maintenance inspection once a year, free of charge for the first two years. After that you can call an emergency hotline and speak to an engineer 24 hours a day. Technicians deal with problems via email or videoconference. (The cost of this is not specified – Ted asks for details and costs of after-sales service to be provided.)
Discounts offered: not mentioned
Payment terms: *to be discussed*

Supplier B: Bot-automation, Japan

Strength(s): They have experience in mobile robotics, motor control and industrial automation. They have won awards and are an ISO-certified company. They say they give customised solutions.
Installation: There is no transition period. They suggest the warehouse stops operations for six to seven days; it can be done Saturday–Friday in a holiday period.
Guarantee: They offer an eighteen-month guarantee.
Training: Two specialist technicians provide training and manuals in English are provided. Basic maintenance can be solved by the client's staff.
Maintenance: Technicians offer help via emergency hotline/teleconference; they will visit the warehouse in 36 hours if complex maintenance is needed in the first 18 months. But there will be an additional cost for after-sales service after that.
Discounts offered: If the client orders a fourth robot, Bot-automation will offer a discount for the after-sales service.
Payment terms: *to be discussed*

4B Put students into pairs to discuss their answers. Go through the strengths and weaknesses of each company with the class.

Possible answers

The Japanese supplier seems to have more experience, they provide customised solutions and perhaps offer better training with two specialist technicians. The Japanese supplier also offers a discount if they buy a fourth robot.

On the other hand, the Singaporean supplier has already worked with clients in Poland, offers a longer guarantee period (two years), and their after-sales service includes a maintenance inspection once a year with a 24-hour emergency hotline.

Extra activities Business workshop 5

B 🔊 BW 5.02 Give students a minute to read the questions. With stronger classes, you could ask students to see if they can answer any of the questions without listening again, then listen to check/complete their answers. Get students to compare answers in pairs before checking with the class.

> 1 S   2 J   3 J   4 S   5 J   6 S   7 J   8 J

C This exercise practises some useful collocations from the recording. Students could do it individually or in pairs, using their dictionaries if necessary. Check answers with the class, clarifying meanings as necessary. As homework, you could ask students to write example sentences using the collocations.

> after-sales service   artificial intelligence
> automated system   customised solutions
> emergency hotline   industrial automation
> specialist technicians   transition period

Task

Students roleplay a negotiation between Meble BDB and suppliers.

5A Put students in groups of four, explain the task and assign roles (or let students in each group choose their roles).

5B Refer students to their information at the back of the book and give them time to read it. Monitor and help them with any unknown words, and answer any questions they may have. Then allow students sufficient time to prepare their questions and answers for the discussion.

5C Divide the students in each group into two pairs (pair A: Tadeusz and Kin; pair B: Anna and Tony). Set a time limit for the negotiation and encourage students to take notes of key information and what is agreed.

6 Students now regroup into new pairs (pair A: Tadeusz and Anna; pair B: Tony and Kin). Go through the questions with students and give them enough time to compare and evaluate their negotiations and discuss the questions.

7 Put students into new groups of four: two students are Meble BDB representatives and the other two represent the chosen supplier – Novarobot or Bot-automation. Explain the task and go through the list of points to discuss with students. Set a time limit for the final stage of the negotiation, and let students do their roleplay.

Writing

Students write a formal email confirming the points agreed during the Task.

8A Students now work in their pairs from Exercise 7 (pair A: Meble BDB representatives, pair B: supplier representatives). Explain the writing task, point out the word limit and set a time limit. While students are writing, go round and provide help as necessary.

8B The Meble BDB representatives now exchange emails with the supplier representatives and check that the terms and conditions are the same.

Model answer

Dear Mr King/Izumi,

Thank you for taking the time to talk to us. Following our recent discussions, we would like to confirm that we have chosen your company, Novarobot/Bot-automation to implement a new automation system using robotics technology in our furniture warehouse in Poznań.

As discussed, we will order four robots, models B 1297Mh_002, for the total amount of €18 m.

Terms and conditions of payment are as follows:

- 20 percent payment on signing the contract.
- 30 percent payment on installation.
- 50 percent payment after a trial period of six months.

We understand there will be a guarantee period of 18 months, after which you will offer us your complete after-sales service at a 20 percent discount. In addition, we have agreed to an installation period of 6–7 consecutive days, which will take place from 27th December to 3rd January.

Could you please send us a copy of the contract with the details? Please do not hesitate to ask if you have any questions.

We look forward to doing business with you.

Yours sincerely,

Tadeusz Walentowicz

Company Director

Meble BDB

MyEnglishLab: Teacher's resources: extra activities

Review ❮ 5

> 1 1 courier 2 postal 3 congestion 4 lockers
>   5 properly
> 2 1 delivery 2 manufacturers 3 distribution
>   4 logistician 5 packaging 6 operate 7 packages
> 3 1 must be bought 2 has already been found
>   3 will be launched 4 has just been changed
>   5 wasn't finished on time 6 couldn't be returned
> 4 1 agree at all 2 I'm not sure that's 3 rubbish
>   4 I'm afraid 5 might work 6 That makes
> 5A 1 sound 2 proposal 3 Good 4 reasonable 5 start
> 5B a 3 b 5 c 2 d 1 e 4
> 6 1 received 2 Unfortunately 3 respond 4 forced
>   5 request 6 resolved 7 satisfaction

6 › Entrepreneurs

Unit overview

	CLASSWORK		FURTHER WORK
6.1 › Fairphone	**Lead-in**	Students discuss the concept of starting up and running a business.	**MyEnglishLab:** Teacher's resources: extra activities; Alternative video worksheet; Reading bank
	Video	Students watch a video about Fairphone, a company that has developed an ethical smartphone.	**Pronunciation bank:** p.116 Consonant-vowel linking
	Vocabulary	Students look at vocabulary related to starting and financing a business.	**Teacher's book:** Resource bank Photocopiable 6.1 p.146
	Project	Students develop a business idea for a start-up company and then present it to the class.	**Workbook:** p.29 Exercises 1–3
6.2 › Young entrepreneurs	**Lead-in**	Students look at adjectives to describe organisations, products, services and businesspeople.	**MyEnglishLab:** Teacher's resources: extra activities
	Reading	Students read a text about an entrepreneur who left university to start a business.	**Grammar reference:** p.123 Reported speech
	Grammar	Students study and practise reported speech.	**Teacher's book:** Resource bank Photocopiable 6.2 p.147
	Speaking and writing	Students roleplay an interview and then write a short email or article reporting the interview.	**Workbook:** p.30 Exercises 1 and 2, p.31 Exercises 1–3
6.3 › Communication skills: Influencing	**Lead-in**	Students discuss influencing in business.	**MyEnglishLab:** Teacher's resources: extra activities; Interactive video activities; Functional language bank
	Video	Students watch a video about different influencing styles and the importance of influencing skills in the workplace.	**Workbook:** p.32 Exercise 1
	Reflection	Students discuss adapting influencing styles and think about their own influencing style.	
	Functional language	Students look at language for dealing with objections.	
	Task	Students practise the functional language from the lesson by roleplaying and then discussing different situations.	
6.4 › Business skills: Presenting facts and figures	**Lead-in**	Students discuss their experience of giving presentations.	**MyEnglishLab:** Teacher's resources: extra activities; Functional language bank
	Listening	Students listen to a presentation and focus on how facts and figures are presented.	**Pronunciation bank:** p.116 Intonation and discourse marking in presentations
	Functional language	Students look at useful phrases for presenting facts and figures using visual information.	**Workbook:** p.32 Exercise 2
	Task	Students plan and give a short presentation using visual information.	
6.5 › Writing: Summarising	**Lead-in**	Students listen to part of a talk and then complete a short summary of it.	**MyEnglishLab:** Teacher's resources: extra activities; Interactive grammar practice; Writing bank
	Functional language	Students analyse a model answer and look at tips for writing an effective summary.	**Grammar reference:** p.123 Order of information in sentences
	Task	Students listen to part of a talk and write their own summary of it.	**Workbook:** p.33 Exercises 1–3
Business workshop 6 › Doable crowdfunding	**Video and listening**	Students watch (or listen to) crowdfunding pitches.	**MyEnglishLab:** Teacher's resources: extra activities
	Speaking	Students look at and discuss the features of a successful crowdfunding pitch.	
	Task	Students prepare and deliver a crowdfunding pitch.	

Business brief

The main aim of this unit is to introduce students to concepts related to **entrepreneurs**.

An **entrepreneur** is someone who develops a new business or product. Most entrepreneurs start on a small scale, often with a group of colleagues or friends. Entrepreneurs can be found in any area of business but recently many of them have come from computer or internet-related businesses, for example, Bill Gates (Microsoft), Steve Jobs (Apple), Mark Zuckerberg (Facebook), Larry Page and Sergey Brin (Google) and Jeff Bezos (Amazon). A lot of them also started their first businesses in a garage!

To become an entrepreneur, first of all you have to have an **original idea**. This could be an idea for a new product or service or way of doing something. For example, Amazon introduced a new way of shopping – purchasing items online rather than buying them in a physical store.

Entrepreneurs need to identify a **business opportunity**, i.e. a market need for their product or service and the potential to make money. They need to make sure their new product or service is of sufficient quality and to be aware of and react to **customer needs**.

A key stage in becoming a successful entrepreneur is to find a source of **funding**. The most recent trend is **crowdfunding** – raising money from a large number of people who invest a small amount of money each for rewards such as discounts and free products. **Business angels** are wealthy individual investors who support new projects that they believe have a good chance of becoming successful and giving them a **return on their investment**. Other sources of funding come from the entrepreneur's own savings or, perhaps the least popular but most common way, borrowing from a bank.

Once investment has been secured, the new business, called a **start-up**, must become **sustainable** – that is, it needs to make enough money to pay costs and repay the loan. This usually requires working long hours, living with insecurity and the possibility of failure. Ninety percent of all start-ups fail to develop into long-term businesses. Entrepreneurs have to be willing to **take risks** and have to be highly **self-motivated**. Another characteristic commonly associated with entrepreneurs is **leadership**. They need to attract a team of skilled and motivated staff who are loyal to the company and willing to work hard.

Once a start-up has established a place in the market that it can maintain, the owner can then start to look at ways of expanding the business – moving from local to international markets, producing in greater volume and **diversifying** its range of products. All businesses must make a profit to be sustainable, but financial profit is not always the main motive. **Ethical** entrepreneurs aim to improve people's lives and create a fairer society, for example, by making sure workers are paid a fair wage or by only using materials from environmentally friendly or politically acceptable sources.

Entrepreneurs and your students

Students who are not yet working should be aware of well-known entrepreneurs as listed above and the importance they have as developers of new businesses and products. Steve Jobs, Apple and iPhones provide the easiest example to understand this concept. Working students need to understand the process of developing a business and the concepts of identifying new business opportunities, developing new products, being aware of customer trends, and how to evaluate the risks involved.

Unit lead-in

Ask students to look at the photo and unit title. Explain or elicit the meaning of *entrepreneur*, then briefly discuss the quote with the class. What does it mean? (Coming up with an idea isn't as important as turning it into reality; making an idea happen is what makes the difference between a *vision* and *success*.) Do they agree? What does this mean in the world of business? How does one 'make an idea happen'?

6.1 ❯ Fairphone

GSE learning objectives

- Can understand a large part of a video on a work-related topic.
- Can use language related to running and financing a business.
- Can express and comment on ideas and suggestions in informal discussions.
- Can give an effective presentation about a familiar topic.

Warm-up

Write the names of some famous entrepreneurs on the board, e.g. Larry Page (co-founder of Google), Steve Jobs (co-founder of Apple and developer of products such as the iPhone), Bill Gates (co-founder of Microsoft), Enzo Ferrari (founder of Ferrari car company). Ask the class what these people have in common (they all started their own businesses – and they all started in a garage!). If you have time, you could ask the class to think of other famous entrepreneurs, possibly from their own country. Use this opportunity to establish the difference between a successful businessperson who works for a big company and an entrepreneur who starts his/her own company.

Lead-in

Students discuss the concept of starting up and running your own business.

1 You could discuss the questions as a class or put students in pairs first and give them a few minutes to brainstorm ideas.

Possible answers

1 Some typical reasons and the kinds of businesses entrepreneurs start tend to fall into three or four categories: a) They have lost their job or want a change so they start a business doing similar work. b) They have identified a business they like and they want to do something similar. c) They can see a common problem and want to introduce a new service or product. d) They take over the running of a family business.
2 Some people feel more comfortable about running their own businesses, others prefer to work for a company. Many people nowadays opt for the stability of a secure job and run their own business as well. These are often online businesses.
3 Attractions include freedom, creativity, being your own boss, the chance to make a lot of money. Disadvantages include risk, loss of money, long hours, stress of responsibility.

2 Discuss the question as a class. Focus on the word *ethical* and how it might relate to smartphones (e.g. recycling old smartphone parts). Do not confirm answers yet as students will check their predictions in the next exercise.

Video

Students watch a video about Fairphone, a company that has developed an ethical approach to producing smartphones.

3 ▶ 6.1.1 Put students in pairs and play the video for them to check their predictions from Exercise 2. Check answers with the class and ask students what they think of the idea.

Possible answers

There are possibly three ways in which Fairphone could be described as ethical. Firstly, the company aims to help the local economies where there are mineral mines. Secondly, the design of the phone helps customers adapt their phones. Thirdly, the company recycles old phones.

4 ▶ 6.1.1 Give students 2 minutes to read the summary. Point out the definition of *turnover* at the bottom of the page. Tell them not to worry about any other unknown words for now – they should just think about what kinds of words are needed for the gaps. With stronger classes, you could ask students to try to guess the missing words based on the first viewing, and then play the video for them to check/complete their answers. Point out the word limit (1–3 words per gap) and play the video. To check answers, you could play the video again and tell students to ask you to pause when an answer is heard. After checking answers, clarify any unknown vocabulary as necessary (e.g. *visibility, conflicts, mines, modular, minerals, mechanism*).

1 campaign   2 (metals and) minerals
3 make a phone/device   4 over forty/40 (people)
5 ten thousand / 10,000   6 exchange and repair
7 over 60,000   8 create change   9 the biggest
10 a market/demand

5 Put students in pairs or small groups to discuss the questions. If your students have access to the internet, you could get them to check the price and design of the phone online, to help them answer some of the questions. Discuss the answers as a class.

Possible answers

1 people who want to build and repair their own phones; people who are concerned about the environment and the conflicts in the Eastern Congo; people who don't see the need to buy the latest smartphone every year or two
2 Students' own answers
3 He wants people to know where the minerals for phones come from, and that people are dying in wars which are being fought for these minerals. He also wants people to know that with a modular phone, you can replace parts of the phone rather than the whole phone.
4 By sales and profits would be the usual measure, but as this is a social enterprise, he will probably also measure its success by the help it brings to local economies and communities in the Eastern Congo, as well as how it reduces the impact on the environment by recycling minerals.
5 He is pragmatic. He feels it's necessary to show that a more ethical business can be a success so that other corporations will follow the example.

Extra activities 6.1

A ▶ 6.1.1 Go through the words in the box with students, then ask them to complete the extracts. They could do this individually or in pairs. You could check answers with the class or play the video again for students to check their answers.

> **1** mining **2** launched **3** bank account **4** Sales
> **5** waste **6** source **7** supply chain **8** demand

❯ Pronunciation bank
p.116: Consonant–vowel linking

Warm-up

Look at the explanation in the box with students and give them an example: write *Can I come in?* on the board. Say each word one by one, then model the consonant–vowel linking in connected speech (*Can‿I come‿in?*). Point out that in *come in*, although the last letter in *come* is a vowel, the sounds are linked because *come* ends with a consonant **sound**.

1 ◀)) P6.01 Play the recording for students to repeat the phrases, paying attention to the linked vowel–consonant sounds.

2 Put students in pairs and ask them to draw the consonant–vowel links in the phrase. Encourage them to say the phrase to each other, to 'hear the links'. In the meantime, write the phrase on the board (without the links). Do not confirm answers yet as students will check them in the next exercise.

> ... that's why we started‿a company instead‿of, you know, doing‿art projects, for‿example.

3 ◀)) P6.02 Play the recording for students to check their answers. Invite students to draw the links in the phrase on the board. Then play the recording again for students to listen and repeat.

4 Put students in pairs to practise saying the phrases in Exercises 1 and 2. Monitor and correct any pronunciation errors as necessary.

Alternative video worksheet:
Looking for investment

1 Put students in pairs or small groups and give them 3–4 minutes to discuss the questions. Remind them to give reasons for their answers. You could then broaden this into a class discussion.

> **Possible answers**
> **1** decide on your target market; check that there is a need for the product/service; create a pitch for your idea; find an investor to develop the idea; decide team roles to organise the start-up; build a prototype; test ideas in a focus group; make changes and develop the product or service with more investment if needed; recruit more people to help the business run smoothly
> **2** Students' own answers
> **3** use savings; borrow money from friends and family; get a loan from a bank; attract investors

2 ▶ ALT6.1.1 Explain to students that they are going to watch a video about a start-up company and go through the questions with the class. Play the first part of the video (0:00–2:10), twice if necessary in weaker classes. Check answers for questions 1 and 2, but do not confirm the answer to question 3 yet – students will check it in the next exercise.

> **1** Gerry is the ideas person. Louise organises practical issues.
> **2–3** Students' own answers

3 ▶ ALT6.1.1 Explain that students are going to watch the rest of the video to check their predictions from Exercise 2. To help students, you could tell them that they need to listen for *four* reasons. Play the video (from 2:10 to the end), then discuss the answers with the class. What reasons does the investor give? Did students mention any of these reasons in Exercise 2? Do they agree with the investor's decision?

> **Reasons given by the investor:**
> They have not built a working prototype.
> The ideas they have do not make a business.
> They have no clear team roles.
> He is nervous they are not capable of delivering their vision.

4 ▶ ALT6.1.1 Go through the table headings with students and check that they understand *enthusiast*, *commission* and *seed capital*. Play the whole video for them to complete the notes and get them to compare answers in pairs before checking with the class.

> **1** cycling/bicycle/bike **2** social e-commerce platform **3** 18,000 **4** £96,000 **5** £3,000 **6** working prototype **7** change name of brand **8** focus group **9 a** graphic design for new name; **b** new logo; **c** intellectual property research **10** no

5 Put students in pairs or small groups and check that they understand *communities* and *monetised*. Give them 2–4 minutes to discuss in their groups, then get brief feedback from the class.

> **Possible answer**
> Online communities where users join because they share an interest do not always find it easy to make money. The members of the online community may not want to be sold products or services when the main aim of joining the community is to communicate with people with a shared interest. It can be a challenge to make money for online communities where it is free to sign up and use the service. Making money from adverts may be difficult if services do not attract enough advertising.

6 Explain that the phrases are used in the video and ask students to do the exercise, individually or in pairs. You may want to let them use their dictionaries. Check answers with the class, clarifying meanings as necessary.

> **1** d **2** f **3** b **4** c **5** a **6** e

7 This activity practises the vocabulary introduced in Exercise 6, so it may be better for students to do it individually.

> **1** working prototype **2** elevator pitch
> **3** investment opportunity **4** focus group

8 Depending on the level of your class, this exercise can be done individually or in pairs. Ask students to read the text quickly first, to get an idea of what it is about. Encourage them to use their dictionaries to check which phrasal verb is needed each time. Check answers with the class, clarifying the meanings of the phrasal verbs. Encourage students to record the phrasal verbs in their vocabulary notebooks. As homework, you could ask students to write an example sentence for each phrasal verb.

> **1** in **2** up **3** out **4** out **5** on **6** for **7** up
> **8** out **9** up **10** on

9 Put students in pairs or small groups to discuss the questions, then broaden this into a class discussion.

Vocabulary: Running a business

Students look at vocabulary related to starting and financing a business.

6 You could go through the words in the box with students before they do the exercise, or ask them to check in their dictionaries and then clarify meanings as necessary during class feedback.

crowdfunding: a method of getting money for something, e.g. a new business, by asking many people to give part of the money needed, often on the internet

set up: start a company, organisation, committee, etc.

start-up: a new small company or business, especially one whose work involves technology

> **1** start-up **2** crowdfunding **3** set up

7 This exercise can be done individually or in pairs. Again, either go through the words in the box with the class or let them use their dictionaries and clarify meanings during class feedback.

> **1** pitch **2** profit **3** go out of **4** business angel
> **5** funding **6** target market

8A You could do the first item as an example with the class. Ask students to read the question and identify the type of word in brackets (verb) and the type of word required in the gap (noun). Elicit the answer, then let students complete the rest of the exercise, individually or in pairs. Remind them to read the questions first, to see what type of word is needed for each gap. Point out that they should also make sure that they use the correct *form* of the word, e.g. if it is a noun, they should check if it needs to be singular or plural.

> **1** advice **2** founders **3** growth **4** financial
> **5** investment, backers **6** entrepreneurial

8B Put students in pairs or small groups to discuss the questions. Give them 3–5 minutes to discuss in their pairs/groups, then get brief feedback from the class.

Extra activities 6.1

B Go through the words in the box with students, then ask them to match the words with the definitions. They could do this individually or in pairs. Check answers with the class.

> **1** sales **2** bank account **3** launch **4** source
> **5** supply chain **6** demand **7** waste **8** mining

C Tell students that this activity will help them check their vocabulary from this lesson, and get them to complete it individually, as a quick vocabulary quiz. Explain that they need to read the definitions and write the words. You could get them to compare answers in pairs before checking answers with the class.

> **1** invest **2** entrepreneur **3** back **4** set up
> **5** start-up **6** founder **7** growth **8** pitch
> **9** crowdfunding **10** profit
> **11** business angel / backer / investor **12** go out of

Project: Setting up a business

Students develop a business idea for a start-up company and then present it to the class.

9A Put students in small groups. Go through the instructions and table with them and answer any vocabulary questions they may have. Explain that they can choose one of the ideas in the table or use their own idea. Point out that they should follow the three steps listed, and give them plenty of time to plan their presentation. If your students have access to computers, you could ask groups to prepare a short presentation using PowerPoint or similar.

9B Groups now present their business ideas to the class. When everyone has had a chance to present their idea, do a class vote on the best one.

MyEnglishLab: Teacher's resources: extra activities; Alternative video worksheet; Reading bank
Pronunciation bank: p.116 Consonant–vowel linking
Teacher's book: Resource bank Photocopiable 6.1 p.146
Workbook: p.29 Exercises 1–3

6.2 》 Young entrepreneurs

GSE learning objectives

- Can express and comment on ideas and suggestions in informal discussions.
- Can extract key details from an article on a business-related topic.
- Can report factual information given by other people.
- Can report what other people have said and asked using appropriate language.
- Can carry out a prepared interview, checking and confirming information as necessary.
- Can write a short article on a familiar business-related topic.

Warm-up

Write *Successful entrepreneurs* in a circle on the board. Put students in pairs or small groups and ask them to think about the qualities of a successful entrepreneur: What do they think is necessary in order for an entrepreneur to be successful? Give students 2–4 minutes to discuss in their pairs/groups. Elicit ideas and write them in smaller circles around the one on the board, in a spidergram. Ask students to give reasons.

Lead-in

Students look at some useful adjectives to describe organisations, products, services and businesspeople.

1 Put students in pairs and give them 1–2 minutes to discuss the question, then get brief feedback from the class.

2 Students could do this in the same pairs as Exercise 1 or individually.

> 1 prestigious 2 well-known 3 fashionable 4 cool
> 5 reliable 6 high flyer

3 Keep students in the same pairs as Exercise 1. Look at the example with the class, then give pairs 2–3 minutes to think of their own examples. When the time is up, elicit examples from different students.

Reading

Students read a text about a successful entrepreneur who left university to start a business.

4A/B Briefly discuss the question in Exercise 4A with the class, eliciting ideas from different students. Then give them time to read the text quickly and check their predictions: Why did Ferry Unardi leave university to start a business?

> Ferry Unardi and his business partners had always discussed the idea of launching a travel search engine. They felt the time was right, with interested investors and a good consumer base. Ferry said he had underestimated the speed of change (in the Indonesian internet industry) when he arrived at Harvard.

5 Students read the article in more detail this time and answer the questions. Get them to compare and discuss their answers in pairs before checking with the class.

> 1 Traveloka is an online travel agency. It operates like a search engine for the travel industry.
> 2 It takes 10–15 percent commission from the airlines and hotels for each booking made.
> 3 It receives 10 million visitors a month, it has partnerships with 33 airlines and hotels.
> 4 It operates in Southeast Asia.
> 5 He thinks computer programming is now more popular and seen as a cool profession.
> 6 He says he is 'interested' to see what type of people enter the industry and how they take it forward. Given that he says the industry is now fashionable and cool, the implication is that good people will be attracted to the industry and he feels positive about it.

6 Put students in pairs to discuss the question. With a weaker class, you could brainstorm general ideas about why companies succeed (e.g. good or lucky timing, luck meeting the right investor, a good business sense). Round up students' ideas in a class discussion.

Notes

This is a subject of debate. Many rich entrepreneurs believe luck has played a part in their success. Others argue it's all down to hard work and determination. The reality is probably somewhere in-between. There are also other common factors students might mention: social class, family wealth, education in prestigious institutions, industry and financial contacts. Some entrepreneurs have not had these advantages but many more have.

Extra activities 6.2

A This exercise practises useful vocabulary from the reading text. You could go through the words in the box with students before they begin or let them use their dictionaries. With weaker classes, you may wish to do the first item as an example with the class.

> **1** partner **2** underestimated **3** rate **4** look up to
> **5** partnership **6** development

Grammar: Reported speech

Students study and practise reported speech.

7A Go through the instructions with students and briefly explain the concept of reporting speech. Explain that there are two ways to report what someone has said: using direct speech (i.e. the speaker's exact words) or reported speech (i.e. changing the speaker's words slightly when reporting them). You could give them an example on the board (e.g. *He said, 'I have decided to leave university and start a business.'* → *He said he had decided to leave university and start a business.*) → Refer students to the three speech bubbles and ask them to scan the text to find the reported speech versions.

> He told me the company had partnerships with 33 airlines and hotels across Southeast Asia.
>
> He said his other partner had been a fellow intern at Microsoft.
>
> I asked him if any businesses had inspired them.

7B Refer students to the Grammar reference on page 123. Go over the grammar with them and answer any questions they may have. Then do this exercise as a whole class, checking and explaining answers as you go.

> **1** The verb tenses 'shift back', e.g. Present Simple changes to Past Simple, Past Simple to Past Perfect, etc.
> **2** The object pronouns change, the verbs *said* and *told* are used, the speech marks are removed.
> **3** The verb *asked* is used, the word *if* or *whether* is used and the tense shift is the same as in reported statements. There is no auxiliary verb (*did*) in reported questions.

8 Students could do this individually or in pairs – the second option might be easier for weaker students. Remind students to refer to the Grammar reference on page 123 if they need help. Check answers with the class, going over any grammar points again if necessary.

> **1** his family didn't **2** me he had won **3** him if he missed
> **4** said e-commerce would grow **5** him how he had got

9A 🔊 6.01 Explain the activity. With a weaker class, you may want to do the first item as an example with the class: play the first extract and go through the answer with students, pointing out the changes required – *you* to *me*, tense shift, omitting the auxiliary *do*. Get students to compare answers in pairs before checking with the class.

> **1** (me) what I liked **2** her (that) I liked
> **3** (me) if/whether I had **4** (that) I took
> **5** thought I would be **6** I had never thought

9B Students could discuss the questions in pairs first, then as a whole class.

Extra activities 6.2

B 🔊 Ext 6.01 There are three options for this exercise: you could play the recording only and have students reconstruct and report the conversation, get students to read and listen or get students to read only. If you use the recording, you may need to pause it to give students time to write. Depending on the option you choose and the level of your class, students could work individually or in pairs.

> Susana told David that she thought (that) there were some unique challenges for young entrepreneurs like her. David asked (her) what she thought they were. Susana said (that) she had had to find finance, which was harder because she had had no experience. And she had had to learn how to manage a team and be a good boss. David asked her if she thought (that) it was stressful. Susana said (that) it could be, but (that) she had learnt ways to deal with it.

Speaking and writing

Students roleplay an interview between an entrepreneur and a journalist and then write a short email or article reporting the interview.

10A Put students in groups of four and assign roles (Students A and B are entrepreneurs; Students C and D are journalists). Go through the instructions, explain the task and answer any questions students may have. If the entrepreneurs need help with ideas for their start-up company, you could refer them to the table on page 59. Give students sufficient time to prepare for their roleplays while you go round monitoring and providing help.

10B Put students from each group in A–C and B–D pairs, so that one entrepreneur is working with a journalist. Set a time limit for the roleplay and ask students to begin. Monitor and make notes of any significant errors or breakdowns in communication.

10C Put students back into A–B and C–D pairs. Go through the instructions and explain the task. Set a time limit for the activity and, again, monitor and note down any points to highlight during feedback. When the time is up, go through any points you noted during this and the previous activity.

10D Explain the writing task and give students 20 minutes to write their emails/articles. Alternatively, if time is short, students could do this for homework.

Model answer

Email

Guess what? I had an interview today with a business journalist which will be great publicity for BIZGO. She asked me what my travel agency did and I told her that we cater for the special needs of business travellers. She asked me what those were, so I gave her a few examples like hotel rooms with big desks so they can work, and 24-hour room service. I also told her we were negotiating partnerships with several hotels and airlines so I could offer my clients the best deals on price. I also mentioned that we were planning to expand into Eastern Europe and Asia. I'll let you know when the article is published!

Article

I interviewed Ruth Grant about her new online travel agency BIZGO, which caters for businesspeople. She told me she had travelled for work for many years and knew about the special needs of business travellers. I asked her what some of these special requirements were and she told me that they needed hotels with fast wi-fi connections, large desks in the rooms and 24-hour room service. She said that she was negotiating partnerships with several hotels and airlines so that she could offer her clients the best deals. I asked her which markets she operated in and she said she mainly worked in Western Europe and the USA. She was also planning to expand into Eastern Europe and Asia.

MyEnglishLab: Teacher's resources: extra activities
Grammar reference: p.123 Reported speech
Teacher's book: Resource bank Photocopiable 6.2 p.147
Workbook: p.30 Exercises 1 and 2, p.31 Exercises 1–3

6.3 ❯ Communication skills

Influencing

GSE learning objectives

- Can use language related to encouraging and persuading.
- Can express and comment on ideas and suggestions in informal discussions.
- Can recognise the use of persuasive language in a simple presentation or lecture.
- Can respond to objections.
- Can raise objections.

Warm-up

Dictate or write the following questions on the board: *Who do you know that is good at influencing people? Why do you think this is? What do they do that makes them good at it?* Put students in pairs or small groups and give them 3–4 minutes to discuss the questions. Then elicit ideas from different students. You could broaden this into a class discussion about the qualities of a 'good influencer': What do students think makes a good influencer?

Lead-in

Students discuss the importance of influencing in business.

1A Put students in pairs to discuss the questions. Encourage them to give reasons and examples. Then invite different students to share their answers with the class.

1B Students could do this individually or you could put them in pairs and ask them to think about what the best thing to say might be in order to influence people in each situation. Invite different students to share their ideas with the class.

Video

Students watch a video about different influencing styles, their advantages and disadvantages and the importance of influencing skills in the workplace.

2A ▶ 6.3.1 If students watched the videos from the previous units, elicit or remind them of the situation and Matt's and Paula's roles (Matt is the project lead, Paula is a member of the Mexico team). Also elicit what project PRO Manage are currently working on (they are launching a series of online project management courses). If this is the first communication skills video for your students, you might want to briefly explain the above before they watch. Go through the instructions and questions with students, play the video and check answers with the class.

> 1 Paula says she can 'make a strong argument, backed with good reasoning.' And 'I expect to get what I want, I haven't failed yet!' (Matt also says, 'Remember not to be too pushy.')
> 2 Matt says that 'Pedro likes to be involved in decision-making, he's quite a collaborative guy and likes to give input.'
> 3 (Possible answer) Paula's natural style of influencing sounds direct and strong. This may not allow Pedro to feel he can give input, which may result in a negative outcome.

2B Give students a minute to read the text and check that they understand *empathy* and *common direction*. Students can then do the exercise individually and compare answers in pairs before class feedback. Alternatively, you may want to do this as a whole class, checking and explaining answers as you go.

> 1 pull   2 push   3 push   4 pull

3A Put students in small groups. Explain that Paula has two options for her pitch, and go through the options with students. Give groups 2–3 minutes to discuss and decide on the best approach for Paula to take in her pitch to Pedro and Susan. Make it clear to students that they can choose which option they want to see first on the video. Elicit ideas from a few students and then, as a class, decide which video to watch first.

3B ▶ 6.3.2   ▶ 6.3.3   Give students a minute to read the statements for Option A or the questions for Option B, depending on their choice. Play the video and get students to compare answers in pairs before class feedback. Do the same for the second video. If necessary, especially in weaker classes, let students watch either or both of the videos a second time in order to complete their answers.

Option A
1 T 2 T 3 T 4 F 5 F

Option B
1 It is most important for Pedro not to have to spend a lot of time integrating the platform and managing the implementation.
2 He is also worried about their budget and the cost of implementation.
3 She asks questions to find out more about Pedro's concerns and then explains how they can help.
4 Yes, she does.

4 Put students in pairs to discuss the learning points from the videos. Round up their ideas in a class discussion.

Notes

In Option B, sensing that she might be pushing it (literally), Paula changes her style and approach and starts asking questions to find out more about Pedro's concerns, priorities and his general perspective. She then suggests a variation to the payment terms, which builds on Pedro's concerns about cost and budget. So, she's using a pull style, and has better results with him. The learning point here is how no single style is best, but a range of styles need to be at our disposal and used according to the situation, context and people involved. This point is made in the Conclusions section, which students will watch in the next exercise.

5 ▶ 6.3.4 Ask students to work individually and note down the answer to the question. After they have watched the video ask students to compare their answers in pairs and discuss to what extent they agree and why.

Possible answer
We need to adjust our style of communication to the people we are trying to influence and the situation.

Reflection

Students discuss the importance of adapting influencing styles and think about their own influencing style.

6 Allow students to work individually first, so that they can reflect on their own preferences and ideas. Then put them in pairs to discuss their answers. As feedback, elicit ideas from different students for each question, and encourage brief class discussion.

Functional language: Dealing with objections

Students look at useful language for dealing with objections.

7 This exercise can be done individually or in pairs. Check that students understand what an objection is, and also the meanings of the headings in the table. Note that an objection in a sales negotiation is positive because it means the customer is identifying issues to resolve before the sale can be closed. By probing, we can rule out 'false' objections and get to the real issues. Most objections centre on three issues: feasibility, value and price.

Acknowledge: 1 **Probe:** 3, 4 **Answer:** 2, 5 **Confirm:** 6

8A Explain the activity and point out that students should look for links in each turn to find the correct order (e.g. a: *It's a lot of money*. e: *When you say* a *lot of money* ... ?). When students have finished, get them to check their answers in pairs and then ask one pair to read the whole conversation so that the rest of the class can check.

1 a 2 e 3 i 4 h 5 f 6 d 7 c 8 g 9 b

8B Put students in pairs and give them 2–3 minutes to practise the dialogue.

Extra activities 6.3

A This activity practises key phrases from the Functional language section. Ask students to do it individually, then check answers with the class.

a What is your main concern?
b I appreciate that you want a pool.
c That's a fair point.
d How does that sound?
e That doesn't have to be a problem.
f Can I ask why we need a pool?
g Do we have a deal?
h The most important thing for you is hygiene.

B Students now use the phrases from Exercise A to complete the dialogue. Get them to check answers in pairs before class feedback and, if there is time, put them in pairs to practise the dialogue.

1 c 2 a 3 e 4 f 5 h 6 d 7 b 8 g

Task

Students practise the functional language from the lesson by roleplaying and then discussing different situations.

9A Put students in pairs and go through the instructions and situations with them. Explain that students need to work individually first, to plan what they will say, and then roleplay the conversations in pairs. Remind students to use phrases from Exercise 7 and set a time limit for the preparation stage. Monitor and help students as necessary. Then set a time limit for the roleplays. Make sure students swap roles for each situation, so that they have a chance to practise both persuading and objecting. Monitor during the roleplays and note down any points to highlight during feedback.

9B Join pairs together into groups of four to discuss the questions. Once students have discussed in their groups, broaden this into a class discussion and also highlight any points you noted while monitoring.

MyEnglishLab: Teacher's resources: extra activities; Interactive video activities; Functional language bank
Workbook: p.32 Exercise 1

6.4 ❯ Business skills
Presenting facts and figures

GSE learning objectives

- Can relate information in a presentation to the same information given in graphs, charts and tables.
- Can refer to pictures, charts, graphs, etc. during a presentation using fixed expressions.
- Can ask for questions or feedback at the end of a presentation.

Warm-up

Put students in pairs or small groups and ask them to think of a presentation they have attended. What did they think of it? What did they like / not like about it? What made it interesting/boring? What do they think makes a good presentation? Give students a few minutes to discuss in their pairs/groups, then get brief feedback from the class. Use this as an opportunity to pre-teach useful vocabulary for Exercise 1 (e.g. *audience, visual data, flipchart*).

Lead-in

Students discuss different features of a presentation and think about using visual data in presentations.

1 Go through the questions with students and check that they understand *audience, adapt, flipchart, visual data* and *distracting*. Give them 1–2 minutes to think about their answers individually first, then put them in pairs to discuss the questions. During feedback, elicit ideas from different students for each question, so that the class gets an idea of the different types of audience, tools, visual data, etc.

2 Write *visual data* on the board and ask students for some examples of how we can present facts and figures in a presentation (e.g. pie charts, bar graphs, line graphs, tables; if students don't know any of these words, use the images at the bottom of the page to teach them). Put students in pairs to discuss the question, then elicit ideas from different pairs.

Suggested answers

- Visual data should support your words when presenting, not distract from them.
- Tell the audience what they're looking at.
- Focus on key points.
- Make it memorable.
- Control what the audience can see. Use animation to reveal data rather than present it all at once (tell a story).
- Keep the audience interested and curious.
- KISS (Keep It Short and Simple).

Listening

Students listen to a presentation and focus on how facts and figures are presented.

3A Explain that the words on the left are all related to business sales and can be useful in presentations. Ask students to complete the exercise individually or in pairs, then check answers with the class, clarifying meanings as necessary.

1 d **2** g **3** a **4** h **5** b **6** f **7** e **8** i **9** c

3B 🔊 6.02 Go through the questions with the class and check that they understand *demographics*. Play the recording, twice if necessary, and get students to compare answers in pairs before checking with the class.

1 They make specialist and high-end cases for mobile phones, tablets and laptops.
2 18–25 years and 25–30 years are their two biggest age demographics.
3 The mobile sector is growing.
4 They don't have enough stock.
5 Mobile cases – they see these as the big winner for the next two years at least.

3C 🔊 6.03 Ask students to look at the charts and tell you what type of chart each pair shows (A–B = line graph; C–D = pie chart; E–F = bar graph). Give students a minute to study the charts before listening, then play the recording. During feedback, you could refer students to the audioscript on page 149 and ask them to find the parts where the speaker talks about each graph.

Market growth: A
Customer age demographic: C
Stock needs: F

Functional language: Presenting visual information

Students look at useful phrases for presenting facts and figures using visual information.

4 Go through the words/phrases in the boxes with students and ask them to do this exercise individually. Remind them that they can use the audioscript on page 149 to help them if necessary. Get students to check answers in pairs before class feedback. You could check answers with the class or play the recording again for students to listen and check.

Part 1: the overview
1 next part **2** slide **3** pie **4** right **5** notice **6** graph
7 chart **8** hand over

Part 2: the details
1 significant **2** details **3** show you **4** interesting
5 fact **6** think **7** closely

5 Put students in pairs. Explain the activity and make sure the students in each pair choose a different chart to describe. Give them a few minutes to prepare individually. Encourage them to make notes and to use phrases from Exercise 4. In their pairs, students then take turns to describe their chart to their partner. Monitor and note down any errors in the use of the functional language phrases. Highlight these during feedback.

Extra activities 6.4

A This is a consolidation exercise, so it might be better for students to do it individually. Explain that the text is an extract from a presentation where the speaker presents visual data, and give students 3–4 minutes to complete it. Check answers with the class.

> **1** target market **2** bar **3** pie **4** revenue
> **5** forecast **6** growth

B Weaker students could do this activity in pairs. If they have access to computers, you could ask them to create their slide using PowerPoint or a similar program. If time is short, this exercise can also be done as homework.

> **Possible answer**
> Target market
> • Sales: more watches than clocks
> • Revenue: €300k
> • Forecast for next year: €450k = 50% growth

C Depending on the level of your class, you could ask students to do this individually or in pairs. Go through the instructions and list of topics with them and give them plenty of time to prepare. They should *not* make notes for their presentation – they need to present the data using the charts they create. Point out that they should prepare *at least* two visuals.

D Students give a mini-presentation using the charts they created in Exercise C. The students listening should make notes for at least two questions to ask the speakers at the end of each presentation.

➤ **Pronunciation bank**
p.116: Intonation and discourse marking in presentations

> **Warm-up**
> With books closed, write the example sentence from the box on the board. Explain to students that this is a sentence from a presentation and ask them a) where they think the speaker should pause and b) what intonation they think the speaker should use. Ask students to open their books and look at the sentence in the box to check their answers. Go through the explanation with them and model the pronunciation of the sentence.

1 🔊 P6.03 Explain the activity and play the recording for students to mark the pauses. Check answers with the class.

> **1** Today, | I'd like to tell you about our latest product.
> **2** I'll begin | by giving you some background.
> **3** In the next part of the presentation | I'd like to present some more technical details.
> **4** As you can see from the chart, | Poland is one of our biggest markets.
> **5** I'm going to finish | by telling you a little story.

2 Put students in pairs to practise saying the sentences, using the correct pauses and intonation. You could let them listen to the sentences once more before they practise them in their pairs.

Task

Students plan and give a short presentation using visual information.

6A Put students in pairs and explain that they are going to plan and give a presentation. Read the context and instructions with them and make sure they are clear about what they have to do. If your students are having difficulty creating their own information, you can use the back-up ideas in the Notes below. Point out the structure of the presentation and explain that students will have to plan theirs using these sections, and that each student will need to present two of the sections – they can decide in their pairs who will deliver each section. If your students have access to computers, encourage them to use PowerPoint or similar presentation software to create their visuals. Otherwise, prepare flipchart paper and pens for each pair. To help students structure their presentation and provide more examples of useful language you can also print out section 2 (Presentation skills) of the Functional language bank (page 185) or refer students to the Functional language bank on MyEnglishLab.

> *Notes*
> **Back-up 1**
> Outline:
> Company name: LuxLife Ltd
> Product: Food products from luxury restaurants
> Target market: 35–50-year-olds
> Market information: The market is growing by 15 percent and the company is growing by 25 percent.
> Stock levels: Running low as you have three times more orders than you expected. You urgently need to order a lot more stock and need investment.
>
> Notes on data and simple visuals:
> • a pie chart to show product types (e.g. frozen meat and ready-made meals, special sauces, cakes, pasta)
> • a line graph to show forecast company growth (You have grown by 75 percent in the past six months and you expect to double in size in the next two years.)

Back-up 2

<u>Outline:</u>

Company name: ICU Ltd

Product: Internet glasses

Target market: 18–40-year-olds

Market information: Wearable technology market is booming. There are a lot of competitors and you have a small company, but you have a very good product.

Stock levels: You have 200 in stock and pre-orders for 900. There is a waiting time of four months for your customers.

<u>Notes on data and simple visuals:</u>

a bar chart to show demographic information

line graphs to show rising sales

6B/C Pairs give their presentations. The rest of the class should listen and make notes on the key points to give the presenters feedback afterwards. You could also ask the 'audience' to note down at least one question to ask the presenters. After each presentation, the 'audience' gives their feedback (and asks their questions) to the presenters.

MyEnglishLab: Teacher's resources: extra activities; Functional language bank

Pronunciation bank: p.116 Intonation and discourse marking in presentations

Workbook: p.32 Exercise 2

6.5 ⟩ Writing

Summarising

GSE learning objectives

- Can recognise that a speaker has summarised ideas in a simple presentation or lecture.
- Can write a simple summary of factual work-related information.

Warm-up

Write the following questions on the board: *What kind of communications do you have to summarise in English? What do you find most difficult about writing summaries in English? Why?* Put students in pairs or small groups to discuss the questions, then get feedback from the class.

Lead-in

Students listen to part of a talk and then complete a short summary of it.

1A ◀) 6.04 Explain the context and the activity. Play the recording, then check answers with the class.

b to explain the background to his business

1B ◀) 6.04 Give students a minute to read the summary and think about the words needed to complete the gaps. Point out that they can use between one and three words, and play the recording. Do not confirm answers yet as students will check them in the next exercise.

1 estate agent   2 wooden toys   3 craft fairs
4 target market   5 larger premises   6 family savings
7 placing an order   8 pitching   9 business angels

1C ◀) 6.04 Refer students to the audioscript on page 149. Explain that they will use the audioscript and listen again in order to check their answers. Play the recording and give students a minute to check/correct/complete their answers. Then check with the class.

Functional language

Students analyse a model answer and look at tips for writing an effective summary.

2 It may be better to do this exercise as a whole class, explaining the tips and checking answers as you go. Note that for tips 2 and 3, students need to look for the synonyms/paraphrases in the audioscript on page 149 (see answer key below). For tips 2–5, give students prompts and ask for more examples to check that they understand (e.g. Tip 2: ask students for a synonym of *very small* (*tiny*) or *significant* (*important*); Tip 3: ask students to paraphrase a simple phrase/sentence, e.g. *They turned down his application.* → *His application was rejected.*; or *The bank didn't like the idea.* → *The bank wasn't interested in the idea.*; Tip 4: ask students for other linking words they know, e.g. *but, although, in addition, for instance, because (of)*; Tip 5: ask students for other reporting verbs they know, e.g. *says, explains, argues.*

1 George Johnson, founder of GJWoodToys, explains how he began his business
2 huge (synonym of *enormous* in the audioscript), soon (synonym of *it wasn't long after this* in the audioscript)
3 both the money and experience (paraphrase of *not only the investment needed but a wealth of experience too*)
4 However, As a result, Finally
5 mentions that

Extra activities 6.5

A Students should be able to do this exercise individually by now, but you may wish to allow weaker students to work in pairs. Remind them that if they need help, they can refer to Exercise 2 on page 66. Check answers with the class.

1 b   2 c, e   3 d, f, h, j   4 i   5 a, g

Optional grammar work

The summary in Exercise 1 contains examples of how to order information in sentences, so you could use it for some optional grammar work. Refer students to the Grammar reference on page 123 and use the exercises in MyEnglishLab for extra grammar practice.

Task

Students listen to part of a talk and write their own summary of it.

3A Put students in pairs and refer them to the summary on page 134. Explain the activity, set a time limit and remind students to refer to the tips in Exercise 2. Note that students should *not* write an improved version of the summary at this point – they should only discuss ways in which it can be shortened and improved. Elicit ideas from different pairs at the end.

3B 🔊 6.05 Explain the writing task and refer students to the audioscript on page 149. Play the recording for them to read and listen to the final part of the talk and set a time limit for them to write their summary. Give them plenty of time and point out the word limit before they begin. Also remind them to use the tips in Exercise 2 and their ideas from Exercise 3A. While students are writing, monitor and provide help as necessary. If time is short, this exercise can be set for homework.

Model answer

George Johnson advises new entrepreneurs to passionately believe in their product or service because, without that belief, it will not sell. His second point is the need for extensive market research and to listen to people's feedback. After that comes good, step-by-step planning and time management. According to him, a good plan is a map which can be redrawn if there are failures. The best advice he was given was to listen to all the advice offered, but to reject what felt wrong, but he believes that asking for advice when it is needed is vital because no one is an expert in everything. Managing finances carefully from the start is fundamental and becomes even more important as the company grows and the amounts increase. When working with large retailers, he tells entrepreneurs to negotiate hard for their desired unit price as retailers will always aim for the lowest price possible. If the retailers want a product, it must be good, so the entrepreneur should not give it away. In addition, close customer relations are crucial because, without the customer, the business will fail. Furthermore, becoming a leader and managing a company is hard, so learning to trust key people and delegating work appropriately is essential, although it is not easy when people are used to having total control. And finally, he concludes that success requires hard work and that the entrepreneur will probably work harder than ever before.

3C If students write their summaries for homework, you could do this exercise in the next lesson. Put them in pairs and ask them to read each other's summaries, compare them, and give each other feedback.

MyEnglishLab: Teacher's resources: extra activities; Interactive grammar practice; Writing bank
Grammar reference: p.123 Order of information in sentences
Workbook: p.33 Exercises 1–3

Business workshop ❯6
Doable crowdfunding

GSE learning objectives

- Can understand the main points of a work-related recorded presentation.
- Can express and comment on ideas and suggestions in informal discussions.
- Can give a short, rehearsed talk or presentation on a familiar topic.

Background

1 Ask students how entrepreneurs find money to start a business (e.g. a bank loan, borrowing money from friends/ family, business angels). Make sure they understand *crowdfunding* (raising money from a large number of people who invest a small amount of money each). Put students in pairs and give them time to read the background and discuss the questions. Check answers with the class.

Notes

4 Note that small backers do not generally get offered equity/shares in a company. This reward is reserved for large investors such as business angels and venture capital firms. Instead, smaller contributors typically receive free samples of products, customised goods, discounts and their names mentioned in film credits.

Getting a backer

Students watch (or listen to) crowdfunding pitches for Doable's website.

2 ▶ BW 6.01 🔊 BW 6.01 Explain to students that they are going to watch (or listen to) three people's crowdfunding pitches from Doable's website. They should watch/listen and identify the type of project each speaker needs the money for. Play the video/recording and check answers with the class.

Ben wants money to replace costumes and equipment destroyed in a fire.

Alison wants money to develop a mobile app for T-shirt design.

Marcos wants money to cover the production costs of a mobile tour guide app.

3 ▶ BW 6.01 🔊 BW 6.01 Give students 1–2 minutes to read the texts before they watch/listen again. With stronger classes, you could ask students to see how many gaps they can fill from the first viewing/listening, then watch/listen again to check and complete their answers. Get students to compare answers in pairs before checking with the class.

1 events and festivals   2 hit by disaster
3 costumes and equipment   4 insurance company
5 world tour   6 design your own   7 organic cotton
8 our mobile app   9 order
10 smartphones (anytime, anywhere)   11 an audio guide
12 free to download   13 (just) ten euros   14 70 percent
15 cover the cost

Extra activities Business workshop 6

A ▶ BW 6.01   This activity provides students with extra listening practice. Give them time to read the sentences first, so they know what to watch for. Then play the video, twice if necessary, and check answers with the class.

1 weren't   2 is not   3 herself   4 before   5 30
6 don't have

Making a successful pitch

Students look at and discuss the features of a successful crowdfunding pitch.

4 Give students time to read the tips and extracts, and help them with any unknown words (e.g. *solidarity*, *incentive*). You could then do the exercise as a whole class, checking answers as you go, or ask students to work individually and then check answers with the class.

1 c   2 e   3 a   4 d   5 b

5A Put students in pairs to discuss the questions. Remind them to give reasons. Then invite a few students to share their ideas with the class.

5B This exercise can be done in pairs, small groups or you could brainstorm ideas with the whole class. If students work in pairs or groups, as feedback, elicit a few ideas from different pairs/groups. The class could also vote on the best idea for each business.

Suggested answers

Ben Fischer's theatre company could ask the public to crowdfund the company's future productions for rewards such as theatre tickets, bit parts in the plays, VIP seats, discounts and a night out with the actors.

Alison's Tees could ask for funding to expand into other products, e.g. own-design jewellery, bags, accessories, other clothes and childrenswear. Rewards could include special discounts on products, fast delivery and first choice on personalised products. Backers could also model the clothes on her website.

Holidapp could extend audio guides into Australia, Asia and Africa in the coming years. Rewards could include free and unlimited access to a percentage of the developed guides, depending on the size of the backer's contribution.

Extra activities Business workshop 6

B Students could do this individually or in pairs. Give them time to read the tips and extracts, and help them with any unknown words (e.g. *infection*, *renovate*, *effortlessly*). If you choose to ask students to work individually, you could get them to compare answers in pairs before checking with the class.

1 d,i   2 b,e   3 a,c   4 g,j   5 f,h

Task

Students prepare and deliver a crowdfunding pitch.

6 Put students in small groups. Explain that they are going to write a crowdfunding pitch for a project of their choice: a new project for one of the companies from the video following the notes given, a project for one of the companies that the groups decide on or a new idea of their own. Go through the list of things to remember with students and give them time to read the texts at the bottom of the page and ask you any questions they may have. Give the groups plenty of time to prepare. Monitor, checking students' pitches for any language errors and helping them with any vocabulary they may need.

7 Students use their smartphones to record their pitches. If your students are uncomfortable videoing themselves, you could ask them to record the pitches as audio only.

8 Groups now watch each other's pitches and decide which project they would back. Give them time to discuss in their groups first and then invite groups to share their decisions with the class, giving reasons.

MyEnglishLab: Teacher's resources: extra activities

Review ◀ 6

1   1 advice   2 set up   3 target market   4 start-ups
    5 go out of   6 profit   7 founders   8 angel
    9 investment   10 funding   11 financial
    12 crowdfunding
2   1 had finished by lunchtime that
    2 what my plan for the new business was / what my
       plan was for the new business
    3 (that) they wouldn't be working here/there
    4 if/whether he had been working in hospitality
    5 (that) the Sales Manager would visit (them) the
       following/next
    6 could finish the report then
    7 where I worked
3   1 address   2 sounds   3 mind   4 aware   5 spread
    6 free   7 appreciate
4   1 part   2 slide   3 pie   4 notice   5 line   6 significant
    7 closely   8 interesting
5   1 a   2 c   3 e   4 b   5 d

7 > Working abroad

Unit overview

	CLASSWORK		FURTHER WORK
7.1 > **Global work cultures**	**Lead-in**	Students discuss different aspects of working/studying abroad.	**MyEnglishLab:** Teacher's resources: extra activities; Reading bank
	Video	Students watch a video about the various aspects and challenges of working abroad.	**Teacher's book:** Resource bank Photocopiable 7.1 p.148
	Vocabulary	Students look at vocabulary for talking about work cultures and adjectives for describing people's personalities.	**Workbook:** p.34 Exercises 1–3
	Project	Students research a foreign culture and then write tips for people from abroad coming to work/study in their own country.	
7.2 > **Cultural anecdotes**	**Lead-in**	Students talk about ways of adapting to working/studying abroad.	**MyEnglishLab:** Teacher's resources: extra activities
	Listening	Students listen to three monologues where people talk about their experience of working abroad.	**Pronunciation bank:** p.117 Phrasing and intonation in past sentences
	Grammar	Students study and practise the Past Simple, Past Continuous and Past Perfect Simple.	**Grammar reference:** p.124 Past tenses
	Speaking and writing	Students practise telling and writing anecdotes using past tenses.	**Teacher's book:** Resource bank Photocopiable 7.2 p.149
			Workbook: p.35 Exercises 1–3, p.36 Exercises 1–3
7.3 > **Communication skills:** Decision-making	**Lead-in**	Students discuss different approaches to decision-making.	**MyEnglishLab:** Teacher's resources: extra activities; Interactive video activities
	Video	Students watch a video about different decision-making styles and preferences, and how these may affect business results and relationships.	**Pronunciation bank:** p.117 Strong or weak?
	Reflection	Students think about their preferred communication style and its effectiveness when making decisions.	**Workbook:** p.37 Exercises 1 and 2
	Functional language	Students look at useful language for expressing preferences.	
	Task	Students practise the functional language from the lesson by discussing their preferences in different situations.	
7.4 > **Business skills:** Relationship-building	**Lead-in**	Students talk about building relationships with new people.	**MyEnglishLab:** Teacher's resources: extra activities; Functional language bank
	Listening	Students listen to a conversation between people who are meeting for the first time and then to a monologue about building relationships with new people.	**Workbook:** p.37 Exercise 3
	Functional language	Students look at useful phrases for keeping a conversation going.	
	Task	Students roleplay making small talk and building relationships with recruits at an induction day in a new company.	
7.5 > **Writing:** Making recommendations	**Lead-in**	Students read a report on company problems and identify examples of suggestions, advice and recommendations.	**MyEnglishLab:** Teacher's resources: extra activities; Interactive grammar practice; Writing bank
	Functional language	Students look at useful phrases for giving advice and making suggestions and recommendations in different registers.	**Grammar reference:** p.124 First and second conditional
	Task	Students practise checking written work by proofreading an email and write a report.	**Workbook:** p.38 Exercises 1–3
Business workshop 7 > Cross-cultural consultants	**Reading**	Students read a blog post on cultural awareness.	**MyEnglishLab:** Teacher's resources: extra activities
	Listening	Students listen to interviews with international staff.	
	Task	Students present a recommendation for working in their culture.	
	Writing	Students write a formal email confirming the outcome of their presentations.	

Business brief

The main aim of this unit is to introduce students to the concepts related to **working abroad**.

People work abroad for various reasons – for example, they may be **transferred overseas** by the company they are currently working for; or they may decide they want to work in a particular country and apply for a job before they go, or they may go to a country and find a job after they have arrived. In all three cases, the person needs a **visa** or **work permit** that allows them to work, **qualifications** that make them suitable for the jobs available and **experience** related to the position or the country. It helps if the person knows something about the **culture** and the **practical aspects** of living there. And last but not least, they need to be able to communicate in the **language** of that country.

The positive aspects of working abroad are having a chance to experience another culture and broadening your perspective. It can also help **personal development** through having to deal with the unique challenges of being 'out of your comfort zone', i.e. in situations which you are completely unfamiliar with. It can also improve you **career development**. Companies, especially international or multinational companies, like to employ people with a wide range of experience and a proven ability to operate in various situations overseas.

Working abroad has its negative side. **Culture shock** – the negative feeling you have when you suddenly experience the differences in another culture – is the most obvious. The shock can be reduced by **good preparation** – having a job to go to, having a visa, having enough savings to cover the first period after moving, researching the culture and information related to daily life such as the transport system, schools, places to live, the food and the climate.

A **positive attitude** once you have arrived, proactively making friends and integrating with the local culture, also helps. However, most people, even those who do their best to adapt, can feel **homesick** – they miss their family and wish to return to their country at some point.

Culture shock often refers specifically to the differences in behaviour which a person discovers when they move abroad. **Local customs** and **etiquette** can be difficult to understand and even harder to copy. People may appear reserved and less friendly than you are used to or the opposite: people may seem too direct. Even small things like touching and physical distance can be different enough to cause embarrassment and stress. At work, there may be different attitudes to **timekeeping** and **interpersonal relationships** that you may find unfamiliar or frustrating – for example, company life may be more **hierarchical**, which means that you have to take orders from a superior when you may be used to working in a flatter sort of culture.

The best cure for culture shock is probably to **keep an open mind** – to avoid **stereotyping**, not to make assumptions about how you want or expect people to behave, to maintain a positive attitude to new relationships and integrate with your new environment by joining a club, taking up a local sport and joining in local cultural and neighbourhood events. And finally, the ability to speak the language of your new country is probably the biggest challenge and benefit of all.

Working abroad and your students

Students who are not yet working need to be aware of the practical aspects of working abroad and the positive and negative sides to living in a new and possibly unfamiliar culture. Working students should be aware of the various intercultural aspects of communicating and working with people whose work culture may be significantly different from theirs.

Unit lead-in

Elicit a brief description of the main photo and then look at the quote with the class. Check that students understand *culture shock* and give students 2 minutes to discuss in pairs or small groups: What do they think the quote means? Do they agree? Once students have discussed in their pairs/groups, you could broaden this into a class discussion.

7.1 > Global work cultures

GSE learning objectives

- Can give or seek personal views and opinions in discussing topics of interest.
- Can understand a large part of a video on a work-related topic.
- Can carry out a prepared interview, checking and confirming information as necessary.

Warm-up

Ask students to think of three things that are typical of their country's culture. Elicit ideas (accept any answers) and write them on the board. Then ask the class to put them into categories (e.g. food, sport, daily life, behaviour, weather). Now put students in pairs and ask them to imagine they are moving to another country. What would they miss if they didn't live in their country? And what would they worry about if they lived in a new country? Give students a few minutes to discuss in their pairs. Then elicit and discuss students' ideas as a class.

Lead-in

Students discuss different aspects of working/studying abroad.

1 Go through the questions with students and, if you didn't do the unit lead-in above, check that they understand *culture shock*. You could give students a few minutes to discuss the questions in pairs or small groups first, before discussing them as a class. For question 1, you could ask students to give details of specific events or incidents.

Possible answers

2 learn the language, get to know the culture from reading travel/cultural guides and watching documentaries, look for accommodation, find a suitable international school for my children, open a bank account in that country, prepare to move house, pack my suitcases, go on a short trip to check out the location before relocating, negotiate a better salary to compensate for relocation, sign up with a networking group to meet new people when I get there

3 Students' answers will vary depending on their culture. They may say that it depends which country the visitors come from, but they could mention differences regarding timetables, local customs, traditions and festivals, food and drink, etiquette when communicating with people (e.g. shaking hands / bowing / kissing when greeting), working times, meal times, etiquette when eating out, making eye contact, personal space when talking to people, things to do / not to do when travelling on public transport, etc.

Video

Students watch a video about the various aspects and challenges of working abroad.

2 ▶ 7.1.1 Explain that students are going to watch a video about working abroad and go through the instructions with the class. Explain that the names of the countries are given in the box but the names of the speakers are not – students will need to listen/watch for them. Play the video, twice if necessary, then check answers with the class.

1 Evelyn, Germany **2** Rodrigo, Brazil **3** Marcus, Sweden **4** Hanna, Poland

3 ▶ 7.1.1 Go through the questions with students and check that they understand *break the ice, tend to be like* and *acceptable*. With stronger classes, you could ask students to try to answer the questions before they watch again, then watch to check/complete their answers. With weaker classes, you may need to play the video twice for students to complete their answers and/or pause at regular intervals to give them time to write their answers. Get students to compare answers in pairs before checking with the class.

1 relocate to offices in different countries
2 It brings challenges. Foreign professionals have to learn about cultural issues like customs and etiquette. They may find the way people communicate and interact at work is different.
3 They will be your friend for life if they make friends with you.
4 They tend to be very friendly and communicative.
5 saying the wrong things at the wrong time but learning the language quickly
6 because Polish people tend to be more direct

4 You could do this exercise as a whole class: get individual students to read out the sentences and ask the class if they can remember the speakers. Tell them not to worry about the words in bold for now. Then play the video for students to check their answers.

1 M **2** E **3** M **4** H **5** R **6** H

Extra activities 7.1

A ▶ 7.1.1 Ask students to do this individually. Give them 1–2 minutes to read the sentences, then play the video for them to complete the exercise. Get them to compare answers in pairs before checking answers with the class. With weaker classes, you could list the gapped words on the board in random order (see answer key below), ask students to complete the sentences using the words on the board, then play the video for them to check their answers.

1 International, career
2 Foreign, customs, etiquette
3 cultures, standards
4 broken the ice, got to know
5 be quiet
6 polite, leave it at
7 practices, nation's culture
8 unwritten, challenging, global

Vocabulary: Working abroad

Students look at vocabulary for talking about work cultures.

5 Put students in pairs. Explain that A, B and C are three possible definitions of each word/phrase in bold in Exercise 4. Students should choose the best one, but they should **not** use their dictionaries at this point. They should use the meaning of the sentence to help them. Check answers with the class and clarify meanings as necessary.

> **1** B **2** C **3** C **4** A **5** B **6** A, C

Adjectives, prefixes and opposites

Students look at adjectives for describing people's personalities.

6A List the adjective prefixes on the board and explain or elicit that they all have a *negative* meaning. Encourage students to give examples for each prefix, or give them a 'positive' adjective for each prefix and ask them to form its opposite (e.g. *satisfied – dissatisfied, possible – impossible, complete – incomplete, fair – unfair*). Go through the adjectives in the box with students and check that they understand the meanings. Elicit or explain that they are all used to describe someone's personality, and give students 3–4 minutes to complete the exercise. Point out that they should use one of the prefixes or find another antonym. Depending on the strength of your class, you could let students work in pairs, using their dictionaries if necessary. Check answers with the class.

> **Possible answers**
> **1** indirect **2** unfriendly/reserved/shy
> **3** informal **3** dishonest **5** unhelpful
> **6** unkind/cruel **7** impolite/rude
> **8** friendly/sociable/communicative/open/outgoing
> **9** unsociable/uncommunicative/unfriendly/reserved
> **10** disrespectful

6B Students should do this individually, then check answers in pairs before class feedback.

> **1** friendly
> **2** sociable
> **3** indirect, dishonest
> **4** helpful, unkind
> **5** respectful, informal, impolite

7 Put students in pairs and give them 3–5 minutes to discuss the questions. Encourage them to think about their own opinions and experiences or experiences of people they know. As feedback, elicit answers from different students and briefly discuss them as a class.

Extra activities 7.1

B This activity practises key vocabulary from the video. Students could do it individually or in pairs. Before they begin, point out that both options are possible in some sentences. Check answers with the class.

> **1** common **2** come across **3** ✔ – Both options are possible and have the same meaning. **4** became fluent, nuances **5** ✔ – Both options are possible and have a similar meaning; alone **6** Did you get used to

C This activity practises personality adjectives from the lesson. You may want to do the first item as an example with the class, then let students do the rest of the exercise individually or in pairs. During feedback, encourage students to give reasons for their choices.

> **Suggested answers**
> **1** shy – The others are all synonyms of being friendly.
> **2** loud – It's the opposite of the other adjectives.
> **3** rude – It has a negative meaning, whereas the other adjectives are positive.
> **4** mean – *Direct, open* and *honest* are (near) synonyms; *mean* is the opposite of *generous*.
> **5** dishonest – It has a negative meaning; the other adjectives are synonyms of being kind.
> **6** indirect – It has a different meaning to the other adjectives, which all mean *impolite*.
> **7** kind – The others are synonyms of *impolite* and are all negative.
> **8** annoying – *Formal, reserved* and *polite* are (near) synonyms; *reserved* is the opposite of *sociable*.

Project: Research a culture

Students research a foreign culture and then write tips for people from abroad coming to work/study in their own country.

8A Put students in pairs or small groups. Go through the instructions with the class and check that students understand the meanings of the words in the box in the third bullet point. Also go through the phrases for checking/confirming information – you could put them on the board for students to refer to during the activity. Before students begin, make sure they are clear about what they need to do in each step. Also check if they all have a phone or other device they can use to record the interview. If they don't, encourage them to take notes. Give pairs/groups plenty of time for each step, while you go round monitoring and helping as necessary. As feedback, ask students to use their recordings/notes to report back to the class; they could do this in a future lesson if time is short.

8B Ask a couple of students to give an example of something people should/shouldn't do if they come to work/study in the students' own country. Then give them time to write their dos and don'ts in their pairs/groups. As feedback, elicit ideas from different pairs/groups.

MyEnglishLab: Teacher's resources: extra activities; Reading bank
Teacher's book: Resource bank Photocopiable 7.1 p.148
Workbook: p.34 Exercises 1–3

7.2 › Cultural anecdotes

GSE learning objectives

- Can express and comment on ideas and suggestions in informal discussions.
- Can understand the details of extended talks or interviews about people's lives and experiences if delivered in clear, standard speech.
- Can tell a simple anecdote.
- Can write a simple anecdote.

Warm-up

Ask students if they have ever worked/studied abroad or if they know someone who has. What did they / the people they know do to help them adapt to living in a new country?

Lead-in

Students talk about ways of adapting to working/studying abroad.

1A Put students in pairs and go through the instructions with them. Check that they understand *region*. Give pairs a few minutes to discuss and put the factors in the box in order of importance. Go round the class and make a note of any interesting questions or comments, and refer back to these when pairs have finished. Ask different pairs to share their ideas with the class, giving reasons.

1B Give pairs a few minutes to brainstorm ideas, then elicit ideas from different students.

Possible answers

reading travel/cultural guides; preparing to move and packing; asking your company/organisation for advice about relocation / studying abroad; going on a short trip in advance to see what it's like; finding a good school for your children (for those students with families); finding out about the culture's values, e.g. religious practices / holidays; talking to work colleagues / students from the other country before you go

Listening

Students listen to three monologues where people talk about their experience of working abroad.

2 ◀) 7.01 Explain the activity, give students a minute to read sentences a–i and answer any vocabulary questions they may have. Check that they understand *offended*, *loss of face* and *optimistic*. Play the recording, twice if necessary, and get students to compare answers in pairs before checking with the class. If time allows, you could refer students to the audioscript on page 149 and ask them to underline the parts that give the answers.

Speaker 1: b, c and g
Speaker 2: e and i
Speaker 3: a, d and h
Item f is not used.

3 ◀) 7.01 Again, give students time to read the statements and ask you about any unknown words. Play the recording and check answers with the class. You may need to play the recording a second time for students to correct the false statements.

Speaker 1
1 F (There was a smell of incense burning.)
2 T
3 T
Speaker 2
4 T
Speaker 3
5 F (Shivani was working hard because her colleagues had fallen ill and she was covering for them. When she didn't send the figures, her American boss sent her an email with a red flag, copying in all the team.)
6 F (Shivani's boss wanted the figures by the end of the month, so when Shivani didn't send them, her boss sent her an 'angry' email. (Shivani hadn't explained the situation to her boss because she didn't want to give a bad impression.))

4 Put students in pairs to discuss the questions. Encourage them to give examples from their personal experience where possible, and allow them to refer to the audioscript on page 149 if necessary. When the pairs have finished, get brief feedback from the class.

Extra activities 7.2

A ◀) 7.01 Ask students to do this individually and then compare their answers in pairs. Play the first speaker's turn for them to check their answers, then check as a class.

1 c 2 e 3 f 4 d 5 a 6 b

B ◀) 7.01 Give students a minute to read the gapped sentences. Play the second speaker's turn, then check answers with the class.

1 Hakuna matata, worries 2 While/When, agree to deadlines 3 frustrating, had previously agreed 4 On the other, atmosphere

C ◀) 7.01 Explain the activity and give students time to read the gapped sentences. Point out that they will need to change the form of some verbs. Play the third speaker's turn, then check answers with the class. With stronger classes, you could ask students to try to complete the sentences before listening, then listen to check/complete their answers.

1 was working, had to 2 had fallen, was going 3 was leaving 4 didn't explain, were having 5 quit

Grammar
Past tenses: Past Simple, Past Continuous and Past Perfect Simple

Students study and practise the Past Simple, Past Continuous and Past Perfect Simple.

5 You could do this exercise as a whole class, checking and explaining answers as you go. You may wish to briefly revise the form of each tense, especially with weaker classes. You could also refer students to the Grammar reference on page 124 at this point, and go through the explanations as a class.

> **1** b, b **2** c, b **3** b, a

> ❯❯ **Pronunciation bank**
> **p.117: Phrasing and intonation in past sentences**
>
> **Warm-up**
> Write the following example sentence on the board and ask students to identify the background information (underlined) and the main information (in bold). _She had had many interviews before_, **so she knew how to answer most of the key questions.**
> Draw arrows to show the fall-rise intonation for the background information, and the falling intonation for the main information:
>
> _She had had many interviews before, so she knew how to answer most of the key questions._
>
> Model and drill the intonation, and explain to students that we often use this pattern in sentences with various past tenses. Go through the explanation in the box with them, referring to the sentence on the board.
>
> **1** 🔊 P7.01 Explain that students have to listen and use the intonation pattern to identify and mark the main information in each sentence. You could also ask students to mark the intonation using arrows. Check answers with the class.
>
>> **1** While José was working in India, <u>he was surprised to see a shrine on the table in the chairman's office</u>. [fall-rise on 'India', fall on 'chairman's office']
>> **2** Even if they'd previously agreed to a deadline, <u>they later admitted they couldn't meet it</u>. [fall-rise on 'agreed', fall on 'meet']
>> **3** Because her boss had copied in all the members of the team, <u>Shivani was so embarrassed that she quit her job</u>. [fall-rise on 'team', fall on 'job']
>
> **2** Put students in pairs to practise saying the sentences. Walk round and check their intonation is following the correct patterns. If necessary, let students listen again before they practise in their pairs.

6 Ask students to do this individually and then compare answers in pairs. Check answers with the class.

> **1** d **2** a **3** e **4** c **5** f **6** b

7 Students could do this individually or in pairs. Remind them that they can refer to the Grammar reference on page 124 if they need help. Check answers with the class, clarifying any points as necessary.

> **1** weren't, were
> **2** was travelling, asked, earned
> **3** was still studying, got, didn't accept
> **4** joined, couldn't, became
> **5** were negotiating, did you find, thought
> **6** were doing / did, were, held

Extra activities 7.2

D This is a consolidation exercise, so it might be better for students to do it individually. Point out that more than one answer may be possible in some cases. Encourage students to read the text quickly before trying to complete the gaps, to get a general idea of what it is about. If time allows, get students to compare answers in pairs before class feedback.

> **1** went **2** hadn't happened **3** was using
> **4** was living / had lived **5** were **6** dealt **7** got
> **8** wasn't **9** were feeling **10** gave **11** was told
> **12** didn't give **13** took **14** was walking
> **15** drove **16** ended **17** were not connected
> **18** had never heard

Speaking and writing

Students practise telling and writing anecdotes using past tenses.

8A Put students in pairs or small groups. Explain what an anecdote is, explain the activity and point out the useful phrases. You could give students an example of your own before they begin (see model answer below). Allow some preparation time before students tell their anecdotes to their partners. As feedback, invite a few students to share one of their anecdotes with the class.

> **Model answer**
> A few years ago I was working in the USA. Working for a huge IT corporation in the States had so many benefits. People could do whatever they liked in their work area – for example, they had lunch at their desks, they played basketball or video games in the breaks, things like that. Once, when I was going into the kitchen, I was surprised when I saw a colleague lying on the floor. I asked him if he was feeling all right. He said he was praying. He was a practising Muslim who prayed at work in the _Sujood_ position. I had never seen that kind of practice in my country. Such activities were tolerated in the USA as it didn't affect business.

8B Go through the instructions with the class. Point out the word limit and refer students to the audioscript on page 149. Students could write their anecdotes in class, which will give you an opportunity to go round the class and give students individual advice and feedback. Alternatively, the exercise could be set as homework. If you set it for homework, students could read their anecdotes to the class in a future lesson.

MyEnglishLab: Teacher's resources: extra activities
Pronunciation bank: p.117 Phrasing and intonation in past sentences
Grammar reference: p.124 Past tenses
Teacher's book: Resource bank Photocopiable 7.2 p.149
Workbook: p.35 Exercises 1–3, p.36 Exercises 1–3

7.3 › Communication skills
Decision-making

Warm-up

Write the following question on the board: *When it comes to decision-making, are two heads better than one?* Put students in pairs or small groups and ask them to discuss the question: Do they prefer making decisions on their own or with other people? What do they think are the advantages and disadvantages of making decisions with other people? (e.g. advantages: diversity of ideas, greater commitment to ideas; disadvantages: may take longer; one person / a few people may dominate the group). Once students have discussed in their pairs/groups, you could broaden this into a class discussion.

Lead-in

Students discuss different approaches to decision-making.

1A Put students in pairs and give them 3–4 minutes to discuss the questions. Get brief feedback from the class.

1B Before students discuss the questions, give them time to read the texts and answer any vocabulary questions they may have. Check that they understand *consensus, deadline, decisive, commitment* and *competence*. Put students in pairs or small groups to discuss the questions, then invite different students to share their ideas with the class.

Video

Students watch a video about different decision-making styles and preferences, and how these may affect business results and relationships.

2 ▶ 7.3.1 If students watched the videos from the previous units, elicit or remind them of the situation and Stefanie's and Paula's roles. Also elicit what project PRO Manage are currently working on (they are launching a series of online project management courses). If this is the first communication skills video for your students, briefly explain the context yourself. Go through the instructions and questions with students, play the video and check answers with the class.

1 Stefanie wants to set a date for the launch. Paula wants to understand more about how Susan and Pedro work, and think about a launch date later.
2 Stefanie wants to suggest a date she thinks is best. Paula wants to talk to Susan and Pedro and collectively decide on the best date.
3 Stefanie and Paula have differing approaches. This may cause friction during the customer meeting.

3A Go through the instructions and the details of Options A and B with the class. Put students in small groups and give them 1–2 minutes to discuss which approach they think Stefanie and Paula should follow to get commitment from their potential customers. Encourage them to give reasons. When groups have finished, elicit ideas from different students. Clarify that they can choose which option they want to see first on the video and then, as a class, decide which video to watch first.

3B ▶ 7.3.2 ▶ 7.3.3 Give students a minute to read the questions and play the video for Option A or Option B, depending on the students' choice. With weaker classes, you may need to play the video a second time for students to complete their answers. Check answers as a class, then explain that students will need to answer *the same* questions for the second option. Repeat the process for the second video.

Option A
1 Susan reacts well to the direct and decisive approach. Pedro seems hesitant.
2 They decide to launch in September. It was Stefanie's idea and supported by Susan.
3 This style is successful in that they made a quick decision, though they might have been too quick to decide and it's not clear if they got buy-in from Pedro. The end result was a decision, but can it be seen as successful if relationships may be damaged because of the process they used?

Option B
1 Pedro reacts well to Paula's flexible and collaborative approach. But Susan becomes impatient with this approach.
2 The launch in September is agreed. It was Susan's idea when she finally came in and took control.
3 This style was good for developing the relationship between Paula and Pedro. However, it may have been too indecisive and time-consuming for Susan, who interrupted and took control. The end result was a decision, but can it be seen as successful if relationships may be damaged because of the process they used?

4 Put students in pairs to discuss the questions. Encourage them to give reasons. Allow 3–4 minutes for the pairwork, then elicit ideas and reasons from different students.

Possible answers

Paula probably felt very frustrated at the end of Option A as she wasn't able to participate at all and didn't have the chance to find out about Pedro's views. Stefanie probably felt happy with the process and the result in Option A as it was driven by her preferred style.

Paula probably felt a bit happier with the process in Option B as she found out more about Pedro's priorities. Although the agreed date was the same as in Option A, Pedro raised the need for a pilot. Paula still wasn't able to discuss all the points she wanted to, though. Stefanie was probably happy with the outcome in Option B but may have been frustrated with the process as it took longer to reach a decision.

5 ▶ 7.3.4 Keep students in the same pairs and explain that they are going to watch the last section of the video, where the speaker discusses the learning points from the video. Play the video and give pairs a few minutes to discuss their answers. Check answers with the class and ask if any students have ever experienced these differences and if so, how they overcame them. Invite individual students to share their experiences with the class.

The three cultural differences are: attitudes to decision-making (target-driven vs. consensus-oriented), time and deadlines (fixed vs. flexible), and hierarchy (flat hierarchy = discussion; hierarchy important = less discussion/disagreement).

The recommendation for overcoming these in business is to observe others, then discuss a preferred approach.

Reflection

Students think about their preferred communication style and its effectiveness when making decisions.

6 Allow students to work individually on this so that they can reflect on their own preferences and communication style. Then put them in pairs to discuss their answers. As feedback, elicit ideas from different students for each question and encourage brief class discussion.

❯ **Pronunciation bank**
p.117: Strong or weak?

Warm-up

Go through the explanation in the box with students. Write the example exchange on the board and explain that in A, *Are* is not stressed and so is pronounced in its weak form (/ə/), while in B, it is stressed to emphasise the affirmative answer, and so is pronounced in its strong form (/ɑː/). Model and drill the pronunciation.

1 ◀)) P7.02 Play the recording for students to repeat. Repeat as many times as necessary until students are pronouncing strong and weak forms correctly.

2 You may want to do the first item as an example with the class. Remind students that strong forms are only used when a word is stressed, and put them in pairs to complete the rest of the exercise. Do not confirm answers yet – students will check them in the next exercise.

3 ◀)) P7.03 Play the recording for students to check their answers. Go through the answers with the class, explaining why each strong form is stressed (see explanations in brackets in the answer key below). Then put students in pairs to practise saying the sentences.

1 The /ðə/ (weak) process is as /əz/ (weak) important as /əz/ (weak) the /ðə/ (weak) result.
2 Deadlines are /ə/ (weak) useful to /tə/ (weak) keep people focused – that's /ðæts/ (strong – it's the subject of the final clause) their main purpose.
3 I think consensus is important – what do /də/ (weak) you /juː/ (strong – contrasts what 'I' think with what 'you' think) think?
4 If we can't all reach an /ən/ (weak) agreement, what do /də/ (weak) you /jə/ (weak) think we should do /duː/ (strong – main verb rather than auxiliary verb)?

Functional language:
Expressing preferences

Students look at useful language for expressing preferences.

7 Ask students to complete this exercise individually and get them to compare answers in pairs before checking with the class. During feedback, check that students understand the meaning of the phrases and encourage them to record the phrases in their notebooks.

1 keen **2** prefer to **3** happy to **4** want **5** sure

8A This exercise introduces more phrases to express preference. Give students a few minutes to match the two parts of the sentences, then get them to compare answers in pairs before class feedback. Again, encourage students to record the key phrases in their notebooks.

1 b **2** c **3** e **4** g **5** a **6** d **7** f

Notes

There are a variety of forms in Exercises 7 and 8A which you could ask students to identify. Point out that each phrase is used in a particular pattern. Write the phrases on the board and ask students to tell you what verb form it is used with. Encourage them to record these in their notebooks.

7

I'm keen + *to*-infinitive
I/I'd prefer + *to*-infinitive
I'm happy + *to*-infinitive
I want + *to*-infinitive
I'm sure + *that* clause

8A

My preference is / would be + *to*-infinitive
I don't mind + *-ing*
I would rather + bare infinitive
I'm (not) keen on + *-ing*
If it were up to me, I'd + bare infinitive
I would rather + object + Past Simple
We'd prefer it if + object + Past Simple

8B Do this exercise quickly, as a whole class.

> I don't mind

9A/B Students could do Exercise 9A individually or in pairs. If you asked students to identify and record the verb pattern for each phrase (see Notes above), you could refer them to the list on the board or in their notebooks. Check answers with the class, then put students in pairs to practise the dialogue.

> **1** booking **2** looked **3** were **4** would cancel **5** to do
> **6** chose **7** not to increase **8** going

Extra activities 7.3

A This exercise practises the functional language phrases from the main lesson. Explain that only one word is wrong in each sentence, which students may need to replace with a new word or change to a different form. Ask students to work individually and then compare answers in pairs before class feedback.

> **1** I'd rather we ~~talk~~ talked about price now.
> **2** If it were up to me, I ~~will~~ would cancel the contract.
> **3** We'd prefer not to ~~discussing~~ discuss that issue in this meeting.
> **4** She's keen ~~for~~ to sign the agreement as soon as possible.
> **5** Our preference would ~~is~~ be to outsource this process.
> **6** We're happy to ~~adapting~~ adapt the software to your specific needs.
> **7** I don't mind ~~change~~ changing the date of the meeting.
> **8** I'd rather ~~started~~ start the meeting at 9 a.m. than 10 a.m.

Task

Students practise the functional language from the lesson by discussing their preferences in different situations.

10A Students could do this in pairs or small groups, depending on the size of your class. Go through the instructions and situations with them and check that they understand the words in the boxes. Remind them that they should use phrases from Exercises 7 and 8 to talk about their preferences. Depending on the time available, pairs/groups can choose one of the situations or work through the situations one by one. If possible, ask students to record their conversations – they can then use their recordings when they do Exercise 10B. While students are working, monitor and note down any errors in the use of the functional language phrases to highlight during feedback.

10B Students discuss the questions in their pairs/groups, using their recordings if they have them. During feedback, highlight any errors you noted during Exercise 10A.

MyEnglishLab: Teacher's resources: extra activities; Interactive video activities
Pronunciation bank: p.117 Strong or weak?
Workbook: p.37 Exercises 1 and 2

7.4 ❯ Business skills
Relationship-building

GSE learning objectives

- Can identify strategies and expressions to maintain a conversation.
- Can use a basic repertoire of conversation strategies to maintain a discussion.
- Can initiate, maintain and close simple, face-to-face conversations on familiar topics.

Warm-up

Write the following two questions on the board: *Do you like meeting new people? How easy do you find it to start a conversation with someone you have just met?* Put students in small groups and give them 2–4 minutes to discuss the questions. Encourage them to give reasons and/or examples from their personal experience. When the time is up, invite individual students to share their answers with the class.

Lead-in

Students talk about building relationships with new people.

1A/B Put students in pairs to discuss the questions. Go round the class monitoring and make a note of any interesting points or comments. Refer back to these when the pairs have finished. Once students have discussed in their pairs, you could briefly discuss the questions as a whole class.

Listening

Students listen to a conversation between people who are meeting for the first time and then to a monologue about building relationships with new people.

2A Go through the list with the class and check that they understand *interrogation* and *assumption*. Put students in pairs and give them 3–4 minutes to discuss. As feedback, elicit ideas from different students.

2B 🔊 7.02 Explain that students are going to listen to the first part of a conversation during an informal dinner at an international networking event. Give them a minute to read the questions, and point out that there are no wrong answers to questions 4 and 5, but students should support their answers with reasons. You may wish to let them read the strategies in Exercise 2A again before they listen. Play the recording, then check answers with the class.

> 1 work, politics (elections)
> 2 work, hobbies/interests, family
> 3 Strategies 1 and 6
> 4 (Possible answer) Tadashi gives very short answers and doesn't ask follow-up questions, so Peter may think he is unfriendly, shy or that he isn't confident speaking in English. Pilar gives very short answers about her job but offers more information about her family and hobbies. Peter may get the impression that she is not very interested in or serious about her work.
> 5 (Possible answer) They may feel that they are being interrogated by Peter. He asks a lot of questions and asks follow-up questions on the same topic even when they have indicated that they are not comfortable discussing it. He doesn't adapt his style to theirs or express interest in the topics they raise. They may therefore think he is uninterested or has poor communication skills.

2C 🔊 7.03 Explain that you are going to play the second part of the conversation and give students a minute to read the questions. Play the recording, then check answers with the class.

> 1 Peter tries to take an interest in the others' interests. He gives Tadashi more time to think, reflect and talk. He tries to identify something Tadashi is passionate about and then lets him talk. He then brings Pilar into the conversation by asking her about her family.
> 2 Tadashi's work, Peter's holiday and family
> 3 strategies 1, 2, 4, 6 and 8

2D 🔊 7.04 Explain that students are going to listen to Peter talking about what happened. Play the recording and get students to compare answers in pairs before class feedback. After checking answers, ask students if they agree with Peter's conclusion in question 1.

> 1 He concludes that first impressions are often based on assumptions and they can often be wrong.
> 2 His reflection included evidence of strategies 1, 3, 5, 6, 7 and 8.

Functional language:
Keeping a conversation going

Students look at useful phrases for keeping a conversation going.

3A Look at the example with the class and point out that the conversation has three parts: the initial question/comment, the response and the follow-up question/comment. Ask students to complete the rest of the exercise individually and get them to check answers in pairs, using the audioscripts on page 150.

> **2** e, iii **3** b, v **4** a, iv **5** d, i

3B Students could do this exercise individually or in pairs. Again, point out that each conversation has three parts.

> **1** c, i **2** a, iii **3** b, ii

3C Put students in pairs and explain the activity. Point out that they should use the three-part structure, as in Exercises 3A and 3B. Tell them that they can use phrases from these exercises to help them. During the activity, monitor and make a note of any errors/points to highlight during feedback.

Extra activities 7.4

A You could ask students to do this exercise individually, comparing answers in pairs before class feedback. Alternatively, you could do it as a whole class, checking answers as you go. The second option may be easier for weaker classes.

> **1** d **2** c **3** a **4** b **5** e

B This exercise can be done individually or in pairs. If time allows, after checking answers, put students in pairs and get them to ask and answer the questions, using the three-part conversation structure they looked at in the main lesson: initial question → response → follow-up question/comment.

> 1 What do you like to do in your free time?
> 2 What's your favourite food?
> 3 Tell me about your best day during your studies or at work.
> 4 What are you most proud of?
> 5 Tell me something new you did this year. How did it go?
> 6 Do you avoid or like to use technology in your free time?

Task

Students roleplay making small talk and building relationships with recruits at an induction day in a new company.

4A Explain the task and give students a few minutes to think of suitable topics and questions they want to ask.

4B Put students in pairs for their roleplays. Explain the task and point out that they should talk about at least 2–3 topics. Also explain that students may need to change their approach during their conversation, using a different strategy from Exercise 2B. With weaker classes, you may wish to do an example with a stronger student first. During the activity, go round the class and monitor, making notes of any errors/points to highlight during feedback.

4C Go through the instructions and questions with the class, and give students plenty of time to reflect on their conversations and give each other feedback. At this point, you could also highlight any points you noted during Exercise 4B.

4D Put students in new pairs to repeat the activity, addressing the feedback they received from their partner (and you) in Exercise 4C.

MyEnglishLab: Teacher's resources: extra activities; Functional language bank
Workbook: p.37 Exercise 3

7.5 ❯ Writing
Making recommendations

GSE learning objectives

- Can use a basic repertoire of conversation strategies to maintain a discussion.
- Can maintain professional etiquette in conversation using simple phrases and fixed expressions.
- Can understand problem and solution relationships in a structured text.
- Can make suggestions and recommendations on work-related topics.
- Can give advice including reasons.
- Can write a short, simple work-related report outlining key issues.
- Can describe hypothetical (counterfactual) results of a current action or situation using the second conditional.

Warm-up

Write the following questions on the board: *In what situations might you need to give advice or make suggestions to colleagues? Have you ever received advice or recommendations from a colleague? If so, explain the situation.* Put students in pairs or small groups and give them 3–4 minutes to discuss the questions. Get brief feedback from the class.

Lead-in

Students read a report on company problems and identify examples of suggestions, advice and recommendations.

1 Ask students to read the report quickly first and identify the main problem (cross-cultural project teams not being familiar with cross-cultural differences) and two suggested ways of dealing with the problem (a cross-cultural training course, team members visiting the other countries). Then ask students

to read the report again and underline all the examples of suggestions, advice and recommendations. Get students to compare answers in pairs before checking with the class.

Recently <u>it has become obvious that staff need to be trained in</u> cross-cultural working as we now have several project teams with members from different countries. <u>For these projects to be most effective, it is advisable that</u> everyone is aware of the cultural background of each team member. If people are not familiar with the differences, then cultural problems will become more complicated. Consequently, <u>to avoid misunderstandings, it is essential that everyone in the team learns</u> how each culture differs. <u>We therefore suggest that all staff in these teams do a suitable cross-cultural training course.</u> <u>You ought to</u> do this quickly because, unless training is arranged with immediate effect, some projects will probably suffer. If this happened, it would be a disaster for the company. <u>Our recommendation would be to organise a course for the staff immediately.</u> <u>Another suggestion is to visit the other countries.</u> If team members visited other members in their own countries, they would get to know each other better and develop better working relationships.

Functional language

Students look at useful phrases for giving advice and making suggestions and recommendations in different registers.

2 Ask students to complete the table using the report in Exercise 1 to help them if necessary. Check answers with the class and go through the phrases in the table with them. Check that students understand the phrases and pay attention to register: point out to students that we use different registers for different types of writing – just as we speak differently to different people – depending on the situation, context and reader. Refer students to the three headings in the table and ask them when we might use each register (e.g. formal: in a report or letter of complaint; neutral: when presenting facts, e.g. in a review or article; informal: in an email to a colleague we know well).

1 advisable **2** would **3** obvious **4** suggest **5** ought

Extra activities 7.5

A Depending on your students' needs, ask them to do this exercise individually or in pairs. Check answers with the class and clarify any errors as necessary.

1 to seek **2** listen **3** you reduce **4** is to build
5 the company recruits more staff **6** were
7 finding **8** be to update **9** could do **10** have

Optional grammar work

The report in Exercise 1 contains examples of the first and second conditionals, so you could use it for some optional grammar work. Refer students to the Grammar reference on page 124 and use the exercises in MyEnglishLab for extra grammar practice.

Task

Students practise checking written work by proofreading an email and write a report.

3A Put students in pairs, refer them to the email on page 131 and explain the activity. Stronger students could do this individually. You may wish to do an example with the class first.

> Hi Josh
> I've just ~~get~~ **got** your email about the supplier problem. Have you tried ~~talk~~ **talking** to Salvador Greco, the boss, about the delivery problems? You ~~ought~~ **should / ought to** speak to him immediately. However, make sure that you aren't too direct about the business. He'll probably ~~will~~ ask about general things first. He'll think ~~your~~ **you're** rude if you start with the business chat immediately. Unfortunately, ~~unless~~ **if** the problem continues, you will have to find a new supplier. We ~~don't~~ **can't** afford to delay production anymore. You'd better ~~to~~ start looking for alternative suppliers if you can't speak to Salvador.

3B Ask students to turn to page 129 and give them time to read the notes. Explain the task and let students ask you any questions they may have. Tell them that they can use the model answer in Exercise 1 to help them, and that they should include formal phrases from the table in Exercise 2 in their report. If time is short, students can write their reports for homework.

> **Model answer**
> **Cross-cultural project teams**
> There have been several problems recently with our cross-cultural teams. It seems that some of the team members are not getting on with each other and this is causing serious delays and misunderstandings.
> Firstly, the most important thing to do would be to get feedback from every team member, focusing on both the strengths and the weaknesses of their teams. I would then advise the company to provide training for all project team members immediately. If possible, the company should also try to arrange for team members to meet face-to-face so that they can get to know each other better and understand their different cultures. If it becomes apparent that there are still problems, then one thing which could be done is to move team members from one team to another. However, it is hoped that this will not be necessary.
> In conclusion, I would strongly recommend that you organise training for current team members and also for anyone else who may be involved in cross-cultural working in the future.

3C If students write their reports for homework, you could do this exercise in the next lesson. Put them in pairs and ask them to read each other's reports and think about the phrases from Exercise 2: How many did they use? Did they use them correctly? Did they use the right register? Could they add any more? Students could then rewrite their reports, taking in their partner's feedback.

MyEnglishLab: Teacher's resources: extra activities; Interactive grammar practice; Writing bank
Grammar reference: p.124 First and second conditional
Workbook: p.38 Exercises 1–3

Business workshop ❯7
Cross-cultural consultants

> **GSE learning objectives**
> - Can identify key information in an extended text or article.
> - Can recognise when examples are being given in a structured presentation on an unfamiliar topic.
> - Can summarise and give opinions on issues and stories, and answer questions in detail.
> - Can express their thoughts in some detail on cultural topics (e.g. music, films).
> - Can write an email giving details of work-related events, facts or plans.

Background

Students read about Betker Finance, a multinational looking for cross-cultural training for their employees, and Connecting Cultures, a consultancy offering this type of training.

1 Put students in pairs and give them time to read the background and discuss the questions. Check answers with the class and clarify any unknown vocabulary.

> 1 Connecting Cultures offers cross-cultural training for businesses.
> 2 Dutch employees often go on business trips and have meetings with colleagues and sales staff from around the world, including Europe, Japan, India and Brazil.
> 3 International employees say some managers are not familiar with working practices in different cultures and often come across as very direct, even impolite. (Dutch managers have also requested cultural training to improve their communication and understanding of international markets.)
> 4 If the course is successful, Betker Finance will offer similar cultural training to all its employees (i.e. more business for Connecting Cultures).

Company blog

Students read a company blog on cultural awareness.

2A Explain that students are going to read an extract from a blog post on the Connecting Cultures website. Remind them of the services the company offers, and ask them to look at the heading and the image on the left and make some predictions about the content (e.g. local business culture compared with business culture in another country, information about the courses Connecting Cultures offers, different attitudes to time). Give students time to read the text to check their predictions and answer the questions – they could do this individually or in pairs. Check answers with the class.

> 1 No, it's 'the way we do things around here. This is true for a region, a community, business sector or any organisation', not just a nationality.
> 2 It can differ in areas such as being direct or attitudes to time.
> 3 No. 'An individual may not share the same characteristics as the "national" character. We should NEVER fall into the trap of stereotyping people.'
> 4 Students' own answers

2B Put students in groups of three and assign A, B and C roles. Explain that there are three more parts to the blog post and students are going to read a different part each. Refer students to the their part of the blog post and explain the activity. Encourage them to make notes. During the information exchange, walk round the class and make sure students have understood the blog post and can communicate the ideas clearly. Give assistance as necessary. When groups have finished, check answers with the class and list the five topics on the board for students to refer to during Exercise 2C.

> The following topics are mentioned:
> Student A reads about 1) time; Student B reads about 2) directness vs. indirectness and 3) individualism vs. collectivism; Student C reads about 4) linear-active, multi-active or reactive cultures and 5) authority and hierarchy.

2C Refer students to the list of topics on the board and ask them to discuss the question. They could do this in their groups first and then as a class. Encourage them to give concrete examples for each topic in their own culture, e.g. *I usually arrive on time for meetings/classes. Being even a few minutes late would be embarrassing.*

Extra activities Business workshop 7

A This activity provides students with extra reading practice. Give them time to read the statements first, so they know what they need to look for in the texts. They could do the exercise individually or, in weaker classes, you could let them work in pairs. Encourage students to underline the parts of the texts that contain the answers.

1 T
2 F (In Southern Europe, Latin America and the Middle East, relationships and the meeting are what count, and schedules are less relevant. Time is flexible because of the business relationship.)
3 T
4 F ('Being direct is a concept that is often admired in cultures such as the USA and parts of Europe, but not necessarily in the UK.')
5 F ('The concept of being (in)direct can also cause friction in business. Remember, not everyone believes you should "say what you mean".')
6 T
7 T
8 T
9 F ('Reactive' cultures are those that value respect and courtesy, as reflected in most Asian cultures. … in China the most important or senior person is treated with a great deal of respect …')
10 F ('Anglo–American countries and the Netherlands tend to be less formal … These cultures will also have companies with flatter and less hierarchical organisational structures.')

What international colleagues say

Students listen to interviews with international staff from Betker Finance.

3A ◀) BW 7.01 Explain the situation and activity to the class. Play the recording, twice if necessary, then check answers with the class.

> **Speaker 1:** c, a, d
> **Speaker 2:** b, e, f, g

3B ◀) BW 7.02 Explain the activity and give students time to read the notes. Point out that students should listen for six mistakes in each summary. Play the recording, twice if necessary, and get students to compare answers in pairs before checking with the class.

> Speaker 3 says the manager seemed very ~~indirect~~ **direct/ abrupt**. She says it's good to have ~~an agenda~~ **a purpose** to a meeting, but in their culture, they always make ~~coffee~~ **conversation / small talk** before getting down to business. It's important to get ~~the number of~~ **to know** the other person to establish a ~~conflictive~~ **good/positive/relaxed** atmosphere and they like to do business with people they ~~don't~~ like.
> Speaker 4 thinks the Dutch sales representative ~~didn't talk~~ **talked** a lot and didn't understand ~~Japanese~~ **their market**. The visitor thought they had finished the ~~meal~~ **meeting**, when they had only started! The sales rep seemed a little ~~emotional~~ **annoyed** when he said he would check with his boss. He was surprised that she quickly confirmed points that they ~~had~~ **hadn't** agreed on. Hopefully, the next meeting will be more ~~musical~~ **harmonious**.

3C Put students in pairs and give them 2–3 minutes to discuss the question. Then invite different students to share their ideas with the class.

Possible answers

Speaker 1: Making small talk and getting to know a business partner is very important in business in multi-active cultures, e.g. Indians will also ask quite direct questions about your family and marital status. Business relationships are built on trust and business visitors should be aware that family members often work together in countries like India and China. To avoid misunderstandings, it is rude to say 'no'. For example, certain cultures will not turn down a request at the risk of offending the other person – this would cause embarrassment or 'loss of face'.

Speaker 2: In order to have successful business relationships, be aware that face-to-face meetings are preferred in multi-active cultures. These cultures are usually not very punctual but there are individuals and regions that are exceptions, e.g. punctuality is admired in the north of Italy. In addition, multi-active cultures such as the Italian one give a lot of importance to first impressions, although this is also true of many business cultures.

Speaker 3: In linear-active cultures like the American one or even in the Netherlands, Switzerland, Austria and Germany, people prefer to get straight down to business without making small talk. However, in multi-active cultures, like Brazil, Argentina or Saudi Arabia, people prefer to get to know their business partner before talking business. To avoid misunderstandings, it would be best to check these preferences before meetings and trips.

Speaker 4: Reactive and linear cultures have very different attitudes to time. A reactive culture like the Japanese one would expect a business deal to consist of various meetings or negotiations before making a final decision. Reactive cultures place a lot of emphasis on authority and will not make individual decisions before consulting a superior. In addition, the collective, or group, has more importance than the individual. They are very used to working in teams and will take decisions as a team, so it's important to make sure that you are talking to the right person, that is, the decision-maker in a meeting. Asian cultures will say 'yes' to confirm they are listening, not that they have agreed. In a meeting, they prefer to listen rather than talk. So, in order to avoid misunderstanding, it's very important to check understanding during and at the end of a meeting or phone call, for example, using open questions, rather than closed questions.

Extra activities Business workshop 7

B ◀) BW 7.01 ◀) BW 7.02 This activity provides students with extra listening practice. Give them time to read the summaries and play the recording. To help them, you could tell them that they need one or two words for each gap. If time allows, get them to check answers in pairs, using the audioscripts on page 153.

Speaker 1
1 traditions 2 food 3 big family 4 trust
5 no problem 6 saying 'no'
Speaker 2
1 face-to-face 2 multi-tasking 3 Europeans
4 one thing 5 interruptions 6 first impression
Speaker 3
1 Sales Manager 2 headquarters
3 direct and abrupt 4 get to know 5 interests
6 getting down
Speaker 4
1 Japanese 2 many questions 3 approval
4 boss 5 email 6 agreed

Task

Students present a recommendation for working in their culture and then write a formal email confirming the outcome of their presentations.

4A Put students in pairs or small groups. Explain that students are consultants, and go through the instructions and questions with them. Explain the task and point out that students need to refer to all four parts of the blog post (pages 100, 136, 131 and 135) and the audioscripts for the interviews (page 153). Make sure students understand what they need to do, and answer any questions they may have. Set a time limit and encourage students to make notes – explain that they will need to present their ideas later, so they need to make clear notes to refer to. Go round monitoring and providing help as necessary. If your students have online access, you could let them research any questions they need more information about.

4B Pairs/Groups now take turns to present their recommendations. Ask the rest of the class to listen and ask questions at the end.

4C As a class, students decide which group would be the best to work with Betker Finance, giving reasons. You may wish to ask students to take notes, which they could use to plan their email in the next exercise.

5 Students now write an email to the director of Betker Finance, explaining their choice. They could do this in class or for homework. Point out the word limit and remind students to plan their email carefully, organise it into clear paragraphs and use appropriate *formal* language.

MyEnglishLab: Teacher's resources: extra activities

Review ◀ 7

1 1 fluent 2 be put off 3 come across 4 tend to
    5 common 6 alone
2 1 unsociable 2 unfriendly 3 disrespectful
    4 dishonest 5 informal 6 unhelpful
3 1 was working 2 made 3 involved
    4 (had) recruited 5 prepared 6 insisted 7 resigned
    8 returned 9 had warned 10 hadn't listened
    11 hadn't been able / wasn't able / weren't able
    12 couldn't
4 1 I'd cancel the meeting 2 We don't mind
    3 I'd prefer it if 4 not pay in advance
    5 The boss isn't keen 6 to change the design
5 1 a 2 j 3 g 4 d 5 l 6 k 7 f 8 b 9 i 10 h
    11 c 12 e
6 1 obvious 2 recommend 3 advisable 4 advice
    5 were 6 ought

8 > Leadership

Unit overview

	CLASSWORK		FURTHER WORK
8.1 > **Learning to lead**	**Lead-in**	Students discuss their views on leadership.	**MyEnglishLab:** Teacher's resources: extra activities; Reading bank
	Video	Students watch a video about a TV show called *Safari Vet School*, where trainee vets test and develop their leadership skills.	**Pronunciation bank:** p.117 Glottal stops
	Vocabulary	Students look at common verb + noun collocations related to work and leadership.	**Teacher's book:** Resource bank Photocopiable 8.1 p.150
	Project	Students research and talk about great leaders and then write an article about one.	**Workbook:** p.39 Exercises 1–3
8.2 > **Neuroleadership**	**Lead-in**	Students look at some useful vocabulary related to work and leadership.	**MyEnglishLab:** Teacher's resources: extra activities
	Reading	Students read an article about neuroleadership.	**Pronunciation bank:** p.117 Phrasing and intonation in relative clauses
	Grammar	Students study and practise defining and non-defining relative clauses.	**Grammar reference:** p.125 Relative clauses
	Speaking	Students talk about themselves and their lives using relative clauses.	**Teacher's book:** Resource bank Photocopiable 8.2 p.151
			Workbook: p.40 Exercises 1–3, p.41 Exercises 1 and 2
8.3 > **Communication skills:** Giving and receiving feedback	**Lead-in**	Students discuss the importance of feedback.	**MyEnglishLab:** Teacher's resources: extra activities; Interactive video activities
	Video	Students watch a video about different approaches to feedback and points to keep in mind when giving and receiving feedback.	**Workbook:** p.42 Exercise 1
	Reflection	Students reflect on the main points and conclusions from the video and discuss their own approach to feedback.	
	Functional language	Students look at useful language for giving and responding to feedback.	
	Task	Students practise giving and responding to developmental feedback by roleplaying different situations.	
8.4 > **Business skills:** Leading meetings	**Lead-in**	Students discuss different aspects of meetings.	**MyEnglishLab:** Teacher's resources: extra activities; Functional language bank
	Listening	Students listen to a meeting and think about strategies for managing and leading meetings.	**Workbook:** p.42 Exercise 2
	Functional language	Students look at useful language for leading and managing meetings.	
	Task	Students hold mini-meetings in groups, taking turns to lead.	
8.5 > **Writing:** Informing of a decision	**Lead-in**	Students read a model answer and practise checking written work for spelling mistakes.	**MyEnglishLab:** Teacher's resources: extra activities; Interactive grammar practice; Writing bank
	Functional language	Students look at useful phrases for business emails informing of decisions.	**Grammar reference:** p.125 Reduced relative clauses
	Task	Students write an email informing of decisions.	**Workbook:** p.43 Exercises 1 and 2
Business workshop 8 > Talent management	**Listening**	Students listen to employees talking about their training needs.	**MyEnglishLab:** Teacher's resources: extra activities
	Reading	Students read five training course descriptions.	
	Task	Students design a development plan for an employee.	
	Writing	Students write a formal email justifying their need for training.	

Business brief	The main aim of this unit is to introduce students to concepts related to **leadership**.

There are many types of leader – from the commander of a large army to the leader of a small project team – and there are many theories about what qualities a leader needs and what sort of person has the potential to become a leader. All leaders need **intelligence**, motivation and **self-belief**, and the ability to communicate their **vision** to their team, group or country. Many leaders also possess **people skills** or **charisma** – an ability to attract and influence other people by the force of their personality. These characteristics can be used for positive aims but they can also have a negative influence.

One definition of a leader is 'a person who can consistently succeed and meet the expectations of an organisation or society'. In the case of a CEO (Chief Executive Officer) of a large company, for example, they are judged by their **performance** in strategic and financial terms – does the company achieve its aims and does it make a sufficient profit? In the case of a President or Prime Minister, can they provide the conditions for a stable economy and a safe society? In more extreme cases this type of leader may show 'autocratic' tendencies, i.e. use their **authority** and power to manipulate people. In some cases, they may have a lack of **empathy** (ability to understand other people's feelings or point of view).

Leaders must be able to visualise an **end goal** and have the **knowledge** and **confidence** to achieve that goal. Some leaders, in contrast to the autocratic type of leader, create a **democratic**, shared sense of purpose, and act in the best interest of others rather than themselves or an impersonal corporate goal. They discuss decisions with their team and **delegate** roles and **responsibilities** according to other's abilities. They **support** their staff and make sure the group has what they need to do the job. They empathise with the individuals in their team and recognise ability and achievement. They are also aware of the benefits of **rewarding** effort and success – praise, promotion or financial reward. They are honest about their own weaknesses and do not hide problems but share them and **motivate** others to **find solutions**.

There is debate about whether leaders are born or made. There are examples where individuals possess **innate qualities** of leadership, such as Nelson Mandela. A person's **family background**, **education** and **life experience** almost certainly make a difference. Power may be inherited, e.g. the Kennedy and the Bush families in the USA, but power does not necessarily equal leadership. Some people are put into positions where they have to lead, e.g. management positions, but they may not naturally be leaders and require **training**. It appears that everyone has a **natural limit** in terms of their ability to manage at a certain level as described by the **Peter Principle** – this suggests that people can lead competently until they are promoted beyond a certain level after which they become ineffective.

There is ongoing debate about gender and leadership. It is only relatively recently that men and women have been viewed equally as potential leaders and the number of female leaders in politics and business has grown significantly.

Leadership and your students	Students who are not yet working need to be aware of the concept of leadership and know some examples of key leaders in their various fields. Working students should be more aware of leadership as they may be asked at some point in their careers to lead teams and take managerial responsibility.

Unit lead-in

Elicit a brief description of the photo and ask students how they think it might be related to the unit title, *Leadership*. Look at the quote with students and check that they understand *legacy* and *inspire*. Students could then discuss the quote in pairs, small groups or as a whole class: Do they agree with the quote? What else do they think makes an 'excellent leader'?

8.1 ❯ Learning to lead

GSE learning objectives

- Can give or seek personal views and opinions in discussing topics of interest.
- Can understand a large part of many TV programmes on familiar topics.
- Can extract specific details from a TV programme on a business-related topic.
- Can use language related to politicians and leaders.
- Can express their opinions in discussions on contemporary social issues and current affairs.
- Can write short, simple biographies about real or imaginary people.

Warm-up

Ask the class to think of five famous leaders in history. Encourage them to think of examples from as many countries and periods in history as possible. Elicit suggestions from different students and write them on the board. Discuss with the class what the leaders achieved, e.g. military success (Julius Caesar), political and social success (Nelson Mandela), business success (Steve Jobs). Ask the class what sort of characteristics these leaders had and whether they had anything in common.

Lead-in

Students discuss their views on leadership.

1A You could ask students to discuss the comments in pairs first, and then broaden this into a class discussion. For question 2, encourage students to think about a variety of areas such as business, politics, social issues, science, the arts and whether leaders in these areas have similar or different characteristics (e.g. Pablo Picasso was a leader in terms of having strong original ideas and creating new genres of art, but did he have anything in common with other leaders at the time?).

Notes

1 The 'great man theory' assumes that leaders are 'born, not made', i.e. they have an innate combination of ability and personal characteristics. Students might want to explore the nineteenth-century great man theory some more, and reflect on how history is taught. More recent theories argue that leadership is not 'a gene' that only a special class of charismatic men and women possess.

2 The core ingredients of leadership may be universal, e.g. good judgement, integrity and people skills. There may also be cultural elements in successful leadership style.

3 A popular answer is that leaders have people who follow them while managers have people who work for them. Many people find themselves promoted into management roles and then have to learn to lead in order to get the team to follow them and share their vision of success.

1B Put students in groups and give them 2–4 minutes to discuss the question, then get brief feedback from the class. Encourage students to explain their answers.

> **Possible answers**
> good judgement, integrity, people skills, good communication skills

Video

Students watch a video about a TV show called *Safari Vet School*, where trainee vets test and develop their leadership skills.

2 Do this exercise as a whole class, eliciting ideas from different students.

3 ▶ 8.1.1   Go through the table with students before they watch the video. After watching, get students to compare answers in pairs before checking with the class.

> **2** (16) veterinary students
> **3** to test their leadership abilities (in real-life situations)
> **4** She is team leader.
> **5** He supervises Nadia and is her mentor.

4 Give students time to read the statements and check that they understand *intimidated*. Play the video, then check answers with the class. In weaker classes, you may need to play it a second time for students to correct the false statements. If time allows, you could check answers by replaying the video, telling students to ask you to pause each time an answer is heard.

> **1** F (They travel to South Africa for the show.)
> **2** F (She admits people can be quite intimidated by her.)
> **3** T
> **4** F (He was unhappy because they took a long time (15 minutes) to complete the task.)
> **5** T
> **6** F (He said she never asked the team for their opinion about what they should do.)

5 Put students in pairs or small groups and give them 3–5 minutes to discuss the questions, then discuss the answers as a class.

Possible answers
1 She has a strong personality, is a high achiever and seems confident, which are useful qualities for a leader. However, she is loud and recognises she intimidates people, so she might not be well liked by her future staff. She likes to be in control, which could make her an autocratic leader who micro-manages her staff.
2 These questions are debatable. One of the students themselves said that 'We needed just one person to (like kind of) control the operation.'
3 It's good to ask questions all the time in order to get feedback from staff on how their work is going. It's also vital to ask questions when you are looking for solutions to problems or trying to make improvements. A good leader knows how to ask the right questions. The leader needs to take control in an emergency, if a quick decision is needed, or if there are vast differences of interests and opinions, if there are employees not doing their job well or bullying other staff.
4 It is entertainment in that there is drama and wildlife. It is educational in the sense that viewers can reflect with the contestants on their leadership abilities and hear Steve's advice.

Extra activities 8.1

A ▶ 8.1.1 With weaker classes, it might be better to allow students to work in pairs for this activity. Stronger students can work individually and then check answers in pairs before class feedback.

1 P 2 P 3 N 4 PM 5 N 6 S 7 N 8 S 9 P

B Students could do this individually or in pairs, using their dictionaries if necessary.

a in your face b the whole point c tough d range
e got a taste of f chatter g high achiever
h advice i comfort zone

❯ **Pronunciation bank**
p.117: Glottal stops

Warm-up
Explain that glottal stops are a feature of some people's accent or speech. Go through the explanation in the box with students and then give them an example: write *got* on the board. Say the word with a strong /t/ sound (with your tongue touching your alveolar ridge, i.e. palate behind your upper teeth) and again with a glottal stop (with your tongue further back in your mouth). Tell students that they do not need to use glottal stops, but they are important for listening because they can make words more difficult to identify.

1 🔊 P8.01 Play the recording and ask students to notice the difference between the two versions of the exchange.

2 🔊 P8.02 Explain the activity and play the recording, twice if necessary, for students to identify the glottal stops. Check answers with the class.

1 Grea**t** leaders are born no**t** made.
2 Nobody really agrees abou**t** wha**t** the characteristics of a grea**t** leader are.
3 We forgo**t** the whole poin**t** was just to get i**t** on the truck.

3 Put students in pairs and explain the activity: they should take turns to say the sentences in Exercise 2 either with the strong /t/ sound or a glottal stop. Their partner should identify the sound used each time. You may want to do an example with a stronger student first: say one of the sentences yourself and ask the student to identify the sound you used.

Vocabulary: Leadership

Students look at common verb + noun collocations related to work and leadership.

6 You could do this exercise a whole class, checking answers as you go, or ask students to do it individually and compare their answers in pairs before checking with the class. Encourage students to record the collocations in their vocabulary notebooks.

1 d (delegate tasks) 2 c (run a team)
3 a (make (key) decisions) 4 b (take on responsibility)

7 Explain the activity and do the first item as an example with the class. Allow students to use their dictionaries if necessary and get them to compare answers in pairs before checking with the class.

1 delegate 2 prioritise 3 trust 4 set 5 run 6 trust
7 cope with 8 win

8 Weaker students could do this exercise in pairs. Encourage them to use their dictionaries to check new words and/or whether a noun collocates with a verb. Explain that the verb must collocate with all the nouns in a group.

1 c 2 f 3 a 4 d 5 b 6 e

9 Put students in pairs and give them 3–4 minutes to discuss the questions. Encourage them to give examples from their personal experience where possible. When the pairs have finished, get brief feedback from the class.

Extra activities 8.1

C This activity gives further practice in verb + noun collocations from the Vocabulary section. Explain that each word/phrase from the box must fit *both* sentences in each pair and point out that students may need to change the form of some verbs. Check answers with the class.

1 **a** Making **b** made
2 **a** gave **b** giving
3 **a** running **b** ran
4 **a** coping with **b** to cope with
5 **a** trust **b** trusted
6 **a** Setting **b** set

Project: Great leaders

Students research and talk about great leaders and then write an article about one.

10A Put students in pairs or small groups. Give them a minute to read the instructions, then go through them with the class. Clarify that students need to work individually for the first two steps, then share and discuss their ideas with their group. If your students have access to the internet, encourage them to research their chosen leaders online. Otherwise, make sure students choose two or three people they know well enough to say what makes them good leaders. Set a time limit for the first two steps. When that time is up, set a time limit for the next two steps, with students working in their groups. Monitor and provide help if needed.

10B Go through the instructions with the class and give students a minute to think about which leader they are going to write about. You could pair up students who choose the same leader and let them research and brainstorm ideas together. If your students do not have online access, it might be better to set this exercise for homework, so students can do their research before they write their article. Highlight the word limit and remind students to plan their article carefully and organise it into clear paragraphs.

Model answer

I think country and western singer Dolly Parton is a great leader in her profession. She was born in Tennessee in 1946. She grew up in a big family and started performing and writing her own songs at an early age. Many of her songs, like *Jolene* and *I Will Always Love You*, are classics. Parton is also a successful businesswoman. Her multimillion-dollar business empire includes the Dollywood theme park in her hometown, which has created jobs for the community. She also owns restaurants, radio stations and publishing companies. She attributes her business sense to her father, a farmer, and her creativity to her mother. I admire her because she's a talented, hard-working woman with a great sense of humour.

MyEnglishLab: Teacher's resources: extra activities; Reading bank
Pronunciation bank: p.117 Glottal stops
Teacher's book: Resource bank Photocopiable 8.1 p.150
Workbook: p.39 Exercises 1–3

8.2 > Neuroleadership

GSE learning objectives

- Can guess the meaning of an unfamiliar word from context.
- Can give or seek personal views and opinions in discussing topics of interest.
- Can extract key details from an article on a business-related topic.
- Can make simple inferences based on information given in a short article.
- Can skim a simple text to identify key concepts.
- Can recognise significant points and arguments in straightforward newspaper articles on familiar topics.
- Can correctly use defining (restrictive) and non-defining (non-restrictive) relative clauses.
- Can take part in routine formal discussions conducted in clear standard speech in which factual information is exchanged.

Warm-up

Write the following quote on the board: *'Great leaders don't blame the tools they are given. Great leaders work to sharpen them.' Simon Sinek, author and motivational speaker.* Discuss it as a whole class. Ask students if they agree with the quote and what 'tools' it might be referring to. Do students think a person's brain is a 'tool' that can be 'sharpened' to make a great leader?

Lead-in

Students look at some useful vocabulary related to work and leadership.

1 You may want to do the first item as an example with the class. Elicit from students the key words in the sentence which could help them work out the meaning of *behaviour* (*good* and *reward*). Ask them what they think the word means. Then refer them to page 129 and ask them to choose the correct definition of *behaviour*. Students can complete the rest of the exercise individually or in pairs. Encourage stronger students to try and work out the meaning of the words without looking at the definitions. Check answers with the class, eliciting from students which words from each sentence helped them work out the meaning of the word in bold.

1 f 2 a 3 e 4 b 5 d 6 c

2 Put students in pairs or small groups and give them 3–4 minutes to discuss the questions. Get brief feedback from the class.

Reading

Students read an article about neuroleadership.

3A Read the question, refer students to the article headline and check that they understand *neuroscience*. Discuss the question as a class.

3B Explain the activity and go through options a–c with students. Check that they understand *in principle, unethical* and *mindset* before they read the text. Give students 2–3 minutes for the activity and explain that they only need to read the text quickly at this point – they should not read in detail. Check the answer with the class.

> **a**

4 Explain that students will now need to read the text in more detail in order to answer the questions. Ask them to work individually and get them to compare answers in pairs before class feedback.

> 1 They are excited and keen to find out more.
> 2 That managers were all the same (interchangeable) and then later studies suggested that different managers' personalities and mindsets had different impacts on an organisation.
> 3 Neuroscience research has the potential to help companies and managers change their personalities and mindsets through new training and development courses.
> 4 frugal, selfish, altruistic, unscrupulous, risk-averse, entrepreneurial
> 5 Because it could be used for unethical reasons, e.g. bad or short-term goals.
> 6 motivation, will, years of practice (time), reflection, feedback

Extra activities 8.2

A This activity looks at useful vocabulary from the reading text. You could go through the words in the box with students before they do the activity or let them check any unknown words in their dictionaries. Check answers with the class, clarifying meanings as necessary.

> 1 appoint 2 work out 3 open up
> 4 take as a given 5 reliable 6 extrapolate
> 7 successor 8 pursue

Grammar
Relative clauses

Students study and practise defining and non-defining relative clauses.

5A Ask students to read the information about relative clauses. To help them, explain that with non-defining relative clauses, the sentence would still make sense if we took out the relative clause. Defining relative clauses give essential information – the sentence wouldn't make sense without the relative clause. Refer students to the underlined relative clauses in the article and do the exercise as a class, checking answers as you go.

> 1 non-defining 2 non-defining 3 defining 4 defining

5B Again, do this exercise as a whole class, checking and explaining answers as you go. Then refer students to the Grammar reference on page 125, give them time to go through the explanations and examples (or go through them as a class), and clarify any points as necessary.

> 1 which 2 who 3 which 4 that
> Other common relative pronouns: *when, where, whose* (also *whom*, though this is not covered at B1+ level)

> ❯ **Pronunciation bank**
> **p.117: Phrasing and intonation in relative clauses**
>
> ### Warm-up
> Go through the explanation in the box with students and give them an example of each type of relative clause. Write the following sentences on the board: *The product, which came out ten years ago, made them famous. This is the product that made them famous.* Model the pronunciation of both sentences, using pauses and a lower pitch for the non-defining relative clause.

1 🔊 P8.03 Play the recording for students to identify the types of relative clause. Ask students what the differences in phrasing and intonation are between the two sentences (the lower pitch for the non-defining relative clause and the two pauses before and after it).

> 1 non-defining 2 defining

2/3 🔊 P8.04 Play the recording and get students to repeat the sentences, chorally first, then individually. Then put students in pairs to practise saying the sentences.

6A This exercise can be done individually or in pairs. Check answers with the class, clarifying any errors as necessary.

> 1 who/that 2 whose 3 which/that 4 when
> 5 which/that 6 who/that 7 where 8 who/that

6B This is a tricky question, so give students time to work out the answer and remind them to refer to the Grammar reference on page 125 if they need help. In weaker classes, you could allow students to work in pairs.

> It is possible to omit the relative pronoun in sentences 3, 4, 6 and 8.
> In a **defining relative clause**, when the relative pronoun refers to the **object of the verb**, we can omit it. However, we cannot omit the relative pronoun in a defining relative clause when it refers to the subject of the verb (as in sentences 1 and 5). Nor can we leave out the pronoun in a non-defining relative clause.

7A/B Look at the example with the class and ask students to work individually. Get them to compare answers in pairs before class feedback. Do Exercise 7B as you check each answer: for each sentence, ask: *Do we need to use commas with the relative clause? Can the relative pronoun be omitted?*

7A
1 The workshop (which/that) she planned to attend was cancelled at the last minute.
2 Leading a team, which I wouldn't like to do, must be very difficult.
3 The university where I studied has a course on neuroleadership.
4 Her book, which was published last year, instantly became a bestseller.
5 The restaurant (where) we often go for lunch has a good selection of desserts. / The restaurant we often go to for lunch has a good selection of desserts.
6 London, which is the capital of the UK, is an expensive city.

7B
1 There are no commas because this is a defining relative clause; you can omit the relative pronoun *which/that* because it refers to the object of the verb.
2 We use commas before and after this non-defining relative clause.
3 There are no commas because this is a defining relative clause.
4 We use commas before and after this non-defining relative clause.
5 There are no commas because this is a defining relative clause; you can omit the relative pronoun *where* because it refers to the object of the verb.
6 We use commas before and after this non-defining relative clause.

Extra activities 8.2

B Students should be able to do this exercise individually by now, but you may wish to allow weaker students to work in pairs. Remind them that if they need help, they can refer to the Grammar reference on page 125. Check answers with the class.

1 who/that 2 which/that 3 which 4 who
5 who/that 6 where 7 when 8 whose
9 which/that 10 who
It is possible to omit the relative pronoun in sentences 2, 5, 7 and 9 because it refers to the object of the verb.

Speaking

Students talk about themselves and their lives using relative clauses.

8A Explain the activity, go through the examples with students and give them time to write their sentences. Monitor and make sure their sentences are grammatically correct.

8B Put students in pairs, explain the activity and look at the example questions with the class. You may also wish to demonstrate the activity with a stronger student. Monitor and make a note of any errors in the use of relative clauses to highlight during feedback.

MyEnglishLab: Teacher's resources: extra activities
Pronunciation bank: p.117 Phrasing and intonation in relative clauses
Grammar reference: p.125 Relative clauses
Teacher's book: Resource bank Photocopiable 8.2 p.151
Workbook: p.40 Exercises 1–3, p.41 Exercises 1 and 2

8.3 〉 Communication skills
Giving and receiving feedback

GSE learning objectives

- Can express and comment on ideas and suggestions in informal discussions.
- Can understand the main points of feedback from clients and colleagues if delivered slowly and clearly.
- Can understand feedback about performance.

Warm-up

Ask students in what situations they have given and received feedback, and who to/from (e.g. in their English course, to/from a classmate; at work, to a colleague / from a manager; at college, to/from a fellow student). Ask students how they feel about giving and receiving feedback. Is it important to them? Do they think receiving feedback really helps them improve? Are they comfortable giving feedback to others?

Lead-in

Students discuss the importance of feedback.

1 Put students in pairs to discuss the questions. If time allows, join pairs together into groups of four to further discuss their ideas. Invite different students to share their views with the class.

1 Students' own answer
2 Possible answer: Feedback is important in business because without it, we don't know what we are doing well or where we can improve. So the risk is that we might become demotivated if we are not aware of success and positive elements of our work. Conversely, if we are not hearing feedback about how we can develop, we may then develop at a slower pace or not at all – this can also be detrimental to the organisation.

Video

Students watch a video about different approaches to feedback and points to keep in mind when giving and receiving feedback.

2 ▶ 8.3.1 If students watched the videos from the previous units, ask them for a short summary of the situation so far. If this is the first communication skills video for your students, briefly explain the situation yourself. Play the video, twice if necessary, then check answers with the class. Check that students understand *developmental feedback*.

Matt is hoping to get some positive feedback which will confirm what he did well and that he was successful in his role. He's also interested in getting some developmental feedback about things the team think he could improve on.

3A Put students in small groups and go through the instructions and details of Options A and B with them. Give groups 2–3 minutes to discuss and decide on the best approach for giving feedback to a manager. Make it clear to students that they can choose which option they want to see first on the video. Elicit ideas from a few students and then, as a class, decide which video to watch first.

3B ▶ 8.3.2 ▶ 8.3.3 Give students time to read the questions for Option A or Option B, depending on their choice. Play the video and get students to compare answers in pairs before class feedback. Do the same for the second video. If necessary, let students watch either or both of the videos a second time in order to complete their answers. For both options, ask students what they thought of Matt's response (question 2).

Option A
1 He did a good job communicating with the team and keeping them informed. He asked Stefanie to help out Kenji when he had some difficulties. He gave Paula some coaching and some tips for presentations.
2 He reacts positively and is motivated.
3 There is a positive atmosphere, Matt feels validated and motivated. However, the exchange of looks at the end indicates that the team had more to say. They may have started with positive comments before going on to make developmental comments. They don't get the chance to make these comments as Matt takes the positive feedback to mean that there are no issues to discuss.

Option B
1 He could have had some individual calls with each team member before the project kicked off, so that everyone had a clear idea of their role. He shouldn't have waited until things were urgent before passing them on to others. He should communicate a timeline in future so that people can plan their workload more effectively.
2 He reacts defensively. He may feel the feedback is only negative and might struggle to maintain motivation if there isn't anything positive.
3 The team members each have an opportunity to give their developmental comments. However, the focus of what each person says is on 'what didn't work' rather than specifics of 'what could be done better next time', and the comments are not balanced with positive comments. As a result, Matt feels defensive and there is a tense atmosphere by the end. This may make it more difficult to work together again in the future.

3C Put students in pairs and give them plenty of time to discuss their answers. Get feedback from the class and list students' ideas on the board.

4 ▶ 8.3.4 Play the video for students to make notes in the table. Check answers with the class before students discuss the question. If time allows, get students to discuss their views in pairs first, then broaden this into a class discussion.

Giving feedback
1 Motivate people by focusing on things which have been done well.
2 Help people improve by focusing on areas in which they can develop.

Receiving feedback
1 Feedback is valuable. Actively ask for it.
2 Listen to feedback first without disagreeing or making excuses about potentially negative points. Then decide later if you want to act on it.

Overall conclusion
Use a balanced approach of both positive and developmental feedback. Positive feedback reaffirms someone's actions and position and is good for their motivation, though without developmental feedback they may not be aware of any areas in which they can improve.

Reflection
Students reflect on the main points and conclusions from the video and discuss their own approach to feedback.

5 Allow students to work individually first so that they can reflect on their own preferred approach to feedback. Then put them in pairs to discuss their answers. As feedback, elicit ideas from different students for each question, and encourage brief class discussion.

Functional language
Giving and responding to feedback

Students look at useful language for giving and responding to feedback.

6 Ask students to look at the table. They should know *developmental* by now, so ask them why they think this word is used instead of *negative* (*feedback*). It is important to get across that feedback should be useful and not critical, even though weaknesses need to be addressed. Get students to do the exercise individually and then compare answers in pairs before class feedback.

Positive feedback: 1, 4
Developmental feedback: 2, 3, 5, 6, 7

7 Give students time to go through the phrases in the table, then do the exercise as a whole class.

1 Thank   2 Explore   3 Respond and reflect

8A Explain the activity and go through the situations with the class. Check that students understand *contribute* and *dominate*. Check that they understand the activity by asking which type of feedback they will use (all three situations require developmental feedback). Give students a few minutes to think of what they would say. Encourage them to use phrases from Exercise 6.

Possible answers
1 I think in future if you contribute a little more in meetings, that might be good for your self-confidence.
2 You did a very good job explaining our position, but you could have given them more of a chance to speak, that would have been good.
3 Not a big deal, but people have noticed that you sometimes arrive later. Remember to get to work on time or please talk to me if there's a problem.

8B Put students in small groups to compare and discuss their ideas. Allow 4–5 minutes for this, then invite students to share with the class the best examples of developmental feedback from their group.

Extra activities 8.3

A Depending on your students' needs, ask them to do this exercise individually, as a quick quiz or in pairs. Check answers with the class and clarify any errors as necessary.

1 b   2 a   3 c   4 b   5 b   6 c   7 c   8 a   9 c   10 b

Task

Students practise giving and responding to developmental feedback by roleplaying different situations.

9A Put students in pairs to roleplay the situations from Exercise 8A. They should swap roles after each situation, taking turns to give and respond to feedback. Give them some time to prepare. During the activity, monitor and make a note of good examples and also any errors you may need to highlight during feedback. Attend to these at the end of the exercise.

9B Join pairs together into groups of four and explain the activity: students roleplay one of the situations first, then discuss their thoughts on giving and responding to developmental feedback. They should consider the balance of not being over-critical but not avoiding dealing with weak areas that need improvement. At the end of the activity, get brief feedback from the class.

MyEnglishLab: Teacher's resources: extra activities; Interactive video activities

Workbook: p.42 Exercise 1

8.4 ❭ Business skills

Leading meetings

GSE learning objectives

- Can extract the key details from discussions in meetings conducted in clear, standard speech.
- Can respond to interruptions in a meeting using fixed expressions.
- Can close a meeting or discussion using appropriate language.
- Can lead a simple discussion if given time in advance to prepare.

Warm-up

Ask students what they think might make a meeting unsuccessful. Elicit ideas and write them on the board. Then put students in pairs or small groups and ask them to think about what the leader of a meeting might do to prevent these issues. Give them a few minutes to discuss in their pairs/groups, then invite different students to share their ideas with the class. Ask if any students have ever attended a meeting which they thought was unsuccessful. If so, ask them what they think went wrong.

Lead-in

Students discuss different aspects of meetings.

1 Put students in pairs. Explain that there are two statements in each item, which give different views on different aspects of meetings. Go through the statements with them and check that they understand *facilitator*, *external* and *interruption*. Give students 3–4 minutes to discuss in their pairs, then invite different students to share their ideas with the class. Note that there is no best option in each pair – either may be valid depending on the culture (corporate, national or otherwise) of your students.

Listening

Students listen to a meeting and think about strategies for managing and leading meetings.

2 🔊 8.01 Explain that students are going to listen to the first part of a meeting and play the recording for them to answer the questions. Check answers with the class.

> 1 They are preparing for a presentation to senior management at the end of the month.
> 2 to decide which information John will present and which tasks each of them will do to prepare
> 3 focus on the goal, collect ideas, discuss the ideas, choose the best options, assign tasks

3 🔊 8.02 Go through the list of rules with students and check that they understand *acknowledge*. Explain that they are going to listen to the next part of the meeting in order to identify the strategies the leader uses to manage interruptions. Play the recording and get students to compare answers in pairs before checking with the class. During feedback, you could play the recording again, pausing each time the leader uses one of the strategies, for students to identify the strategy. Alternatively, you could ask students to find examples of each strategy in the audioscript on page 150.

> 2, 3, 4, 7

4 🔊 8.03 Tell students that they are going to listen to the last part of the meeting and identify the action points for each person. Write the names of the participants (*Angela, Philippe, Bettina, John*) on the board and play the recording. With weaker students, you may need to play the recording a second time or pause after each answer is heard to give them time to complete their answers.

> **Angela:** prepare two slides on the designs update
> **Philippe:** prepare an overview of the media campaign and the timeline for what will happen
> **Bettina:** prepare an overview of the market research results
> **John:** prepare some brief information on the overall timeline and where they expect to be in the next two months

4B 🔊 8.03 Play the recording again for students to tick the things John did in the last part of the meeting. Check answers with the class.

> 1, 4, 5, 6

Functional language
Leading and managing meetings

Students look at useful language for leading and managing meetings.

5A Students could do this individually or in pairs. They should be able to complete the phrases without looking at the audioscript, but tell them they can refer to it if they need help.

> **1** called **2** goal **3** focusing **4** thinking

5B Explain the function of the phrases (dealing with interruptions) and ask students to do the exercise individually. Check answers with the class.

> **1** important **2** limit **3** back **4** concern **5** agenda

5C Explain that these are useful sentences for the closing stages of a meeting and go through the functions in the table with the class. Students could then do the exercise individually, checking answers in pairs before class feedback. Encourage students to record the phrases from Exercises 5A–5C in their notebooks.

> **1** This has been a very productive meeting.
> **2** It was useful to talk through both our successes and areas for concern.
> **3** The action points from this meeting are …
> **4** Philippe, you'll prepare an overview of the media campaign.
> **5** Is everyone OK with their tasks?
> **6** Does anyone have any questions about what they have to do?
> **7** Let's meet again to finalise everything at 2 p.m. on Friday next week.
> **8** Please send me your completed tasks before close of business on Thursday.

Extra activities 8.4

A This exercise practises and expands on useful phrases for leading and managing meetings. Students could do it individually or in pairs. The second option might be easier for weaker classes.

> **1** d **2** c **3** g **4** a **5** e **6** b **7** f

B This exercise introduces useful phrases for interrupting politely. Before students begin, explain that it is generally a good idea to avoid interruptions, but when students do have to interrupt, it is important that they do so politely. Give them time to complete the exercise individually or in pairs, then check answers with the class. Encourage students to record the phrases in their notebooks.

> **1** c **2** b **3** d **4** a

C Go through the tips with students and answer any vocabulary questions they may have. Then put students in pairs and give them 3–4 minutes to discuss and decide if the tips are helpful. When the time is up, invite different students to share their views with the class, giving reasons.

> **Helpful:** 2, 3, 4, 8
> **Unhelpful:** 1, 5, 6, 7

Task

Students hold mini-meetings in groups, taking turns to lead.

6A–C Put students in groups of three and explain that they will have three mini-meetings, taking turns to lead. Go through the instructions and topics in Exercise 6A with them. Ask students to assign roles for the first meeting, and go through the preparation steps with them. Explain that they will need to follow the same steps for each meeting. Then go through the instructions and checklist in Exercise 6C with them. Explain that after each meeting, the participants should give feedback to the leader, using the checklist to help them. Allow 3–5 minutes' preparation time for each meeting and also set a time limit for each meeting and feedback session. Stop students when the preparation time is up and ask them to hold their meeting and then give feedback to the leader before holding the next meeting. Repeat the process for the other two meetings. During the activity, monitor and make a note of any points to highlight during feedback, but do not interrupt the meetings. It would be better to hold a brief feedback session at the end of Exercise 7.

7 In their groups, students now discuss how easy or difficult it was to lead each meeting. When the groups have finished, broaden this into a class discussion. Ask students what problems they had and how they might learn from their experience, and highlight any points you noted during Exercises 6A–6C.

MyEnglishLab: Teacher's resources: extra activities; Functional language bank
Workbook: p.42 Exercise 2

8.5 ▶ Writing
Informing of a decision

GSE learning objectives

- Can check and correct spelling, punctuation and grammar in simple written texts.
- Can use language related to decision or indecision.
- Can write an email, giving details of work-related events, facts or plans.
- Can construct reduced defining (restrictive) relative clauses with verb + -ing.

Warm-up

Write the following questions on the board: *1 Have you ever had to inform people about important decisions? How did you do it? 2 Why do you think it's important for companies to inform staff / customers / the general public about their decisions?* Put students in pairs or small groups and give them a few minutes to discuss the questions. Then invite different students to share their answers with the class.

Lead-in

Students read a model answer and practise checking written work for spelling mistakes.

1 Explain to students that this is a *formal* email in which a CEO is informing managers of important decisions. Ask them to read the email quickly first and tell you what the three main decisions are (1 new CEO appointed; 2 all managers to have hands-on experience within the company; 3 the number of current managers will not be reduced). Then give students time to read the email and find the spelling mistakes. They should do this individually, then compare answers in pairs before class feedback.

1 leedership – leadership **2** succesor – successor
3 apointed – appointed **4** subsidary – subsidiary
5 bored – board **6** experiense – experience
7 finaly – finally **8** departement – department

Functional language

Students look at useful phrases for business emails informing of decisions.

2 Explain that these are useful phrases students can use in emails informing people of important decisions. Point out the formal and semi-formal registers before students begin and ask them to complete the table. Depending on the level of your class, they could do this individually or in pairs. During feedback, you could highlight some common differences between formal and semi-formal emails, e.g. use of full forms in formal emails (*We are pleased*) and use of short forms in semi-formal emails (*I'm writing*); use of impersonal phrases in formal emails (*This is to inform you, It was agreed that*) and personal phrases in semi-formal emails (*I'm writing to, Let me tell you*); omitting part of a phrase in semi-formal emails (*(This is) just to let you know*) and use of full phrases in formal emails (*This is to inform you*).

1 inform **2** announce **3** consensus **4** agreed **5** reach
6 came **7** tell **8** know **9** couldn't

Extra activities 8.5

A This activity gives further practice of key phrases from the lesson. Ask students to complete it individually, then check answers with the class.

Optional grammar work

The email in Exercise 1 contains examples of reduced relative clauses, so you could use it for some optional grammar work. Refer students to the Grammar reference on page 125 and use the exercises in MyEnglishLab for extra grammar practice.

Task

Students write an email informing of decisions.

3A Put students in pairs and refer them to the email on page 131. Allow plenty of time for them to rewrite the email. While students are writing, monitor and provide help as necessary.

Model answer

Dear José
As you missed this morning's sales department meeting, here is a summary of the decisions made. Firstly, it was decided that Sylvie du Martin would be the best person to chair the International Sales Mangers' meeting next month. Unfortunately, with regard to improving communication between Production and Sales, we were unable to reach a consensus, so it appears that the same problems with Production will continue for now.

Finally, a social event has been arranged on Friday evening next week in order to try and resolve the situation informally.

3B Refer students to the notes on page 135. Set a time limit for the writing task and remind students to use phrases from Exercise 2. With weaker classes, you could allow students to write their emails in pairs, and then work with a different partner for Exercise 3C. If time is short, students can write their emails for homework.

Model answer

Dear Team,
This is to inform you of the decisions made at Monday's sales meeting.
Firstly, regarding the point about customer feedback on the new product range, it was agreed that all customers will be asked to do an online survey as soon as possible. It was also thought that we could encourage them to participate by offering some kind of incentive.
With regard to the replacement team leader for national sales, we are very happy to announce that we decided that John Hedges should take on that role. He has been a regional team leader with us for two years and we are sure he will do an excellent job.
The lack of staff training for new staff was also discussed and we reached an agreement about giving more training to new team members. We agreed that we would contact the training company immediately to arrange this. Unfortunately, we were unable to come to an agreement on conference dates for this year, so they are still to be confirmed. However, we agreed on two potential venues for the conference.

3C If students write their emails for homework, you could do this exercise in the next lesson. Put them in pairs and ask them to read each other's emails and think about the functional language phrases from Exercise 2: How many did they use? Did they use them correctly? Did they use the right register? Could they add any more? Students could then rewrite their emails, based on their partner's feedback.

MyEnglishLab: Teacher's resources: extra activities; Interactive grammar practice; Writing bank
Grammar reference: p.125 Reduced relative clauses
Workbook: p.43 Exercises 1 and 2

Business workshop 8 ❯
Talent management

GSE learning objectives

- Can distinguish between main ideas and supporting details in familiar, standard texts.
- Can scan several short, simple texts on the same topic to find specific information.
- Can briefly give reasons and explanations for opinions, plans and actions.
- Can express opinions as regards possible solutions, giving brief reasons and explanations.
- Can make suggestions and recommendations on work-related topics.
- Can make and justify a simple point of view in a work-related document.

Background

Students read about Grupo Tula, a distributor of consumer electronics.

1 As a warm-up, ask students what training courses they have done or would like to do when they start their first/next job. Then put students in pairs and ask them to read the background and discuss the questions. Explain that the questions require students to generate their own ideas and opinions as well as using information from the text. Check answers with the class.

Possible answers

1 Consumer electronics products include washing machines, dishwashers, fridge-freezers, microwaves, toasters, food mixers, TVs, computer consoles, etc.
2 Adopting English makes it easier to recruit globally (including board members), reach global markets, work in global production teams and integrate foreign staff
3 A new graduate may need lots of basic on-the-job skills training as well as more formal courses such as giving presentations, time management and use of a company's software and intranet.
4 Managers might need different types of training (including peer training, coaching and mentoring) as their careers develop and they take on different roles. Employees today also need access to continual training in order to perform better as well as keep up with trends, e.g. in technologies, global markets, the changing workforce and new management theory. Training helps to keep staff motivated and focused on the company's goals.
5 Pros: Internal recruits know the company's business well and have 'grown' with the organisation. It also motivates staff to know they have a career path within the company. It is quicker to find a suitable replacement when a member of staff retires or leaves the company. Cons: It takes time and money to develop staff so it could be quicker and easier to recruit people externally with the appropriate skills. Also, people from outside the company will come with a different perspective and ways of thinking and working.

Training needs

Students listen to employees talking about their training needs.

2 ▶ BW 8.01 Explain the activity and check that students understand the job titles in the box before they listen.

Cris Martinez is Senior Finance Manager. (He says he reports to the Chief Financial Officer.)
Alex Cortés is Operations Manager. (She has to make sure the day-to-day business runs smoothly and she negotiates with suppliers and clients.)
Danni Lee is a Trainee Sales Manager. (He graduated and joined the company recently, so we can assume he is in a relatively junior position.)

3 ▶ BW 8.01 Give students time to read the notes so they know what they need to listen for. Play the recording and get students to compare answers in pairs before class feedback.

1 (generic) training 2 network 3 (other) senior managers 4 talent development 5 better results 6 suppliers and clients 7 communicating in English 8 fluency 9 the right things 10 (quite) stressed 11 Excel 12 lead a team

4 Check that students understand *resistant* and discuss the question with the whole class. Make sure students give reasons for their answers. With weaker classes, you may wish to allow students to refer to the audioscript on page 153 or let them listen again.

Cris Martinez seems most resistant because he has done a lot of training in the past and wants something different. His suggestion for a network of mutually supporting senior managers is something many top companies have implemented.

Extra activities Business workshop 8

A ▶ BW 8.01 This exercise can be done individually or in pairs. You could ask students to check the words in the box in their dictionaries or, with weaker classes, go through the words as a class. Play the recording for students to check their answers and clarify any queries about vocabulary as necessary.

1 core 2 tie 3 pass on 4 day-to-day 5 overseeing 6 adopted 7 on-the-job 8 pick it up

Training options

Students read five training course descriptions.

5 Explain that the five texts are extracts from adverts for different training courses. Check that students understand the course titles in the box and give them time to read the descriptions and do the matching activity. Check answers with the class.

1 time management 2 coaching 3 presentations 4 executive decision-making 5 team-building

6 Ask students to do the exercise individually and get them to compare answers in pairs before class feedback. They should highlight the parts of the texts that gave them the answers.

> **a** 4 **b** 1 **c** 2 **d** 2, 3 and 5 **e** 2 and 5

7 If time allows, get students to discuss the question in pairs or small groups first, giving reasons for their answers. Then get brief feedback from the class. Alternatively, discuss the question briefly as a whole class.

Extra activities Business workshop 8

B This activity gives further practice of key vocabulary from the texts in Exercise 5. It can be done individually or in pairs. As homework, you could ask students to write their own example sentences for the words/phrases.

> **1** e **2** i **3** h **4** c **5** f **6** j **7** a **8** g **9** d **10** b

Task

Students design a development plan for an employee and then write a formal email justifying their need for training.

8A Put students in small groups and go through the instructions and list of points to think about with them. Explain that they should look back at the *Training needs* section and choose one of the employees. They should read the notes about them and check the audioscript. Based on this information, they should then put together a development plan, bearing in mind the list of points in this exercise. They can use their own ideas and/or the texts in Exercise 5. Give students plenty of time to read the background material and brainstorm ideas. Monitor and provide help as necessary.

8B Groups now take turns to present their development plans. Ask the groups listening to make a note of any ideas from the other groups which they could use to improve their own plans. Then give groups time to revisit their plans.

9 Explain the writing task and give students 20 minutes to write their emails. Alternatively, if time is short, students could do this for homework.

Model answer

I would like to apply for the three-day intensive presentation skills course. In my role as a Project Manager I regularly have to give presentations to colleagues throughout the company. I therefore feel comfortable when giving talks in my own language. However, I have recently started working on a new international project and I realise that I am out of my comfort zone when I have to present to a group in English. I feel particularly uncertain about the language I need to describe graphs and the strategies I could use to deal with audience questions. I would welcome the opportunity to practise my English skills so that I can gain more confidence and sound more persuasive.

MyEnglishLab: Teacher's resources: extra activities

Review ◀ 8

1 **1** make **2** cope **3** delegate **4** gives **5** takes
   6 trust **7** won **8** prioritise **9** sets **10** praise
2A **1** which **2** where **3** which **4** who **5** whose
   6 who/that **7** whose **8** when
2B We can use *that* in sentence 6.
   We can omit the relative pronoun in sentence 8.
3 **1** job **2** feel **3** bear **4** impressed **5** appreciate
   6 account
4 **1** coming **2** called **3** goal **4** focusing **5** concern
   6 agenda
5 **1** d **2** e **3** g **4** a **5** f **6** b **7** c

Resource bank

Photocopiables

Reading bank

Writing bank

Functional language bank

1.1 > Vocabulary

Student A

1 You are going to talk about roles and responsibilities. Work in groups. Complete the table with the words in the box and your own ideas.

> auditing   brand image   cash flow   chasing payments   company image   customer service
> designing products   invoicing   managing director   managing products   market research
> production department   quality control   sales team   supply chain

	Finance Supervisor	Head of Operations	Marketing Manager
responsible for			
in charge of			
take care of / look after			
work closely with / coordinate with			

2 Work in pairs. Follow the instructions.

1 Choose one of the jobs in Exercise 1 and talk about it for one minute without saying what your job is. Student B has to guess your job. He/She can ask you up to three questions before guessing.

2 Listen to Student B and try to guess what job he/she is describing. You can ask him/her up to three questions before guessing.

Student B

1 You are going to talk about roles and responsibilities. Work in groups. Complete the table with the words in the box and your own ideas.

> customer service   employee relations   health and safety   interviewing
> managers of other departments   manufacturing   marketing team
> operations department   payroll   pricing   production processes   promotion campaigns
> providing raw materials   recruiting and training   sales strategies

	Director of Human Resources	Production Supervisor	Sales Director
responsible for			
in charge of			
take care of / look after			
work closely with / coordinate with			

2 Work in pairs. Follow the instructions.

1 Listen to Student A and try to guess what job he/she is describing. You can ask him/her up to three questions before guessing.

2 Choose one of the jobs in Exercise 1 and talk about it for one minute without saying what your job is. Student A has to guess your job. He/She can ask you up to three questions before guessing.

1.2 ❯ Grammar

1 Look at the card and complete the conversation with appropriate future forms.

Scheduled event
all-day meeting – Tuesday – discuss next year's marketing plans
Plan/Arrangement
give presentation 9.30
Personal intention
spend all day Monday preparing
Prediction
interesting day, learn a lot

A: What are your plans for next week?

B: Well, we ¹_____ (have) an all-day meeting on Tuesday to discuss next year's marketing plans.

A: Really?

B: Yes, and I ²_____ (give) a presentation at 9.30. It's the first of the day.

A: Are you nervous?

B: A little. But I ³_____ (spend) all day on Monday preparing!

A: That's a good idea!

B: Well, I hope so. I think it ⁴_____ (be) a really interesting day and I'm sure I ⁵_____ (learn) a lot.

2 Work in pairs. Pick up a card each about your plans for next week. Look at your scheduled event, your plan/arrangement, your personal intention and your prediction. Then have a similar conversation with your partner.

Scheduled event	**Scheduled event**
sales conference in Miami – flight 3.45 p.m. Monday	two-day finance meeting – Tuesday and Wednesday
Plan/Arrangement	**Plan/Arrangement**
stay Beach Hotel 4 nights attend conference meetings – Tuesday and Wednesday	give presentation, explain latest financial figures – Wednesday 3 p.m.
Personal intention	**Personal intention**
do lots of networking	check financial figures, prepare presentation – Tuesday
Prediction	**Prediction**
learn about new products, useful and fun	difficult decisions, productive day
Scheduled event	**Scheduled event**
new computer systems training day – Thursday	team-building away day – Friday
Plan/Arrangement	**Plan/Arrangement**
attend morning session meet new Systems Manager after lunch	get lift from manager
Personal intention	**Personal intention**
read about the new computer systems – Wednesday evening	get to know the team better, do lots of networking
Prediction	**Prediction**
challenging day, helpful in future	fun day, improve working relationships

2.1 › Vocabulary

1 Choose the correct option in italics to complete the questions.

1 In what ways can a company improve its *brand / product* image?

2 What can companies do to increase *brand / customer* engagement?

3 What two examples of interactive *engagement / marketing* can you think of?

4 What *fast / ultra-* luxury products are you familiar with?

5 How important do you think brand *awareness / approach* is to the success of a product?

6 What one product has your continued customer *loyalty / placement* (for example, shampoo, shoes, toiletries)?

7 What do you think makes a brand *image / logo* like VW on Volkswagen cars successful?

8 If you are in the hospitality industry, what is your *base / core* business?

9 Is a cautious *approach / awareness* to expansion always the best way to run a business?

10 What is your opinion of product *marketing / placement*? Do you think it works as an advertising technique? Are there any dangers?

11 What are some advantages and disadvantages of *fast / ultra-* growth in a company? Give one or two examples.

12 Can you think of an example of *bad / cautious* history about brand extensions?

13 Why might you look *further / fast* afield for customers?

14 What kind of products do you think will appeal to an aspirational *base / core* of clients without much money?

15 Can you think of examples of *brand / further* stretching which have been very successful?

2 Choose five questions from Exercise 1 to ask a partner. Then work in pairs and ask and answer your questions. Take notes.

_____
_____
_____
_____
_____

3 Ask another partner five different questions from Exercise 1. Take notes.

_____
_____
_____
_____
_____

4 Look at your notes. Choose an answer you found surprising or interesting and share it with the class.

2.2 ❯ Grammar

1 Choose the correct option in italics to complete the quiz. Then work in pairs or groups and do the quiz.

Are you a luxury brands expert?

1 *As well as / While* men and women's clothing and accessories, Burberry also sells

   a children's clothing.   **b** food and drink.   **c** electronic devices.

2 *However / Although* Chanel is best known today for clothes, handbags and fragrance, Coco Chanel, the founder, started her career selling

   a scarves.   **b** hats.   **c** gloves.

3 *When it comes to / In addition to* luxury cars, Rolls-Royce are famous for manufacturing

   a jet engines.   **b** computers.   **c** trams.

4 Louis Vuitton has been associated with luxury for over 100 years. *However / Then*, when he first arrived in Paris in the 1830s, its founder, Louis Vuitton, got a job as a

   a tailor.   **b** shoemaker.   **c** box maker.

5 *Also / While* Louis Vuitton was taking his first steps in business in the 1830s in Paris, Thierry Hermès, the founder of the famous fashion house Hermès, was starting his own company selling

   a harnesses and saddles for horses.   **b** silk scarves for women.   **c** toys.

6 *In recent years / To start with*, the Italian luxury brand Gucci has contributed over $20 million to the children's charity UNICEF, and has founded Chime For Change, a global campaign for

   a the empowerment of girls and women.   **b** universal education.   **c** a widespread vaccination programme.

7 *Now / When* it comes to luxury Swiss watches, few brands are as well known as Rolex, Vacheron Constantin and

   a Longio.   **b** Patek Philippe.   **c** Konstantin Chaykin.

8 These days, Cartier is famous not only for jewellery, but also for luxury accessories *such as / previously* handbags, sunglasses and

   a scent, including women's perfumes and men's fragrances.
   b footwear, including shoes and boots.
   c outerwear, including jackets and coats.

9 The Italian luxury brand Prada has expanded its business *in recent years / now* by acquiring other brands, including Church's English Shoes, Car Shoe, and 80 percent of Marchesi 1824, the famous

   a Roman hotel.   **b** Florentine restaurant.   **c** Milanese café.

10 Today, the Spanish luxury fashion house Loewe has stores all over the world selling bags, clothing and accessories. However, *for instance / to start with*, Loewe produced only leather goods and was based in

   a Barcelona.   **b** Malaga.   **c** Madrid.

2 Work in pairs. Write three similar quiz questions about luxury brands. Use connectors to express contrasting ideas, to refer to time, to give examples or to sequence ideas. Give your questions to another pair to answer.

3.1 › Vocabulary

1 Find someone who:

	Name	Notes
1 has got an up-to-date CV.		
2 is a full-time employee.		
3 is good at sorting out problems at work or at home.		
4 is naturally very competitive.		
5 is motivated by enjoyment of work rather than money.		
6 thinks he/she has the skills to become a manager.		
7 needs a job with flexible hours.		
8 would like a job with lots of responsibility.		
9 would like to have an internship.		
10 thinks he/she would probably come across well in interviews.		
11 hasn't got any work experience.		
12 has recently applied for a job.		
13 has had more than five job interviews.		
14 has interviewed jobseekers.		
15 would like to interview potential interns for his/her company.		
16 would like to be a recruiter for a large company.		
17 wouldn't like to be responsible for interviewing new candidates at work.		
18 would like to have a position in a large international company.		

2 Work in pairs and compare your notes. Have you found out anything which has surprised you?

3.2 ⟩ Grammar

Student A   **1** Write one or two indirect questions for each of the topics below to ask a partner. Use the table to help you.

Can you tell me	if whether
Could you tell me	**what** **who** when **where** why
I'd like to know	**how** how many how often how long

1   home / living arrangement

_____

2   brothers and sisters

_____

3   university studies / degree

_____

4   studying English / doing English homework

_____

5   favourite book/author/film

_____

2 Ask and answer your questions with Student B.

- -

Student B   **1** Write one or two indirect questions for each of the topics below to ask a partner. Use the table to help you.

Can you tell me	if whether
Could you tell me	**what** **who** when **where** why
I'd like to know	**how** how many how often how long

1   learning English

_____

2   school

_____

3   hobbies and pastimes

_____

4   holiday/travel

_____

5   fitness regime: gym, sport, etc.

_____

2 Ask and answer your questions with Student A.

4.1 › Vocabulary

competitive *(adj)*	**emerging** *(adj)*	**major** *(adj)*
cut *(verb)*	**make** *(verb)*	**make** *(verb)*
solve *(verb)*	**miss** *(verb)*	**take** *(verb)*
develop *(verb)*	**come up with** *(phrasal verb)*	**tackle** *(verb)*
product *(noun)*	**profit** *(noun)*	**takeover** *(noun)*
prices *(noun)*	**markets** *(noun)*	**player** *(noun)*
costs *(noun)*	**money** *(noun)*	**a profit** *(noun)*
problems *(noun)*	**opportunities** *(noun)*	**risks** *(noun)*
strategies *(noun)*	**a plan** *(noun)*	**problems** *(noun)*
lines *(noun)*	**margin** *(noun)*	**bid** *(noun)*

Business: _____

1 In order to succeed in emerging markets, we should …

2 The product lines which make the most profits are …

3 The best way to cut costs and offer competitive prices is to …

4 If our profit margins are very small, we are in danger of …

5 If we don't tackle employment problems quickly, we probably won't …

6 If we don't take risks, our company will probably / probably won't …

7 The best way to make sure we don't miss opportunities is to …

8 If our company decides to make a takeover bid, we should make sure …

4.2 ❯ Grammar

Student A   **1**   Work in pairs or small groups. Read the problems and think of possible solutions. Make notes. Use modal verbs to talk about obligation, necessity, prohibition and recommendation (*have to / don't have to, must/mustn't, should/shouldn't*).

Problems		
1 The country where our silver jewellery is being manufactured has become politically unstable. We think there is going to be a revolution.	**2** I work in a very smart shop selling luxury goods. One of my colleagues has started coming in wearing old, dirty clothes. He doesn't shave and his hair is very messy. I think he's giving a bad impression, but I don't want to tell my boss about it.	**3** I've heard that the rent I have to pay for my clothing shop on the High Street is going up by 50 percent. I'm afraid this is going to mean that I'll have to close my shop.

2   Read the solutions to some problems and try to work out what the problems are. Make notes.

Solutions		
4 You mustn't ignore the problem. She has to know that people have started to notice. You should ask her why this is happening and if there are any problems at home, for example. Maybe she has to drop off and collect a child from school. Whatever her excuse, you should explain that she mustn't be late or leave early again. She has to work a full day like everybody else.	**5** You don't have to close it. You shouldn't sell it either because you will need it if you come back home. You should get a manager to look after it while you are away, or you could promote someone to run it. You must make sure the rest of the staff are happy with your choice.	**6** You will have to think about developing an online business. You should also think about getting your goods from exclusive suppliers. You shouldn't stock goods which are cheaper and easily available elsewhere or online.

3   Now work with Student B and match the problems with the solutions. Then discuss your ideas. Were they similar?

Student B   **1**   Read the solutions to some problems and try to work out what the problems are. Make notes.

Solutions		
A You don't have to accept the situation. You must talk to your landlord as soon as possible and explain that you can't afford to pay so much per month. You should tell him/her that you'll have to close if he/she goes ahead.	**B** You should move your factory to another, more stable country. You must give your staff enough warning so they can find other jobs or move with you. You have to make sure you follow employment law, but you mustn't wait too long.	**C** You mustn't let this continue because your manager will wonder why you didn't tell her about it. You should talk to your colleague and find out if there's a reason for the way he looks at the moment. Perhaps there is a problem at home. But if his appearance doesn't improve after your conversation, then you must talk to your manager.

2   Work in pairs or small groups. Read the problems and think of possible solutions. Make notes. Use modal verbs to talk about obligation, necessity, prohibition and recommendation (*have to / don't have to, must/mustn't, should/shouldn't*).

Problems		
D We have a small shop selling leather goods. There are similar products online for lower prices than ours. Our client base is decreasing and our business is in trouble.	**E** One of my employees has been late for work every day for the last couple of weeks. It's causing problems with other colleagues and creating a bad atmosphere. Now she has started leaving early as well.	**F** I have a restaurant in my home town which is doing well, but I want to go abroad and start another business – either a restaurant or a café. I don't want to close my restaurant as all the people who work there are friends or family.

3   Now work with Student A and match the problems with the solutions. Then discuss your ideas. Were they similar?

5.1 > Vocabulary

1 Choose the correct option in italics to complete the statements about online shopping, delivery and logistics.

Statement	✓/✗	Classmate who agrees with me
1 When you order something online, it often arrives in a huge box with lots of unnecessary extra *package / packaging*. This is really bad for the environment.		
2 I think that in the future, everything will be automated in *distributer / distribution* centres like Amazon warehouses, and even delicate and breakable goods will be packed by robots rather than people.		
3 *Automate / Automation* in warehouses means that products can be found, tracked, packed and distributed efficiently and more quickly than in the past. Soon there won't be any people working in warehouses at all.		
4 I've often had goods delivered to *collector / collection* lockers and it's worked really well for me. It's much better than home delivery.		
5 Most big supermarkets offer online shopping and a home *deliver / delivery* service, or you can 'click and collect', which means you collect your online shopping already packed for you in the store. 'Click and collect' may be cheaper and more convenient if you aren't going to be home, but it's worse for the environment.		
6 *Manufacturing / Manufacturers* need to think about how their products are going to be packaged and distributed before they produce them. Otherwise their products might not be suitable for new methods of distribution like drones and robots.		
7 I don't think there's any way we'll go back to shopping the way we used to – on the High Street and in shopping malls. I think online *retailer / retailing* is here to stay.		
8 Delivering medical and other emergency *supplies / suppliers* by drone in the future is a bad idea. It may be quicker, but it will take away thousands of jobs.		
9 I doubt that drones will be allowed for the *transporter / transportation* of goods in my country. I think they are dangerous.		
10 When it comes to *fulfilling / fulfilment* orders efficiently and economically, I think courier companies are more reliable than the postal service in my country.		

2 Decide if you agree (✓) or disagree (✗) with the statements in Exercise 1. Then try to find someone who agrees with you.

5.2 ❯ Grammar

1 Read the text about a product. What do you think it is?

What is it?

Most people have one of these. The one I've got is probably manufactured in China or maybe Brazil. I'm pretty sure mine was designed in Finland, though. I know the first one was invented by an American engineer called Martin Cooper. It's been around since the 1980s and has become an essential device for most people. It's been used by a whole generation of young people who don't know a world without it. Mostly, it is required for communication, but it can also be used for entertainment. It's made mostly of plastic but minerals are also used in its manufacture. These are often extracted from mines in Africa. These days, if it's ordered online, it will probably be shipped the same day, and should be delivered to your door the next day. It's breakable, so it will need to be packaged really well – probably in a box. In the future, I think it could be delivered by drone because it's really light.

2 Read the text in Exercise 1 again and underline the passive forms.

3 Work in pairs. Think of a product which everybody in the class will be familiar with. It could be something you use every day, something you buy often or something you only buy once or twice in a lifetime. Use the prompts below to write sentences describing your product.

It was invented in …

It is produced in/by … In the past it was manufactured in …

Nowadays, it's made in/of …

It used to be made of … It was designed in/by …

If it isn't carefully packaged, it could be …

Lots of these products have been shipped to …

If you order it online, it will be …

It can/can't be delivered by drone because …

4 Work with a different partner. Read your sentences about your product and answer questions about it until your partner guesses what your product is. Then swap roles.

6.1 ⟩ Vocabulary

1 Choose the correct option in italics to complete the questions.

> **1** Do you think *crowdfunding / crowdfounding* is more or less risky for investors? Why?
>
> **2** If you *found / set* up your own business, what would it be?
>
> **3** Can you think of any *set-ups / start-ups* which have done really well? What do they have in common?
>
> **4** Would you be interested in becoming *a business / an entrepreneur* angel in the future? What would you invest in?
>
> **5** Do you know any companies which have *gone / set* out of business? What happened?
>
> **6** If you had a good business idea, who would you *pitch / target* it to first: family, friends or strangers?
>
> **7** Why do you think it's difficult for new companies to *do / make* a profit? Think of two reasons.
>
> **8** Imagine you have a company making leather goods. Who is your *business / target* market?
>
> **9** What is the greatest challenge for someone who is thinking of *finding / founding* their own company?
>
> **10** What are some advantages and disadvantages of fast *growth / target* for a start-up?
>
> **11** How difficult or easy is it to get financial *backing / investment* for a new business in your country?
>
> **12** What two qualities does a business need in order to become a good *funding / investment*, in your opinion?
>
> **13** What *advice / advise* would you give someone who is thinking about starting a business?
>
> **14** If you could invest in any successful company worldwide, which company would you choose to *fund / found*? Why?
>
> **15** Can you think of someone with *entrepreneuring / entrepreneurial* talent? What did they do?

2 Choose five questions from Exercise 1 to ask a partner. Then work in pairs and ask and answer your questions. Take notes.

_____
_____
_____
_____
_____

3 Ask another partner five different questions from Exercise 1. Take notes.

_____
_____
_____
_____
_____

4 Look at your notes. Choose an answer you found surprising or interesting and share it with the class.

6.2 ❯ Grammar

I'm studying economics. I really enjoy it. Are you a student too?	I love my job. It's really interesting. Do you enjoy what you do?
I've just started my own business. Where do you work?	I spent last year working in an office. I didn't really like it. Do you work in an office?
I've got an internship at an investment bank. I'm really looking forward to it. Have you done any internships?	I'll give you a lift to the restaurant. What time do you want to leave?
I've just moved into a new flat on my own. It's exciting. Where do you live?	We must go now if we're going to get to the meeting on time. Have you called a taxi?
I've never lived in a big city. I'd like to find a job in a city. Do you live in a city or in the country?	I'm leaving tomorrow morning. When are you going back?
I must go now and prepare a talk for tomorrow. I'm feeling a bit nervous. Are you giving a talk at the conference?	I really admire your new start-up. It's so original. When did you get the idea for it?
I'll phone tomorrow to arrange a meeting. What time do you want to meet?	We opened our new offices last year. Where are your offices?
I'm interested in becoming an entrepreneur. How long have you had your own business?	I work for my family's business. We have three restaurants in our town. Have you been to one of our restaurants?
We didn't drive. We took a taxi. Do you want to share a taxi back to the hotel?	We met last year at the conference in Rome. How long are you planning to stay this time?
I'll meet you tomorrow to talk about our ideas for a start-up. What time do you want to meet?	I've never been to a conference like this before. How many times have you come to one of these conferences?

7.1 ❯ Vocabulary

A

in-	in-	in-	in-
un-	un-	un-	un-
un-	un-	un-	un-
un-	un-	dis-	dis-
dis-	im-	im-	im-

B

direct	friendly	formal	honest
helpful	kind	polite	reserved
sociable	respectful	cool	convenient
correct	fashionable	important	patient
perfect	popular	reliable	satisfied

7.2 ❯ Grammar

Student A

1 **Complete the anecdote with the Past Simple, Past Continuous or Past Perfect Simple form of the verbs in brackets.**

A really embarrassing thing happened to me the other day. I ¹_____ (work) on a new contract when one of my colleagues called and asked if I could send her some sales figures. Her exact words were, 'I know you're really busy, but if you've got a moment, could you send me the sales figures for last month?' I said, 'Sure, no problem,' and carried on writing the urgent report my boss ²_____ (ask) me for that morning. To be honest, I completely ³_____ (forget) about the sales figures as I ⁴_____ (focus) all my attention on the report. It had been a really difficult week, with lots of deadlines, and I ⁵_____ (feel) stressed and exhausted.

The next day I got an angry email from my colleague saying I'd put her in a very difficult position because I ⁶_____ (not send) her the sales figures. She'd needed them urgently for a meeting with new clients and thanks to me, she'd made a very bad impression. She said she ⁷_____ (think) of making an official complaint. I was amazed! I was also terribly embarrassed, but I ⁸_____ (think) she was being very unfair. I know she'd asked me to send the figures, but only if I had time. And I'd been really busy with the report ...

Later on, I saw an email she ⁹_____ (send) the day before to remind me to send the figures. I ¹⁰_____ (feel) very bad then and, of course, I apologised. It's OK now. I think she understood, because yesterday she ¹¹_____ (ask) me to send her a copy of a product presentation I ¹²_____ (give) the week before. Her exact words were, 'Please could you send me the presentation immediately? I need it urgently.'

2 **Read the anecdote again and try to remember it. Imagine this happened to you and tell Student B. Then listen to Student B's story. In what way are your stories similar/different?**

Student B

1 **Complete the anecdote with the Past Simple, Past Continuous or Past Perfect Simple form of the verbs in brackets.**

A really annoying thing happened to me the other day. One of my colleagues ¹_____ (ask) me for a report I was writing about one of our new products. His exact words were, 'I must have the marketing report you're writing. Thanks!' It ²_____ (sound) urgent and although I ³_____ (work) on something else, I knew I had to finish the report for him.

My boss ⁴_____ (ask) me to update some sales figures, so I worked on that until lunchtime. Then, all through my lunch hour, I worked on the marketing report. I ⁵_____ (not have) time to finish it, so instead of going home at 5.30, I continued working on it. By 7.30, I still ⁶_____ (not finish), so I took it home and worked on it until midnight. By this time, I was exhausted, so I went bed. Then, at about 3 a.m., I ⁷_____ (wake up) in a panic because I remembered that I ⁸_____ (not send) the report! So I got up, logged in and sent the report.

I was really tired the next day at work, but happy I'd finished the report. Later that morning, when I ⁹_____ (walk) to the canteen, I bumped into the colleague who'd asked me for the report. When he ¹⁰_____ (not say) anything, I asked him if he ¹¹_____ (get) it. 'What report?' he asked. I couldn't believe it! 'The marketing report you said you *must* have!' I replied angrily. 'Ah, yes,' he answered. 'Actually, I don't need it until next week. But thanks anyway!'

I was very upset! But later that afternoon, I ¹²_____ (receive) some flowers and a note of apology. Someone had told him I'd spent my lunch hour and half the night on the report and he said he'd felt really guilty.

2 **Read the anecdote again and try to remember it. Imagine this happened to you. Listen to Student A's story and then tell him/her your story. In what way are your stories similar/different?**

8.1 › Vocabulary

1 How important do you think these leadership qualities are? Rank them 1–20 (1 = most important, 20 = least important). Then compare your answers in pairs.

What makes a good leader?

- coping well with stress
- coping well with criticism
- coping well with change
- giving clear instructions
- giving support
- giving praise when people deserve it
- giving constructive feedback
- knowing when to delegate
- making good decisions
- making an effort to understand others
- making people feel safe
- running a business efficiently
- running meetings successfully
- running a team of people well
- setting a good example
- setting high standards
- setting priorities
- trusting his/her instincts
- trusting his/her team
- winning the respect of his/her team

2 Do a class survey: find out which quality the majority of students ranked as the most and least important.

3 Complete the sentences. Then compare your answers with other students.
- A good leader _____ .
- A bad leader _____ .
- I would like my boss to _____ .
- If I become a leader, I'll try to _____ .

8.2 〉 Grammar

Student A　**1** Work in pairs. Join the sentences about famous businesspeople using relative clauses.

1 **Mary Barra** is the first woman to run a global motor company. She is Chief Executive of **General Motors**.	**2** **Warren Buffet** is a famous American entrepreneur and head of the American multinational holding company **Berkshire Hathaway Inc**. Warren Buffet said, 'You can't make a good deal with a bad person.'	**3** **Ana Maiques** is the Spanish CEO of Neuroelectrics. **Neuroelectrics** is a company. It develops technologies to treat the brain.	**4** **Pierre Omidyar** was born in Paris. His parents are Iranian. He is the founder of **eBay**. eBay is an online auction and shopping website.

1 _____
2 _____
3 _____
4 _____

2 Do you know any of these people and companies? Discuss with your partner.

Wu Yajun　Jeff Bezos　Ursula Burns　Leonardo Del Vecchio

Longfor Properties　Amazon　Xerox　Luxottica

3 Work in new pairs. Student B has information about the people and companies in Exercise 2. Ask him/her about them. Take notes.

Who is Wu Yajun? Is she Chinese?

Is Longfor Properties a Chinese company?

Did Jeff Bezos found Amazon?

4 Use your notes to write sentences about the people and companies in Exercise 2. Use relative clauses. Then check with Student B.

Student B　**1** Work in pairs. Join the sentences about famous businesspeople using relative clauses.

1 **Wu Yajun** is one of the richest women in China. She is the Chairwoman of Longfor Properties. **Longfor Properties** is an investment-holding company based in Beijing.	**2** **Jeff Bezos** is the founder and Chief Executive of Amazon. **Amazon** is one of the largest online retail companies in the world.	**3** **Ursula Burns** was the first African-American Chief Executive of a top U.S. corporation. She is now Chairwoman of **Xerox** and has been listed as one of the 100 most powerful women in the world.	**4** **Leonardo Del Vecchio** is one of the richest men in Italy, after Michelle Ferrero. Del Vecchio's company, **Luxottica**, is the biggest producer and seller of glasses in the world.

1 _____
2 _____
3 _____
4 _____

2 Do you know any of these people and companies? Discuss with your partner.

Mary Barra　Warren Buffet　Ana Maiques　Pierre Omidyar

General Motors　Berkshire Hathaway Inc.　Neuroelectrics　eBay

3 Work in new pairs. Student A has information about the people and companies in Exercise 2. Ask him/her about them. Take notes.

Who is Mary Barra? Is she an American executive?

Is she an engineer at General Motors?

Is Warren Buffet an entrepreneur?

4 Use your notes to write sentences about the people and companies in Exercise 2. Use relative clauses. Then check with Student A.

1.1 ❯ Vocabulary

- Tell students that they are going to talk about roles and responsibilities and practise vocabulary from Lesson 1.1.
- Divide the class into two groups, A and B.
- If you think students might not be sure about the meaning of some of the words in the boxes, write them on the board first and check as a class or get students to check in their dictionaries before they start.
- Hand out a worksheet, A or B, to each student and ask them to complete the table. Encourage them to come up with some of their own ideas as well. Point out that there are no right or wrong answers.
- Put students in A–B pairs and tell them they should not show their worksheet to each other. Ask them to choose one job from their table and imagine it is what they do. They then talk about their role and responsibilities for about one minute, without using their job title. Their partner can ask up to three questions before guessing what the job is. Point out that Student A and Student B have different sets of jobs. Monitor students as they are speaking and encourage them to use the vocabulary they have learnt in Lesson 1.1. Go over any difficulties as a class.

Possible answers
Student A

	Finance Supervisor	Head of Operations	Marketing Manager
responsible for	auditing chasing payments	designing products managing products	brand image market research
in charge of	cash flow	supply chain	customer service
take care of / look after	invoicing	quality control	company image
work closely with / coordinate with	managing director	production department	sales team

Student B

	Director of Human Resources	Production Supervisor	Sales Director
responsible for	interviewing recruiting and training	manufacturing	promotion campaigns
in charge of	health and safety payroll	providing raw materials	pricing sales strategies
take care of / look after	employee relations	production processes	customer service
work closely with / coordinate with	managers of other departments	operations department	marketing team

1.2 ❯ Grammar

- Tell students that they are going to practise future forms from Lesson 1.2.
- Put students in pairs and hand out one copy of the top half of the worksheet to each student. Ask pairs to complete the conversation with appropriate future forms. Check answers with the class and then get students to practise the dialogue in their pairs.
- Explain that students are now going to have similar conversations about next week, using similar cards. Hand out a set of cards to each pair. Students take turns to pick up a card and have a similar conversation.
- Monitor students and check that they are using future forms correctly. Make a note of mistakes and go over them as a class at the end of the lesson.
- As a follow-up activity, you could ask students to write one of the dialogues. They could do this in class or for homework.

1 have   2 'm giving   3 'm going to spend
4 's going to be   5 'm going to learn

2.1 ❯ Vocabulary

- Tell students that they are going to talk about marketing and brands and practise vocabulary from Lesson 2.1.
- Hand out a copy of the worksheet to each student and get them to complete Exercise 1. They could do this individually or in pairs. Check answers with the class.
- Ask students to choose five questions from Exercise 1 they would like to ask another student. Put students into (different) pairs and ask them to take notes of their partner's answers.
- After a few minutes, put students into new pairs and get them to discuss five different questions.
- Students share one answer they found interesting or surprising with the class.

1 brand   2 customer   3 marketing   4 ultra-
5 awareness   6 loyalty   7 logo   8 core   9 approach
10 placement   11 fast   12 bad   13 further   14 base
15 brand

2.2 ❯ Grammar

- Tell students that they are going to talk about luxury brands and practise using connectors.
- Before you start, if you think your students might need extra help, write the luxury brands on the board and ask students what they know about them (e.g. *What do they sell? Where did the company start?*):
  - Burberry: British clothing and accessories, famous for its raincoats
  - Chanel: French clothing and accessories, famous for its clothing and perfume, e.g. Chanel No. 5
  - Rolls-Royce: cars, motorbikes and jet engines – British originally, now owned by BMW, the German car manufacturer

- Louis Vuitton: French, most famous for its suitcases, bags and accessories
- Hermès: French, famous for its scarves
- Gucci: Italian, famous for its clothing and shoes
- Rolex: Swiss watches
- Vacheron Constantin: Swiss watches
- Patek Philippe: Swiss watches
- Longio: Chinese watches
- Konstantin Chaykin: Russian watches
- Cartier: French jewellery, watches and fashion accessories
- Prada: Italian leather goods, clothing and accessories
- Loewe: Spanish leather goods, clothing and accessories

- Hand out a copy of the worksheet to each student and get them to choose the correct connectors, individually or in pairs. Check answers as a class.
- Put students in pairs or groups and get them to do the quiz. This could be a competition: the pair/group with the most correct answers wins.
- After discussing the quiz answers as a class, ask students to write their own multiple-choice questions in pairs. Encourage them to use connectors. Monitor and check the questions before students hand them over to another pair to answer. Students could also do this as homework. You could use it as a warmer at the beginning of your next lesson.

> **1** As well as, a **2** Although, b **3** In addition, a
> **4** However, c **5** While, a **6** In recent years, a
> **7** When, b **8** such as, a **9** in recent years, c
> **10** to start with, c

3.1 ❯ Vocabulary

- Tell students that they are going to talk about jobs and internships, and practise vocabulary connected with jobs.
- Hand out one copy of the worksheet to each student and explain that these are all 'find someone who' questions: they will need to mingle in order to find the people listed in the table.
- Before students begin, point out that they shouldn't just ask 'Who- questions'; for example, for question 1, they should ask: *Have you got an up-to-date CV?* and not *Who has an up-to-date CV?*
- Get a few students to ask you or each other a few questions in open class to begin with. Encourage them to ask more questions of their own and write notes, e.g.
  A: Have you got an up-to-date CV?
  B: Yes, I have.
  A: When did you last update it? / What did you put under ('interests')?
- Give students 10–15 minutes to mingle and ask as many people as possible questions about jobs, internships and work experience, taking notes. Encourage them to expand on and explain their answers.
- Put students in pairs to compare their notes.
- Invite different students to share any surprising findings with the class.

3.2 ❯ Grammar

- Tell students that they are going to practise using indirect questions to ask each other questions which could sound rude if asked too directly. Give an example: *How old are you?* vs. *Could you tell me how old you are?*
- Divide the class into two groups, A and B, and hand out an A or B worksheet to each student. Put students in A–A/B–B pairs or groups and give them time to write their indirect questions. Check with each pair/group before students ask and answer.
- Now put students in A–B pairs and get them to ask each other their questions. Point out that if they would rather not answer, they can say something like: *Actually, I'd rather not say. / I'm sorry, I can't remember. / I don't know, I'm afraid.*
- You could then ask students to write two more indirect questions to ask their partner.

> **Possible answers**
> **Student A**
> **1** Can you tell me where you live? / Could you tell me who you live with? / I'd like to know if you live on your own or with your family.
> **2** I'd like to know whether you've got any brothers or sisters.
> **3** Could you tell me what university you go/went/would like to go to? / I'd like to know how long you've been studying … / Can you tell me what your degree is in?
> **4** I'd like to know how often you study English. / Can you tell me how long it usually takes you to do your English homework?
> **5** Could you tell me what your favourite book/film is? / I'd like to know who your favourite author is.
>
> **Student B**
> **1** Can you tell me how long you've been learning English?/ I'd like to know when you started learning English.
> **2** Could you tell me where you go/went to school? Can you tell me how long you've been/were at that school?
> **3** Could you tell me what your hobbies are? / I'd like to know how long you've been [doing that hobby].
> **4** I'd like to know where you've been on holiday this year. / Could you tell me what your travel plans are? I'd like to know who you're going on holiday with. / Can you tell me how many countries you've visited?
> **5** Can you tell me what you do to stay fit? / I'd like to know what sports you do / what gym you go to.

4.1 ❯ Vocabulary

- Tell students that they are going to practise making and using collocations related to business strategy.
- Put students in pairs or groups of three. Give each pair/group a set of word cards and tell them to spread them out face up on the table. Give them three minutes to make up as many collocations as possible by matching pairs of grey and white cards. The group with the most correct collocations wins. Check as a class and write the collocations on the board.
- Put students in groups or three or four and give one copy of the business strategy card to each pair/group. Before they begin, you could ask them to look at the sentence stems and underline the collocations they formed in the first part of the activity.

- Ask them to choose a business (e.g. a supermarket chain, a food company, a hotel group, a boutique hotel, a restaurant, a fast-food outlet, an independent grocery store) and write it at the top of the card.
- Explain that each group has to create a business strategy for their company by completing the sentences on the card.
- Groups present their strategies to the class and then do a class vote for the best one.

competitive prices   emerging markets   major player
cut costs   make money   make a profit   solve problems
miss opportunities   take risks   develop strategies
come up with a plan   tackle problems   product lines
profit margin   takeover bid

4.2 〉 Grammar

- Tell students that they are going to practise using modal verbs to talk about obligation, necessity, prohibition and recommendation.
- Divide the class into two groups, A and B, and hand out an A or B worksheet to each student. Each group has three problems and three solutions which they need to match to the other group's solutions and problems. Make sure students realise that the problems on their sheet do **not** match their solutions.
- Put students in A–A/B–B pairs or groups and give them time to think up problems and solutions. Encourage them to make notes.
- Now put students into A–B pairs and tell them that they should not look at each other's worksheets. Pairs work together to match the problems with the solutions and then discuss and compare their ideas.

Problem 1 - Solution B   Problem D - Solution 6
Problem 2 - Solution C   Problem E - Solution 4
Problem 3 - Solution A   Problem F - Solution 5

5.1 〉 Vocabulary

- Tell students that they are going to talk about online shopping, delivery and logistics.
- Put students in pairs or groups of three. Hand out one copy of the worksheet to each student and give them time to complete Exercise 1. In stronger classes, you could ask students to do this individually. Check answers with the class, making sure students pronounce the words correctly.
- Ask students to work on their own to decide if they agree or disagree with each statement. Tell them not to show their handouts to each other.
- Students now mingle and try to find at least one other student who agrees with them. Before they begin, point out that they shouldn't just read out the statements to each other – they should exchange opinions / ask each other questions (e.g. for 1: *Do you think too much packaging is used when you order something online?*). Encourage them to explain why they agree or disagree with each statement.

1 packaging **2** distribution **3** Automation **4** collection
5 delivery **6** Manufacturers **7** retailing **8** supplies
9 transportation **10** fulfilling

5.2 〉 Grammar

- Tell students that they are going to practise using passive forms to talk about a product.
- Hand out one copy of the worksheet to each student and give them two minutes to read the description and try to work out what the product is. Check the answer with the class.
- Then, working individually or in pairs, get students to read the text again and underline the passive forms. Check answers with the class.
- Put students in pairs. Explain that they will write similar sentences about a product they have chosen with their partner. Point out that the product has to be familiar to all the other students – it can't be something unusual or very new. Before students start writing, go over the list of prompts, making sure students know what everything means.
- Monitor and help students to write their sentences.
- Once students have finished, put them in different pairs to read out their sentences about their mystery products. They ask each other questions to find out more about the product. To make it more challenging, you could tell students that they can only ask *yes/no* questions.

1 The product is a mobile phone.
2 Most people have one of these. The one I've got is probably manufactured in China or maybe Brazil. I'm pretty sure mine was designed in Finland, though. I know the first one was invented by an American engineer called Martin Cooper. It's been around since the 1980s and has become an essential device for most people. It's been used by a whole generation of young people who don't know a world without it. Mostly, it is required for communication, but it can also be used for entertainment. It's made mostly of plastic but minerals are also used in its manufacture. These are often extracted from mines in Africa. These days, if it's ordered online, it will probably be shipped the same day, and should be delivered to your door the next day. It's breakable, so it will need to be packaged really well – probably in a box. In the future, I think it could be delivered by drone because it's really light.

6.1 〉 Vocabulary

- Tell students that they are going to talk about starting and running a business and practise vocabulary from Lesson 6.1.
- Hand out a copy of the worksheet to each student and get them to complete Exercise 1. They could do this individually or in pairs. Check answers with the class.
- Ask students to choose five questions from Exercise 1 they would like to ask another student. Put students into (different) pairs and ask them to take notes of their partner's answers.
- After a few minutes, put students into new pairs and get them to discuss five different questions.
- Students share one answer they found interesting or surprising with the class.

1 crowdfunding **2** set **3** start-ups **4** a business
5 gone **6** pitch **7** make **8** target **9** founding
10 growth **11** backing **12** investment **13** advice
14 fund **15** entrepreneurial

6.2 ❱ Grammar

- Tell students that they are going to practise using reported speech.
- Ask students to imagine they are at a conference party. Tell them you are going to give them a card with a statement and a question on it. Hand out one card to each student. (Depending on the size of your class, you may not need to use all the cards.)
- Students look at their cards and roleplay the situation as a class or in groups of six to eight, depending on the size of your class.
- Tell students that you want them to network. They should talk to all the other students and try to get their statement and question across in a natural way. Point out that the order in which they use them is not important. Once they've said what's on their card, they move on to another person.
- Tell students that they should try to remember what everybody said so that they can report it back to the rest of the class later.
- After six to eight minutes, put students in small groups to report back on what the other students told them and also on what they were asked. Get them to write as many sentences as they can remember, e.g. *Antonio told me he was studying economics. He said he really enjoyed it. He asked me whether I was a student too.*
- You could make this a competition. The group with the most correct reported statements and questions wins.

7.1 ❱ Vocabulary

- Tell students that they are going to play *Snap* with prefixes. Explain that they will have a pile of prefixes (pile A) and another of adjectives (pile B). The aim is to make negative (opposite) adjectives using the correct prefixes.
- Put students in pairs and give each pair two sets of cards, A and B. Ask students to shuffle each set and put the cards in two piles face down on their desks.
- Students take it in turns to pick up a card from each pile. If the cards aren't a match, they go back under each pile. If the cards are a match (e.g. *indirect*), the student who shouts out 'Snap!' first gets to make a sentence with the adjective (e.g. *My manager's comments were an indirect way of blaming me for the problem.*). If the sentence is correct, the student who made it keeps the cards. If it is incorrect, the other student keeps the cards. If there is any doubt, students should ask you for help.
- The student with the most cards at the end wins.
- Check as a class that students have all the correct opposites. Write them on the board if students need extra help.
- Follow up by asking students to share some of their sentences with the class.

indirect, unfriendly, informal, dishonest, unhelpful, unkind, impolite, unreserved, unsociable, disrespectful, uncool, inconvenient, incorrect, unfashionable, unimportant, impatient, imperfect, unpopular, unreliable, dissatisfied

7.2 ❱ Grammar

- Tell students that they are going to practise using past tenses.
- Divide the class into two groups, A and B.
- Hand out a worksheet, A or B, to each student and give them time to complete the text; they could do this individually or in A–A/B–B pairs. You could check answers with each group at this point, or after students have completed Exercise 2, as a whole class.
- Put students in A–B pairs for Exercise 2. Allow six to eight minutes for this activity. Explain that students can refer to their text if necessary, but they should not read – they should tell their story in their own words.
- You could ask students to discuss the similarities and differences in the anecdotes in their pairs or you could do this as a whole class discussion.

A
1 was working 2 had asked 3 forgot 4 was focusing
5 was feeling 6 hadn't sent 7 was thinking 8 thought
9 had sent 10 felt 11 asked 12 had given
B
1 asked 2 sounded 3 was working 4 had asked
5 didn't have 6 hadn't finished 7 woke up
8 hadn't sent 9 was walking 10 didn't say
11 had got 12 received

8.1 ❱ Vocabulary

- Tell students that they are going to practise talking about leadership qualities.
- Give each student a copy of the worksheet and allow three to five minutes for the ranking activity. Then put students in pairs to compare and discuss their answers. You might like to go through the list as a class before they begin, to check students understand all the points.
- The class survey in Exercise 2 can be done with students working in large groups or you could let them mingle and find out which quality their classmates ranked as the most and least important. Encourage students to ask lots of different questions (e.g. *Do you think giving clear instructions is really important? What's more important than that? I'm not sure giving praise is important. Do you agree?*). Discuss the results of the survey as a class.
- Put students in pairs and ask them to complete the sentences about leadership. They can come up with their own ideas or use the ideas in Exercise 1. You could then put pairs into groups of four to share and discuss their ideas. Alternatively, you can do this as a class discussion, asking different students to share their sentences with the class.

8.2 ❯ Grammar

- Tell students that they are going practise talking about famous businesspeople using relative clauses.

- Divide the class into two groups, A and B, and hand out an A or B worksheet to each student. Put students in A–A/B–B pairs and give them time to join the sentences using relative clauses. Explain that there is more than one possible way of combining the sentences. In weaker classes, you might want to do an example on the board.

- Students work in the same pairs for Exercise 2 and discuss what they know about the companies and people in the boxes.

- Put students in A–B pairs for Exercise 3. They exchange information about the people and companies on their lists. They should not show each other their sentences, and the student asking the questions should take notes of his/her partner's answers.

- Students use their notes from the previous exercise to write their own sentences and then check with their partner. If time is short, students can do this exercise for homework. You could ask them to check with their partners in the next class or get them to research the people and companies online.

Possible answers

A

1 Mary Barra, who is the first woman to run a global motor company, is Chief Executive of General Motors.

2 Warren Buffet, who said, 'You can't make a good deal with a bad person', is a famous American entrepreneur and head of the American multinational holding company Berkshire Hathaway Inc.

3 Ana Maiques is the Spanish CEO of Neuroelectrics, which is a company that develops technologies to treat the brain.

4 Pierre Omidyar, who was born in Paris and whose parents are Iranian, is the founder of eBay, which is an online auction and shopping website.

B

1 Wu Yajun is one of the richest women in China and the Chairwoman of Longfor Properties, which is an investment-holding company based in Beijing.

2 Jeff Bezos is the founder and Chief Executive of Amazon, which is one of the largest online retail companies in the world.

3 Ursula Burns, who was the first African-American Chief Executive of a top U.S. corporation, is now Chairwoman of Xerox and has been listed as one of the 100 most powerful women in the world.

4 Leonardo Del Vecchio, whose company Luxottica is the biggest producer and seller of glasses in the world, is one of the richest men in Italy, after Michelle Ferrero.

Unit 1 〉

1 Before you read, choose the correct definition (a or b) for the words in bold in these sentences.

1 Some people say that money is a good **incentive** to work hard.

 a something that motivates you to work more or do something new

 b something you give to someone who works hard

2 Eduardo is a very good footballer and knows a lot about game tactics, so now he would like to become a **coach**.

 a someone who trains and advises a person or team

 b the manager of a team

3 An inspector is coming to our school tomorrow to **evaluate** the quality of teaching; I'm sure they will think it's very good.

 a make something better

 b decide how good or bad something or someone is

4 This document provides a **framework** for future cooperation with Canada.

 a a set of ideas and rules that you use to decide what to do and how to do it

 b an official decision which allows you to do something

5 I love working with my Korean colleagues but sometimes I find it difficult to understand their **mindset**.

 a a group of computer programs which can perform a lot of different tasks

 b the way in which people think about things and make decisions

6 It is better for teachers to give students some **autonomy** instead of always telling them what to do.

 a a reward that you give to someone who works hard and never causes problems

 b the opportunity to make your own decisions without being controlled by anyone else

2 Read the article and match the sub-titles (1–5) with the sections of the article (B–F).

1 What are the dangers? Section ____

2 What are the results? Section ____

3 When was it introduced? Section ____

4 What are the limits to independence? Section ____

5 How does it work? Section ____

3 Decide if the statements are *true* (T) or *false* (F).

1 Before 'responsabilisation', Michelin had already experimented with giving workers more autonomy.

2 At Le Puy, workers on the factory floor work in teams, but there are no team leaders.

3 At Le Puy, the teams' performance is assessed by the executive committee.

4 Mr Senard does not believe everyone is ready to support the idea of worker empowerment.

5 There were similar initiatives to Michelin's in Japan and in the USA more than 20 years ago.

6 Michelin's programme has influenced both large and small companies.

4 Match 1–5 with a–e to make collocations used in the article.

1 team   **a** programme

2 training   **b** companies

3 quality   **c** member

4 chief   **d** executive

5 small- and medium-sized   **e** control

5 Complete the sentences with collocations from Exercise 4.

1 A lot of customers say our new office chairs are not very good. I think we really have a problem with _____ _____ .

2 _____ _____ _____ _____ are usually based in only one place and are owned by only one person or by a small group of people.

3 The new _____ _____ is planning to reorganise our company.

4 I would like to follow a _____ _____ to improve my computer skills.

Michelin's 'responsabilisation': Power to the workers

A What is 'responsabilisation'?
It is a French word which describes how Michelin, the tyre-manufacturing company, wants to organise the way people work together. The company wants to involve workers more when it needs to make decisions. It also wants to give workers more control over what they do, and also to make
5 them feel responsible for what they do.

B Many years ago, Michelin had already introduced flexibility to allow certain team members to step in for an absent team leader. Some time later, the company tried giving greater autonomy to entire teams. The experiment was a success, so the company started extending the practice to more and more factories in the group.

10 **C** Michelin's plant in Le Puy-en-Velay, in South-central France, is one of six factories involved in the latest phase.
At Le Puy, a short training programme prepares workers for the switch to greater operational responsibility. They learn, for example, the basics of teamwork, how to manage conflicts, how to communicate positively and how to structure a project.
15 Team leaders do not give detailed orders on how to organise production or provide solutions to difficult situations. Instead, they act as coaches or they help to resolve disagreements.
Workers in the ten-strong teams divide responsibility between themselves. For example, one team member manages production, another oversees safety, a third, quality control. Together, they evaluate their own performance.
20 The teams work within a framework, which includes the vision and values of the group and the behaviour expected of Michelin staff.

D Group strategy is still decided at the top by the Chief Executive and executive committee. But some teams are already examining how they can handle more sensitive non-production issues such as recruitment, incentives and rewards.

25 **E** Individual workers at Le Puy say people are more engaged in their work, they deal with production line problems more quickly and they find their jobs more interesting. Michelin says the factories whose workers took on operational responsibility are happier. Besides, Le Puy's production is increasing.

F The Chief Executive, Mr Senard, says the biggest risks are not moving fast enough and not being
30 able to change the mindset of staff used to greater hierarchy.
Some managers may dislike losing status and power, and some workers have said that the granting of limited independence is just a cheap alternative to increasing wages.

G How different is Michelin's programme from previous management initiatives?
Giving decision-making power to front-line workers is not unusual. Taiichi Ohno, chief production
35 engineer at Toyota after the Second World War, insisted that teams should work out how to solve production line problems themselves. He called it 'autonomation' or 'automation with a human touch'.
In the USA, Tom Peters, the management writer, introduced the idea of 'liberation management' in the early 1990s, which had a big influence on companies such as W. L. Gore,
40 manufacturer of Gore-Tex fabric, and Harley-Davidson, the motorcycle group.
Over a decade ago in India, Vineet Nayar, then Chief Executive, turned the hierarchy of HCL Technologies upside down, with an 'employees first, customers second' approach that put managers at the service of valuable front-line staff.

H Do other companies experiment with 'responsabilisation'?
45 Some experts regard the Michelin programme as part of a wider movement towards giving workers more autonomy. Some small- and medium-sized companies in France and Belgium have gone further and no longer have any hierarchy at all.
Some big French companies, such as privately owned Decathlon, the sports equipment retailer, now have similar programmes.

Unit 2 >

1 Before you read, look at the words in bold in the article. Match them with their definitions (1–7). Use a dictionary if necessary.

1 the knowledge or skill necessary to do something _____

2 designed for or used by people who have a lot of money _____

3 an agreement to become business partners _____

4 when the value of the money of a country goes up and down _____

5 think that something is less big or important than it is _____

6 show the truth about something bad _____

7 make something less strong or effective little by little _____

2 Complete the article with the connectors in the box.

> as well as   for instance   however   such as

3 Read the article and number these topics in the order they are mentioned.

a the start of an alternative form of trade in luxury goods in China

b a forecast of the growth of online sales

c the influence of social media on price awareness

d how some companies have tried to adapt to the changes

e a list of the changes that have affected the luxury business

f two online fashion retailers striking a major deal

4 Decide if these statements are *true* (T) or *false* (F).

1 Net-a-Porter and Yoox's combined annual sales will reach €13 million.

2 The luxury industry had not predicted that so many people would be expert at using social media to check prices around the world.

3 People have different views about how the luxury industry should adapt to the changes caused by the digital age.

4 Some luxury brands sponsor artists and museums.

5 Chinese consumers are aware that Western companies' special pricing policy is good for them.

6 Some luxury companies are thinking of opening more new stores in Asia.

5 Check your answers to Exercise 4. Correct the false statements.

6 Find words and phrases in the article which mean the same as the following.

1 set up, established (Section A)

2 income from business activities (Section B)

3 make something continue without changing (Section B)

4 information you get by someone telling you (Section C)

5 make a problem or subject easy to notice so that people pay attention to it (Section D)

6 think about an idea or a plan again in order to change it (Section D)

Technological revolution in the luxury industry

A The internet changed the buying habits of the rich. A clear sign of the changes to the luxury industry in the digital age came from the **tie-up** between the two online fashion retailers Net-a-Porter and Italy's Yoox.

5   This major deal made Federico Marchetti, the entrepreneur who founded Yoox, Chief Executive of an online business with annual sales of €1.3 billion and 2 million customers.

    The tie-up showed how the luxury industry would change in the future. Traditionally, luxury companies had avoided the internet because they thought the web's democratisation of shopping **undermined** their exclusive, **upmarket** values.

B But luxury brands **underestimated** several factors, [1]_____ : how the internet
10 changed the habits of the rich; the rise of the Chinese as significant online shoppers; the increasing digital **know-how** of the general public, who use social media to compare prices; falling advertising revenue at fashion magazines; [2]_____ the fact that, through smart devices, the internet can be present everywhere. All indicated that the industry needed to change rapidly.

    Luca Solca, Managing Director and Head of Luxury Goods Research at Exane BNP Paribas, an
15 investment company, says that by 2020 online sales combined with digitally driven in-store sales – when customers have used the internet for research before they visit a store – will represent 50 percent of sales. Mr Solca says that if luxury brands want to survive and be successful, they need to keep up to date with changing digital technologies and practices.

    Not all people agree about how to adapt to the constantly changing consumer environment.
20   Groups such as Prada and Louis Vuitton, [3]_____ , have tried to preserve brand value by opening contemporary art museums in cultural centres such as Milan, Paris and Venice. Prada has also sponsored women directors at the Venice Film Festival.

C It is in the matter of pricing that the dramatic effect of social media and the internet is most noticeable. The internet has made it totally clear to consumers that the same handbag is on sale in
25 Beijing for a higher price than in Paris. Through social media, people can **expose** pricing policies in a click.

    Erwan Rambourg, Luxury Analyst at HSBC, says: 'Blogs, forums, word of mouth and travel are spreading knowledge of brands and what consumers should pay for them. This will probably force Brand Managers to stop thinking that they can charge Asian consumers more.'
30   '[4]_____ , Chinese consumers already know that they pay more and feel that Western companies are not fair to them,' says a Business Consultant based in Shanghai.

    The price gap has also caused a special kind of trade in luxury goods in China – the *daigou* industry – where the Chinese buy luxury goods outside China to resell at home, often on the internet.

D **Currency fluctuations**, the challenge of the internet and of attracting tourist shoppers highlight the
35 need for companies to rethink some of the main elements of their strategies.

    For example, some luxury companies which have spent millions of euros on opening new outlets in Asia in recent years are asking themselves whether they now need to reduce their physical networks and focus more on the internet.

Unit 3 ❯

1 **Read the article and choose the sentence which best summarises it.**

1 In this article, a middle-aged consultant explains in detail why he doesn't completely agree with Lucy Kellaway's views on job interview questions.

2 This text is about a *Financial Times* journalist who gives an employer advice about what questions to ask or not to ask job applicants.

3 In this article, Lucy Kellaway explains with some humour why she thinks it is not very useful to ask an applicant about the class of degree they obtained at university.

4 In answer to a reader's letter, Lucy Kellaway provides a list of the reasons why she thinks the most stupid question to ask a job applicant is 'What grade did you achieve for your degree?'

2 **Choose the correct option (a, b or c) to complete the sentences.**

1 Lucy Kellaway believes that you can be very successful in your career
  a even if you don't work hard.
  b even if you didn't get a top degree at university.
  c only if you got a top degree and work very hard all the time.

2 She believes that even if you know your colleagues very well,
  a you will not easily guess how well they did at university.
  b you should not ask them what grades they got at university.
  c they will not happily tell you what kind of students they were.

3 In her opinion,
  a it is a good idea to ask a job applicant to describe a situation in which they showed leadership.
  b talking about creativity is not interesting.
  c 'What class of degree did you get?' is not the most stupid interview question.

4 Lord Winston only hired applicants with upper second-class degrees because
  a he couldn't find anyone who did better than that.
  b he himself hadn't spent enough time at university.
  c he thought they were probably more interesting and curious.

5 According to the author, people who get a first-class degree
  a do not usually keep quiet about it.
  b are usually happier than other people.
  c do not ask other people how well they did.

3 **Match 1–6 with a–f to make collocations from the article.**

1 application
2 consulting
3 master's
4 career
5 paid
6 job

a success
b form
c employment
d applicant
e firm
f degree

4 **Complete the sentences with collocations from Exercise 3.**

1 Could you tell us how many undergraduates have to work in _____ during term time in order to finance their studies?

2 A _____ that has relevant work experience often has a better chance of being hired.

3 If you want to achieve _____ , it is important to build relationships and also to keep an open mind and seize all opportunities that present themselves.

4 The first stage of our admission test requires you to fill in a long _____ .

5 I'd like to know how I can prepare for a _____ in management.

Should an employer ask about a candidate's class of degree*?

Reader's question:

I was thinking of changing jobs and I went online to apply to one of the big five consulting firms. I really disliked the first question on the application form: 'What class of degree did you get at university?' I have more than ten years' experience, two master's degrees, several professional
5 certificates and enough to show professionally. I just don't feel it should matter whether you worked hard at university when you're mid-career – or even in your first job. Do you agree?
Consultant, male, 36

Lucy Kellaway's answer:

I do. The grades a student gets at university do not really show how good they will be at their job.
10 That is partly because the grade could be the result of one of two very different things. A high mark might mean the person is very bright; a low mark might mean the person is, well, not so bright.

Equally, it could mean they spent their student years working very hard (or just being lazy). But even if an employer knew why a student got a high grade or a low one, it wouldn't be particularly useful. This is because academic intelligence doesn't necessarily lead to career success. I'm often
15 surprised that some of the most intelligent people I know are not very good at their jobs, and some of them even seem rather stupid professionally.

Even if the grade reflected hard work (or lack of it), that still doesn't prove that the person would continue to work really hard when they are in paid employment. Most of us work much harder at some points in our lives than at others. I know lots of people who were lazy university students but
20 have been exceptionally hard-working ever since.

A couple of years ago, I did a test of my *Financial Times* colleagues: I tried to guess the class of degree they had received. I know most of those colleagues very well, but I was really bad at guessing who got what grade. Besides, there was not necessarily a link between the best degrees and the finest journalists.
25 Yet, despite all this, I don't think that the question is quite as idiotic as you evidently do. Or at least I don't think it is as idiotic as the other questions that were probably on the form.

I bet they asked you to describe situations in which you showed leadership. Or maybe they asked you about 'creativity', so you had to talk and talk using a lot of big words but not really saying anything meaningful.
30 At least a grade is a fact, and employers can do with it whatever they choose. It's possible that they didn't want to hear that you got a top degree at all. A couple of years ago the scientist Lord Winston announced that he only hired job applicants with 2.1s (upper second-class degrees). Anyone who did better than that, he reasoned, hadn't spent enough time at university becoming the sort of interesting, curious person he was looking for.
35 As an aside, it is obvious from your question that you didn't get a first-class degree (neither did I). In my experience, the people who did are more than happy to tell employers – or anyone at all – forever and ever, just how well they did.

---

*In the UK, there are usually four classes of degree, depending on academic achievement and students' grades throughout their study time. In order from highest to lowest: first-class [1st]; upper second-class [2:1]; lower second-class [2:2]; third-class [3rd].

Unit 4 ❯

1 Before you read, choose the correct definition (a or b) for the words in bold in these sentences.

1 Google has just opened a new **physical store** in my hometown.
   a a shop that sells body-building equipment
   b a real shop, not an online shopping site

2 Shopping online is OK, but there's nothing like a good **brick-and-mortar** bookshop.
   a real, not virtual
   b antique

3 Our corner shop is open 24/7 and sells all the **convenience items** you need.
   a things like food, drinks, magazines, soap, toothpaste, etc. that people buy frequently
   b things like gadgets, souvenirs, etc. that people buy as presents

4 I haven't got enough money for luxuries. I spend it all on **groceries**.
   a second-hand clothes
   b food and other things used in the home

5 Zara has retail **outlets** in many cities around the world.
   a shops
   b advertisements

6 Our company has an annual **revenue** of about €12 million.
   a amount of tax companies have to pay every year
   b money received from selling goods or services

2 Read the article and complete the gaps (1–4) with the sentences (a–e). There is one extra sentence you do not need.

a So, from Amazon's point of view, the grocery market is very attractive.
b Amazon also built a network of smaller warehouses close to city centres.
c U.S. retailers must evolve to succeed in the next decade.
d For example, it opened its first physical bookstore in Seattle in 2015 and later opened more in several other cities.
e Instead, they order their goods online in advance, then drive to the store and wait in their car.

3 Choose the sentence which best summarises the article.

1 Excellent overall sales figures make it possible for Amazon to experiment with physical stores in new areas such as groceries.
2 Because its main competitors have difficulty finding growth in their grocery sales, Amazon has decided to focus on bookstores instead.
3 Amazon's growing network of warehouses close to urban centres is evidence that the company is giving up on online sales.

4 Decide if the statements are *true* (T) or *false* (F).

1 Amazon's new strategy means it is no longer exclusively an online company.
2 Over three quarters of U.S. retail sales are already online.
3 Retailers can sell groceries at a much higher price than what they buy them.
4 At the Seattle store, customers can drive up and down the aisles to choose the items they want to buy.
5 Amazon's Prime Now programme is now available outside the USA.
6 Analysts think Amazon will experiment with physical clothes shops as well.

5 Complete the sentences with prepositions.

1 Amazon is one of the most valuable businesses _____ the world.
2 Grocery is probably Amazon's biggest potential for a rise _____ revenue.
3 I order my groceries online _____ advance, then I go to the drive-in store.
4 Amazon's warehouses are usually close _____ city centres.
5 Our courier will deliver your order _____ your office within two hours.
6 Amazon has developed an excellent strategy to compete _____ its brick-and-mortar rivals.

FT

Amazon's drive-in grocery stores continue offline strategy

A Amazon's online-only strategy was so successful that the company quickly became the world's largest online retailer and one of the most valuable businesses in the world. Encouraged by its success and rapidly increasing overall sales, the company decided to start testing out new strategies.

5   Despite the growth of the U.S. online retail market, more than 80 percent of U.S. retail sales were still offline. People familiar with Amazon's thinking knew that it would start looking for new ways to get a piece of such sales.

Indeed, Amazon started to experiment with brick-and-mortar outlets. [1]_____ Very soon, it also started to increase its brick-and-mortar presence in other areas.

10 **B** Amazon set itself a key new goal: mastering the grocery market. Although the difference between what it costs retailers to buy groceries and what they sell them for is relatively small, shoppers buy grocery items more frequently than any other category of products. [2]_____ A financial analyst also said that grocery was the company's biggest potential for a rise in revenue.

C The retailer's first step into physical stores for grocery and convenience items was its innovative
15   grocery store in Seattle. It is a drive-in store, so customers do not have to walk up and down the aisles looking for the products they want to buy. [3]_____ When their order is ready, an Amazon employee takes it to their car, and that's it.

D [4]_____ These warehouses are used as bases for its one-hour and two-hour delivery programme, 'Prime Now'. How does this programme work? First, customers have to have an
20   Amazon Prime account; they also need to make sure Prime Now is available in their area. They can then order online their selection of groceries, convenience items, electronics, etc., and an Amazon courier will deliver the order to the customer's house or workplace within two hours. Delivery is completely free for members of the Prime Now programme but there is something to pay if the customer wants to get the items within one hour of ordering.
25   Amazon's futuristic 'Prime Now' programme expanded to many U.S. cities, as well as to other cities in other parts of the world such as London and Paris.

E Analysts expect that it is only a matter of time before Amazon starts testing out brick-and-mortar strategies in other areas, starting with clothing. With the success of its online model, Amazon has already turned the traditional retail market upside down, and now it continues to adapt its
30   strategy to compete with its brick-and-mortar rivals.

Unit 5 ❯

1 Before you read, look at the words in bold in the article. Match them with their definitions (1–4). Use a dictionary if necessary.

    1 follow the movement or development of something _____

    2 the things you buy _____

    3 machines with a long, flat, moving band of rubber, often used in factories and airports to move things from one place to another _____

    4 the way from one place to another _____

2 Read the article and choose the best subtitle for it.

    1 Postal operators invest in small e-commerce and technology companies

    2 Parcel companies fail to meet online shoppers' expectations

    3 From drones to tracking software, the aims are speed and convenience

    4 Modernisation no longer a priority for parcel companies

    5 Delivery apps disappoint consumers

3 Complete the gaps in the article (1–4) with the phrases (a–f). There are two extra phrases you do not need.

    a within 90 seconds of entering the centre

    b how the vans should be packed

    c for consumers to cancel orders

    d and the robots are controlled using a mobile app

    e and displays the van's location on a map in real time

    f for a next-day delivery

4 Decide if the statements are *right* (R), *wrong* (W) or if the text *doesn't say* (DS).

    1 Speed of delivery is the only thing that matters for online shoppers in the UK.

    2 DPD is the leader in innovation in the market.

    3 DPD has an app that lets customers contact the driver.

    4 Some companies use software that enables drivers to find the best route for delivery.

    5 Couriers working for Hermes will soon work Saturdays and Sundays as well.

5 Put the letters in brackets in the correct order to complete the sentences.

    1 Our new software helps our workers _____ (acpk) the vans in the most efficient way.

    2 A lot of companies _____ (netsiv) large sums of money in innovation and technology.

    3 An increasing number of people now choose to _____ (dorre) things online, but many still prefer to go to a shopping centre.

    4 More and more customers now expect parcel companies to _____ (redveil) their goods within a few hours of ordering.

    5 We plan to _____ (vledpoe) new software that will enable our customers to track their order in real time.

Parcel services plan to deliver any time, any place

A Online shoppers in the UK increasingly expect that they can click on 'Place order' late into the night and still take delivery of their purchases the next day. Shoppers demand speed and they also want to get the goods they have ordered at a convenient time and place. 'You can buy online later and later in the day [1]_____ ,' says Mark McVicar, Transport Analyst at Barclays Bank.
5 'Because a lot of retailers can take orders up to midnight, there is now a much shorter time to get products from an online retailer to a local distribution centre and then on to a particular parcel **route**,' McVicar explains.

B The response by parcel companies is to invest tens of millions of pounds in technology, from machinery to software.
10 DPD, part of French state-owned group La Poste, is among the companies leading the innovations. Last year the express delivery group opened one of Europe's biggest parcel centres, a £100 million facility in England, with the latest technology. Inside the 470-metre-long building, parcels are loaded onto **conveyor belts**. As soon as the parcels are on the belts, they are directed by electronic scanners to one of 172 exits [2]_____ .
15 A lot of changes are happening in Britain's £9 billion parcel market. For example, Amazon is experimenting with flying drones to drop off **purchases**. The U.S. technology company's programme is still in development, but it hopes the small, pilotless air vehicles will eventually deliver packages up to ten miles from its warehouses within half an hour.

C Companies have also started to develop more and more innovative software. One of their goals is to
20 try to shorten delivery times. Another goal is to develop ways for consumers to **track** orders, select a specific time period for delivery or choose a collection point other than home.
DPD now has an app that gives customers until 1 a.m. on the day of delivery to select a one-hour period. Later, customers can change the collection point to a neighbour or 'pick-up shop', or change the date. The app sends information when a driver is 30 minutes away [3]_____ .

25 **D** Giving consumers flexibility on timing sometimes makes it difficult to plan routes for drivers. Larger companies use special software to find the most efficient routes and [4]_____ . Hermes, one of the UK's biggest parcel companies after Royal Mail, is investing £18 million in 21,000 handheld devices for couriers and parcel shops. The devices will include route-planning software to help the company deliver within two hours. In the past, its couriers worked weekdays using
30 paper documents, and tracking information became available 48 hours later, says Hermes UK. Soon, it adds, its couriers will work any day of the week, 'have the latest technology to do their job and real-time tracking will be available.'

Unit 6 ❯

1 Before you read, look at the words in bold in the article. Match them with their definitions (1–5). Use a dictionary if necessary.

1 an aim, belief or organisation that a group of people support (e.g. by raising money) or fight for _____

2 borrow money from a bank _____

3 a course in which you learn a lot about something in a very short time _____

4 in large amounts, to sell to individual people _____

5 talking a lot to other people about all the good and great things you have done _____

2 Read the article and match the headings (1–4) with sections A–C. There is one extra heading you do not need.

1 Writing books: the best way to promote oneself

2 Dynamism, generosity and flexibility

3 Learning from both success and failure

4 Never too young to start learning how to do business

3 Read sections A and B again. Choose the option (a, b or c) which best completes each sentence.

1 As a young child, Mr Devlyn often crossed the border into Texas because he wanted

a to visit his American father, who was an eye doctor in El Paso.

b to look for other children who could work for him.

c to buy goods that he could then sell back home.

2 Two of the things Mr Devlyn learnt as a young child were

a buying wholesale and promoting one's business.

b selling houses and translating from English into Spanish.

c examining eye patients and making glasses for them.

3 The main reason for Mr Devlyn's success seems to be that

a he never failed in anything.

b he took risks and had some good opportunities.

c he adopted innovative ideas from Japan.

4 One of the most important things Mr Devlyn learnt is that

a first-class service makes your customers want to come back.

b strong competition in business is in fact better than no competition at all.

c very few people learn from their mistakes.

4 Decide if these statements are *true* (T) or *false* (F).

1 Mr Devlyn opened a small shop in Ciudad Juárez to sell imported chocolate bars.

2 He was not an only child.

3 He can speak both Spanish and English.

4 He began to learn how to make glasses when he was a teenager.

5 He advertised the family business only in Ciudad Juárez.

6 He has shops in more than three different countries.

7 Mr Devlyn is not a shy, reserved person.

8 He has helped people in need.

Hyperactive businessman builds opticians' empire from Mexico

A As an adult, Frank Devlyn built his parents' small optician's into the biggest chain in Latin America. But it was selling U.S. sweets in Mexico as a young boy in the 1940s that gave the president of Devlyn Group his first taste for business.

'Mars, Snickers, Milky Way – they didn't exist in Ciudad Juárez,' says Mr Devlyn. At the age of
5 eight, he would cross from the northern border town into El Paso, Texas, buy the chocolate bars and sell them to his neighbours back home. 'I was selling house to house,' he says, recalling that he got a good price: 'I had no competition.'

It was a **crash course** in business. 'I learnt how to buy **wholesale**,' he says, and within two years he had eight other children working for him selling the sweets.

10 At the same time, as the eldest of six children, he was beginning to learn the family business, which was set up in 1936 by his American father and Mexican mother, both opticians, in Ciudad Juárez. He translated while 'the American eye doctor', who had never learnt Spanish, examined patients. By the age of nine he had learnt how to make glasses.

He also learnt the benefits of publicity and promotion by knocking on doors both sides of the
15 border and giving out advertisements and calendars to shopkeepers.

B After his father died when Mr Devlyn was 22, he was asked by American Optical to take over a factory. He accepted, **took out** his first **loan** and then went from success to success. Now he is the president of a business with 1,200 opticians' shops, mainly in Mexico but also in Guatemala, El Salvador and the USA.

20 An early lesson was to go where there was no competition and 'to offer such good service [that] people are customers for life.' He was also open to new ideas, such as conducting eye tests in the middle of a shop, not behind closed doors – something he had seen in Japan.

But there have been downs as well as ups. Mr Devlyn at one point wanted to use only frames that he had manufactured himself. It was a failure. 'I learnt from that. I learnt like crazy,' he says.

25 **C** Now in his late 70s, Mr Devlyn is not afraid of **self-promotion** and says he wants to stand out. He talks easily and with confidence, telling anecdotes and showing off selfies, including one with Mexico's president, Enrique Peña Nieto. Melanie, his eldest daughter and president of the board of Devlyn Holdings, says her father is an internet addict: 'I don't think his brain is ever off. He's a hyperactive adult, which is very good for the business,' she says.

30 The former president of charitable body Rotary International, Mr Devlyn is also the author of a series of books, including *Frank Talk, Frank Talk on Leadership* and *Frank Talk on Public Speaking*. He also wants to write several more books, including one on the history of the optical industry.

He has helped a number of social **causes** and has provided free glasses to one million Mexicans who can't pay for eye care.

35 He has experienced the transformation of Ciudad Juárez from a sleepy town to a busy centre manufacturing a lot of goods for export.

Mr Devlyn also understands the need to keep moving with the times. In 2014, his company merged with Opticas del AH, which is owned by Linzor Capital Partners. 'You've got to move forward. What got you here won't get you there,' he says.

Unit 7 >

1 Before you read, choose the correct definition (a or b) for the words in bold in the sentences.

1 He made a serious **blunder** when he told everyone that he thought the new manager was no good.
   a a short public presentation
   b a careless or stupid mistake

2 A teacher should **praise** students when they work hard.
   a say nice and positive things about
   b give more work to

3 They often **criticise** the government for not investing enough in the health service.
   a request a special meeting with
   b say that someone or something is bad in some way

4 He finally agreed to sell his car although it was very difficult to **persuade** him.
   a make someone do something by asking them many times to do it
   b say nice and positive things about

5 One of my grandmother's dreams was a more **egalitarian** society. A lot has changed since her days but in some places some people have more rights than others.
   a a system in which all people are equal
   b a system in which some people have more power than other people

6 Boris says he will **bypass** his manager and go straight to the director.
   a communicate directly with his manager
   b communicate directly with someone above his manager

2 Read the article and complete the gaps (1–3) with the paragraphs (A–C).

3 Read the article and number the topics in the order they are mentioned.

   a academic work that can help businesspeople understand different cultures
   b how a South-American businessman adapts to local circumstances in Europe
   c the most important piece of advice from Lenovo's Chief Diversity Officer
   d what the Chinese like to do before getting down to business
   e a frequent reason why people misunderstand each other
   f a company where employees are relaxed about cultural differences

4 Complete the collocations from the article with the verbs in the box.

| build   call   deal   get   give   keep   play   socialise |

1 _____ with a problem   5 _____ by the rules
2 _____ a meeting   6 _____ things done
3 _____ feedback   7 _____ trust
4 _____ to a schedule   8 _____ with colleagues

5 Complete the sentences with collocations from Exercise 4.

1 I think it's much better to _____ as soon as it occurs rather than wait until it gets more serious.

2 Safety at work concerns all of us, so I suggest we _____ for Wednesday morning to discuss those important issues together.

3 When you _____ on an employee's performance, make sure you include both positive points and things to work on.

4 In China and in many Arab or Latin American countries, you need to _____ before you do business.

5 I generally like to be as efficient as possible and to get things done, but I also like to make time to _____ .

How to fix culture clashes in global teams

1 ____

Language blunders are a common problem but, once discovered, mostly easy to deal with. Erin Meyer, a professor at Insead, believes relations are really tested when we forget that how we praise, criticise, persuade and get things done is an expression of the culture in which we grew up – not simply our personality.

2 ____

Yolanda Lee Conyers, an American and Chief Diversity Officer at the Chinese computer maker Lenovo, knows how easy it is to start a relationship badly. After Lenovo purchased IBM's PC business, her job was to bring East and West together. So, she started calling a lot of meetings, but very soon some people told her that the Chinese did not like her.

3 ____

For successful team-working, it is also very important to recognise that what gets the job done in one culture might lead to problems elsewhere. Philip Rooke, the British CEO of Spreadshirt, a global online clothing business based in Germany, has a team with 20 different nationalities. They do not avoid talking about their differences – instead, they joke about them. 'We say if a German isn't criticising, it's praise.' Some nations, like the Germans and the Dutch, are taught to give open and honest feedback, while others are less direct.

Those who wish to understand cultural differences better can turn to research such as Geert Hofstede's study of national differences at IBM, and Professor Meyer's Culture Map.

The map shows what kinds of behaviour are considered more or less standard in work styles around the world. For example, in many advanced economies, an effective manager is one who always keeps to a schedule. But in countries where the electricity might suddenly fail, the best time managers are those who can quickly change or adapt their plan when something unexpected happens.

With so many differences, how can organisations function peacefully? Ms Lee Conyers' advice is simple: 'We say: before judging people, let's first be sure that we understand their intention.'

But 'when in Rome', should a manager from overseas 'do as the Romans do'* or stay true to his or her own business practices? Professor Meyer recommends you should 'know how to do in Rome' and then decide which behaviour will produce better results. Jose Carvalho, a Brazilian who heads the commercial payments division of American Express in Europe, agrees. He thinks egalitarian workplaces are great, but he says: 'If I went straight into a hierarchical market and bypassed three layers of management, I'd upset quite a few people and wouldn't get anything done.' Obviously, understanding when to play by local rules is extremely useful.

---

*If you say 'When in Rome, do as the Romans do', you believe that when people are in a foreign country, they should behave like the local people – not like people from their culture.

A She so much wanted to get things done that she had forgotten one thing: for the Chinese, it is very important to build trust first by socialising with colleagues. Another problem was her use of the word 'request'. 'To us, "request" sounds polite; but the standard translation in Mandarin Chinese is more like "demand", which naturally upsets people,' she says.

B As she puts it, 'When misunderstandings happen, it's often not because we assume people from other cultures are different from us, but because we assume they are like us.' So we may have the impression that the answer we get to a question or a request was unfriendly or even rude when in fact it was intended to be helpful.

C Teams that are in different corners of the world have become part of working life. Organisations that bring nationalities together are often interesting and creative places to work. But cross-cultural working can be difficult, even when nations might superficially seem similar.

Unit 8 ❯

1 Before you read, check that you know the meaning of the words/phrases in bold. Match 1–6 with a–f to make definitions. Use a dictionary if necessary.

1 A **top-down** way of organising a business is one in which

2 A **bottom-up** way of organising a business is one in which

3 When you **justify**,

4 **Idealism** is the belief that

5 **Optimism** is a tendency to believe that

6 If someone is **assertive**,

a you give an acceptable explanation for something that other people think is unreasonable.

b you should live according to high standards and principles, even when they are very difficult to achieve in real life.

c employees are involved in decision-making and can make suggestions about how the organisation should be led.

d they behave in a confident way.

e the most important people make decisions and tell people below them what they should do.

f good things will always happen.

2 Read the article and choose the sentence which best summarises it.

1 Interviews with senior leaders and future leaders show that leadership styles haven't changed much over the past ten years and are not likely to change much in the future.

2 In this article, various senior and future business leaders explain why they believe a top-down style of leadership is best, although the relationship between leaders and followers is changing quickly.

3 Influence rather than titles and position; collaboration rather than hierarchy; dialogue rather than authority – this is what 'leadership' means for both senior and younger leaders today.

3 Read sections A and B again. Decide if these statements are *true* (T) or *false* (F).

1 The author found that both senior and younger leaders hold similar views about the future of leadership.

2 According to Dame Athene Donald, female leaders today usually lead by giving orders.

3 The author found that the new generation of leaders are in fact still in favour of hierarchical structures.

4 Members of the next generation do not think it is important for leaders to be willing to explain their actions or to be criticised for them.

5 It seems that in future people will think that someone's networks are more important than their position.

4 Read section C again. Choose the option (a, b or c) which best completes each sentence.

1 According to the author, the next generation of leaders
   a are too ambitious and idealistic.
   b will probably be unable to deal effectively with economic and financial crises.
   c might feel the need to go back to a more traditional style of leadership.

2 The author believes that hierarchical structures will probably come back because
   a the younger generation is not optimistic enough.
   b such structures usually come back even if they disappear for a while.
   c too many organisations have a weak leader.

3 Some of the young leaders the author met
   a were not keen to adopt an assertive style even when necessary.
   b worried about having too many responsibilities if they were in a position of power.
   c had already had their dreams destroyed by inflexible organisations.

4 The author suggests that
   a today's senior leaders would like to use the same leadership style as their predecessors'.
   b today's young leaders will probably bring about a lot of changes over the next decade.
   c leaders generally lack a clear vision of what they want to achieve.

5 Match 1–6 with a–f to make collocations from the article.

1	hold	**a**	about people
2	develop	**b**	an approach
3	care	**c**	a position
4	justify	**d**	influence
5	lose	**e**	(one's/your/their, etc.) decisions
6	destroy	**f**	(someone's/your/their, etc.) ambitions

6 Complete the sentences with the correct form of a collocation from Exercise 5.

1 There are many different ways to encourage staff development. You just have to _____ that works for you.

2 Federico had _____ of authority and influence for many years, so he found it difficult to have to work as an assistant in his new job.

3 Good business leaders, teachers and doctors all have something in common: they genuinely _____ .

4 Never tell your children that they are too ambitious because you might _____ .

5 The idea that government is responsible for the well-being of people began to _____ about 50 years ago.

The new leadership

A I asked a group of senior leaders – men and women who hold or have held senior positions in the military, business, science, academia and the arts – and a group of 'next-generation' leaders in their early twenties what 'leadership' meant to them. Increasingly, they suggest, influence is more important than power and position, networks more than hierarchies, and intelligence more than force.

Sir Jeremy Greenstock, former UK Ambassador to the United Nations and Chairman of geopolitical advisory group Gatehouse Advisory Partners, says leaders must find a balance 'between leading and listening, between top-down and bottom-up, between short-term and long-term.'

Dame Athene Donald, Professor of Physics and Master of Churchill College (University of Cambridge), says that leaders today have to give people reasons why they should do something, rather than give them orders. She links this development to the rise of more women to leadership roles.

Harriet Green, former Chief Executive of travel group Thomas Cook and now head of three IBM business divisions, says that just being the oldest, longest-serving or next in line is no longer good enough to be a leader. Organisations are starting to develop the more collaborative approach that Sir Nicholas Kenyon, Managing Director of the Barbican arts centre, calls 'responsive leadership': in other words, a good leader is one who 'listens to the audience' and can feel in advance the kind of things they might be interested to discover.

B The next generation has the ambition – and the tools – to make these changes happen more quickly. They want to work in organisations that have a far flatter structure, in which leaders really 'care about the people who are following' them, according to Fatima Islam, who is studying war and psychiatry at King's College, London,

and already leads 200 people in the university's Officers' Training Corps.

Members of the next generation say they will expect leaders to create a culture based more on trust, fairness and honesty, to offer clearer feedback, and to be able to justify their decisions to their followers. Titles will be less important, but influence over wider networks of people will be more important.

C Clearly sooner or later the ambition and idealism of the next generation of leaders will come face to face with the complex realities of our world. They will meet a world in which leadership failures have caused global financial and economic crises and wars in various regions. For this reason, it is not impossible that at some point a crisis leader of the more traditional type will be needed again. Despite the younger generation's optimism, hierarchies and relationships based on power may lose influence for some time, but then – as they usually do – come back again stronger than before. I have met – though not in this group – young leaders who are not willing to take on positions of power, even when it seems clear that a more assertive style is what is needed. Finally, and very sadly, two things may destroy the younger generation's dreams and ambitions. On the one hand, there is the growing number of responsibilities that they will have; on the other hand, there is the fact that existing leadership models are so difficult to stop or even to change.

But since the senior leaders I interviewed all made clear they had to lead differently from how their predecessors led, it seems likely that the next ten or twenty years will see even greater transformation. As Lawrence Baker, who works at a consultancy developing novel medical devices, says: 'It's about, "This is what this place might look like – how should we get there?"'

Unit 1 ›

1 1 a 2 a 3 b 4 a 5 b 6 b

2 1 F 2 E 3 B 4 D 5 C

3 1 T 2 F 3 F 4 T 5 T 6 T

4 1 c 2 a 3 e 4 d 5 b

5 1 quality control
2 small- and medium-sized companies
3 Chief Executive
4 training programme

Unit 2 ›

1 1 know-how
2 upmarket
3 tie-up
4 currency fluctuations
5 underestimate
6 expose
7 undermine

2 1 such as 2 as well as 3 for instance
4 However

3 1 f 2 e 3 b 4 d 5 c 6 a

4 1 F 2 T 3 T 4 T 5 F 6 F

5 (Model answers)
1 Net-a-Porter and Yoox's combined annual
sales will reach ~~€13 million~~ **€1.3 billion**.
5 Chinese consumers are aware that Western
companies' special pricing policy ~~is good~~ **is
not good** for them.
6 Some luxury companies are ~~thinking of
opening more new stores in Asia~~ **asking
themselves whether they need to focus
more on the internet**.

6 1 founded 2 revenue 3 preserve
4 word of mouth 5 highlight 6 rethink

Unit 3 ›

1 Sentence 3

2 1 b 2 a 3 c 4 c 5 a

3 1 b 2 e 3 f 4 a 5 c 6 d

4 1 paid employment
2 job applicant
3 career success
4 application form
5 master's degree

Unit 4 ›

1 1 b 2 a 3 a 4 b 5 a 6 b

2 1 d 2 a 3 e 4 b

3 Sentence 1

4 1 T 2 F 3 F 4 F 5 T 6 T

5 1 in 2 in 3 in 4 to 5 to 6 with

Unit 5 ›

1 1 track
2 purchases
3 conveyor belts
4 route

2 Subtitle 3

3 1 f 2 a 3 e 4 b

4 1 W 2 W 3 DS 4 R 5 R

5 1 pack
2 invest
3 order
4 deliver
5 develop

Unit 6 ›

1 1 cause
2 take out a loan
3 crash course
4 wholesale
5 self-promotion

2 2 C 3 B 4 A

3 1 c 2 a 3 b 4 a

4 1 F 2 T 3 T 4 F 5 F 6 T 7 T 8 T

Unit 7 ›

1 1 b 2 a 3 b 4 a 5 a 6 b

2 1 C 2 B 3 A

3 a 4 b 6 c 5 d 2 e 1 f 3

4 1 deal
2 call
3 give
4 keep
5 play
6 get
7 build
8 socialise

5 1 deal with a problem
2 call a meeting
3 give feedback
4 build trust
5 socialise with colleagues

Unit 8 ›

1 1 e 2 c 3 a 4 b 5 f 6 d

2 Sentence 3

3 1 T 2 F 3 F 4 F 5 T

4 1 c 2 b 3 a 4 b

5 1 c 2 b 3 a 4 e 5 d 6 f

6 1 develop an approach
2 held a position
3 care about people
4 destroy their ambitions
5 lose influence

1 ❯ Emails

Lead-in

The content and style of emails may differ from country to country. Here are some questions to think about before you write work-related emails:

1 Think about who you are writing to. In general, emails are either informal (more like spoken English) or formal/semi-formal (similar to a business letter). Emails to senior staff or people outside of your organisation may use more formal language than those sent to work colleagues.

2 Think about the style you need to use. Should your email be a) short and direct or b) longer with polite introductions and endings? Sometimes this depends on the recipient's country/culture.

3 What information are you going to communicate? Check the tone and organisation to make sure that the end result is polite and clear.

Model answers

Informal email

> Hi Deenesh,
>
> Just a quick email to say that we've arranged an informal presentation for project managers to introduce the new computer system. Are you free on Friday at 11 a.m? Let me know if you're available and I'll send details.
>
> We've decided to run a series of longer training sessions at the end of the month for all staff members. I've attached a list of software training course dates which might be of interest for your team.
>
> Let me know if you need anything else on this. Otherwise, hope to see you on Friday!
>
> All the best,
> Kasia

Formal email

> Dear Ms Park,
>
> Further to our telephone conversation yesterday, we are pleased to invite you to an open day for candidates applying for intern positions at Godrey & Maine. Attendees are requested to report to reception at 9.30 a.m. on 21 June. Please confirm by email whether you will be able to attend.
>
> The attached document contains full details of the events and seminars taking place throughout the day.
>
> We are delighted to confirm that we will be welcoming distinguished speakers from Harvard Business School, Singapore Management University and Instituto Tecnologico de Mexico (ITAM).
>
> Please do not hesitate to contact me if you have any further queries.
>
> Yours sincerely,
> Adriana Borges
> Training Coordinator

Functional language

Opening and closing an email

	Formal/Semi-formal	Informal
Greeting	Dear Sir or Madam, Dear Ms/Mrs/Miss/Mr/Dr Jamal,	Hi/Hello Norbert, Good morning Maria,
Concluding	Please do not hesitate to contact me if you have any queries. Do let me know if I can be of any further assistance on this matter. Please let me know if you require any further details/information. I look forward to hearing from you.	Feel free to contact me if you have any questions. Hope to see you / hear from you soon. Let me know if you need anything else / more information on this.
Signing off	Yours sincerely, Kind regards, Regards, Sincerely, Yours,	Best wishes, All the best, Best,

Reasons for writing

Function	Formal/Semi-formal	Informal
Linking to previous communication	Further to our conversation/ meeting, ... In response to your email, ... With reference to our conversation on Monday, ...	Thanks for your email. It was good to speak yesterday.
Saying why you are writing	I am writing to inform you that your application has been accepted. I am writing regarding / with regard to our meeting on 23 January.	I'm writing to let you know that the meeting has been changed from 2 p.m. to 3 p.m. I just wanted to confirm the date of our next meeting. Just a quick question about the schedule.
Referring to attachments	Please find attached a list of clients. You will find attached the itinerary. Please sign the contract attached.	I've attached the project update. You'll find the document/file attached.
Requests and offers	I would be most grateful if you could update your contact details. Please confirm if/whether you are able to attend. I would appreciate it if you could send me the file. I would also like to know when Mr Lee would be available for a call.	Could/Can you let me know if you're available? I was just wondering if you could join our meeting on Friday. Would you mind filling in the attached form?
Informing of a decision	We are delighted to confirm that Sara West has agreed to accept the role of Vice President. We are pleased to announce that work on the new building will begin in July. We are sorry / regret to inform you that your application was not successful.	We've decided to change the logo to improve brand image. We thought that it was best to discuss this at the meeting next week. I'm sorry to have to tell you that your proposal was not approved.

Invitations

Function	Formal/Semi-formal	Informal
Inviting	Godrey & Maine invite you to a fundraising auction on 29 August. We are pleased to invite you to a communications seminar. We hope that you will be able to join us for refreshments after the ceremony.	I'd like to invite you to a product demonstration. Are you free on Thursday? Would you like to come to a talk on career progression? It would be great if you could join us.
Thanking / Responding to thanks	Thank you for your kind invitation. It was my pleasure.	Many thanks / Thanks for the invitation. No problem!
Accepting	I would be delighted to attend the debate. I can confirm that I will be able to attend the videoconference.	I'd love to come. I'm looking forward to attending the workshop.
Declining	Unfortunately, it will not be possible to attend. Sadly, I will have to decline your kind invitation as I have a prior engagement.	Sorry, I won't be able to make the team meeting this week. It's not going to be possible to go to the seminar as I already have an appointment.

2 ❯ Letters

Lead-in Letter writing style and layout may differ from country to country. In general, letters have a more formal style than emails, and use of contractions, idioms and slang are avoided. Short paragraphs and clear language will make letters easier to read. Letters often include a subject line, which helps the reader understand important details.

Model answers Covering letter

Dear Mr Weber,

Re: Social Media Coordinator vacancy

I am writing in response to your recent advertisement on the Schloss Tours website regarding the planned expansion of your social media team. Please find my CV enclosed.

I have had two years' experience in the travel sector and also studied German at Edinburgh University. I have also gained additional post-graduate qualifications in computing and marketing. In my current position, I gained experience in IT and was the project leader for the team which developed the company website. For the last six months I have been in charge of social media and promotions while the department manager has been on maternity leave. The temporary post has been very successful and I would like to pursue a permanent position in the same field.

My main interest relates to the use of social media in the travel industry to promote sales, and the coordinator role would be an excellent opportunity to use both the marketing and language skills that I have developed. You will find detailed examples of the social media projects I have worked on in my CV.

I have also taken the opportunity to study your current social media presence and have some ideas which I would be interested to discuss with you. I would be grateful for the opportunity to learn more about the role and your company.

Thank you for taking the time to consider my application.

Yours sincerely,
Theresa Gonzalez

Letter of complaint

Dear Sir or Madam,

Subject: Catering quality issues

I am writing regarding a problem which occurred during a recent training session at the Greenlanes Outdoor Pursuit Centre in Eastbourne, Kent. Your company was asked to arrange lunch at the venue for 25 people, including 3 vegetarians.

However, there were serious issues with the service supplied. No vegetarian option was available. The quantity of food was insufficient (for 15 rather than 25 people). The quality of food was unsatisfactory (cold and inedible).

As a result, we had to pay extra to have food delivered from a local restaurant. I have tried to contact Alan Conway, who made the initial arrangements, but he has not answered my emails nor returned my calls. As a result, I am now contacting customer services in an attempt to resolve the issue.

We have used your company on previous occasions and have been pleased with the service. However, as you can imagine, we are disappointed both with the problems described and also with the communication breakdown that we have experienced.

We will not be able to pay the invoice submitted by your company until these concerns have been addressed and a suitable discount has been agreed.

Your prompt response will be appreciated.

Yours faithfully,
Alex Tekin

Functional language

Opening and closing a letter

Greeting	Dear Sir or Madam, Dear Ms/Mrs/Miss/Mr/Dr/Professor Kline, To whom it may concern,
Highlighting the subject	Re: Subject:
Referring to documents	Please find enclosed my CV. The enclosed documents/contract ...
Closing	I look forward to hearing from you. I look forward to (receiving) your reply.
Signing off	Yours sincerely, Yours faithfully, Kind regards, Sincerely, Yours,

Covering letters

Saying why you are writing	I am writing in response to / with regard to your advertisement on your website. I am writing to enquire about the position of Sales Manager you advertised on your website.
Providing information	I have completed a degree in computer science / a computer science degree. Additional qualifications have been gained in accounting. I have experience in the insurance sector.
Reasoning/ Skills	As you can see from my enclosed CV, my qualifications and experience match this position's requirements. My professional qualifications appear to be well suited to your company's requirements. These skills make me a perfect candidate for the job. I work well under pressure and enjoy working in a team. My native language is Italian, but I can also speak Spanish and German.
Closing remarks	I would appreciate / be grateful for the opportunity to discuss the position. If you require any further information, please do not hesitate to contact me. I would be happy to attend an interview at any time convenient to you. I can supply references from previous employers if required. Thank you for your time and consideration.

Letters of complaint

	Complaint
Referring to the problem	I am writing regarding a late order. I am writing to express my dissatisfaction with one of your products. I am writing to complain about a holiday you arranged for me.
Giving / Asking for details	There were serious issues with the service supplied. The goods were damaged. Several parts of the order were missing. The agreed delivery day was 25 April but the goods did not arrive until 11 May. Unfortunately, the products were nothing like we had been led to expect.
Describing results	Because of this, we were unable to use the product. As a result, we had to find another supplier. Due to this, the event had to be cancelled.
Requesting action	We would be grateful if our money was refunded. It seems only fair that you should offer a full refund. I would appreciate it if you could look into this matter as soon as possible. I would appreciate your immediate attention to this matter.

3 > Reports

Lead-in

The content and style of reports may differ from company to company. Reports are usually written using formal style and clear language. Here are some questions to think about before you write reports:

1   Will the reader be from inside or outside the company? Company style, layout and content may differ for internal and external reports.

2   What length is appropriate for the report? A short report might be a single page but longer reports require more detail. It is important to organise the information so that it is easy to read, using headings and subheadings. Longer reports may also include a summary or executive summary at the start, which contains key information, decisions or recommendations included in the report.

3   It is important to read and edit your report, checking punctuation, grammar, spelling and data before sending.

Model answer

Introduction

The purpose of this report is to consider requests by staff representatives to move over to flexible working hours from September. We will explain the reasons that the changes have been requested and look at the potential problems and effects. Finally, the report will offer recommendations regarding limited changes to working hours.

Reasons for changes to working hours

Staff representatives have raised employee concerns that the current working hours are leading to problems in staff retention. The HR department has also noted that it is currently proving difficult to attract new staff. After studying our competitors in the industry, the following ideas were put forward for consideration:

- Increase salaries by five percent or offer a performance-related annual bonus scheme.
- Offer flexible working hours to attract employees with young families back to the workforce and retain current employees.
- Include an additional two days to current annual paid leave after one year's service.

Feedback from a recent board meeting indicated that it would not be possible to increase wages, offer a bonus or extend annual leave, but that it would be possible to explore the possibility of flexible working hours.

Problems and effects

While staff would support flexible working hours, concerns have been raised by management. A series of consultation meetings found that during the next six months, three major projects will begin which will require intensive teamwork. A key issue raised by team leaders and project managers is that flexible hours would cause problems scheduling meetings and working hours for collaborative tasks, which could have an impact on productivity.

Recommendations

While full flexible hours would not be practical, it is recommended that staff should be offered the option of starting and ending the day an hour earlier or later. Discussion with management teams indicate that these arrangements are unlikely to cause problems with current or future projects and would prove popular with staff. The Marketing department has agreed to take part in a one-month trial and the findings will be reported back to department heads at the next interdepartmental meeting. If the trial is successful, limited changes to working hours would then be recommended to the board of directors.

Conclusion

This report has looked at requests by staff representatives to move to flexible working hours for staff. We have considered views that working hours are one of the factors which make our company less attractive to potential new staff when compared to competitors.

Consultation with management teams highlighted the fact that moving over to fully flexible work patterns could cause problems with projects which require team collaboration and common schedules. Instead, it was recommended that staff are offered limited flexibility in the start and end times of the working day. A trial period has been agreed and findings will be presented in the next interdepartmental meeting. If the trial is successful, we would then recommend moving to implement these changes in all departments across the company.

Functional language

Starting and ending a report

Most reports will contain an introduction, a main body and a conclusion. Some longer reports may also include a summary, an appendix (additional data or information at the end of the report), references or a table of contents.

Section	Function	Example
Summary	It is found at the start of a report and it tells the reader what type of information the report will contain. It is usually short (less than 150 words). The summary can be written after the rest of the report is complete.	**This report explores** global trends in workplace design. Each year over 3,000 small companies close due to problems with financing new ideas. **The report looks at ways** in which the financial sector can support small businesses and encourage growth.
Introduction	It states the purpose of the report and briefly outlines what the report intends to do.	**The purpose of this report is to** outline the advantages and disadvantages of using green energy and recommend ways to improve environmental strategy in line with company policy. **The aim of the report is to look into** the cause and effect of stress in the workplace **and suggest solutions** for both employers and employees. **This report looks into** the main reasons for customer service complaints **and proposes changes** to staff training in order to resolve the issues.
Conclusion	It restates and summarises the main points of the report. Bullet points or numbered lists may be used to highlight key information.	**In this report we have looked at** ways to improve productivity **and outlined** key areas which need to be improved. **In conclusion,** it is essential to communicate the relationship between exercise, diet and health to educational organisations.

Main body of a report

The main body of the report expands key points or findings, outlines problems or issues and makes recommendations. Headings and subheadings are used to organise information and bullet points can highlight key points.

Reporting problems, reasons and results	**The main problem is** pollution which is destroying sea life. **The key issue seems to be** lack of housing to attract a skilled workforce. **This was because of** changes in the exchange rate. **There are two main reasons for** the increase in prices. The new logo was unsuitable **due to** the style and colours. **As a result,** the supplier was unable to meet the deadline. **The consequence of this was that** interest rates rose by 1.5 percent. **This could have a negative impact on** brand loyalty. **The most important effect was that** communication improved significantly.
Making recommendations	**To** improve delivery times, **we should** employ more drivers and change our main delivery routes. The warehouse **needs to** be extended to allow for the proposed increase in supplies which will take place from next year. **The following recommendations** are designed to answer the question 'How can we increase tourism using a minimal marketing budget?' **It is suggested that** health and safety procedures are reviewed annually and that safety training is offered to all staff.

4 ❯ Note-taking and summarising

Lead-in

A summary is a shortened version of factual information (e.g. a talk or text). Reporting and paraphrasing skills are useful in order to avoid repetition, and the writer presents the information in his/her own words. When writing a summary, it is useful to:

• include key points.

• leave out unnecessary detail.

• use your own words.

It can be useful to take notes before you summarise information. Begin with general notes which focus on the main points, and then go back to organise the information before you write your summary.

Model answers

Notes

> **Seminar:** Key skills of the modern entrepreneur
>
> **Article by:** F. M. Miller (note: find out which uni?)
>
> **Research methods:** 1,000 questionnaire participants / 250 face-to-face
>
> **Aim:** identify common traits = key to success
>
> **Key skills:**
>
> raise/mnge $
>
> hire/train/mnge staff
>
> new trends
>
> **Other views:** Prof Saito – Kyoto uni:
>
> questions M's research methods
>
> Did questionnaires + F2F interviews use same subjects?
>
> **Important:** don't use in publications – gather info first re: methodology

Summary

> <u>**F. M. Miller: Entrepreneurship**</u>
>
> F. M. Miller developed the article from a paper given at a seminar titled 'Key skills of the modern entrepreneur'. He reports that over 1,000 entrepreneurs were approached to complete a questionnaire and a further 250 were interviewed face-to-face. Data was gathered relating to common advice and qualities which the participants recognised as being key to success. The three top skills identified were:
> • the ability to raise and manage finances.
> • hiring, training and managing staff.
> • recognising and responding to new trends.
>
> However, these findings have now been challenged by Ayako Saito, Professor of Business Management at Kyoto University. Professor Saito argues that the research methods used by F. M. Miller need to be reconsidered as participants from the face-to-face studies also took part in the questionnaires. It is recommended that we should avoid including F. M. Miller's research data in any of our publications until further research is carried out into the methodology.

Functional language Note-taking techniques

Technique	Description	Examples
Abbreviations	Notes leave out words or shorten words and use abbreviations. Useful abbreviations include: e.g. for example i.e. that is cf. compare etc. and the rest vs. versus	Contracts sent to ~~Head office~~ HO 18/7 Deadline: ~~Thursday~~ Thurs ~~morning~~ a.m. or ~~Friday~~ Fri ~~morning~~ a.m.? ~~An example of this is the previous budget~~ e.g. last budget Peak season prices increase ~~during the~~ in summer, ~~that is~~ i.e. July–Aug. ~~This~~ affects Finance, HR, Marketing, ~~and the rest of the departments~~ etc. ~~Compare~~ cf. bank loan ~~versus~~ vs. investment ~~for~~ finance strategy.
Highlight key information	Make the important information stand out by underlining, highlighting or using asterisks.	<u>Key reasons new business ideas succeed</u> discovery made by J. N. Zaleski in 2018 five <u>most urgent</u> areas for change good communication is vital**
Bullet points and numbered lists	There are different styles of bullet points (e.g.• or –). Bullet points are often used to list information where the order is not important. When the order is important, numbered lists are usually used.	Main probs with project: – communication – change to schedule Three key markets: 1 Turkey 2 Mexico 3 Korea
Use of symbols	Common symbols include: = equals @ at < less than > more than & or + and C20 twentieth century $/£/€ currency symbols	result = increased employment marketing: not enough € in budget changes @ HO <10% key inventions of C20

Summarising

Technique	Examples
Using synonyms and paraphrase	*The article was written by F. M. Miller following a seminar delivered by the Professor of Sociolinguistics at the University of Uppsala in Sweden, which was titled 'Key skills of the modern entrepreneur'.* F. M. Miller developed the article after a university professor's seminar titled 'Key skills of the modern entrepreneur'.
Reporting	*'We need to reconsider the research methods,' says Professor Saito.* Professor Saito argues that the research methods used by F. M. Miller need to be reconsidered.

1 > Conversation skills

Lead-in
Some business practices may differ from country to country. Here are some questions to research before you meet new business contacts:

1 How do people usually greet each other in business situations in the country you are in or are going to visit? For example, is it more usual to shake hands or bow?

2 How do people exchange business cards? Do people usually receive the card with one or two hands? Are you expected to read the card carefully? Are business cards usually exchanged at the beginning or end of the conversation?

3 How important is small talk in different business situations (e.g. during first meetings)?

Introductions

Introducing yourself

Hi/Hello, my name's …
Can I introduce myself? I'm …
May I join you? I'm … from …

Introducing others: two-step introduction

- Introduce people by saying their full name and title.
- Follow with brief information about the person.

Formal/Semi-formal	May I introduce … I'd like to introduce …
Less formal	This is … Let me introduce you to …

Professor Kim, this is Clare Williams. Clare will be leading the design project. Clare, this is Professor Kim from Seoul National University. Professor Kim is advising the project team on smart technology.

Responding to an introduction

- Use the person's name in your response.
- Add a brief comment.
- When you are introduced to someone using a title or surname (Ms, Mrs, Miss, Mr, Dr, Professor, etc.) it is polite to continue using the title/surname until the person suggests using their first name (e.g. *Please, call me Sarah.*).

Formal	It's a pleasure to meet you (too). Delighted to meet you.	You too.
Less formal	Great/Nice/Good to meet you.	And you.

It's good to meet you, Professor Kim. I'm looking forward to working with you on this project.

Welcoming

		Initial comment (host)	Response (guest)
Welcome		Thank you / Thanks for coming.	Thanks for inviting me. / It's good to be here.
		It's good to see you again.	Good to see you too.
		How are things? / How are you? / How's business?	Good / Not bad, thanks. And you?
Offer help/ hospitality		Can I take your coat?	Yes, please. / No, thanks.
		Would you like a drink?	Could I have a coffee, please?
		How do you take your tea/coffee?	Black, no sugar, thanks. / With milk and sugar, please.

Small talk

It can be useful to think about a few brief comments or questions on a few small talk topics before a meeting. Acceptable topics include business/work, current affairs, the weather, sport, interests, travel, etc.

Initial question or comment	Response
Is this your first visit to … ?	Yes, it's a great city. / No, I was here for a conference last year. How long have you been here?
This is a great space, isn't it?	Yes, it's a great venue. Have you been here before?
What are you working on at the moment?	A new research project. It's challenging but interesting. And you?
What do you think of the news about … ?	It was surprising/interesting/awful, wasn't it? What are your thoughts on it?
Did you catch the news today?	No, what happened?
It's great/awful weather today, isn't it?	Yes! Is it meant to continue?
Did you see the match last night?	No, I missed it. Who won? / Yes, it was great, wasn't it?
So, what do you do in your free time?	I'm interested in / I play … . And you?
Do you travel much on business?	Yes, quite frequently. / No, rarely. What about you?
What are you doing over the holidays?	I'm hoping to travel round Japan. What are your plans?

Keeping a conversation going

It is polite to show interest in what the other person is saying and respond with a follow-up comment or question to keep the conversation going.

Initial question or comment	Response	Follow-up question or comment
This is a great space, isn't it?	Yes, it's a great venue. Have you been here before?	Yes, I was here for a conference last month. What about you?
Do you travel much on business?	No, rarely. What about you?	Actually, I travel quite frequently. But this is my first time in Japan.
What are you doing over the holidays?	Actually, I'm hoping to visit Rome.	Really? I hear it's beautiful this time of year.

2 ❯ Presentation skills

Lead-in

Some business practices may differ from country to country. Here are some questions to research before you prepare presentations for different audiences:

1 How much detail should you include in the presentation? What does your audience already know about this topic? How much background, explanation or technical understanding will be required? Should some of the information be presented visually?

2 Does your presentation answer key questions such as *who, what, why* and *when*?

3 What is the appropriate level of formality for this audience? Should the presentation be relaxed and informal or structured and formal? Should humour be included or would the audience prefer a more serious delivery? Would you prefer questions during the presentation or at the end?

Beginning a presentation

	Formal/Semi-formal	Less formal
Opening and welcome	Thank you for inviting me to speak to you today.	It's great to be here today. Thank you for coming.
Providing a brief outline of the talk	I'm here to talk about the retail supply chain. I'd like to give you a brief outline of my presentation. The talk consists of three main sections.	Shall we get started? I'd like to talk to you about strategies to improve productivity. The talk is divided into three main parts.
Telling the audience when they can ask questions	I will be happy to answer any questions during the presentation. There will be an opportunity after the presentation to ask questions.	Feel free to ask questions during the presentation. I'll be happy to answer any questions at the end of the presentation.

Transitions and signposting		
	Sequencing	Let's start by looking at … Firstly, … / Secondly, … / Then … / Next … / Finally, … First, let's start with … Following this, … Last but not least, …
	Moving from point to point	Which leads me on to my next point. My next point covers … Moving on to … Turning to … Now, I'd like to talk about / discuss / look at … Now, let's move on to …
	Emphasising	The most important thing to remember is that … So what is the key information here? Now, why is this important? This point is vital. The thought I'd like to leave you with is …
	Checking understanding	Before we move on, can I check that everyone understood? Are you all with me? Is everything clear so far? Would you like me to go over anything again?
	Giving examples	For example, … For instance, … A good example of this is … To give you an example, … Let me give you an example.
	Adding	In addition, … Added to this, … Furthermore, … Also, …

Presenting visual information and figures		
	Drawing attention to visuals	As you can see from our first slide, … This graph shows … Can I draw your attention to this chart? Let's move on to the next slide. Now, I would like to show you … Let's look at …
	Presenting figures	We interviewed **around** 2000 people. This is **about** a third of the population. This represents **approximately** 20 percent of the average salary. There were **precisely** 912 different brands. **Exactly** 69 percent of our customers reported that they were satisfied with the service.

Closing		
	Summing up	To sum up, … To summarise, … I'd like to summarise the main points. Now let's summarise briefly what we've looked at.
	Closing	In conclusion, … To conclude, … Let me end by saying … Finally, I'd like to say …
	Thanking the audience	Thank you for listening. Thank you for your attention/time.
	Inviting questions	Does anyone have / Are there any questions? Any questions or comments? I'm happy to answer any questions. If you have any questions, I'll be happy to answer them now.
	Dealing with difficult questions	That's a good question and I'd like to come back to it later. I'll need to get back to you on that. Thanks for highlighting that and I'll speak to you after the presentation.

3 ❯ Interview skills

Lead-in

Here are some areas to research before an interview:

1. **Prepare:** Read about the job role and the company. Identify the skills, qualities or experience that make you a good candidate for the role. Think about the questions the interviewer might ask and practise your answers. Before the interview, use some techniques, such as deep breathing, to relax.

2. **Know what to expect:** Will the interview be with one person or with a group of people? Will you need to sit a test?

3. **Be confident:** When you walk into the interview, shake hands, smile and listen carefully to the questions before you respond.

Beginning the interview

	Interviewer	Interviewee
Welcome	Thank you for coming along today. My name is … and this is my colleague … Please take a seat.	Thank you for taking the time to see me. It's nice to meet you. Thank you.
Small talk	Did you have any trouble finding us? Is this your first visit to … ?	No, the instructions were very clear. Yes, I've never been here before. / No, I was here for a conference last year.
Getting started	Shall we begin? Let's get started.	Certainly.

Typical interview questions

Interviewer	Interviewee
Tell me about yourself. (Possible follow-up questions: *Where did you do your work placements? / Tell us about your internship. / What did you learn from the experience?*)	**Tip:** Don't go into too much personal detail. Focus on information that is useful for the job role. Give the interviewer enough information to ask follow-up questions. I've been studying at [the Indian Institute of Science] and recently completed my degree. I graduated from [Oxford University] in [2017]. I carried out two work placements with [pharmaceutical companies]. I also completed an internship to gain wider experience in the field. Now I'm looking for a position which will allow me to fully use these skills, which is why I applied for this role.
Why did you leave your last position?	**Tip:** It's unlikely that you will be asked this question if the interview is for your first job. If you are currently in work, don't use negative language or go into detail about things that are wrong with your current position. I wanted a position which would offer more challenge. I felt that I had outgrown the position and there wasn't room for advancement. I'm looking for a position where I can fully use my skills and qualifications. I'd like to take on more responsibility.
What are your strengths/ weaknesses?	**Tip:** For both questions, focus on positive qualities which relate to the position or company. My main strengths are that [I am focused and hard-working and work well in a team]. I'm also a [good problem solver and I enjoy challenges]. I perform well under pressure. I'm used to working [in a busy environment]. I'm good/skilled at [working to a deadline]. I've always been [very organised].
	In the past, my main weakness was organising time, but I developed a system which helped my organisation skills. One skill I am currently working on is [sharing responsibilities]. I am not very good at [managing my time]. To address this problem, I have joined a time-management course at my local community college. I work too hard sometimes.

Why do you think you're right for this role? / Tell us why we should hire you.	**Tip:** Don't focus on why the company is right for you. Point out why *you* are right for the role or company. Use research that you have done about the job or company.
	I think that [my computing qualifications] would help me contribute to this role. I think that [my experience in the industry] would make me a good match for this position. I have [excellent administrative skills] and I believe I'd be an asset for the company. I believe that I will be successful in this position because …
Where do you see yourself in five years' time?	**Tip:** This is where you can show that you are ambitious but are not planning to take the CEO's job!
	I want to improve my key skills and industry knowledge so that I can be effective in my role. I'd like to rise to a team leader position and contribute to the success of the company. My long-term career goal is becoming a project manager.

Dealing with questions

That's a good question.

I'm pleased that you asked me that.

Could you repeat the question, please?

There are two ways to answer that question.

May I take a moment to think about that before responding?

Asking questions about the role/ organisation

Do you offer training opportunities for staff?

What type of projects would I work on in this position?

Are there opportunities for advancement for employees?

Do you have an induction program and could you tell me a little about it?

How much travel is expected?

What are the most important skills of the person who does this job?

Who would I be working with?

Ending the interview

Interviewer	Interviewee
I think we've covered everything. Shall we end there?	Could you talk me through the next steps? Would you like a list of references? When can I expect to hear from you?
We'll contact applicants by the end of the week with the decision.	That's great. I look forward to hearing from you.
Thank you for coming in today.	It's been a pleasure. Thank you for seeing me.

4 > Meeting skills

Lead-in

Here are some questions to consider before organising or attending a business meeting:

1 What is the purpose of the meeting? What do you want to accomplish? Who will attend?

2 Is there a meeting agenda? What topics need to be discussed? How long will you need for each topic?

3 During the meeting, are you keeping to the schedule? Are you keeping the comments on topic? Is everyone participating and contributing?

4 How will you keep record of the key points, action points or items that require further discussion? Do you need to identify someone to take minutes? Have you ensured there is a meeting summary to send out to all participants?

5 What are your next steps? Do you need to set up a follow-up time and date to meet again?

Introductions and opening

Welcoming participants	Thank you all for coming today. It's great to see you all here today. Thank you all for coming at such short notice.
Introducing participants	I think we all know each other, don't we? Could we go round the table and briefly state our roles? Before I get started, I'd like to welcome Luke, from our office in Paris. Firstly, I'd like to introduce Emil, our new Finance Manager.
Opening the meeting	Good morning, everyone. If we're all here, let's get started. Since everyone is here, shall we begin? OK, let's begin by looking at the first point on the agenda.
Stating the meeting objectives	The goal of this meeting is to agree on the new logo design. We are here today to discuss our presentation to senior management. The meeting was called to give an update on the project tasks. By the end of the meeting we should have ideas for the new website.
Introducing the agenda	You'll see from the agenda that we are here to discuss the findings from the customer satisfaction survey. We have five main items on the agenda that we need to discuss today, so let's stay focused. Firstly, we'll discuss … / After that, we'll be looking at … / If time allows, we will also cover …

Managing a meeting

Keeping to the point	That's a good point, but we will discuss it in more detail at a later date. This is not on today's agenda, so let's leave it for our next meeting. Let's save this for next time. I'm afraid we'll have to come back to this later. Let's talk more about that next time.
Managing time	We're running out of time, so let's move on. That's all the time we have on this topic. We can discuss additional points in our next meeting. I'm afraid we're running out of time. Does anyone have anything important to add before we move on? We only have ten minutes left, so let's talk about the next item on the agenda.
Managing interruptions	I understand your point, but it might be better to discuss this at a later date. Your point has been noted but please let Amal finish. We'll come to you next, Chris. Karl, please continue with what you were saying. Let's let Nadia finish her point.
Inviting comments/ feedback	Sara, what are your thoughts on this? Do you agree with this viewpoint, Emil? Maria, it would be useful to have your opinion on this. What do you think, Ulrich? Does anyone have anything to add?
Clarifying and asking for clarification	What I meant to say was that the figures aren't reliable. To put it another way, we need to spend less on marketing. What I'm trying to say is that we'd need to talk to our design team about this. Could you explain how that is going to work? So, what you're saying is that we need to look at other options? Can I check what you mean by cost cutting?
Agreeing	That's a good point. I agree with Jean Luc. That's a really good idea. That would work. That's true. Absolutely./Exactly.
Disagreeing	I can see your point but I'm not sure that would work. I'm afraid I don't agree. Not necessarily. That's not always true / the case. I'm not so sure about that.

Problem solving

Explaining the problem	The main problem is that the supplier can't deliver the order. The issue is that we don't have enough staff. The thing is that the equipment is broken and so we won't be able to finish.
Suggesting solutions	Why don't we find a new supplier? We could hire some short-term staff for the project. Have you considered replacing the old equipment? What about adding this information to our website?

Closing

Summing up	That's all we have time for today. Let's sum up the main points. Shall I summarise the key points from today's meeting? Before we close the meeting, I'd like to summarise the main points. Let me quickly go over today's points.
Referring to action points and next steps	Please send Anna the completed reports by Friday. Please don't forget to hand in your reports by the end of the week. Is everyone clear about what they need to do? We'll meet again in a week to discuss progress. I look forward to hearing your views at the next meeting. Everyone will be sent a copy of the minutes and action points. We'll meet again next Thursday to discuss next steps.
Closing	Thank you for coming, everyone. It was a very productive meeting. Thank you for your contribution and ideas. Thank you all for your input today.

5 ❯ Negotiation skills

Lead-in

Some business practices may differ from country to country. Here are some points to research before you prepare for a negotiation:

1 Most negotiations are about both discussion and relationship building. Some cultures prefer a more direct form of communication and speak about business early in the conversation. In other cultures, the introduction and small talk part of the negotiation is important for a successful outcome. Check what type of negotiation to expect before you prepare.

2 Negotiating styles such as ways of expressing agreement and disagreement or decision-making can differ from culture to culture. Nodding might not have the same meaning in all countries. Check that your understanding is the same as the person that you are negotiating with.

Opening and welcoming

Good to meet you / see you again. Are you well?

How's business?

Can I get you anything?

How was your journey?

Thanks for agreeing to meet today.

Proposals

Stating the agenda	What I'd like to discuss today is the terms and conditions for the order. OK, let's start by looking at the agenda. Shall we have a look at the main points of today's discussion?
Making a proposal	We think the best way is to reconsider delivery times. It might be possible to increase the quantity. Would it help if we reviewed the monthly payment terms? If we lower the price, perhaps you could agree to increase the volume? How do you feel about increasing the discount? Do you think you could consider invoicing in dollars? We propose/suggest a four percent discount.
Requesting a proposal	Would you like to outline your proposal? What do you have in mind? Do you have any suggestions? We welcome any offer/suggestion that you would like to make.

Clarifying and checking	Just to clarify, you mean increasing the payments? What do you mean by extending the deadline? Let me make sure I got your point. I'm not sure I understood your position. Do you mean you are prepared to lower the unit price? Let me see if I understand what you're saying.
Compromising	We could offer you a ten percent discount if you think you can order more than 2,000 units. In exchange for a bigger volume, would you be willing to reconsider payment terms? We might be able to work on the price if you think you can pay within a month. How flexible can you be on that? Would you be willing to accept a compromise?

Bargaining/ Discussion

Suggesting alternatives	What about improving quality control? How about increasing the price by five percent rather than eight percent? Can we look at the delivery dates? Could you accept payment in euros? Would you be prepared to increase the order? How would you feel if we extend the deadline?
Agreeing to a proposal	That seems reasonable. That's acceptable. We can work with that. I'm happy to agree to those terms. That sounds great to us. We have a deal!
Refusing a proposal	I'm afraid we can't agree to that. We'd find it difficult to complete the project by your proposed deadline. I'm afraid we can't agree to deliver twice a week unless you increase the volume of the order. That won't be possible, I'm afraid. I'm sorry, we can't accept that.
Explaining concerns	My main concern is that quality will suffer. The main issue is it will take longer by sea than by plane. It's important that we consider whether the changes will increase the budget.
Checking for agreement	Does that sound reasonable? How does that sound? What do you think?

Closing a negotiation

Agreement has been reached	It's been a pleasure doing business with you. Thank you very much for your time.
Agreement has not been reached	I'm sorry that we couldn't reach an agreement. Unfortunately, we haven't been able to reach an agreement. Perhaps we can discuss this again at a later date.
Outlining next steps	So, we'll send you a contract by email. We'll put in writing the terms and conditions we agreed today. If you confirm that in an email to me, we will draw up an agreement. I'll be in contact in the near future to see if we can discuss this again. I'll send you an email confirming all this in writing.

1.1.1 P = Presenter A = Arti N = Nick J = John M = Melanie R = Ray

P: The structure of an organisation is key to its success. It is important that individuals and teams understand their roles and responsibilities within the organisation. Business leaders have to ensure that different departments and operations coordinate and work together. The principle of clear structure applies to all companies – start-ups, small and medium enterprises as well as multinationals.

This company is one of the world's leading news organisations. It creates and distributes news and information on television and digital platforms, 24 hours a day, 7 days a week. Its teams operate all over the world.

The newsroom is the hub of the operation. Staff here are responsible for coordinating the teams gathering news.

A: My name is Arti Lukha and I'm a news editor. My job involves news-gathering for a major news organisation in Britain. I'm in charge of our daily news-gathering operations. I am responsible for how we deploy our reporters, our producers, our cameras and our satellite trucks.

P: When Arti decides to follow a particular news story, she gives a reporter the task of covering it. The reporter is then in charge of the team that produces a report on that story.

N: Hello, I'm Nick Thatcher and I'm one of the general news reporters here and I work to the main bulletins that go out throughout the day. It's all about teamwork. If you're working with a camera operator then together you're making sure you're getting the right pictures on the ground. Back at base you're being supported in ensuring that if you need pictures from the library – from file if you like – then those are available to you in good time as well. And those conversations are ongoing all the time between you and the editor to make sure you're telling the story in the best possible way.

P: The news bulletins are broadcast live.

J: My role as programme director is to lead the production team and to be responsible for the technical and creative execution of the programme. Teamwork is absolutely crucial in the build-up and during the programme. There is no real one role who can do it by themselves, so we are very tightly coordinated. My role as director is to be conductor of that orchestra.

P: In a large organisation like this there are a number of departments working behind the scenes to ensure the company runs well. Managing the staff is a key function.

M: I'm Melanie Tansey and I'm the director of human resources. So I'm responsible for running the human resources team, making sure that we're delivering on all our strategic and operational priorities for the company.

P: The finance department is another important part of the organisation.

R: I'm Ray Snelling and I'm the finance supervisor. I look after all of the billing for our customers and also collection of debts and maintaining customer queries and making sure our customers are happy. It's important that we make sure the payments are coming in on time – it can impact on payments we are making to our suppliers. So if we've got a lot of costs we're incurring on a specific project, we need to make sure we're getting cash in to support that. So it can affect us quite a lot.

P: These are just some examples of the roles in some of the departments in the company. There are many more such as marketing and support all working together to ensure the organisation runs smoothly and successfully.

1.3.1 M = Matt S = Stefanie J = James A = Alistair

M: Pro Manage is a global company, providing project management training qualifications. I'm Matt Farnham, head of UK operations ... based here in London. We're in the middle of launching some new online project management courses ... I'm the project lead, but the team are in Germany, India, Japan, Mexico ... it's an international effort.

Pro Manage is a great place to work, great people. I suppose you'd describe me as the boss, but I don't like people to think of me that way ... I try to be quite open and flexible in the way I do things. I'm pretty informal really ...

S: I'm Stefanie Hatke and I run the Pro Manage German office ... based mainly in Cologne, but I also work from time to time in Switzerland. We're in the middle of a very important product launch and as the main technical expert, I've been asked to travel to London to meet with the project lead.

We're very busy at the moment ... which is positive. I consider myself to be efficient and effective, I like to be well organised and focus on getting the job done – that's what the company pays me to do.

M: Morning, boys.

J: Oh, Matt, hold up. I've got a hard copy of the prospectus that needs approving. It's just a sample, but if you could let me know that the layout's basically OK ...

M: Sure, have to wait until later though, Stefanie from the German office is coming in this morning ...

J: Ah, Stefanie! I know her, she's excellent.

A: She's rude, if you ask me. Everything's urgent with her; she's always on the phone demanding – never asks how you are or has a human conversation.

M: That's a bit alarming, she doesn't sound very much like a team player.

J: I get on fine with her. She's just very work focused, that's all, but she gets results, she's a good person to have on your team.

1.3.2 M = Matt S = Stefanie

M: Stefanie, hi, I'm Matt.
S: Hello.
M: Coffee?
S: What?
M: Can I get you a coffee?
S: Oh, no, thank you. Do you have power?
M: Listen, why don't you come with me? I can show you the office and introduce you to a few people.
S: But I've got everything ready to discuss ...
M: Yeah, but it'll only take a few minutes ... do you know the design guys?
S: No. Well, yes, a bit, I met James in Germany.
M: Great, well, let's go and say hello. So ... first time in London?
S: No, I was here several times.
M: Great. Good trip over?
S: Yes.
M: Great. Ah, here they are. Guys, this is Stefanie. You've met before, right?
J: Yes, in Cologne, *Guten Tag*, great to see you again.
S: Hi.
A: I'm Alistair. Good to finally meet you in person.
S: Ah, yes, hello Alistair. Excuse me.
M: No worries.
J: How's it going so far?
M: Hard work, to be honest. She's been very quiet, a bit ... serious. You need people skills for a job like this.
A: Told you.
J: Honestly, I wouldn't worry about it, she is a bit serious, but just needs time. She's actually very nice, just very results focused.
M: I was trying to be informal, friendly, positive ... you know, focus on relationships first. But Stefanie really didn't seem very comfortable at all. As it turns out, though, I think she's starting to understand how we do things at the London office, she sent me an email to say that she really enjoyed the visit.
S: It was a bit unclear and confusing for me at the beginning, I'm used to getting down to work, not socialising in the office. But I do see that having strong relationships is a benefit when working on a project like this ... I'm planning on moving to London for three months, it will be good to get to know the team better and know more about Matt's way of working.

1.3.3 C = Charlotte M = Matt S = Stefanie

M: Stefanie, hi. I'm Matt Farnham, Head of UK Operations. I'm glad we could arrange this meeting.
S: Yes, me too.
M: OK, shall we make a start? You've only got two hours – is that right?
S: Yes, that's right.
M: OK well, let's focus on getting up to date with the project, there are a few issues I'd like to discuss.
S: Very good.
M: If we have some time at the end, I can introduce you to a few of the team. I've prepared a short agenda, if that's OK?
S: Ah, excellent.
M: Let's start with India; as you can see, we might be about to run into a problem ...
S: By when did you say?
M: 24th of November ....
C: Sorry to interrupt.
M: No, that's OK.
C: Taxi's waiting outside.
M: Thanks, Charlotte. OK, so we need to leave it there. I'll email you all those dates later on and we can continue on the phone tomorrow.
S: Thank you. Sorry to be in a rush like this.
M: No, don't worry ...
S: I need to organise another visit to meet everyone ... maybe we could discuss that tomorrow?
M: Yes, let's do that. Thanks for coming and ... have a safe trip!
S: I will, thank you.
I very much enjoyed my trip to London, yes. I had a very productive meeting with Matt. I think that we'll work well together.
M: She seemed fine, but I can't say that I learnt anything about her. She's clearly very capable, but I'm not sure that she's the right person to take on a project like this ... I need to get to know her better as a person ... We won't have a chance to meet again for at least a couple more months so, no, it's not ideal really.

1.3.4

So, we've seen that people have very different ways of managing first meetings. One is not better than the other. In fact, both have advantages and disadvantages depending on the situation. With the relationship style, you can start to build trust; but it can look unprofessional to be too friendly for too long. With the work style, you can be more efficient more quickly. But maybe you can look rude or impolite to others.

So, to handle first meetings is not easy. But there are a few things you need to think about.

Firstly, know your own communication style; know how you like to do things.

Secondly, understand the communication style of the other person. You can do this in different ways. You could ask someone who knows the person in advance of the meeting, like Matt did. Or, just observe carefully when you meet the person – what they say, what they do.

Finally, think about and decide on the best communication style to have a positive impact on the other person.

2.1.1 J = Jean-Christophe Babin S = Silvio Ursini P = Peter York

J: To pave the way for growth we needed to speak to a–, a broader and aspirational base of clients, which probably with jewellery would come much, much later, and so we have added products at a much lower price point as you would ever dream for a piece of jewellery.

S: At the end of the '90s the company had jewellery, watches, accessories and fragrances. And then we–, we thought about uh how can we interact uh in a more intimate way with our customers. And uh this idea of doing a very small collection of ultra-luxury hotels came about. I was in a taxi, and an artist who's a friend of mine gave me a call and said, 'You have to see this place,' so I turned the taxi around and it was love at first sight. The area used to be monasteries and cloisters, and adjacent to our garden is the Botanical Gardens in Milan, which is a hidden gem in–, in the city. There was a building which uh used to be a convent, uh part of it uh very old, from the 1600s, part of it more recent from the 1970s, and uh we set about uh redesigning it, completely changing its image.

J: In London we have a 25-metres pool that you would never expect uh from a hotel that small, so in that way uh you create, I mean, a sequence of unexpected experience which eventually will create uh a unique emotional memory when you get out of it.

P: There's a lot of bad history about brand extensions. If you over-extend your brand, you spread it thin, you go into areas where you're less credible. At the end, if you overdo it, your brand is devalued. I think the brands which are most careful have the longest future.

S: The most frustrating thing in this project has been um the fact of uh finding so few locations that were appropriate. My strongest advice would be do something only if you have something to say. If you see an opportunity to do something in novelty and relevant, then that's a–, you know, that's a beautiful energy that will make it into a success. If you sit cold-blooded and start saying, 'OK, let's venture into this business, and what are we gonna do? Let's copy the competitors,' for me the customer ultimately will read between the lines and–, and punish you.

2.3.1 M = Matt D = Dan S = Stefanie P = Paula

M: It's a busy time, we're right in the middle of launching a new series of online project management courses … exciting, but also very challenging … International projects can complicate life in so many ways … everyone working separately and in different time zones … for me, the number one priority at this stage is to create a real team …

D: I've got October 12th, 24th and then November 8th, so if those are the dates that you have …

S: One minute Dan, Matt has arrived.

M: Hi, Dan.

D: Hey there.

M: Not late am I?

S: No.

D: Not at all, we're just running a bit ahead of time.

P: Hello! It's Paula!

S: Hi Paula.

M: Hi Paula, it's Matt, we've got Dan and Stefanie with us.

P: Hi. Hi, everyone.

M: Excellent, everyone's here. So this is our first meeting as a team. As I'm sure that you all have seen on email, most of the programming work for the Mexico part of the project will be handled by our U.S. IT department. We're having a call with them next week so I thought we could have a brief chat today to plan our priorities for that conversation. Dan is from the US, and knows the people in IT, and is on the call because I would like his advice. But, Stefanie, do you want to start? Priorities for you?

S: OK. I've worked on similar online projects to this in Germany, also working with the US sometimes, I think that we need to be careful about time and budget. These are the top priorities; making sure that they respect the schedule and don't go over budget; we can discuss other things as the work moves forward. But we need the US to deliver on time and on budget for Mexico.

P: That sounds like great advice. This project is really exciting for Mexico as online learning is starting to become big here … I've never worked with the US, so I really think your experience can help us, Stefanie.

D: Totally disagree. I respect your experience, Stefanie, yes, budgets and timing are important, but I was actually an IT lead over here in the past;

I've delivered over a hundred projects to the US market and in Mexico; and I'm telling you, our focus should absolutely be on quality. If you get the quality wrong, you've got very unhappy customers. And we want happy customers.

P: Mmm, a high standard of final product is very important for us …

D: It's key. Quality should be your number one priority.

S: But I think that we have to focus on timeline and costs. We can evaluate the work later …

D: Sure, but they're not the main thing …

M: OK. Look, I think we can all agree that standards are important, but delivering on time is important too, budgets for projects are very tight at the moment so …

D: Quality is what wins customers, quality is what will get their attention.

M: … So, Stefanie, let's take a look at your proposed schedule and costing, and then we can discuss quality. Is that OK?
Right then, thanks everyone, we'll all meet again at the same time next week. Bye.

P: Thank you.

S: I'm not sure, I'm really not sure.

M: About what?

S: Dan. He's just so arrogant. 'Quality', 'quality', 'quality'. I'm not sure that I can work with him.

M: Look, this is the first time you've talked. I'm sure you'll find a way. Why don't you just try?

S: Could *you* manage the US IT side of things? I'd prefer to work with Paula and the Mexico roll-out. I really like Paula.

M: Well, hang on, let's take some time to think about this …

2.3.2 S = Stefanie M = Matt

S: But how can we be a team if we don't listen to each other? I'd be happier if I could take Mexico and leave you to deal with Dan and the US.

M: Look, Dan's a strong character … but I know him pretty well and can handle him. Maybe it would be better for you to just focus on Mexico and let me worry about Dan. It'll be easier if you work with Paula, the two of you get on well.

S: We do. Thanks Matt, I just think that Dan and I are too different, you know, sometimes personalities just clash a bit.

M: OK, let's do that … I'll call Dan and explain.

S: Thanks, Matt.
Oh, Matt, do you have a moment?

M: Sure, what's up?

S: I have a problem with the project.

M: What is it? Problems with schedule or costs?

S: Not exactly. It's quality. And I know, I know, this was Dan's big concern. He was right, the quality isn't good enough.

M: Have you tried talking to him?

S: I spend all my time with Mexico.

M: Do you want me to set up a call?

S: Please.

M: OK. You need to be able to keep in touch with Dan yourself, we're all on the same team, don't be afraid to ask his advice where you need it.

2.3.3 S = Stefanie M = Matt

S: But how can we be a team if we don't listen to each other? I'd be happier if I could take Mexico and leave you to deal with Dan and the US.

M: I'm not comfortable with that … I think it's important for you to work with Dan.

S: We're just so different.

M: Yes, you are, but that's why I think you'll make a strong team, you have different skills. C'mon … why don't you try?

S: … It's just always all about him.

M: Look, I agree that he sometimes communicates a little … strongly. But he knows what he's talking about … and it would be a great opportunity for you to learn about the U.S. market … y'know, that could be career-changing for you … As you move up it's important to show that you can manage different kinds of people, different personalities. Look, if you need any help, I'm here to support you.

S: OK. Sure. I'll try.

M: I think it's the right decision. Let's have another chat with him, I'll organise a call.
Stefanie!

S: Good morning.

M: Just wanted to ask how things are with Dan.

S: Hmm. It's OK. I find it much easier working with Paula, we get on really well together. It's a bit more difficult with Dan but, to be fair, I am learning from him.

M: Oh yeah?

S: Yeah, we did end up having some issues with quality control. There are some delays.

M: Ah.

S: Yes, as Dan said … but he's really on top of it, and with the two of us working together … we'll be fine, I'm sure.

M: Great, let me know if you need anything from me.

S: Will do.

2.3.4

Successful teamwork depends on many things: a clear task, competent people, enough resource, and different people with different skills. But it's not always so easy to work with people who are different from us. So what do we need to do to make a diverse team really work?
Firstly, we have to make an effort. When Stefanie worked with Dan in Option B, she found it really challenging and she didn't like Dan's communication style at the beginning. She had to work really hard to build that relationship. She needed to be patient and make an effort, but in the end, she learnt a lot and the team did much better.
Secondly, people will need advice and support when working in an international team with different people – it can be really tough. So we need to be there for others with support, sometimes advice, sometimes just listening – either as a manager or as a colleague.
And finally, if you're giving colleagues advice about dealing with other people, you can advise them to be safe – to just work with people like them – as Matt allowed Stefanie to do in Option A – it's easier in a way. My own advice would be to encourage people to think positively about diversity, and try to engage with different types of people – it's more challenging, but may be a better learning experience and may be better for teamwork.

3.1.1 P = Presenter JC = James Caan S = Simon Dolan E = Esther J = John Lees I = Interviewer

P: The job market is very competitive. People who want to progress their career need to stand out from the crowd. Usually, the first thing a potential employer sees is a CV or a résumé. This is the jobseeker's opportunity to advertise experience and skills, and also to show an employer their character or personality. So, what do the experts say about writing the perfect CV or résumé?
This is Esther. She is a nineteen-year-old student. She is applying for internships to gain experience in the business world.
James Caan is an entrepreneur who founded a successful recruitment business. He has agreed to help Esther.

JC: I think one of the biggest problems, I think when you're young, is that everybody says 'But you've got no experience, how do you add any value?' I think what you've got to be able to do is present yourself as somebody who can walk in and make a difference now.

P: But James doesn't think that Esther is selling herself well with her CV. Esther needs to sort out her CV. Simon Dolan is a very straight-talking entrepreneur. Esther goes straight to Simon's office. The first thing Simon notices on Esther's résumé is a spelling mistake.

S: What's the main thing that strikes you on here? So, if we've got … this second line down, have a look there. That word. What is it?

E: Intermediate.

S: If you can't spell that right, what hope have I got employing you and expecting you to get your first few emails and go through the door to a client?

P: The next key point is staying focused in what you say on the CV or résumé.

S: I don't really care about the fact that you enjoy socialising with your friends, you go to the gym. What I care about is how you're going to help me run my business better.

P: Expressing personality is a key to getting employed. Companies look for so-called soft skills like commitment, flexibility and imagination, as well as hard skills like knowledge and diplomas. Next stop for Esther is a careers coach who can help her get that kind of soft information across. John Lees has read thousands of CVs and résumés and knows all the mistakes.

L: I saw a CV where the candidate listed under interests, 'I enjoy eating pizza'. It's not impressive.

P: The next challenge is how to stand out from the competition.

L: Graduate CVs make the same mistakes over and over again. They use clichéd language. So everyone says 'I'm a team player', 'I'm a self starter', 'I'm highly motivated'. And if you use the same language as everyone else, all that shows is that you are exactly the same as every other candidate.

P: Esther has taken all the advice and presents her reworked CV back to Simon.

E: I would very much appreciate the opportunity of an interview to find out more about the role and to demonstrate how I believe I could be of value to your company.

S: Perfect. That's better than 99.9 percent of the CVs that we get in. You would definitely, definitely, definitely get an interview, here or anywhere. Really good job.

P: Two weeks later Esther's new CV has already had an effect. She has an interview for an internship. It has gone well.

I: I thought Esther came across as very well prepared for the role and I'll certainly be recommending her to my partners for a second interview here.

P: Getting a job is a job in itself. You've just got to get out there and make it happen.

3.3.1 P = Paula   M = Matt   A = Alistair   J = James

P: I flew into London from Mexico City yesterday. The first thing in my diary is to meet with Matt, who wants to go over the Mexico launch of our new online courses.
Matt sounded a little tense when we spoke on the phone, but British people always sound tense! I'll tell him exactly what I feel about how things are going – I can focus on results when I need to, but we Latin Americans like to always express our feelings first. You need to be honest in life, don't you?

M: I bumped into Paula's old line manager at an international event recently and quite frankly I have some concerns. Paula's over in the UK this week so I've asked her to come in and see me. He mentioned issues raised around Paula's ability to meet targets and perform as part of a team … I'm a little worried about it so I need to understand what's gone wrong … if I need to replace her, I need to do it soon.

P: Hi!

A: Paula! Where did *you* come from?

P: Mexico, of course … I came all the way …

J: How long are you here for?

P: … just to bring you these! I'm just here for the week, but I have to see Matt now and I'm already late. Let's catch up later, bye … Good morning!

M: Good morning, how are you?

P: I'm good thanks.

M: How was the flight?

P: Long, but good. And I'm excited to be here in London.

M: Excellent, come on, let's go and get a coffee and catch up.

3.3.2 M = Matt   P = Paula

M: I wanted to talk to you this morning about the online courses launch. Obviously you know how important it is.

P: Of course. We're working really hard every day to make sure that it's a success in Mexico. And everywhere else too.

M: I know. How about timing? Do you think you're going to have everything ready by the deadline?

P: Yes. Everything's fine.

M: Confident about that?

P: Yes. Where's this coming from?

M: After you. I recently bumped into Julio Gonzales, and he mentioned something about deadlines on your last project. Is there anything I need to be concerned about?

P: Oh, not this again. Julio's incompetent. Totally incompetent. And he likes to blame other people for his mistakes.

M: But … Do you want milk?… It *is* true that you missed all of your deadlines last quarter, isn't it?

P: That wasn't *my* fault. I wanted to take extra time to make sure we weren't rushing a complicated project. Julio didn't want to listen to me. Everything got delayed and so we missed the target, yes.

M: Right. So you had a disagreement with your manager and held up the project?

P: Er … no, that's not what I said. And I don't see what it's got to do with the online launch in Mexico.

3.3.3 M = Matt   P = Paula

M: I wanted to talk to you this morning about the online courses launch. Obviously you know how important it is.

P: Of course. We're working really hard every day to make sure that it's a success in Mexico. And everywhere else too.

M: I know. How about timing? Do you think you're going to have everything ready by the deadline?

P: Yes. Everything's fine.

M: Confident about that?

P: Yes. Where's this coming from?

M: After you. I recently bumped into Julio Gonzales, and he mentioned something about deadlines on your last project. Is there anything I need to be concerned about?

P: Oh not this again. Julio's incompetent. Totally incompetent. And he likes to blame other people for his mistakes.

M: OK, why don't you tell me a bit more? You say he's incompetent. How would you describe a competent manager?

P: Well, a good manager should support their team and listen to their team. If someone thinks that something should be done differently, maybe they're right.

M: OK … Do you want milk? … So it's important for you, as a team member, to be involved in decision-making, right?

P: Yes, of course. We missed those deadlines because I wanted to take extra time to make sure we weren't rushing a complicated project, and Julio didn't want to listen to me, so everything got held up.

M: Why? Why did you have concerns about the project being rushed?

P: There were too many things that all had to happen at the same time, it was just moving too quickly. It was obvious that we were going to miss things.

M: What do you mean by 'too many things'? Do you think you might have managed a bit better if there had been greater planning or more support, for example?

P: Probably. It was just too much at the time.

M: OK, that's useful to think about. I'm sure we'll make a success of this project … you know I like to involve the team in decision-making, so I'm trusting you to let me know if there's anything we need to change or do differently for Mexico. Thanks for the chat. I think it was important to talk this through.

P: No problem. I think it's good that we can talk like this and, yes, I'll let you know my thoughts on how things are progressing in Mexico.

3.3.4

Listening actively isn't easy. We often focus too much on facts and potentially miss key information that's being communicated about feelings. On the other hand, if we focus too much on listening for feelings, we might miss important facts.
There are a number of things we can do to become more effective listeners.
Firstly, we can listen carefully to identify those key words in a sentence which can give us more information about how someone is feeling and what's important for them. So when Paula was talking to Matt she used words like *incompetent* and *rushing* and said they were trying to do *too many things*.
Following on from that, once we've identified these key words, we can try to understand what the person really feels by asking clarifying questions, such as 'Why do you say "too many things"?' Another point to make is that it's very useful to summarise and to check our understanding before moving on, like Matt did in Option B when he said, 'So it's important for you, as a team member, to be involved in decision-making, right?'
And finally, be open. Truly listen to what the other person is saying. If we only focus on what we want to talk about, we might miss something important.

4.1.1 P = Presenter   J = Joel Hills   I = Irene Rosenfeld

P: When business leaders develop strategies to tackle problems, they often have to take risks. Nobody can predict the future, but businesses do have to anticipate it and make judgements. The Kraft Heinz company based in the US is a major player in the food industry. Over 90 years, Kraft built up a portfolio of well-known food brands including confectionary, biscuits, snacks and dairy products. In the first decade of the 21st century, Kraft's performance was poor. Markets lacked confidence in the company's growth prospects. Its profits were disappointing. Kraft's products were less appealing to a new generation of consumers.

J: It was seeing demand for the processed food and drinks that it manufactured from Dairylea all the way to Oreo biscuits decline. And that the profit margin – the amount of money it was making for every unit of sales – had been squeezed almost to the thinness of a piece of paper.

P: This was only the first of Kraft's problems. The second issue that Kraft had to tackle was that it relied too heavily on its home U.S. market. That meant it was missing opportunities in fast-growing emerging markets around the world. The company's third problem was that its costs were too high. That meant it was not making enough profits on its sales. Kraft's management came up with a bold plan to tackle these issues. It started with a takeover bid for the chocolate maker Cadbury. Cadbury had a 200-year history of making chocolate in the UK. Its products were well established around the world, especially in emerging markets.

J: There was clearly an attraction of having an even larger portfolio of internationally recognised brands that they could seek to take into different markets. So inevitably attracting a bigger international audience was part of Kraft's interest in Cadbury's.

P: Kraft took a gamble that combining the operations of two established companies would be successful and solve another one of its problems.

J: Kraft's primary interest in Cadbury was it enabled it to – because it became a bigger company – essentially cut costs. Where there was overlap between the two companies it found a way of saving money and increasing therefore the profit margin that it was able to get from each one of its products.

P: The second stage of the strategic solution was a merger. Kraft merged with another food giant – Heinz – and became the Kraft Heinz company. The merger created the world's fifth-largest food company. As with the Cadbury deal there was an opportunity to cut costs. There were other potential advantages which helped to solve Kraft's problems. Heinz was considered more innovative in its development of new product lines that met changing consumer preference.

The immediate results were positive. The Kraft Heinz company's share price rose seventeen percent on news of the merger. The combined company has been successful in cutting costs. Looking at the Kraft story it is clear the solutions involved considerable risks. Takeovers and mergers do not always work. Irene Rosenfeld was Kraft's chief executive. She was responsible for the company's strategy.

I: I think there were a number of folk that were questioning our acquisition of Cadbury. We said it was going to be important to us to expand our portfolio, to expand our footprint, particularly in developing markets. And it's played out that way. We're very much on track with the integration. It's enabled us to outperform our peers around the world.

P: For Kraft Heinz it seems that the risks paid off. But finding solutions to large corporate problems is not straightforward and taking risks can lead to business failures as well as successes.

4.3.1 K = Kenji A = Alistair M = Matt J = Jack

A: Good morning.

K: Good morning, how are you?

A: Yeah, fine thanks, you alright?

M: Life is very busy at the moment. There's just so much to do and coordinate. Here, Germany, Mexico, Japan. I spend half my time on the phone these days, dealing with the project ... it's like my workload just doubled overnight. Plus, as project lead, I have to host the regional managers when they come to London. We had Paula in from Mexico recently and now Kenji's over from Japan ... it must be tough on Paula and Kenji, they're completely new to international projects.

J: Knock, knock ... are you not answering your phone today?

M: Jack. Sorry. Was that you a few minutes ago?

J: You look a bit tired mate, what's up? Having fun with the new markets project?

M: No. I mean yes. Overall, so far so good. I've just got loads of work and I'm getting more and more concerned about what's going on in Japan.

J: What do you mean, 'concerned'? Isn't Kenji here at the moment?

M: They're running about three weeks behind schedule, and I just don't see how we're going to make up the time.

J: Three weeks is not a concern, it's a disaster. What's going on?

M: Well, hold on. It's complex. Kenji doesn't have a great deal of experience, Stefanie is busy with Mexico, so no time for Japan and, yeah, we're behind.

J: Three weeks behind.

M: I'm going to talk to Kenji about it later.

J: I suggest you go over there and have some strong words sooner rather than later. Tell him that he needs to perform or he's out. A bit of straight talking wouldn't do any harm.

M: I know, I know. But it's Japan, you can't do 'straight talking' or you'll offend everyone.

J: Matt, you can't stereotype like that. Kenji's a professional. You need to tell him to his face what you expect and when you expect it.

M: Look, you may be right ... but the guy's trying. Shouting at him isn't my style; I think I'd prefer to take a more gentle approach.

J: Yeah, but being gentle often gets you nowhere. If you don't fix this soon, you're going to have senior management complaining. Anyhow, it's your call ... you know what I would do.

4.3.2 M = Matt K = Kenji J = Jack

M: Kenji, I need to have word.

K: Yes?

M: I'll come directly to the point as we need to find a solution. I've been going over our schedules this morning and the Japan side of this project is running more than three weeks late. It's a major delay, I'm not happy about it.

K: Aha, OK, I understand it is not ideal but I am working very hard to put things right. It's not necessary to worry.

M: I do worry Kenji and, no, it's not simply 'not ideal', it's a serious problem. As I'm sure you've seen since you've been over here, we have a lot of resources dedicated to Japan. If you delay, there's a planning impact here.

K: OK, I understand your concern, but we don't have all the required resources in Japan.

M: I don't agree at all. We discussed resources in detail at the start of the project and it's very late in the day to be having this kind of discussion. I've had a word with Stefanie and I'm going to send her over to Tokyo for a couple of weeks. I think that you could benefit from her experience. If we don't resolve this now, we are risking the whole project.

K: OK.

M: Right. Stefanie has been briefed and she will talk to you about this tomorrow and make arrangements.

K: OK. And thank you ... see you later.

J: Hey.

M: Oh, hi, how're things?

J: I was thinking about you, how did that Japan business go?

M: It wasn't easy. I took your advice and was pretty tough on Kenji.

J: Tough guy. And?

M: He was pretty quiet, actually, didn't say much. I sent Stefanie over there last week and I've spoken to him since then, he seems very grateful, said it was strong feedback but that he'd learnt from it. He said that he'd try to be more open about issues, going forward.

J: Good stuff. What did I tell you?

4.3.3 M = Matt K = Kenji J = Jack

M: Morning Kenji, how are you doing? How's the family?

K: Very well, thank you.

M: Listen, Kenji, have you got a few minutes for a quick chat?

K: Certainly.

M: I know that you're very busy, and I hear that things are going very well in some areas, but I think it's good to update on the project. It's a very demanding situation for you and there's a slight delay on your part of the project, right? Just over three weeks.

K: Yes. We are struggling a bit with resources. There are some other projects that management in Japan wants to take priority, it's difficult to balance.

M: I understand. Look, how do we go forward to get back on track. Any ideas?

K: Er ... I think we can manage.

M: I'd like to help. Is there any further support from our side which can help?

K: Maybe Stefanie, is she available? Her expertise would be very helpful, but I understand that she's in Mexico?

M: Not a problem, I can ask her to travel to Japan for when you get back, stay for a week or so until things are back on track? Would next Friday be good for her to visit?

K: Yes, that would be good.

M: Excellent, so we are in agreement. In fact, why don't you call Stefanie and arrange for her to go over, and we can talk again in a couple of weeks? I'm sure that we can get things back on track.

K: OK, I'll call her. Thanks for the support, Matt, I appreciate it.

J: Hey.

M: Oh, hi, how's things?

J: I was thinking about you, how did that Japan business go?

M: Good. I tried to keep things positive.

J: Oh yeah? How did that go?

M: Slowly. Kenji was supposed to coordinate with Stefanie, but didn't. I had to pick up the phone and ask – very nicely again – if he *could just please* call Stefanie.

J: And?

M: He did. She's there. It's going well, I think we're back on track, team spirit is high.

J: You're too nice. You know, Kenji's lucky I'm not managing the project.

4.3.4

It's important to be aware that people communicate differently depending on their culture, as well as their personality.

So firstly, be aware that a direct style can be useful and effective. It makes things clear – it's honest and fast, and some people actually like it. So we see Matt in the first video, partly on the advice of Jack, say very clearly that he's not happy and what needs to happen, and he gets Kenji to understand the situation quickly; that's useful for the team. But, we all know, a direct style can be dangerous. It can close down conversation; it can even cause conflict.

Indirect communication can also work; it's more polite for some, but it can take longer to be effective. So, in Option B, Matt asks Kenji to take the next steps to call Stefanie. However, Matt has to step in again later and make the call himself as Kenji was slow to do it. So in the end, the same result is achieved as Option A, but with the indirect style, but Matt possibly has a happier team without any conflict.

In the end you have to decide. Choose the style which best fits the situation, and not simply the style you prefer.

5.1.1 P = Presenter AL = Allen Lyall
JR = Jukka Rosenberg JM = Jim McAuslan

P: Online shopping is now a major part of the retail sector. It's convenient and often cheaper than buying in traditional stores. E-commerce operators have invested heavily in their logistics systems so that consumers receive a quick and efficient service. An online shopper only has to make a couple of clicks on a website. It is so easy. But behind the scenes, retailers rely on complex logistics operations to fulfil orders. Systems have to handle millions of orders efficiently. Many of the operations in Amazon's giant warehouse are automated. Each order is placed in a separate yellow container. The containers are tracked with their own barcodes. It is a complex operation.

AL: My role is to make sure that the fulfilment centres and the thousands of people we employ in the UK are busy making sure that our orders are delivered on time.

P: Allen Lyall is Amazon's Vice President of European Operations. He explains the scale of the work that the warehouse is capable of.

AL: We dispatched on our busiest day 2.1 million items. There was a truck leaving this building, one every two minutes thirty seconds last year. There was a thousand one hundred tonnes of equipment on that peak day.

P: The orders then have to be packed. This stage in the process is still done by hand. Good packaging is essential to prevent goods getting damaged in transit. With the orders packed they are ready to leave the warehouse and begin the next stage in the process – delivery to the customer. Delivery can be undertaken by the postal service or by courier companies. Frequently, customers are able to track the progress of their package online. Consumers enjoy the convenience of having goods delivered to their homes. But of course customers are not always at home to receive their package. One solution is to use these. They are called collection lockers. Packages can be left inside and the customer can pick them up at any time by entering a PIN number. The logistics that e-commerce relies upon are developing all the time. In the future we may see some changes in the way our online shopping is delivered. This robot has been designed to deliver packages. Customers can arrange to collect their goods from the robot via a mobile app. Some companies are also considering using drones to transport goods to customers. This drone is being developed by the postal service in Finland. Jukka Rosenberg is the Project Director.

JK: This is part of the testing of new technologies in our parcel delivery and post deliveries and this could be an opportunity which we are now testing.

P: Amazon says that in the future, customers could order goods and they would be delivered by drone in as little as thirty minutes. However, are all these changes really for the better? There are concerns about the widespread use of drones. For example, will they create congestion in the sky? Airline pilots are worried about the safety issues raised by drones. Jim McAuslan is a spokesperson for commercial pilots.

JM: There is an issue about the safety of their operation. But our bigger concern is where this technology is going for the future. We're not against the technology but we want it to be properly regulated.

P: As drone technology develops, issues like safety and congestion will need to be balanced against the convenience of delivery by air. It is a discussion that is certain to continue.

5.3.1 S = Stefanie   M = Matt

S: Another day in paradise?

M: We're going round in circles here. Unbelievable.

S: Been talking to Raj?

M: No, IT downstairs. Trying to get some understanding of an email I received from Raj this morning. Of course, they were very happy to point out that if it was *their* responsibility in house, and not 'my expensive external provider', there wouldn't be any of these issues. They told me to cancel the contract with Raj and let *them* handle the project.

S: They may be right.

M: I know they're right. But it's still not very helpful.

S: But I thought you discussed this with Raj last week.

M: I did. We had, what was it, a three-hour conference call? Look, I know they have their issues, Raj is under a lot of pressure over there in India, but he made promises about where we'd be by now. And then he suddenly went very quiet … and then I get an email this morning that there are these issues, and they need more time … more money … You know, maybe it's cultural, Raj didn't feel that he could say no to me in the first meeting, when I asked him if he could solve things.

S: People love to go on about cultural differences but it's too simple, just stereotyping. To be honest, I think it's you. I think you're too soft on Raj. If the platform is not ready, and the project is going over budget, you need to put some pressure on him. He needs to make *us* his number one priority. Call his manager.

M: I don't know … bringing in management … it changes the atmosphere. I don't want to make it more difficult to work with Raj.

S: It's a waste of time, Matt. You need to get tough. We're the customer here. Demand some action.

M: Raj is pretty sensitive; he might not react too well to that kind of thing. Look, I have a call with him later, I'll try and negotiate some kind of solution on the pricing at least. Costs are getting out of control. What?

S: Nothing …

5.3.2 R = Raj   M = Matt   S = Stefanie

R: Hello?

M: Raj, it's Matt Farnham.

R: Hi, Matt. Good to hear your voice. How are you?

M: Not great actually, Raj. I got your email this morning, it wasn't exactly what I wanted to read. There are now really significant problems with

increased cost and no clear timeline to sort out the technical problems. We can't run the project like this. Things have to change.

R: OK, I'm surprised to hear this. You know we're talking about a complex project and we have many other contracts happening over here.

M: Raj, you need to deal with these issues. There's a risk we have to delay the pilot to customers … that means we might even lose customers. And my management is going to complain about these costs. Basically, what I need is for you to cover the extra costs for additional work on the project. What you're billing us is unacceptable … these costs are just out of control.

R: But not all the technical problems that we have were discussed at the beginning, this is a lot of extra work for us.

M: Look, this is how it is: we have a contract, we're not going to accept an open budget. If that's a problem for you, then we need to involve your management. You have to bear the costs, all these delays aren't our problem, we shouldn't pay for them.

R: Erm. OK. Look, let me have a look at the numbers.

M: OK, fine. Send me something by this evening.

R: OK.

M: Right, I have to go to a meeting, I'll talk to you tomorrow.

R: OK.

S: Hello.

M: Hi.

S: Did you speak to Raj?

M: Yes, we had a chat yesterday. Wasn't easy at first. But he was pretty open in the end, and we had a very direct conversation. I had a chat to his manager as well.

S: And?

M: No extra costs on the project … so the money is back under control … we've agreed to have a phone call every day, just to track and manage the fixes. We should be OK in about a week.

S: Good.

M: It *is* good, yes, but I still had to go over Raj's head and talk to his manger … he doesn't seem very happy about it.

S: It's not about making people happy, there's a job to do.

M: That's one way of looking at it, but he's told me he's struggling with a young family and all these problems are a bit demotivating. And if he gets demotivated and decides to walk off the project, we'll have a major, major problem on our hands. To be honest, I'm a bit worried that he's going to walk.

5.3.3 R = Raj   M = Matt   S = Stefanie

R: Hello?

M: Raj, it's Matt Farnham.

R: Hi, Matt. Good to hear your voice. How are you?

M: I'm good thanks but, to be honest, we've got some difficult issues to discuss, Raj, this project is really challenging for everyone at the moment.

R: Yes, it's a real headache.

M: But I want to work with you to resolve things. Now, I appreciate that you're working very hard to deliver, but as we talked about a week or so ago, all these delays are creating financial and commercial issues for us … first there's the cost, all this extra work, and also there's going to be a problem for our customers.

R: You mean being late with the pilot phase?

M: Exactly. Now I want to work with you to resolve this, I don't want to be the bad guy, but I think we need to negotiate on your fees. This is really down to you, not us, so I think it is reasonable to ask to split the costs, we'll take 10 percent, OK?

R: I don't think it's fair to blame us in this way, your team changed some of the requirements, added things, that meant more work, more people from our side …

M: OK. Could I suggest something? What about, if we help from our side and give you one of *our* IT guys, and then *you* should have everything that you need to clear this up quickly.

R: OK. With an extra resource from you, that would be a good solution, I can agree to that.

M: Good stuff. I'll give you another call tomorrow.

R: OK, talk to you tomorrow.

M: Have a good one.

S: Hi. Did you speak to Raj?

M: Yes. We spoke yesterday.

S: And?

M: Good, I think. He's very cooperative. I agreed to take 10 percent of the extra costs … so that should bring the money back under control … I also suggested we send someone from IT *here* to work on this. There's a young guy down there, Mike I think it is, seems keen. He could also help track things a bit in case this happens again …

S: That makes sense.

M: We need to work with these guys, keep them on our side. You know, we need to think about the big picture … there are more countries on the horizon, and my boss is already talking to Raj's boss about the next contract, so …

S: Good thinking.

M: You see, I'm not just a pretty face … Anyway, let's see. I want to keep things positive at this stage. The only thing I have to do now is convince my boss about the extra costs on our side … not going to be easy.

5.3.4

There are a number of learning points in these videos about collaborating with people outside of your team.

Firstly, in professional life, it's important to be demanding sometimes with external partners, to get to a result which is good for your team and your organisation. In Option A Matt communicates powerfully to get Raj's company to pay extra costs. A good result financially. But demanding has risks. Raj is demotivated and might leave the project. An alternative to the demanding style is to use a supportive approach – external partners can respond very positively to this; they support the solutions and they remain very motivated. But, you may need to invest time and money to achieve an outcome that is acceptable for everyone. Matt found this in Option B – he reached an agreement with Raj, but to do this he had to provide extra money and resources.

When communicating internationally, be flexible, and choose the style that best fits the situation.

6.1.1

The phone is really, really – you know, core element of our everyday life, but on the other hand we don't know anything about it. We didn't start as a company, we started as a campaign and the campaign question was how can we give visibility to er the situation in Eastern Congo?

Millions of people died in, in, in wars related to the mining of these minerals we use in, in our mobile devices. So what we thought is, and you know with my background as a designer, is that you know what, why don't we make a device, make a phone? We've been announced the, the fastest growing start-up, tech start-up of Europe by *The Next Web*, which says something about the, the speed in which we grew. We grew from two people to over forty people in two and a ha, two years. Uh we made, in the first one and a half years of our existence, we made a turnover of sixteen million euros. First actually was through crowdfundings, and then in three weeks more than 10,000 people bought the phone. So we had over three and a half million euros on the bank account, we didn't know how to make a phone, you can imagine me laying in bed at night crying and my wife, you know, going at me like, 'Bas, come on! You can do it, you, you started this so you have to, you really have to go for it now,' – it's a success.

All components are actually uh, built up as modules, and people can actually exchange those modules, repair those modules themselves. We work with mines, local mines, in Eastern Congo and where we get our tin, our tantalum, from, so we contribute to the actual economic situation in the Congo instead of, you know, avoiding the country which a lot of companies are doing. If you produce phones, you produce waste, right? And by doing that, you know, by making a Fairphone you're already kind of in the paradox. So what we said is we want to take back phones as well to source minerals. So we've collected over 60,000 phones in the, you know, in the Ghana and we er, we, we got them back to er, Belg, to a Belgian refinery to, you know, to take back to, the minerals to be used in the supply chain again. I might call myself an idealist but I also know, you know, that the world works in a certain way and you have to, you know business is, is an important mechanism to actually create change, um you know that's why we set up Fairphone –that's why we started a company instead of, you know, doing art projects for example. And um, you know a fellow er designer of me, er of mine has, has once said, you know, we're all hippies with business plans. The mechanism we use to change things is a commercial model, and by being part of the economic system and a market mechanism, we are able to actually, you know, put those idea, idealist kind of values into the core of what moves the world. So we're not in it to become, you know, the biggest phone company in the world, but by doing what we do we show that there's a market, we grow demand and if the demand grows the market will follow –that's the way the world works, right?

6.3.1 P = Paula M = Matt

P: I think I'm quite good at influencing people. I'm usually able to make a strong argument, backed with good reasoning. We have some potential buyers from a Mexican chain of business schools coming to London this week.
M: When will they be here?
P: About twenty minutes. … They want to look at partnering with online training and education providers from the UK and I'll be pitching … I expect to get what I want, I haven't failed yet!
M: Remember not to be too pushy … go easy on them.
P: Stop worrying! I've thought of everything, really. Remember we've designed this just for them.
M: I know, I know … but Pedro likes to be involved in decision-making, he's quite a collaborative guy and likes to give input.
P: I'm sure it'll be fine.

6.3.2 Pa = Paula M = Matt S = Susan
Pe = Pedro

Pa: So that brings me to the end of the presentation. I'm sure that you've been able to see the many, many benefits that partnering with us and introducing our online courses will bring to your business schools. I'm sure that you'll agree that our courses are among the best currently available in the global marketplace. Their success and quality are demonstrated by the fact that a number of other business schools and universities in other countries already use them.
M: Well, I'm sure we'd love to hear your thoughts.
S: Yes, I'm really impressed. I like the approach, it feels very new … I can see how it would fit very well in our business schools.
Pe: Hmmm … I'm not sure, I think that there are a lot of technical matters to think about. Who will manage it? How long will the platform take to integrate? We're already quite busy for the rest of this year at least … there's also money to think about … it's the same story with our budget.
Pa: I totally understand your concern. We put together this proposal just for you, so this doesn't relate to anyone else's institution – just yours. We've done an analysis of your business schools and we're aware of the challenges that you mention, but that's why we're so confident that it will be a great success …
Pe: Maybe, but there's a difference between analysing on paper and how things are in practice, this year is …

Pa: Sure, but that's why there's provision for us to support the platform, it's not all just left to you …
Pe: Yes I understood that in your pitch, but …
Pa: And you just won't find a better price anywhere on the market. Not for something like this, nothing more competitive exists.
Pe: OK. Well, I think Susan and I have a lot to think about. I think we can have a discussion over the next few weeks … and we'll get back to you.

6.3.3 Pa = Paula M = Matt S = Susan
Pe = Pedro

Pa: So that brings me to the end of the presentation. I'm sure that you've been able to see the many, many benefits that partnering with us and introducing our online courses will bring to your business schools. I'm sure that you'll agree that our courses are among the best currently available in the global marketplace. Their success and quality are demonstrated by the fact that a number of other business schools and universities in other countries already use them.
M: Well, I'm sure we'd love to hear your thoughts …
S: Yes, I'm really impressed. I like the approach, it feels very new … I can see how it would fit very well in our business schools.
Pe: Hmmm … I'm not sure, I think that there are a lot of technical matters to think about. Who will manage it? How long will the platform take to integrate? We're already quite busy for the rest of this year at least … there's also money to think about … it's the same story with our budget.
Pa: Pedro? Sorry, the most important thing for you is not to have to spend a lot of time integrating the platform and managing the implementation?
Pe: Yes.
Pa: OK, well, we can help with that. We can take on the work of looking at your set-up and creating an implementation plan. On top of that we'll also fully manage implementation … and support it. And of course we'll make sure that any disturbances will be kept to an absolute minimum. Would that be a good solution for you?
Pe: That sounds fine, but there's also cost … I just don't think it's going to work financially.
Pa: Can I ask why you don't think the finances will work out?
Pe: Cash flow. Cash flow and the fact that we allocate budget a couple of years ahead … most of what we have over the next year is already assigned.
Pa: I understand. That doesn't have to be a problem. We would be able to plan and test now, but set the launch for next year and spread the cost. So you could go ahead now, but put it into next year's budget and we could probably agree quarterly payments. How does that sound?
Pe: Well that makes a big difference. If we could agree to those conditions … I think we would be happy to go ahead.
S: Let's do it.
Pa: Great!
Pe: Thanks for being so flexible, Paula.
M: Right, let's take you both to lunch.

6.3.4

When we're just being ourselves, we often try to influence people using our own natural style, and this potentially limits our success. We saw this with Paula in Option A – her 'push' style seemed to suit Susan, but it wasn't working on Pedro. He felt frustrated in the end and Paula wasn't able to close the deal.
In Option B, she adapts to a 'pull' approach and asks Pedro questions to find out more about his needs, while still guiding the conversation to a positive result.
Both 'push' and 'pull' are valid and positive approaches. But they each have advantages and disadvantages depending on the situation. Overall, we have a better chance of communicating successfully if we understand the needs and preferred style of others in specific situations. Then we can choose an influencing style which suits the situation and also the person.

7.1.1 P = Presenter E = Evelyn R = Rodrigo
M = Marcus H = Hannah R = Rennie

P: Working abroad is now a fact of life for many people in business. Multinational companies often require their staff to relocate to offices in different countries or even on different continents. And international experience can be a valuable asset in career development.
The prospect of moving to a new country is exciting. It brings the opportunity to see new places and to get to know different cultures. But going abroad to work is not the same as travelling for pleasure. It brings challenges. Foreign professionals have to learn about cultural issues like customs and etiquette. They may find the way people communicate and interact at work is different.
One of the first things that someone in a new job overseas has to encounter is interacting with co-workers. In different cultures, different standards apply.
E: When you are in Germany people are a bit more reserved to begin with. Once you've broken the ice and got to know them, they will be your friends for life, if they make friends with you. But initially they are a bit more reserved, so don't be put off by that.
P: The workplace culture in Brazil is quite different.
R: When it's time for lunch, you always have lunch with someone – you never have your lunch alone – there's always, usually more than one person. So it tends to be very face value and very friendly, which can be unhelpful at times because you want to do some work and be quiet, but people tend to be interactive, communicative. But at the same time you have a very strong sense of team spirit because everybody's together there doing the same things.
P: Good communication is essential in a work environment. It can present some challenges as Marcus found when he relocated from Sweden to the UK.
M: I thought I was very fluent in English when I, you know, when I lived at home in Sweden. But then when you actually come to live here, you realise (that) the nuances and phrases that you don't know at all. And, you know, doing your mistakes and saying the wrong things at the wrong time, but quickly learning, was fun.
P: The etiquette of communication can also vary. In Poland people tend to be direct when they talk to each other.
H: You might be a little bit shocked that the Poles tend to be more abrupt, or that's how they will come across. The use of 'thank you' and 'please' – it's probably less widely used. The linguistic elements, the cultural element doesn't demand that. So it's absolutely polite if you just say 'yes', 'no' and leave it at that.
P: Many of the rules of a culture remain unwritten. Learning them can be challenging but it is also rewarding and is one of the keys to success in the global workplace.

7.3.1 S = Stefanie P = Paula

S: Today is a big day for our project. We have some clients coming in who are thinking about making a major purchase for the Mexican market …
Paula has responsibility for Mexico, but I'm a bit more experienced so Matt has asked me to lend her some support. The important thing in these kinds of conservations is to make sure that things keep on moving ahead. I'm keen to keep the focus on our launch date, and sticking to the plans that we have between now and then. After that we can worry about group decisions and small details.
I think with the important points we should use our expertise and let our clients know what's best.
S: Hi, Paula.
P: Hi, Stefanie.
S: The first thing I'd like to do is go over all the dates we have for the next three months … can we start there?
P: When we're talking about making decisions, I would say that I prefer to try to find consensus … It's a huge project … in Mexico! There are so many

things to think about ... How will we register students? When to register students? What are we going to do about marketing? Are we going to assist with that? We need to ask them all these questions and take decisions together, we can't know everything about everything ourselves ... So, yes, for me this meeting is about getting to understand more about how they work ... we can think about a launch date later.

7.3.2 St = Stefanie Su = Susan P = Pedro

St: We think that the next step is to decide when exactly we would want to plan the launch.
Su: Yes, I'm happy to have that conversation.
St: Great, well we think that it would be a good idea to keep things moving ...
Su: Absolutely ...
St: ... so I suggest we plan to launch this year.
Su: OK.
St: In our experience it's a good idea to use the summer. When the students aren't around we can implement and test everything ... hopefully your IT guys will have a bit more time then ... it's just easier to set everything up. So my advice is that we aim for a launch date in September.
Su: I totally agree. Let's do that.
P: OK. That's not far off ... I think we should know a little bit more about the process ... I just want to make sure that we're all being realistic.
Su: It's realistic. Let's just do it, we can get into the process later. OK great, we're all agreed then.
St: Fantastic.

7.3.3 St = Stefanie Su = Susan Pa = Paula Pe = Pedro

St: We think that the next step is to decide when exactly we would want to plan the launch.
Su: Yes, I'm happy to have that conversation.
Pa: Great, when would be the best time for you? It would probably be a good idea to keep things moving and plan for sometime this year, but we're happy to work around your needs.
Su: September time would be good.
Pe: I think that we should do a pilot first ... let's just trial it in one of our business schools and, then, if it all runs smoothly, we can roll it out to the rest of the group.
Pa: We could do that, certainly ... sounds logical ... have you thought about how and when you'll register your students, or how we're going to market the courses in advance?
Pe: No, not yet ... I guess we would need to discuss those things internally to start with ... let's keep it flexible for now. You know, sometimes things change, let's keep talking.
Pa: Sure, after all, we're here to facilitate what works best for you.
Su: Thanks, Paula, but I'm sure we don't want to waste your time or ours in meeting after meeting. I'm happy to make a decision now and stick to it ... let's say September. If we don't go live in that semester, there'll be another six-month wait, which no one wants. So can we launch in September? And fix an exact date? You can do whatever piloting you want between now and then.
St: Absolutely, that sounds perfect.
Pe: OK.
St: Great, well, we'll start looking at dates.

7.3.4

Everyone's decision-making behaviour is shaped in some way by their culture; it could be national culture, corporate culture or some other form of culture.
Firstly, some people can take a very target-driven approach while others may prefer a more collaborative approach. For example, in Option A, Stefanie and Susan dominated the discussion and were very target-driven, while in Option B we see that Paula and Pedro are clearly more consensus-oriented.
Another difference is how people view time and deadlines. What's fixed for one person may be flexible for another, and this can cause problems.

As we saw in the videos, Stefanie was keen to have a fixed decision on the launch date while Paula was happier taking a more flexible approach.
Thirdly, we can look at attitudes to status and hierarchy. In some places, hierarchies are flat and you can openly discuss and debate ideas with your manager. Elsewhere, status and hierarchy are more important, and you probably shouldn't openly disagree with your manager.
In this story, Susan is ranked higher than Pedro, and Stefanie has more experience than Paula. These factors could have enabled them to push through their decision in both video options.
So, how can we overcome these challenges? We can first observe others, then discuss our preferred approach. This can help us achieve better business results while protecting relationships at the same time.

8.1.1 P = Presenter N = Nadia
PM = Park Manager VS1= Vet Student 1
VS2 = Vet Student 2 S = Steve Leonard

P: Leadership in business requires a range of skills. These include an ability to make decisions, good communication and knowing when to delegate tasks. Leadership skills such as these are just as important in running a team as they are in managing a multinational. Learning to lead a team can be a challenge.
In *Safari Vet School*, sixteen veterinary students take that challenge and test their leadership abilities in real-life situations with dangerous wild animals. The students have been selected from thousands of applicants to travel to South Africa where they will be supervised by specialists, including experienced TV vet, Steve Leonard.
Nadia is studying at Cambridge University. She's a high achiever – used to getting top grades. The Vet School selectors were impressed by her determination.
N: Failure is not something I cope well with. If you want me to boss you, I will! People can be quite intimidated by me I think. I mean I've had people say they're scared of me, which I don't understand why, but obviously I must be quite 'in your face' maybe. I kind of have one volume and it's 'loud'.
P: Nadia's sense of purpose means that she is chosen as team leader for the first task. An animal must be sedated, treated, put on a truck for transit and then woken up.
As team leader, Nadia has to make key decisions, motivate the group and ensure they all work together. If the animal is not revived quickly, it may be harmed or even die.
It does not run smoothly. Luckily the team manages to administer the reversal drug to wake up the animal. The Park Manager is critical of Nadia's management style in the team debriefing session.
PM: There was far too much chatter going on. And running around. Everyone a bit disorganised. It took you fifteen minutes from when the trailer arrived up to when you actually gave the reversal. OK? Far too long.
VS1: I think we just needed just one person to like kind of control the operation. Because I, literally, didn't know what you guys were doing. I was just on ...
VS2: I was just focusing on the heart rate, the lung field ...
VS1: I didn't know the trailer was there ...
N: Yeah we all got so side-tracked with immobilising it that we forgot the whole point was just to get it on the truck. And I felt that the team was disappointed with how I behaved as the team leader.
P: Nadia receives feedback from Steve, her mentor. She admits that leading and motivating a group is different from motivating herself.
N: I normally cope really well with adrenaline. But looking back I think I cope well with adrenaline when there's just me and I just have to think, 'Right! I have to do this. I'm going to do it'. Whereas when you've got a group of nine people that you're

trying to control and when ...
S: You're trying to control nine people?
N: Well ... because ... it was a group of nine and I was supposed to coordinate them
S: When you look back at this, how many questions did you ask of your team that were advice questions?
N: How do you mean?
S: In terms of 'What do you think we should do?'
N: I can't remember.
S: I didn't hear any. Do you think you'd taken on too much responsibility?
N: Yeah definitely! That was the problem. I was completely out of my comfort zone.
S: You've just got a taste of what it's like to be in charge. How did that make you feel?
N: Awful.
S: Did it? What you experienced was very, very difficult. I don't think you did that bad a job.
P: It has been a tough learning experience for Nadia. She now understands that leadership involves a range of skills – such as motivating all the team members, keeping focused on the main objectives of the task, and communicating clearly.

8.3.1

So this is it ... It's been a long journey, but very successful in the end, I think. All that's left now is to wrap everything up with the team. It's always important at the end of long and detailed projects like this to take the opportunity to learn lessons. As project manager, I'm keen to get some feedback from the guys, so we've set up a brief session while they're still all here in London ... hopefully it won't be too brutal. Obviously I hope they give me some positive feedback. Everyone likes to feel that they've done well ... But it would also be interesting to get some developmental feedback, to hear where they think I could improve.

8.3.2 M = Matt S = Stefanie K = Kenji P = Paula

M: I'd like to ask you all for some personal feedback. As you know, this is one of the first times I've worked on an international project like this so I'm keen to know how you all feel ... so don't be shy, who wants to go first?
S: I'm happy to go first.
M: OK great, go ahead.
S: Well, I think you did a very good job communicating with the team and keeping us all informed ... once we knew each other's roles it was very easy to work together.
M: Great! Thanks Stefanie, I'm happy you feel that I was able to ... pull everyone together, even though we were all in different parts of the world.
K: I agree. And it was good that you asked Stefanie to help out when I had some difficulties.
M: Sure, it just seemed like a sensible idea to me at the time. Paula?
P: I agree. I thought you were a good project manager ... thanks for all the coaching you gave me and for the tips about making presentations ... I felt like you were there to support me.
M: Excellent. Thanks, Paula. Well, I'm looking forward to the next big project already, thanks guys.

8.3.3 M = Matt S = Stefanie K = Kenji P = Paula

M: I'd like to ask you all for some personal feedback. As you know, this is one of the first times I've worked on an international project like this so I'm keen to know how you all feel ... so don't be shy, who wants to go first?
S: I'm happy to go first.
M: OK great, go ahead.
S: Everything was OK in the end and I think the project was a success ... but I have to say ... I thought it was a bit chaotic at the beginning. I think that it was your responsibility to make sure that we all knew each other and communicated ... but I don't think we did have a clear idea of who was on the project or our roles ... I think that was a problem.

M: That's interesting ... I thought I had done that. If you remember I sent around some email intros and I set up a virtual conference?

S: You did, but it came too late and was also a bit short ... It was difficult to know how to get started without knowing my role and everyone else's. I think if you could have called each of us *before* the project began, that would have been good.

M: Right, I'll bear that in mind. Anyone else? Kenji?

K: Everything was fine.

M: Are you sure? You looked like you were thinking about something there. I'd like to hear anything that's on your mind.

K: This project was just one of many tasks that I had. I'm always very busy, but I don't think you understood that, you always asked me to do things urgently. I'm sorry that I was not always able to act so quickly.

M: OK. I really had no idea that you had a lot of other jobs on, you must tell me things like that ... otherwise there's no way that I can know ...

P: But I think what Kenji's saying is that you often waited until things were urgent before passing them on, and that puts us under pressure and creates a lot of stress ... it's just a question of being organised. I think in future if you gave us all a timeline or something, that might help us to plan better.

M: OK, I get the point. We've all been under pressure, and it's not like *your* work was perfect, I had to spend a lot of time fixing other people's mistakes. Anything else?

8.3.4

When giving or receiving feedback, we must always remember that our approach to feedback is usually driven by our own personality and preferences. And that no single approach is best. There are a few points that we should keep in mind: When *giving* feedback, firstly motivate others by focusing on things which have been done well. Also, remember to help them improve by focusing on areas in which they can develop. We saw the team do each of these in the videos, but was their positive intention clear in Option B? I'm not so sure. And in terms of *receiving* feedback, remember that feedback is valuable so, when you're not hearing any, you should actively ask for it, as Matt did. Then when you do get feedback, listen to it first without disagreeing or making excuses about any potentially negative points. Then decide later if you want to act on it. Matt may have missed some valuable information when he started making excuses in Option B.

Finally, use a balanced approach to giving positive and developmental feedback. Positive feedback reaffirms someone's actions and position, and is good for their motivation. But, without developmental feedback they may not be aware of areas in which they can improve.

BW3.01
Amalia

Is this webcam on? Oh, right! So, why should you hire me? Well, I have to say I think I'm hard-working, I'm reliable and, and ... I'm highly qualified. I have a background in marketing and a lot of experience in different sectors. I also speak various languages, so that will be very useful for an international company like Media Solutions.

I would like to work for you because I think I'm good at communicating, especially writing, and I could contribute to your Communications department with my ideas and improve the presence of your clients in social media. Err, ... that's all really. Thanks for listening. Oh, and please call me if you'd like me to come in for an interview.

Birte

Why should you hire me? Because I'm a 'people person': I'm not only sociable, but also really creative and if you hired me, I would give 110 percent and I would get on with all the team and the clients, too. Another thing you should know about me is I'm really into sports and martial arts, as you can see. You can check out some of my videos in social media on how-to-do sports training. I love social media and dedicate a lot of time to it. It's the way everyone communicates nowadays.

What else? I've got a degree in marketing. I did an internship at my dad's company and I learnt *a lot*. I'm a fast learner. I don't have lots of experience but I think it's more important to have the right attitude and just get out there and do it! Why should you hire me? Because I'm worth it! Call me for an interview and please give me the chance to tell you more.

Cindy

So, you'd like to know why you should hire me? That's a good question. Looking at my CV you might think I don't have any relevant experience but I *do* have experience in managing people. I have to communicate in my job every day, where I'm responsible for a team of forty people, talking to different departments and dealing with difficult customers. I'm good at working under pressure, so you can depend on me to write those reports on time!

Err, just a minute .... Another consideration is that I'm a big fan of social media. I write a blog in my free time, although I don't have that many followers yet. I'm also studying marketing online in the evenings. So, if you hire me, I will help you to find the best solutions for you and your clients and improve their online presence with the contributions of key opinion leaders and influencers.

Thank you for considering my application and I look forward to your call!

BW6.01
Ben Fischer

Hi guys! I'm Ben Fischer and my award-winning theatre company performs at events and festivals all over the world. We bring the works of famous German writers and dramatists, such as Bertolt Brecht, to audiences across the globe.

In true dramatic style, our latest production of Brecht's *The Good Person of Szechwan* has just been hit by disaster. An electrical fire destroyed the arts centre where we were performing in London and took with it all our costumes and equipment. Fortunately, nobody was in the building at the time and nobody was injured in the fire.

We know one day the insurance company will eventually pay the compensation to rebuild and replace everything, but we need to complete our world tour now and can't wait around for the money to arrive.

Can you help us? We need to raise €10,000 in the next few weeks to replace everything. I promise all donations to our cause will be repaid when we receive the insurance payout. Not only that, depending on the size of your donation you will receive discounts on tickets and even free tickets to see our play in any city of your choice on the tour. Just see our website for more details.

As Brecht himself once said, 'Everyone needs help from everyone.' By contributing to our disaster fund, you will be doing your bit to support community arts and help our young theatre group to literally rise from the ashes. Thank you!

Alison Chadwick

My name's Alison Chadwick and this is my story. I started my T-shirt business, Alison's Tees, back in university as a hobby. Friends and fellow students used to ask me where I got my T-shirts from and when I told them I designed them myself everyone said that was cool.

Then I thought, you know anyone can design their own T-shirt. It's simple, it's fun and it's creative. On my website you can choose the colour and style but more than that, you can have any design or logo you like printed on it including photos to make your very own unique T-shirt. Friends will be amazed. Before we finally produce the T-shirt, you'll receive a photo of the design for final approval.

No more shopping for hours looking for something you actually like. No more low-quality shop-bought products. All our T-shirts are 100 percent organic cotton and ethically sourced. We're helping independent cotton farmers. We work hand-in-hand with our suppliers to ensure highest-quality tees.

Thanks to previous crowdfunding our business has been a big success. Now we need your support and your money to help us develop our mobile app so our users can design and order their own tees on their smartphones, anytime, anywhere.

Marcos López

If you like travelling, you'll love our new tour guide mobile app. It's like an audio guide but on your mobile phone, so you carry it with you all the time. I'm Marcos López and I'm one of the founders of Holidapp. It's the ultimate travel companion. It's like having an audio guide but on your smartphone. You'll never want to buy another guidebook or tourist map again in your life. You'll find out about the places you're visiting whenever you want in a new, original and entertaining way. Our app is free to download and quick and easy to use. Enter the desired location and for just €10 you will get an expert guide to one of over 30 destinations in Europe and the USA. And the list of places is growing longer each month.

The guide features audio tours by experts in their towns, from qualified tour guides to local storytellers of all ages with a passion for the place where they live. Our platform is free to our guide contributors and they receive 70 percent of the revenues generated by their guides.

Each travel guide on our app comes with high-quality photographs and can use your geolocation to help you get the most from your guide.

We need your backing to help us cover the cost of production, audio recording, programming and photography. We'd also love to hear what you think of the guides so we can keep improving our service.

1.01 DR = David Robinson JW = Janet Wood

DR: In this part of the show I'm talking to organisation consultant, Janet Wood. Janet, the tall organisation structure is still typical in companies today, isn't it?

JW: Yes, and this traditional pyramid hierarchy has many problems.

DR: Such as …

JW: Well, decision-making is generally slow. This type of company can be very bureaucratic and inefficient. It's slow to change and innovate, which is a real danger in today's world.

DR: But is there really any alternative in a large corporation?

JW: Yes, there are examples of successful innovative organisations which do things differently. One of the most famous is W. L. Gore, a multinational manufacturing company.

DR: W. L. Gore is probably best known for the fabric Gore-Tex, isn't it?

JW: That's right. Bill and Genevieve Gore started the company in the USA back in the 1950s with a flat structure. Today, the company still has no traditional organisational chart. Gore believes that if people are passionate about their work, they're going to be highly self-motivated.

DR: So, how does the company operate?

JW: Well, there are over 10,000 employees in 30 countries divided into teams of 8 to 12 people, who work on projects and products together. The staff at Gore are actually called 'associates'. They don't have job titles. And they don't have managers. Instead they choose to 'follow' leaders. Basically, you decide what you are going to contribute to the team and you establish your own work and pay.

DR: I hear the associates actually *elected* the company's chief executive, Terri Kelly.

JW: Yes, she's one of the few people at the company who has a job title.

DR: There's been a lot of talk in the business news recently about a concept called 'holacracy'. Can you tell us what that is exactly?

JW: Yes, the expression comes from the Greek word *holos*, meaning 'whole'. Holacracy is essentially a system with no bosses at all.

DR: How does this manager-free system work in practice?

JW: Well, it's probably too early to know. Just two years ago Zappos, the U.S. online shoe and clothes store which was started in 1999, introduced 'holacracy'. Now all the functions of the company have been delegated to teams called 'circles'. Zappos has about 1,600 employees distributed among some 500 circles. Each circle has a 'lead link' who has a similar role to a project manager.

DR: Does this person, the 'lead link' decide who does what tasks?

JW: No, circle members decide their roles and responsibilities in meetings. Larger teams have circles within circles. Staff can either start a new circle or join a circle depending on the type of work they'd like to do.

DR: Sounds complicated.

JW: Yes, the CEO of Zappos, Tony Hsieh, says it could take another two to five years to complete the transition. In fact, Zappos has a training session next week, called a 'Culture Camp', and I'm flying to Las Vegas tomorrow for that.

DR: I'm sure that's going to be a very interesting experience. Janet, thank you for coming into the studio today.

Ext1.01

1 Well, decision-making is generally slow.

2 This type of company can be very bureaucratic and inefficient.

3 … there are examples of successful innovative organisations which do things differently.

4 W. L. Gore is probably best known for the fabric Gore-Tex, isn't it?

5 Today, the company still has no traditional organisational chart.

6 … she's one of the few people at the company who has a job title.

7 Now all the functions of the company have been delegated to teams called 'circles'.

8 Staff can either start a new circle or join a circle.

1.02

A: Hi, Juliana. What time does the department meeting start tomorrow?

B: At 10 o'clock as usual, but I think I'm going to be about fifteen minutes late. I have a dentist's appointment.

A: Are you going to be able to talk after your trip to the dentist's?

B: Yes, it's just a check-up. In fact, I'm giving a presentation on the company restructuring.

A: I'm sure that's going to be interesting. Is it true we're moving to offices outside the city?

B: I'm not going to tell you anything before the meeting. You know that.

A: Well, I'm going to sit right at the front. I don't want to miss anything.

1.03

First meetings in an international business setting can often be difficult. Two strangers come together. Often, they both have to speak a foreign language, English. So you have strangers who aren't sure what to say to each other. And they aren't sure how to say it. The result is pretty predictable: a difficult silence. Now, silence isn't necessarily bad. In some cultures, silence is good; it's positive because it signals respect. But for me, if you want to get to know someone, to understand them as a person and as a professional – which is essential for doing business together – then silence is a risk, because you stop this process.

If you want to learn about the other person, and build a relationship, you need to ask questions. And this is the real value of asking questions – you learn stuff about the other person.

So … Which questions do you ask? I would say, in terms of style, keep it short and simple, just ask simple starter questions. If you are meeting a visitor, you can say things like, 'Did you have a good trip?' Is this your first time here?' These kinds of questions are good because they allow an easy answer, they're not too personal, but they can quickly break the ice and get the conversation flowing.

You know, sometimes the specific questions don't really matter; you just ask a question to get the ball rolling. And then it's important to ask follow-up questions – if you don't, small talk can feel very mechanical.

In terms of what you ask about in those first few minutes, I think in business you need to have a mix of personal and work topics. On the work side, asking about roles and responsibilities is good, and the organisation behind the person, and where people work and travel … all these questions are easy to answer and give you useful background. And if you listen to what people tell you, you'll find more ideas for other questions.

And all this asking questions, well, it builds understanding and in the end … trust. Remember, it's impossible to trust someone if you don't know them well. And how can you know them well? You've got to ask questions! Oh, one final thing: if possible, find something you have in common with the other person – maybe you visited the same place, you like the same food, the same music or sport. When you and the other person have similar interests, the conversation often goes better.

1.04 P = Paul E = Eva

P: Hi, is it Eva?

E: Yes.

P: Hi, Eva. Nice to meet you. Welcome.

E: Thank you. It's nice to be here.

P: Did you have a good trip? Hotel OK?

E: Yes, no problems. I haven't seen the hotel yet. I came straight here from the airport.

P: OK, well, follow me. My office is just through this door. So, here we are. Can I take your coat?

E: Thank you.

P: Good. Take a seat. Can I offer you something to drink? Coffee? Tea?

E: Just water would be nice, thanks.

P: OK. Here you go. So, is it your first time here in the London office?

E: Yes, it is. But I've been to London once before.

P: OK. For work?

E: No, just a holiday that time.

P: So, where do you work exactly? Are you in the Zurich office at the moment?

E: Yes, I'm responsible for sales support there. I work 20 percent in Geneva, though.

P: OK, and, do you report to Paul Blaettner?

E: Yes, I do. You know him?

P: Yes, I worked with him on a sales project last year. I was thinking of inviting him to join us later. Are you free for dinner this evening?

E: Yes, that would be nice.

P: Fine, so I'll organise that. And, funny, you know I also worked in Geneva. When did you join the company?

E: End of last year.

P: OK, then I just missed you. I moved to this job here in October. So you know, I'm now Head of Customer Service, and also this new international project around Service Excellence, which is why we're here.

E: Yes, I'm really looking forward to this project. It's going to be a lot of work, but I'm ready.

P: It's really good to have you on the project. So, shall we make a start? I know you have a busy schedule and lots of other people to meet.

2.01

1 Good morning, everyone. My name is John Hawkins, and what I want to do today is give you a short introduction to the company. I won't take more than ten minutes because we have a lot to get through today. But if you have any questions, please feel free to interrupt.

2 I would like to start by offering a very warm welcome to everyone here today. Thank you very much for coming. I know many of you have travelled a long way to be here. As you know, I'm Pam Ellis, Managing Director here. What I want to do today is give you an introduction to the company. Firstly, a little information on operations; secondly, more about the people; and finally, the culture we have here. But to begin, I want to look at operations.

3 Good morning. I'm Paolo Orlandi, Managing Director of Production here. Er, sorry for my poor English. But I must, before we take a tour of the factory, give you an introduction to health and safety, so that everyone is safe here. Please, do ask questions if there is anything you don't understand. I know some things I say may not be so clear. But, it's important everyone understands what to do and what not to do in the production area. So, please, ask me questions. Any questions, any time, if anything is not clear. I'd like to start with some rules on where you can walk and where not to walk. As you can see …

2.02

1 So, before I begin and tell you why I am here, I would like to start with why you are here. And how can I know that? Well, I asked a couple of you during coffee this morning. Jackie, over there, yes, she wants to learn about which countries we are active in, as she wants to work abroad one day. Good, I'll talk about that. Peter, he's a finance guy and wants to know more on the numbers. Are we profitable? Important question, Peter, and I'll talk about finance too. And Samir, the interest there is how to become a leader as quickly as possible. And I will talk about that too – what kind of organisation we are, and what kind of people do well here.

2 To begin, before I say anything, I'd like to ask you a few questions, find out what you know about this organisation. Who knows how many people work here? OK … put your hand up if you know the

answer to these questions. Which countries are we active in? ... OK. What are our main products? ... Hmm, so, not so many of you. That's fine. That's why I'm here. My name's Pam Ellis and I want to tell you a little bit about ...

3 Now, to start, I'd like to share a story with you, about a young man, around twenty years ago, who was sitting right where you are standing, new to the company, a little nervous on the first day, not knowing what to expect. Well, that was, as you can probably guess, me all those years ago. On that day, I listened, and I continued to listen and learn, and now I'm Managing Director. So, welcome.

2.03   JH = John Hawkins
Au = Audience member

JH: So, let's begin with the most important part of the company, and that's its people. And there are three important points I want to make here. Firstly, we're a very young company. It was set up only three years ago and the average age is only twenty-nine. This means we're fresh and energetic and we really like innovation, which is our main strength. Secondly, we're a small company, with only fifty-six people at the moment. This is also important because we want to stay personal; people know each other here, we have a family atmosphere, which our customers also feel and love about us. And finally, and as I said earlier during lunch to some of you, we are very international. In fact, we now have twenty different nationalities in the company, working in five countries. For me, on a personal note and speaking very openly, this is important as I believe very much in being international and the value of working across different cultures. So, if you can take a look at this slide, you will see the nationalities in the company. I hope I haven't missed anyone. Truly international. Great. Yes, a question?

Au: Is the company growing? Getting more international?

JH: Great question. Really good question, in a number of ways. Yes, we are growing, probably to around sixty-five people this year. But I don't want to grow much more or we become too big, too much a large corporation. So, yes but no. We are small. We want to be small. And we plan to stay small. But I'll say more about that a little later. Are there any other questions now on that? So, I'll close there. Thank you very much for listening. And I'll hand over to Paul to tell you something about products and services.

3.01
1 What are your strengths and weaknesses?
2 Are you working at the moment?
3 How long have you worked as a chemical engineer?
4 Do you have any experience in green technologies?
5 Why would you like to work for us?
6 What would you do on your first day at work?
7 Do you have your original certificates with you?
8 Where do you see yourself in five years' time?

3.02
1 You've told me about your strengths. Can you tell me what your greatest weakness is?
2 Could you tell me about your work experience?
3 You write in your CV that you have good leadership skills. Can you tell me about a time when you showed leadership skills?
4 Although you have the right qualifications, you don't have much work experience in this sector. I'd like to know if you've ever done any voluntary work.
5 Could you tell me how you would add value to our company?
6 This job involves visiting waste-water facilities around the country. I'd like to know if you are prepared to travel for the job.
7 Right. Finally, I'd like to know who I should contact for a reference.

3.03   I = interviewer   C = candidate
1
I: You've told me about your strengths. Can you tell me what your greatest weakness is?
C: I'm not sure, but my friends tell me I'm quite demanding.
I: Are you a bit of a perfectionist?
C: I don't know. Sometimes perhaps.
I: Anything else?
C: Erm, err ...
2
I: Could you tell me about your work experience?
C: I'm afraid I don't have much experience, but I have a PhD in waste water management.
3
I: You write in your CV that you have good leadership skills. Can you tell me about a time when you showed leadership skills?
C: Sure. I was responsible for a large team of researchers while I was doing my PhD in the States. And in my last job I was the assistant project manager for a waste water facility. That was a temporary position because someone was on maternity leave.
4
I: Although you have the right qualifications, you don't have much experience in this sector. I'd like to know if you've ever done any voluntary work.
C: Erm, let me think now ... Well, when I was at university, I did voluntary work visiting schools. I was working on a project together with teachers and children, raising awareness about water consumption and waste water processes.
I: I see.
5
I: How would you add value to our company?
C: Sorry, I didn't catch that.
I: Could you tell me how you would add value to our company?
C: That's a difficult question. As I said before, I think I'm highly qualified for the job, I'm a fast learner and I'm really passionate about green technologies. It isn't just a job. It's a lifestyle.
6
I: This job involves visiting waste water facilities around the country. I'd like to know if you are prepared to travel for the job.
C: Yes, of course. That will be very interesting.
7
I: Right. Finally, I'd like to know who I should contact for a reference, in case we decide to offer you the job.
C: References? Well, there are two or three contacts. I'll need to check and get back to you. Is that all right?
I: Fine. Do you have any questions for me?

3.04
1   S = Sue   M = Max
S: Thanks for coming in today, Max. ... So tell me, why do you think you're the right person for this job?
M: Well, I'm hard-working, ... I'm flexible, ... I'm good at working with colleagues and customers, and I have the relevant experience and skills.
S: OK. That all sounds good. Have you ever worked in a regional sales team?
M: No, I haven't.
S: Oh, OK ... Do you have a driving licence?
M: Not yet.
S: I see. If you get this job, you will need to have a driving licence. So ... You've told me about your strengths and experience. Can you tell me about your weaknesses?
M: Hmm. Well, ... I'm not very organised, like with paperwork and other things.
S: I see.
M: So, what are the next steps? When can I expect to hear from you?
2   S = Sue   J = John
S: Thank you for coming in today, John. I invited you here because Anna has told me a lot about you and your abilities.

J: That's great. Thank you for your time today.
S: Of course. So tell me, why do you think you're the right person for this job?
J: Well, I'm hard-working, I'm flexible, I'm good at working with both colleagues and customers, and I have the relevant experience and skills.
S: OK. That all sounds good. Have you ever worked in a regional sales team?
J: That's a good question. I haven't, but I do have many transferable skills. I've worked in different local offices of the same company, so I understand the balance between local and regional priorities. So, while my experience is local, I have a good awareness of the sales focus from regional perspectives too. I've also indirectly supported a regional project with local information.
S: That's good. Anna told me about the project you worked on. So, moving on ... Do you have a driving licence?
J: It's good you asked that. I'm currently learning to drive, and I have my test in two weeks' time.
S: OK, that's good. If you get this job, you will need to have a driving licence. Now, you've told me about your strengths and experience. Can you tell me about your weaknesses?
J: Well, I'm very good at dealing with people, which as you know is essential in sales, but I sometimes struggle with the administrative work and paperwork. I am aware of this, though, and I'm working on it so that I can improve.
S: OK, it's good that you're working on this. Do you have any questions for me?
J: Yes, I do. Could you tell me what a normal day or week in this job would be like?
S: Sure, it would start at about 8 o'clock and initially what you'll be doing is ...

4.01
Why is it difficult for companies to plan for the future? Because it isn't easy to know what's going to happen in this complex world we live in. How can a business ever know what will have an impact on its performance and success? In today's session we'll look at a popular tool to plan business strategy called PEST analysis. That's P-E-S-T. PEST is an acronym and the four letters stand for the different types of external factors that a business has to face and generally has no control over. By external factors I mean influences outside a company that can however impact a business. So, what do the letters P-E-S-T stand for? Well, P stands for 'Political' as you might guess. E means 'Economic'. S stands for 'Social factors' and finally T refers to 'Technological factors'. I should mention there is also an extended version of PEST analysis called 'PESTLE' – that's P-E-S-T-L-E, which puts 'Legal' and 'Environmental' factors into additional categories. Anyway, going back to PEST, let's look at some examples we can put into each category so you get a clearer picture. Then later I'll get you to apply PEST analysis to a company you know well. You don't have to take notes as all of this information is on the intranet.

4.02
So, examples of political factors are the stability or instability of governments in a company's markets which will affect business growth. Another example is the employment laws in each country, which are obviously decided by politicians, and thirdly corporate taxes, also decided by government. Economic factors are often closely related. An economic recession is clearly going to affect demand for a company's products. High inflation is going to affect costs and prices. A third example is exchange rates, which will affect exports and imports. Social factors, as the name suggests, are about people and society. For example, changing consumer preferences and the age demographics of the population can affect demand for products. Also, is the population growing and how fast? As for technological factors, we all know the impact technology has on our

lives. Businesses have to analyse the possible uses of emerging technologies, for instance automation on production lines. Another example is the impact of the internet, such as online shopping, and thirdly the smartphone revolution which allows a company to reach customers faster than ever.

4.03

Obviously, a PEST analysis is not only about collecting lots of data. The next step is to prioritise the most relevant factors and identify any business opportunities these offer. For example, can a new technology improve production processes and reduce costs? It's also crucial to identify any significant risks, or threats, to the business. For instance, if consumer demand is falling in one part of its market, should the company develop new product lines? Finally, managers have to go beyond analysis into action. A company mustn't miss any opportunities for the business so these must form part of the business plan. If there are significant threats, the company must come up with a strategy to deal with these risks too. I should mention that PEST is used with other tools which also analyse internal factors, but we won't go into that today. OK, let's look at a PEST analysis of a well-known footwear company.

4.04 R = Roel B = Bibi P = Peter A = Annette

R: OK, let's get started. Good morning, everyone. Great to see you all here today. Now, what I want to look at today is a problem, a nice problem in a way, but a problem, the fact that we're now getting a lot of telephone and email enquiries from new countries: Belgium and France, and Germany, of course, but also the Czech Republic, Poland and Hungary. I think the new website is helping; it's very attractive and it's generating traffic. But it is creating a problem.
B: Can you explain again what the problem is, exactly? New customers – that isn't a problem, is it?
R: No, the problem is that in many of the emails that people are sending, particularly, but also some phone calls, people are not using English; and we don't have the skills in house to deal with customer enquiries in Polish and Czech, etc.
P: OK, so the real problem is a lack of language competence here in the company, which we need to solve or we will lose potential customers. I guess that's the point.
R: Exactly. So, I wanted to take a few minutes of your time to discuss this. Any ideas?
P: Um, would it be possible to train our people here to use the different languages? It's a cost, but it's a solution.
R: OK, intensive training could be a solution. I'll note that down, thanks. What else can we do? Bibi?
B: How about using a call centre service for different languages? People who call us, they can choose the language they work with, and we contract a call centre to handle first contacts, and then they contact our sales staff.
R: That sounds like a possible solution.
A: OK, but I'm not sure how that would work. If we do that, it will just increase our costs.
R: Let's just stick with ideas for the moment. So Annette, anything to add?
A: Maybe we recruit some people with the languages we need.
R: I think that's a nice idea; simple and doable. I don't know the cost, but I like the fact that we might be able to do it relatively quickly.

4.05 R = Roel B = Bibi P = Peter A = Annette

R: So are there any more ideas? No? Well, I think recruitment is the best option.
B: Why do you think recruitment is the solution?
R: Well, we are looking for new salespeople anyway, at least two. And so it's a very easy thing to just add languages to the profile required.
B: I'm not sure that it's the best solution. I prefer training.
P: Bibi, just building on Roel's idea, I think it's easier to hire someone than train them in language

skills. For our staff to learn Czech or Hungarian, it would take a very long time … years!
B: You may be right.
R: OK, then I think we need to look at recruitment as the quick solution. Agreed?
B: OK, I can live with this.
P: Yes.
A: Agreed.
R: Shall I take this on, or do any of you have time to do this? Annette, you normally handle people topics.
A: Do you want me to do that? I'm happy to take it on.
R: Great. So if you could get a job description done by the end of this week for us to discuss, then we can advertise next week, maybe hire by the end of the month. Problem solved in … what, three weeks?
B: If you need any help with this, just ask, Annette. It's quite a lot of work.
A: Great, thanks.
R: Great. That's what I love about you guys – such a great team.

5.01 A = Anne And = Anders

A: Anders. Good to see you again. Are you well?
And: Not bad. Just back from a weekend to see family in Copenhagen.
A: Very nice. We're just in here. Please, take a seat. Coffee?
And: No, I'm fine with water, thanks.
A: Please, help yourself. So, firstly, I should apologise for pushing. I really needed to have this meeting this morning. So, sorry about the very short notice but we have some new financial objectives in the company, from the board, so I have a lot to do on this end by the end of the month – all very urgent.
And: No problem. We need to discuss next year, anyway.
A: We do. So, as I said in my email to you, I think there are some important things we need to talk about. What I'd like to discuss today is, firstly, of course, price of service. Secondly, our cancellation policy. We have more and more cancellations, and we need to discuss how to handle this.
And: OK.
A: Thirdly, quality. You know, we've had a few issues with late taxi pick-ups, some hotels have been a little below standard.
And: OK, very happy to talk about that.
A: To start, I'd like to hear from you first. We talked about these topics last time we met, was it the end of last month? And you said you would have some discussions with your management. So perhaps it's useful to update first on how that went, and you can give me your first ideas on these topics.

5.02 And = Anders A = Anne

And: Yes, we did have some discussions. So, OK, firstly let me just check here, yes, OK, on the pricing side, my proposal would be that we go with an inflation-level price rise, which means just 2 percent, because I think we both appreciate that the economic situation is difficult, so I think this is probably fair to both of us. On the cancellation side, the policy is currently that you need to inform us eight hours before a taxi or a flight needs to be cancelled, or we will charge you for the booking. This is something we want to keep. We think eight hours is reasonable. And then, on the quality side, well, which is more on hotels, we only book as per your instructions, three- or four-star hotels, and we use the national rating system as a guide. The problem we find with hotels and experience of hotels, some people like one hotel and some people another. I realise some people are unhappy with some of the three-stars, but some are happy. So we would recommend no change here.
A: We've had some very unhappy executives.
And: I realise that, but as I said, in some of the same hotels, we have happy executives, even from your company. So, I think this is more around what

some people like and don't like, and it's not really a quality issue. So, how does that all sound to you?
A: Thanks for that. So, going through the three points … Just to clarify, do you mean a 2 percent increase on both taxi and hotel accommodation prices?
And: Yes, that's right.
A: OK, I think the 2 percent, that's a little high; we were hoping for something lower. Would you consider 1.5 percent? That is more or less in line with the current company policy on vendor prices. Before you answer that, on the flight cancellation side, because business is less and less predictable, and more and more trips are being cancelled, we need to agree a different policy on this; we're paying for too many cancelled flights. My proposal would be that we go to three hours pre-warning of a flight problem from our side. I think that would really help us. Most trips are cancelled the morning of travel, so three hours would deal with this fine.
And: But three hours is very short notice.
A: It is. But it's reality. So we need to find a way around this. On the hotel quality side, I think we need to change how we do things and just go for four-star instead of three-star. Assuming we did this, we would want a three-star price on all our bookings; I think this is justified by the volume of bookings.

5.03 And = Anders A = Anne

And: OK, thanks for this. I think this is very fair, overall. On pricing, I can agree to 1.5 percent. We will need to review it again in the future but for next year, fine. On the flight cancellation problem, your proposal is very difficult for us to accept. If we make a flight booking, and then cancel it, we have a cost. This isn't something we can accept.
A: OK, but then you need to negotiate with the airlines.
And: We do talk to the airlines, of course, but they're not always so flexible. And any negotiation on this takes time; so it's very difficult for me to accept this shift to three hours. We could maybe go to six.
A: Six? OK, that might work. It's better than the eight – it makes it easier to cancel on the day of travel … so let's agree to that.
And: OK, good. And then on hotels, I think we can do this but we will need to limit the range of hotels. That will help us to be more flexible on price. You have a big choice of hotels in some locations. Can we change this to two hotels per location, for example?
A: That seems reasonable. OK, fine. Two hotels per location. I think we have six in some cases. And that's too many.
And: OK, good. Yes, so two hotels per city location, and we have a deal.

5.04 And = Anders A = Anne

And: So, is that everything?
A: Yes, I think that we have an agreement. We said that prices would go up by 1.5 percent. We agreed to change flight cancellation time without penalty to six hours before scheduled travel.
And: Correct.
A: And we are going for four-star hotels at three-star rates, but with just two hotels per location.
And: Yes.
A: What do we agree as the three-star rate?
And: That's actually going to be difficult because the rates actually vary a lot. Can we take the average three-star hotel rate in that location, just to use as a benchmark?
A: Fine. Great. So, thanks very much, Anders. If you confirm that in an email to me, then I will get agreement internally with my manager. Then we can draw up a new contract.
And: Very good. I'll email you by the end of this week.
A: Excellent. Well, that was quick and efficient. We have a little time for you to tell me all about your weekend in Copenhagen.

6.01

1 What do you like doing in your free time?
2 I like hanging out with friends.
3 Do you have any previous work or voluntary experience?
4 I take the dog for a walk every day.
5 What do you think you'll be doing in five years' time?
6 I've never thought about that.

Ext6.01 S = Susana D = David

S: I think there are some unique challenges for young entrepreneurs like me.
D: What do you think they are?
S: Um, I had to find finance, which is harder because I had no experience. And I had to learn how to manage a team and be a good boss.
D: Do you think it's stressful?
S: It can be, but I have learnt ways to deal with it.

6.02 and 6.03

Part 1: the overview

In this next part of my presentation, I'm going to tell you more about the target market for our new company as well as market growth and our forecast for the next quarter. As you know, we produce specialist and high-end cases for mobile phones, tablets and laptops in a range of sizes for each product line.

On this slide you can see three charts. This pie chart shows us the age demographic of our target customers. You can see which ages the colours refer to on the right. You'll notice that the 18- to 25-year-old age group is our biggest target group. Next, you can see the growth of our market in terms of annual revenue on this line graph. The main point is that the mobile case sector is both our largest and fastest-growing sector. Finally, on this bar chart, you can see the stock levels we have and our forecast for the next quarter year. At the end of Q4 we'll have this much stock and you can see from our projected sales that we're not going to have enough. We'll need more stock to be able to fulfil the orders that will come in. For that reason, we need a short-term loan so that we can buy more stock. I'd now like to hand over to my colleague, who will give you more details.

Part 2: the details

So coming back to the growth development graph. It is significant that the growth of the tablet product line has been slow and the laptop line has fallen slightly. On the other hand, you can see that the mobile sector has risen sharply and is projected to continue. These details confirm that mobile devices, in general, are outselling both tablets and laptops combined.

I'd also like to show you something on the customer age demographic pie chart. Although our cases are high-end and not exactly cheap, it's interesting to see that almost half of our customers are in the 18-to-25 age group, and almost a quarter are in the 25-to-30 age group. This means that around 70 percent of our customers are in the 18-to-30 age group and are willing to pay high-end prices for our cases. This fact proves that our cases are highly desirable for this age group and they're willing to spend, even though they might not have a lot of disposable income.

The last thing I want you to think about is our current stock levels. The stock is the quantity of product we have ready to sell in our warehouse. Looking more closely at the bar chart, you can see that we have greatly underestimated the growth of the mobile sector. For that reason, we don't have enough stock to meet the demand. We need more, but we'll need money, like a loan, to be able to buy more stock. If we can secure this loan, we will be investing in further stock, especially mobile cases. We see mobile cases as the big winner for the next two years at least.

6.04

Good evening everyone, I'm George Johnson and I started my business, GJWoodToys, while I was still working at my full-time job at an estate agent's,

selling houses. Although I quite liked my job, ever since my kids were born I'd been making wooden toys for them as a hobby. But then other parents saw the toys and wanted to buy them and kept telling me that I should set up my own business. I started by selling the toys at craft fairs and they sold out every time. My target market was enormous: parents and their children, because kids are usually the ones to persuade the parents to part with their money. Parents like something that is well made, durable, reliable and above all safe, and the bright colours and versatility of each piece appeals to the children. It looked like we were onto a winner.

I continued making the toys in my garage for a while but then, when a couple of local stores approached me, I realised that I needed funding to expand my production and move into slightly larger premises. In order to do this and invest in more tools and employ more people, I had to use family savings and remortgage my house, which was a big risk because I could've lost all their money.

However it wasn't long after this that a big department store became interested in the toys after one of their directors had bought some at a craft fair. They started talking about placing an order for 50,000 units. It was at this point that I realised I had a potentially very successful product on my hands. However, this next step would require a huge investment and I just didn't have the money. With the promise of the order from the store I tried pitching to various potential backers to find the funding. The bank wasn't interested, so I started looking at the possibility of crowdfunding, although I eventually decided against this. I also talked to business angels. I was very lucky to meet a business angel who'd been looking for a start-up to invest in and he brought not only the investment needed but a wealth of experience, too.

6.05

So I know you're interested to hear any advice I can give you about setting up your own business. I think it's different for everyone but there are some common points you need to focus on.

Firstly, in the early days it's very important to believe passionately in your product or service. If you don't believe in it, you won't be able to sell it. You have to love what you do.

Once you know that you love the product, conduct as extensive market research as you can and listen to people's feedback. It's no good trying to take a product or service to market if nobody's going to be interested.

Thirdly, I think that good planning is key, especially time management, but also planning every step of the journey. A good plan acts as a map for your business. And if something fails, you can go back to the drawing board and redraw that map.

The best piece of advice someone gave me at the beginning was to be open to advice, but remember that not all advice will be helpful so, if it doesn't feel right for you, ignore it. And don't be afraid to ask for advice or help when you need it. Remember you're not an expert in everything.

Another vital thing is to manage your finances carefully and make sure you know how your money's being used, how much you're spending and earning at all times. As you get bigger and the amounts of money involved get larger and the money is no longer just yours, this becomes even more important, so start off as you mean to go on. And talking about money, if you end up working with large retailers, like me, don't let them beat you down on unit prices as they'll always try to push the price down as far as they can. When you know what price works for you, stick to it. If the retailers want to sell your product, you know it must be good so don't give it away.

With everything else that's going on, don't forget your customer. The customer is the source of your inspiration and rewards, so developing close customer relations is absolutely vital. As soon as you start forgetting the customer, your business is likely to begin to fail.

Furthermore, the frightening thing is that suddenly you become a leader and managing a company and its personnel is not easy. So my advice to you here is to learn to trust your key people and delegate work appropriately. When you've been the only one responsible for everything for so long, I think this is the hardest thing to do – handing it over to others.

And finally, above all, never underestimate how hard it is to succeed. You'll probably find yourself working harder than you've ever worked in your life.

7.01

1 Let me tell you about my experience of working abroad. At the time, I was working as the Regional Financial Director of a construction company with a division in India. Part of my job consisted of meeting senior bank executives to arrange bank guarantees and credit facilities. Once, I went to a meeting with the chairman of a bank in Mumbai and when I went into his office, I was surprised to see a shrine set up on the table where discussions were going to take place and incense was burning in the room. After the customary greetings and introductions, the chairman then turned on some chanting music. I asked what the music was and he told me that it was Indian mantra music to help create a good atmosphere in the meeting. The Indians believed it encouraged a positive outcome. It was quite a different experience to doing business back at home. I had never seen this kind of thing before!

Another thing is that in countries like India, employees will hardly ever tell their bosses that something is not possible. Saying 'no' is often considered 'loss of face'. By 'loss of face', I mean embarrassing a person in front of others, or offending them, and this can of course lead to problems in the workplace. While I was working in India, I often experienced this problem first hand. For instance, employees didn't report problems because they didn't want to give a bad impression to their bosses.

2 While I was living in Kenya, I discovered that optimism is highly valued in Kenyan society. It's reflected in the popular catchphrase 'Hakuna matata', which means 'No worries'. This idea of 'Hakuna matata' sometimes caused conflict at work and led to missed deadlines, you know, people didn't finish a task or a report by a given time.

When I was working in the office in Nairobi, workers preferred to agree to deadlines without questioning them. Later, they admitted that they couldn't meet the deadline, even if they had previously agreed to it. I found it very frustrating. On the other hand, being surrounded by optimistic people helped lighten the office atmosphere and often diffused stressful situations. So, that was the positive side of 'Hakuna matata'.

3 While I was working as a supervisor in a call centre in Delhi for a multinational, I had to report to my boss in Los Angeles. It was very stressful working in customer service. We had to deal with complaints on a daily basis. The last week of the month my American boss was insisting on me sending a report with our latest figures for resolving complaints, and I had promised to send them to him. But then we got very busy. A lot of my co-workers had fallen ill with a virus that was going round and I was working really hard: I was going to work early and I was leaving late at night to cover for them. So I didn't have time to reply to my boss. It was unlucky because he had wanted the figures by the end of the month, but I had to prioritise. Then he started sending me urgent emails with red flags and written in big, capital letters and that was the equivalent of shouting at me. He had also copied in my colleagues. I mean, he shouldn't have written in capital letters, right? He should have picked up the phone and talked to me. Of course, that wasn't easy because of the time difference. And I know Americans are stricter

about time, but he didn't have to shame me like that! Thinking about it, I wanted to create a good impression because the company culture was very competitive, so I didn't explain all the problems we were having. That was my mistake. But the worst thing was he had copied in all the team – it made me look really bad. It was so embarrassing. I couldn't work there after that, so I quit my job. I didn't go in the next day.

7.02 T = Tadashi   Pe = Peter   Pi = Pilar

T: Hello.
Pe: Hi, I'm Peter. I'm from D2 Logistics.
T: I'm Tadashi.
Pe: Nice to meet you, Tadashi. So ... I'm a finance specialist. What do you do? Are you working on any interesting projects?
T: I'm in marketing. I design marketing campaigns.
Pe: Oh. ... Er, so what do you think of the elections? Who do you think will win?
T: I don't know.
Pe: But you must have an idea. What do you think?
T: I'm not sure.
Pe: Oh.
Pi: Hi, I'm Pilar.
Pe: Hello Pilar, it's nice to meet you. I'm Peter.
Pi: It's nice to meet you too, Peter.
T: Hello, I'm Tadashi.
Pe: So, Pilar. What do you do?
Pi: I'm an accountant during the day and I play in a local band at weekends ... in Mexico City ... that's where I live at the moment ... We practise a lot during the week which doesn't give me too much time with my family. I have two brothers, and we all still live at home.
Pe: You're an accountant. Really? I'm a finance specialist. Who do you work for?
Pilar: Oh, er ... I work for ACC Products. I'm a property accountant.
Pe: OK. I ... er ... don't know much about property. Well, I think I'll go back to the buffet to ... get some more ...

7.03 Pe = Peter   T = Tadashi   Pi = Pilar

Pe: So, Tadashi, you're in marketing. What sort of campaigns do you design?
T: I'm working on one at the moment for a hotel chain. We're making ads that will run in planes, on the little screens. Er, is that OK?
Pe: Er, sure. That project sounds really interesting. I saw ads like that the last time I flew on holiday.
T: Maybe they were my ads.
Pe: Yeah, maybe ... It's a very good place to run ads, everyone on the plane sees them.
T: Yes. We try to make the ads specific to the country, if possible, and we always try to put in a little humour.
Pe: Yes, flying and going through airports can be stressful. It's good to have a little humour.
Pi: So Peter, where did you go on holiday?
Pe: I went to Brazil. It was a very long flight, but I had a really nice time with my family. It was a special trip for my father's 60th birthday.
Pi: Great!
Pe: You know, I also have two brothers, like you. One older and one younger.
Pilar: So you're in the middle, then?
Peter: Yes, that's it.

7.04

That was a really nice evening. At the beginning it felt a bit awkward, it wasn't that easy to talk to Tadashi or Pilar. I thought that Tadashi's English wasn't very good and that he was shy and insecure. But I was making assumptions and I was wrong on both points. He was quite fluent, and very enthusiastic when we were talking about things he likes and he's good at. He thinks a lot about what other people say before he reacts. When I realised that, I stopped talking so much. Then he had more time to think, and he spoke more too. And Pilar? I didn't really take her seriously at first; I thought she just wanted to talk about her free time. But when I stopped talking about work and talked

about my family and travel, the conversation really developed. We connected more, and then it was easier to find out more about her job and what she does. I guess first impressions can often be wrong, especially with people from different cultures. Anyway, I'm glad I adapted my approach and got to know them a bit better.

8.01 J = John   P = Philippe   B = Bettina   A = Angela

J: Thanks, everyone, for coming to this special meeting today.
P: No problem. Happy to be here.
B: Sure.
J: There is a management meeting at the end of the month and I have to present a short update on our team and our current project. I called this meeting because I need your help to prepare the presentation, and I want to give the most accurate update, while also representing the successes our team has had recently.
A: OK, how can we help?
J: Well, ideally, the goal for this meeting is to decide which information we want to present to senior management, and which tasks each of you will do to prepare.
P: OK, sounds good.
J: So, we have one hour. Let's start by first focusing on our goal in a little more detail. Then, I'd like to collect your ideas on what we should present. After that, we can discuss your ideas and mine. Next, we'll choose the best options, and then finally we can assign tasks for each of you to do in advance of the management meeting. Does that process sound alright?
All: Yes.
J: OK, let's begin by thinking about the management meeting and what our goal actually is.

8.02 A = Angela   P = Philippe   J = John   B = Bettina

A: So I think we should include some information about the delay in finishing the new designs as that has had a ...
P: No, we shouldn't do that. We don't want to draw attention to our mistakes. I think we should focus on different facts of the ...
J: Philippe, I understand what you're staying is important, but please let Angela finish. We can come to you next, OK?
P: OK, sure, fine.
J: OK, Angela, back to you. Could you try to limit your overview to about two minutes? We need to keep an eye on the clock.
A: No problem. Thanks, John. So, as I was saying, I think we should at least explain that there were delays because they had an effect on the next steps of the project, which meant that we all had to work overtime to get back on track.
J: Yes, that's a good idea, I'll need to explain the increase in costs due to overtime. OK, back to you Philippe.
P: Thanks, John. Well, as I was trying to say, we need to be careful about the negative information we present. We don't want to focus on the negative elements of the past, risk getting in trouble or even worse, we could have our budgets cut.
B: Wait a minute. Who said anything about budgets being cut?
P: Don't interrupt me, Bettina.
J: OK, OK, you two, take it easy. I know you're both passionate about this, but we need to allow each other time to speak.
P: Yes, I agree. And I am not finished. I just wanted to say that I think we should instead focus on the fact that we ran into some difficulties, but we got the designs finished and the project is now running smoothly.
J: OK, thanks, Philippe. Good idea.
B: I need my budget to pay for the market research we already agreed on.
J: Bettina, I understand your concern, but the market research has already been commissioned

and the results are also expected back next week. No one has said we need to reduce the budgets. The market research results aren't on today's agenda, so can we talk about that when the results come back in? In the meantime, can you give us a brief update on what you'll be working on in the project for the next couple of weeks?

8.03 J = John   P = Philippe   A = Angela   B = Bettina

J: Thanks, everyone. This has been a very productive meeting. It was useful to talk through both our successes and areas for concern. I need to be able to present a realistic, but positive, picture of our team's activity at the management meeting.
P: Thanks, John. Yes, it's been good to talk through everything.
J: OK, so the action points from this meeting are: Angela, you'll prepare two slides on the designs update. I'll mention that there were delays that we are now on top of, but the main focus should be on the positive outcome of the designs and the next steps.
A: Right.
J: Philippe, you'll prepare an overview of the media campaign we're planning and the timeline for what will happen.
P: OK.
J: And Bettina, you'll prepare an overview of the market research results. Hopefully they'll confirm what we think about the market and give some further information.
B: Sure. I hope to have them on Wednesday, so that will give me time to review them and send you the most important points.
J: Great. So, is everyone OK with their tasks?
All: Yes./Sure.
J: Does anyone have any questions about what they have to do? Or need any support?
All: No.
J: OK, great. And I'll prepare some brief information on the overall timeline and where we expect to be in the next two months. Let's meet again to finalise everything at 2 p.m. on Friday next week. Please send me your completed tasks before close of business on Thursday.
A: Sure.
P: No problem.
B: Fine.
J: OK, thanks, everyone.

BW1.01

1 As the company's grown we've squeezed more and more people into the same space. It's just so cramped now. And people have different work styles. I don't like being tied down to a desk all the time – moving around helps me to think, like when I'm talking to people on the phone. But this open-plan office makes this impossible for me to do without disturbing other people. Likewise, it's sometimes difficult for me to do any work where I really have to concentrate due to noise levels and visual distractions.
It'd be great to have a more flexible work environment – more meeting rooms, you know, breakout spaces for teamwork and quiet zones where you can work alone and really focus.
2 There isn't anything special about our current office space that differentiates it from any other office right now. It doesn't say anything about our business. We say we're innovative, fun-loving and tech-savvy so that message should be loud and clear in our office design, in the furniture and in the artwork on the walls. Let's make sure potential clients and recruits see and feel what we're about when they walk through the doors.
The company values work-life balance for staff and I'd like more flexible working hours and the chance to work from home a few days a week rather than the current presenteeism, so I can pick my young son up from school every day.
3 The kitchen is a tiny, windowless room with grey walls. Nobody wants to spend more time there than strictly necessary. Then there are

vending machines in the corridor but no seating areas. I'd provide free fruit in public areas and let's get away from people eating at their desks. Apart from anything else, it's smelly!

The best ideas aren't going to come when sitting in front of your monitor, but from those chance interactions and exchanges between staff. We need to create welcoming public spaces, such as a kitchen/dining room where staff from different departments can actually mingle and communicate. Let's make sure to have plenty of space for socialising and collaboration. How about a ping-pong table and attractive outside spaces as well?

BW2.01

1 So, you're asking about window displays? Well, I think this is something the company could improve. Kloze-Zone's design and quality are great, but I'd like to see more innovation in the window displays because it's what makes you go into a store when you're walking down the High Street.

2 We have some special offers and promotions, but our competitors, for example, organise special days in their stores every season, with clothes at 50 percent off. That attracts a lot of interest. I know this heavy discounting doesn't increase sales that much, but it works really well to raise brand awareness. We did have a special event for the store opening – it was a lot of work, but it was great; there was a local band playing and staff gave out free T-shirts to customers. Another thing is, I think we should organise some kind of promotional event in months like November and February, to promote the store. Those months are very quiet for us.

3 I think fast-fashion retailers do a lot to market their clothes at mostly women. I get bored with seeing the same kinds of adverts that are targeted at girls. I think they should aim their campaigns at guys, too. For example, I like going shopping with my girlfriend. Also, when men go shopping, we often buy two of the same thing if we really like it, so that's good business. Perhaps they need more engaging marketing campaigns for guys?

4 What do I think of their customer service? Well, shop assistants sometimes seem too busy to help customers when you're trying on clothes in the fitting rooms. I mean, you might want to try on a different colour or size, and you're not with a friend, so it's difficult. I think they need to employ more staff in the store. But I love their mobile app and it's dead easy to use. The design is really cool because you can check out the clothes and mix and match them online before you come to the shop.

5 Well, I work in the Berlin store. It's difficult because there are a lot of High Street fashion stores in Berlin – it's very competitive. But we work really hard. When we first opened, it used to be fun, then a couple of my colleagues left last month because of the long working hours. We have to work from nine to seven, and Saturdays, too. And even some Sundays. I don't know about Japan – I think they only get two weeks of holiday every year there. But in Germany workers expect a break and longer holidays, you know?

6 What could we improve at Kloze-Zone? The main problem I have as a store manager is that staff turnover is pretty high. Some young people start working in fashion thinking it's going to be good fun, trying on clothes all the time. They don't realise you're on your feet all day and you have to be polite to the customers all the time – even when they complain and return items. I need staff who understand fashion, although, to be honest, a lot of the people I interview aren't even aware of our brand. They confuse us with other High Street stores! I think we need to improve brand awareness to attract both more customers and staff.

BW3.01
Amalia

Is this webcam on? Oh, right! So, why should you hire me? Well, I have to say I think I'm hard-working, I'm reliable and, and … I'm highly qualified. I have a background in marketing and a lot of experience in different sectors. I also speak various languages, so that will be very useful for an international company like Media Solutions. I would like to work for you because I think I'm good at communicating, especially writing, and I could contribute to your Communications department with my ideas and improve the presence of your clients in social media. Err, … that's all really. Thanks for listening. Oh, and please call me if you'd like me to come in for an interview.

Birte

Why should you hire me? Because I'm a 'people person': I'm not only sociable, but also really creative and if you hired me, I would give 110 percent and I would get on with all the team and the clients, too. Another thing you should know about me is I'm really into sports and martial arts, as you can see. You can check out some of my videos in social media on how to do sports training. I love social media and dedicate a lot of time to it. It's the way everyone communicates nowadays.

What else? I've got a degree in marketing. I did an internship at my dad's company and I learnt a lot. I'm a fast learner. I don't have lots of experience but I think it's more important to have the right attitude and just get out there and do it! So why should you hire me? Because I'm worth it! Call me for an interview and please give me the chance to tell you more.

Cindy

So, you'd like to know why you should hire me? That's a good question. Looking at my CV you might think I don't have any relevant experience but I do have experience in managing people.

I have to communicate in my job every day, where I'm responsible for a team of forty people, talking to different departments and dealing with difficult customers. I'm good at working under pressure, so you can depend on me to write those reports on time! Oh sorry, just a minute …. another consideration is that I'm a big fan of social media. I write a blog in my free time, although I don't have that many followers yet. I'm also studying marketing online in the evenings. So, if you hire me, I will help you to find the best solutions for you and your clients and improve their online presence with the contributions of key opinion leaders and influencers.

Thank you for considering my application and I look forward to your call!

BW3.02
Amalia

My proudest achievement? Oh, err … that's a difficult question. I think it was the time when I graduated from university … no, sorry, I think my proudest moment was when I organised a charity event for homeless people in my town. It was a lot of work, but the response from the public was tremendous and we raised over £4,000. I was responsible for organising the social media campaign and talking to the press. I think I did a good job and my family told me they were very proud of me. It was a brilliant experience that made me want to work in social media.

Birte

My proudest achievement has to be when I started a social media campaign about young people with eating disorders. I started posting a video every day with tips for having a healthy diet but it was all about feeling good, not making life more difficult for yourself. There's a lot of contradictory advice about health tips on the internet. You know, people say different things and that confuses people. Then I suddenly got thousands of followers on social media and I realised that my videos and advice on doing exercise and having a healthy diet were making a difference. To give you an example, I received one post from a young woman who was in hospital at the time and she wrote saying that I was an inspiration to her. And that made me feel really proud of what I was doing, my blog was really helping people, you know?

Cindy

That's an interesting question. I'm not sure … I think it was when there was a problem while I was still working as an intern. There was a public transport strike and lots of people were phoning the department and complaining. There was a lack of information and we were getting very negative comments on social media and from the press and a lot of my colleagues didn't seem very interested. Then we had a crisis meeting and the team decided to work hard until late at night to solve problems and to deal with all the emails and phone calls from the public. But I took the initiative to start writing replies to the negative posts on social media, so we improved our company image and my boss thanked me in front of the whole team. And because of me, the department started taking social media more seriously. I felt really proud. I was just the intern.

BW4.01

As the supermarket wars continue we take a look at three major supermarket chains to find out about their strategies.

Upmarket food retailer White's has introduced a loyalty scheme to provide better value to members rather than lowering its prices and entering into a price war with discounters.

It has also expanded its own-brand range and promises 'price matches' with the own brands of other major supermarket chains, like Mulberry's. However, the CEO has announced that it will also continue to invest £400 million each year on weekly special offers and price promotions rather than cutting prices permanently.

She said White's will continue to focus on an excellent in-store service, as well as high-quality product ranges. The supermarket is making a major move into food-to-go to meet the needs of busy consumers.

Food retail giant Mulberry's is still finding it hard to adapt to both increased competition from discounters and changing consumer shopping habits.

Its 'back-to-basics' strategy includes selling off non-core activities, such as in-store restaurants, and it will also stop selling clothes and consumer electronics.

The chain is also spending less on special promotions in order to simplify its strategy and is cutting the number of products to 20,000 to cut costs. Mulberry's smaller convenience stores and its online store have seen good sales growth but falling food prices continue to reduce profit margins. Latest figures show its market share remains flat, at 16 percent.

The discounter C&C has achieved spectacular sales growth in recent years. While the other main players in the retail food market have been closing supermarkets, C&C has just announced its ambitious expansion plan including the construction of fifty new stores.

The chain also said that it will refurbish 150 existing stores over the next three to four years in order to attract more customers. The retailer is also doubling its product range and including more fresh meat and a new own-brand low-price luxury range to rival the main supermarket chains. With these major investments, it remains to be seen if C&C will also have to change its lowest price strategy.

BW5.01 **AW = Anna Woźniak**
TW = Tadeusz Walentowicz

AW: So, Ted, what I'm saying is we need automation for selecting and lifting heavy furniture from high shelves.

TW: But we've been doing that with fork-lift trucks for years.

AW: The thing is, there have been more accidents in the warehouse recently because of the increased numbers of orders. Staff are constantly doing overtime, they can't handle the work and goods are damaged, …

TW: OK, but the items have to be packed carefully and this should still be done manually.

AW: Yes, I agree.

TW: And if we introduce robotics technology to avoid breakage, we have to make sure the supplier provides training. If not, we'll have robots going out of control!

AW: Don't worry, both suppliers say they'll provide training.

TW: So, tell me about these providers. Were they recommended?

AW: Yes, I had recommendations from my contacts in car companies. One here in Poznań and one in Germany.

TW: Good.

AW: One of the providers is a robotics developer from Singapore and the other is Japanese.

TW: Japan, eh? They are going to be expensive.

AW: Both offer quality automation and training. We have to move with the times, Ted.

TW: I know, but I'm worried about costs *and* maintenance. What do we do when the robots break down? What happens if we need maintenance? Are there local people who can fix it, or will they send a guy from Singapore?

AW: Those are good questions. That's why I've arranged interviews with the suppliers tomorrow. You have a teleconference with the supplier from Singapore and I'll talk to the one from Japan. Then we'll compare notes.

TW: All right. And what are *your* main concerns, Anna?

AW: I think there will be some problems with the transition, when we'll have to deal with the old system and the new technology at the same time.

TW: Mmm, Human Resources say there will be a negative reaction from the employees – people are worried about robots taking their jobs.

AW: I know, but we need this automation if we're going to stay competitive. And they'll learn new skills.

TW: Well, Human Resources want to discuss possible job losses. Unfortunately, I don't see all of our workers continuing with robots. But I agree some employees can be retrained. So, tell me a bit more about these suppliers.

AW: Well, Novarobot is based in Singapore. They do industrial automation.

TW: And the Japanese one?

AW: The Japanese supplier is called Bot-automation. They're based in Osaka and also focus on robotics design and ...

TW: We are going to be taken over by robots. If my father saw this company now ...

AW: Your father would want the company to be successful. It's going to make everything much easier, Ted! Trust me.

BW5.02

Supplier A

TW = Tadeusz Walentowicz   TK = Tony King

TW: So, I understand you are specialists in industrial automation, Mr King. And you have worked with clients in the automotive industry in Germany.

TK: That's right. And we have worked with clients in Poland, too.

TW: Good. That will be an advantage.

TK: As I explained to your logistics manager, I'm sure we can help you manage your logistics more efficiently using artificial intelligence.

TW: So, how do you work? How will the robots be installed?

TK: The way we work is that automation systems are installed in two phases.

TW: Two phases? Why is that?

TK: This allows for an easy ... , a smooth transition between manual and automated systems. Your warehouse will have to stop operations for three days during each phase of the installation.

TW: But we can't lose six working days!

TK: We appreciate that, so to minimise the effects on production, this work can be done at the weekend.

TW: From Friday to Sunday?

TK: That's right.

TW: And what happens if something goes wrong? Do you have technicians who can do maintenance, at no extra cost?

TK: Err, ... first of all, we offer a *two-year* guarantee. Many robotics companies offer less. There are sometimes technical problems, usually because operators are not used to the system. Any failure will be repaired by Novarobot technicians during this period. We also do a maintenance inspection, free of charge, once a year.

TW: That's good to know. But what happens when this two-year guarantee ends?

TK: Our robots are made to last for years, Mr Walentowicz. But I recommend you contract our after-sales service. That way you can call an emergency hotline and speak to an engineer 24 hours a day.

TW: Mmm, I'll need to talk to our logistics manager. Could you send me the details and costs of your after-sales service?

TK: Yes, of course.

TW: And I'd like to know about training.

TK: Basic training is provided during installation. After that, our technicians deal with any problems via email, or videoconference. You'll also have a maintenance inspection, once a year.

TW: Well, I think we are going to consider your proposal. And then, if we accept your offer, you can visit our warehouse and discuss what we need.

TK: Can I ask, when do you think that will be?

TW: The logistics manager will contact you.

TK: We hope we can do business with you. Thank you for your time, Mr Walentowicz.

TW: You're welcome, Mr King. Goodbye.

Supplier B

AW = Anna Woźniak   KI = Kin Izumi

KI: Thank you for showing an interest in us, Ms Woźniak.

AW: I see your team has won awards.

KI: That's right. We are innovators in robotics design.

AW: But I'd like to know how your company differs from the competition.

KI: Err ... If you choose us, we can provide solutions in many areas: mobile robotics, motor control and industrial automation. We are an ISO-certified company.

AW: I see.

KI: And we give customised solutions.

AW: That's good to hear.

KI: And specialist engineers assess your needs and then adapt the mobile robotics to your warehouse.

AW: Great, so you adapt to our specific needs.

KI: That's right.

AW: And what about installation? How will that work? I imagine there will be a transition period when we still operate manually, while the employees learn to use the new system.

KI: Mmm, ... not exactly.

AW: Could you clarify that?

KI: Sorry, but we don't have a transition period. We find it causes confusion. We suggest your warehouse stops operations for six to seven consecutive days.

AW: Seven days! That much time?

KI: Err, ... we recommend, for example, from Saturday to Friday. This can be done over a public holiday or in the summer.

AW: Well, that's not ideal. And what about training?

KI: Two specialist technicians provide the training after the installation period. Manuals in English are also provided. That way, any basic maintenance can be solved later on by your own staff.

AW: Good. And what about the guarantee?

KI: We offer an 18-month guarantee.

AW: Only 18 months! But what happens after that? Or if the equipment breaks down?

KI: Technicians from Bot-automation can help via an emergency hotline and teleconference. We guarantee our technicians will visit your warehouse in 36 hours if complex maintenance is needed during the first 18 months.

AW: But not after that?

KI: That depends.

AW: Do you mean there will be an additional cost for the after-sales service when the guarantee ends?

KI: That's correct.

AW: Mmm, well, I'd like to discuss your offer with our director, and then we'll get back to you.

KI: Of course. But remember if you order a fourth robot, we will offer you a discount for the after-sales service.

AW: That's good to know. Excuse me. I'm afraid I have another meeting now.

KI: Please contact me if you have any questions, Ms Woźniak.

AW: Thank you, Mr Izumi. We'll be in touch.

BW6.0.1

Ben Fischer

Hi guys! I'm Ben Fischer and my award-winning theatre company performs at events and festivals all over the world. We bring the works of famous German writers and dramatists, such as Bertolt Brecht, to audiences across the globe.

In true dramatic style, our latest production of Brecht's *The Good Person of Szechwan* has just been hit by disaster. An electrical fire destroyed the arts centre where we were performing in London and took with it all our costumes and equipment. Fortunately, nobody was in the building at the time and nobody was injured in the fire.

We know one day the insurance company will eventually pay the compensation to rebuild and replace everything, but we need to complete our world tour now and can't wait around for the money to arrive.

Can you help us? We need to raise €10,000 in the next few weeks to replace everything. I promise all donations to our cause will be repaid when we receive the insurance payout. Not only that, depending on the size of your donation you will receive discounts on tickets and even free tickets to see our play in any city of your choice on the tour. Just see our website for more details.

As Brecht himself once said, 'Everyone needs help from everyone.' By contributing to our disaster fund, you will be doing your bit to support community arts and help our young theatre group to literally rise from the ashes. Thank you!

Alison Chadwick

My name's Alison Chadwick and this is my story. I started my T-shirt business, Alison's Tees, back in university as a hobby. Friends and fellow students used to ask me where I got my T-shirts from and when I told them I designed them myself everyone said that was cool.

Then I thought, you know anyone can design their own T-shirt. It's simple, it's fun and it's creative. On my website you can choose the colour and style but more than that, you can have any design or logo you like printed on it including photos to make your very own unique T-shirt. Friends will be amazed. Before we finally produce the T-shirt, you'll receive a photo of the design for final approval.

No more shopping for hours looking for something you actually like. No more low-quality shop-bought products. All our T-shirts are 100 percent organic cotton and ethically sourced. We're helping independent cotton farmers. We work hand-in-hand with our suppliers to ensure highest-quality tees.

Thanks to previous crowdfunding our business has been a big success. Now we need your support and your money to help us develop our mobile app so our users can design and order their own tees on their smartphones, anytime, anywhere.

Marcos López

If you like travelling, you'll love our new tour guide mobile app. It's like an audio guide but on your mobile phone, so you carry it with you all the time. I'm Marcos López and I'm one of the founders of Holidapp. It's the ultimate travel companion. It's like having an audio guide but on your smartphone. You'll never want to buy another guidebook or tourist map again in your life. You'll find out about the places you're visiting whenever you want in a new, original and entertaining way. Our app is free to download and quick and easy to use. Enter the desired location and for just €10 you will get an expert guide to one of over 30 destinations in Europe and the USA. And the list of places is growing longer each month.

The guide features audio tours by experts in their towns, from qualified tour guides to local storytellers of all ages with a passion for the place where they live. Our platform is free to our guide contributors and they receive 70 percent of the revenues generated by their guides.

Each travel guide on our app comes with high-quality photographs and can use your geolocation to help you get the most from your guide.

We need your backing to help us cover the cost of production, audio recording, programming and photography. We'd also love to hear what you think of the guides so we can keep improving our service.

BW7.01

1 Oh, when the Dutch managers visited our office, it was very nice. We had good conversations about our respective traditions, our families and food. They loved our Indian food. Regarding business, I would say that we're like one big family here. I have cousins, uncles and aunties in the office working here, and so we work very well together. I realise it's different in Europe but this is how we work in this country. We trust each other. It's just the way it is. Our business relationships are based on trust. The only thing is that they kept insisting about the report for the latest sales figures. And I said, it wasn't a problem, no problem at all. We'll have the report ready soon. I told them not to worry about that. You can't say 'no', or 'that's not possible' to a visitor, can you? That would be terribly impolite!

2 We got on very well with the managers from Betker Finance. It was great seeing them face to face. Perhaps here in the south we're not as punctual as they are. But that doesn't mean we're less productive. In fact I think we're much better at multi-tasking. I find Northern Europeans tend to do only one thing at a time. You know, they're only focused on one thing, which seems a bit limiting if something important suddenly comes up. For example, as the Sales Manager in my region, I have to manage a large team of people and juggle different tasks at the same time. So, it's normal that when I'm in a meeting with a colleague, I might have interruptions, like an urgent phone call, or someone from the office comes in to ask me something. It's the way we work. But I don't think our Dutch colleagues had a good first impression of us. And we're great believers in first impressions.

BW7.02

3 When the sales manager came from headquarters, he just said: 'Hi, how's it going?' and he got down to business right away, talking about figures and KPIs. You know, key performance indicators. Actually, there was no time to reply, or even for me to ask him the same thing. It was very direct and abrupt, which surprised me. I know it's good to be efficient and have a purpose in a meeting, but in our culture, we always make conversation before getting down to business. I often ask the visitor about events in their country, and find out about their interests and maybe their family. It's important to get to know the other person to establish a good atmosphere. I mean, we all want to do business with people we like, don't we?

4 When the sales representative came from Betker Finance, it was quite erm, quite difficult because she talked a lot about the new products which were very erm … interesting, but I had the impression that she didn't understand our market so well. And at the end of the first meeting, she thought we had finished, we had just begun! She also asked me many questions, which I couldn't answer because I needed to get approval from my boss. So when I said at the end of our conversation that I needed to check everything with him, she seemed a little erm … annoyed. I felt bad about that. And we thought she was staying for the week, so we would have time to discuss the new products with the team, and adapt them for our market, but she left after a couple of days. Then she sent me an email confirming points that we hadn't agreed on. I tried to explain that we do business as a team, and everything has to be confirmed by my bosses. I hope our next meeting will be more harmonious.

BW8.01   **HR = Human Resources Manager**
CM = Cris Martinez   AC = Alex Cortés
DL = Danni Lee
1, Cris Martinez
HR: Have you had any thoughts about your current training needs, Cris?
CM: Well, these days I'm responsible for formulating our long-term business plans and, as you know, I report directly to the Chief Financial Officer. I've done a lot of generic training courses in core management skills over the years. Now I need something more practical than sitting down all day in a training room looking at PowerPoint slides and doing roleplays.
HR: I see. So, regular training courses are not of interest to you?
CM: No, no, no. I want to tie my leadership development to my real-world projects. It'd be good to be able to build up a network with other senior managers in Grupo Tula around the world to share ideas, … and problems and solutions.
HR: So, a support network of peers would interest you?
CM: That's right! We can learn a lot from each other's experiences. One key role of senior executives is managing change and I think we can support each other with this. It would be good to get the perspective of executives with diverse cultural and business perspectives.
HR: At the same time, you have a great deal of knowledge and expertise which you could pass on.
CM: Yes, that's true. Of course I believe that talent development should be a part of a senior manager's job. It's just getting the time to do it, isn't it?
2, Alex Cortés
HR: What type of training would interest you Alex, and why?
AC: My job essentially is to make sure the day-to-day business runs smoothly, which includes overseeing a lot of staff. I know the technical side of my job well. So, I'd like to do something new to improve my leadership skills. I want to help my staff develop, get better results from them, and not just focus on completing the task.
HR: Right. So you want to help your staff improve their performance?
AC: That's it!
HR: Anything else you might like to do?
AC: Yes, well, a big part of my work is negotiating deals with suppliers and clients and more and more of them are outside Mexico nowadays. I can

see why the company has adopted English as the official language since the merger, but I don't feel as confident communicating in English as I do in Spanish, particularly in meetings and when I'm giving presentations. I know I'm really going to need to do something to improve my fluency if I'm going to progress through management levels in the future.
HR: Yes, I think a lot of people are going to want more English language training now. By the way, have you been back to Spain recently?
AC: No, but my parents are coming here next month. It'll be good to see them again!
HR: I can imagine.
3, Danni Lee
HR: So, Danni how are you adapting to life in Mexico? A bit different from Wisconsin, right?
DL: It's been great! Everyone's so helpful and friendly.
HR: That's good to hear. Now tell me a bit about yourself. I see you have a degree in business administration and started here six months ago in the sales division. How's that going?
DL: I really love the work, but I'm not always sure what I'm supposed to be doing or if I'm focusing on the right things. I have so many demands on my time and I feel quite stressed by it all. I work really long hours but I don't think that's what I should be doing either because I have no life outside the office at the end of the day.
HR: I see. That's not good. It sounds like you need some help with those issues.
DL: And you know, I don't know why they didn't teach us more practical computer skills at university, like Excel. It would really help me a lot with my job now.
HR: Maybe some on-the-job training would be an idea or an online course?
DL: Yeah, I'm sure I could pick it up quickly enough with some help. I'm really keen to learn as much as I can. At the moment I don't manage any staff but I'm quite ambitious. I'd like to lead a team one day so I'd like to know more about what that involves.

P4.02
1
OK, let's get started. Good morning, everyone.
2
A: How about using a call centre service for different languages? People who call us, they can choose the language they work with, and we contract a call centre to handle first contacts, and then they contact our sales staff.
B: That sounds like a possible solution.
C: OK, but I'm not sure how that would work. If we do that, it will just increase our costs.
3
A: Bibi, just building on what Roel said, I think it's easier to hire someone than train them in language skills. For our staff to learn Czech or Hungarian, it would take a very long time … years!
B: You may be right.
C: OK, then I think we need to look at recruitment as the quick solution.
4
I'll send Stefanie over to Tokyo for a couple of weeks, OK?

P8.03
1 The workshop, which I was planning to attend, was cancelled.
2 The workshop which I was planning to attend was cancelled.